THE RANGE OF ETHICS

Introductory Readings

THE RANGE OF ETHICS

Introductory Readings

HAROLD H. TITUS
Denison University

MORRIS T. KEETON
Antioch College

Van Nostrand Reinhold Company
New York   Cincinnati   Toronto   London   Melbourne

VAN NOSTRAND REINHOLD COMPANY Regional Offices:
Cincinnati New York Chicago Millbrae Dallas

VAN NOSTRAND REINHOLD COMPANY International Offices:
London Toronto Melbourne

Published by VAN NOSTRAND REINHOLD COMPANY
450 West 33rd Street, New York, N.Y. 10001

10 9 8 7 6 5 4 3 2

PREFACE

This book of readings has been prepared for use either as a supplement to an expository text or as a basic text—possibly with other writings in a particular area or areas. While there are a number of books of readings in the field of ethics, they tend to deal exclusively with ethical theories or with contemporary problems but not with both. A few books that do not fall in one or the other of these classifications present papers of a more technical nature written for the specialized journals and the mature philosopher. This book opens the general field of moral philosophy for beginning students most of whom will be taking only one course in this all-important but often neglected discipline.

We have made every effort to select material that is clear and readable, as well as relevant. Our aim has been to acquaint the reader with the broad range of ethical principles and problems that he is almost certain to meet as he lives in today's rapidly changing world. Among the questions treated are these: How civilized is our society? Can human nature be changed? Why is right right? How do we test our moral standards? How can we make sense of competing moral theories and standards? What are the main moral philosophies and what insights can we gain from them? What principles do we need to keep in mind as we enter business and the professions, listen to the mass media, engage in politics, and face many new and baffling problems in the thermonuclear and space age? Can we bring our morals up-to-date and construct a moral philosophy that will bring us a reasonable degree of fulfillment and enable us to live like mature men and women? In the selections we present, some of the ablest and wisest leaders of the past and present share their convictions with us.

The length of the chapters and selections has been determined in part by adaptability for classroom use or daily assignments. In some cases there is a single selection for a chapter or topic. When two or more selections are used in one chapter, these have been chosen so as to develop the line of thought or to present contrasting positions. When parts of selections are omitted, care has been taken to preserve the argument or point of view while eliminating less relevant, repetitious, or dated material.

We wish to thank the many authors and publishers who have given permission to use the selections reprinted.

HAROLD H. TITUS
MORRIS T. KEETON

CONTENTS

vii

PART ONE

INTRODUCTION: PRELIMINARY CONSIDERATIONS

CHAPTER 1

THE PLACE OF MORALITY
IN CONTEMPORARY SOCIETY

How Civilized Is Our

*Civilization?**

JAMES P. WARBURG

James P. Warburg (1896-   ) has held various
business and government positions. Besides *The West
in Crisis*, his twenty-fifth book, he has written *The
United States in a Changing World*, 1954, and *Disarmament—The Challenge of the Sixties*, 1961.

I

You and I belong to that segment of the human family which, for
want of a better term, is commonly referred to as "Western Man."
This somewhat misleading designation is applied to that small minority
of the world's population which first gathered in the eastern Mediterranean basin, spread from there over most of Europe, settled the two
Americas, the southern tip of Africa and the antipodes, establishing in
these widely separated regions of the earth something of a common way
of life which we call "Western civilization."

2

Western Man is accustomed to ascendancy. He thinks of himself as having brought civilization to its highest point. Both his ascendancy and the hypothesis upon which it rests are now on trial.

Racially, there is no such thing as Western Man. The Mediterranean basin was originally populated by peoples of many racial and tribal strains. Over the centuries, Western Man has conquered and absorbed, and been conquered and influenced by many other ethnic groups, including Goths, Vandals, African Negroes, and American Indians. Western civilization is not a white civilization by any means, but it is strongly permeated by the notion of white supremacy. Because of this notion, the community of Western Man is divided within itself and, because of it, the influence of Western civilization has been impaired. If we ask ourselves why the majority of mankind is apparently indifferent to the survival of Western civilization, a part of the answer lies in Western Man's assumption that he is somehow superior to other human beings because of the lighter pigmentation of his skin.

But that is not the whole answer.

For the past five centuries at least, Western Man has dominated the course of world history. Western Man originally acquired his ascendancy because he gained a head start over the rest of mankind in the struggle against his physical environment.

Western Man's material heritage derived from many earlier Mediterranean civilizations, such as those of the Persians, Egyptians, Phoenicians, and of course the Greeks and Romans. These peoples were the first to emancipate themselves from the shackles of a primitive nomadic or agricultural subsistence economy, to discover the division of labor, to learn how to trade, to manufacture, to accumulate capital, and to achieve mobility over land and sea.

Through his more rapid material progress, Western Man was able to acquire more and more relative military and economic power and also more and more relative knowledge and freedom.

Western Man's spiritual heritage derived from Judaism, from the humanism of the ancient Greeks, and from the teachings of Jesus Christ. Judaism gave Western Man the concept of a single, universal God and of a human society based upon justice under God's law. Greece gave Western Man the belief in the human individual as a rational being and, hence, the concepts of freedom of thought, freedom of expression, and political democracy. Judaism, however, embodied a contradiction between belief in a single, universal God and a religious setting in which that God appeared as the God of only a single, chosen people. Christianity resolved this contradiction by its assertion of the brotherhood of man, from which flowed its teaching of brotherly love, compassion, and non-violent resistance to aggression.

Our civilization has for centuries practiced neither the Jewish teaching of justice under moral law nor the Greek teaching of rational thought and behavior, and least of all the Christian teaching of love, compassion, and human brotherhood. Since the birth of Christ, the West has produced no great apostle of non-violence equivalent to Mahatma Gandhi. Our civilization has spawned crusaders, inquisitors, conquerors, and tyrants—Torquemadas, Napoleons, Hitlers, and Stalins—but not a single great prophet of brotherhood and peace.

The Western world, which we like to think of as "the cradle of civilization," has been the breeding ground of most of the fratricidal conflicts with which the human race has been afflicted for the past two thousand years.

The fatal weakness of Western Man have been his insatiable acquisitiveness and his inability to live at peace with himself. Both are the products of a materialism insufficiently restrained by humanitarianism and moral sensibility. The component parts of Western society did not unite in order to guide mankind toward progress in peace and justice. They quarreled ceaselessly among each other over their religious dogmas, their possessions, and their opportunities for aggrandizement. They fought over the hegemony of Europe, over the ownership of newly discovered parts of the world, and, finally, over the domination of the world itself.

In his endless quarrels, Western Man has reached forever more deadly weapons of murder and destruction. His moral sense has been more and more subordinated to expediency and to false concepts of patriotism. In World War I it was still considered a moral atrocity to bombard an open city with long-range artillery. In World War II scarcely a moral protest was raised against thousand-bomber raids upon sleeping cities. Today a single plane or missile can carry more destruction than was inflicted by all the air raids of World War II. Every hour of day and night, planes or missiles, each carrying this lethal load, are ready, at a moment's notice, to slay innocent millions and to make the earth uninhabitable for the human race.

Ironically, Western Man, in his materialism unrestrained by moral scruple, has now all but destroyed the foundations of his own supremacy. In so far as his ascendancy rested upon superior force of arms, he has developed weapons to the point where they have become useless as a means of enforcing his will. To the extent that his power was economic, he has wasted his strength in fratricidal conflict. Where his advantage derived from knowledge and skill not possessed by other peoples, his own inventions have so reduced time and distance as to make the maintenance of his monopoly impossible. Where Western Man might have gained the respect and admiration of the masses of mankind through empathetic understanding and co-operation, he has undermined his own influence by his selfishness, his callous inhumanity, and his failure to live up to the moral standards of the religious beliefs which he so militantly proselytized.

Thus Western Man missed his great opportunity to establish what might have been a world leadership based upon consent rather than conquest.

II

In contrast to the materialistic development of Western civilization, most of the great Asian civilizations turned inward, emphasizing man's spiritual development rather than his material progress. Some authorities say that this was due to the inherently different nature of Eastern Man. Others maintain that this view puts the cart before the horse—that Eastern Man turned inward because his harsh physical environment compelled him to seek solace in contemplation. Whatever the original cause, it is a fact that in most Asian societies the study of the past, the observance of family, tribal, caste, or religious customs, and the contemplation of man's nature and his relation to the universe have, until very recently, overshadowed the pursuit of material progress. Broadly speaking, Eastern Man has for the past five hundred years been passive and nonaggressive by comparison with Western Man's aggressive activity.

Under the impact of the Asian revolution, this pattern is rapidly changing, most markedly in China.

Africa is only a step or two behind Asia. Africa and Asia contain two thirds of the world's population.

Most students of history would agree that Tsarist Russia belonged to the Western world, even though it had been subjected to Asian influence and, geographically, was as much a part of Asia as of Europe. Tsarist Russia was one of the European powers which quarreled among each other for centuries over dynastic rights and territorial possessions; it bore its share of responsibility for World War I. Tsarist Russia's Asian empire was essentially no different from the colonial empire of Britain, except that it was not separated from the mother country by water; part of it had been acquired by conquest and part by Russian settlement of relatively empty Siberian space.

Tsarist Russia was a devoutly Christian country. Its cultural heritage, though not identical with that of Europe, was certainly more like it than like that of its Asian neighbors.

But what of Soviet Russia?

Karl Marx was a German. *Das Kapital* was written in the British Museum. Communism, as now practiced in the Soviet Union, is a distorted offshoot of West European socialism. Like socialism, it originated as a protest against nineteenth-century capitalism and exploitative imperialism.

However, since the Bolshevik Revolution, Soviet leadership has increasingly turned its back upon the West, orienting itself more and more toward Asia. The Soviet Union is now a multi-national state rather than a European nation with a colonial empire in Asia. In some respects this multi-national state is more Asian than European. Soviet leadership has rejected Christianity and has adopted a theory of the relationship of the individual to the state which is antithetical to the Western concept.

Soviet Man has detached himself from the West. He conceives of Western Man as his enemy, yet the materialistic standards by which he measures his accomplishments are largely the materialistic standards of the West. Soviet Man challenges Western Man with the latter's own weapons. Together with Western Man, he stands on trial before mankind, on the charge of holding the entire human race at the brink of destruction. Against this indictment Soviet Man can plead that it was not he who opened the door into the atomic age and that, unlike Western Man, he has not yet used a single nuclear weapon.

The fact is that Soviet Man has adopted our own crass materialism and added to it an explicit repudiation of the moral restraints in which we still have the grace to profess belief.

We have betrayed the Judaeo-Christian heritage. Soviet Man has rejected it altogether.

III

The dawn of the atomic age robbed physical power of its significance as an instrument of rational policy. Yet Western Man and Soviet Man have entered upon a struggle for preponderance of physical power, as if neither of them realized what has occurred.

To describe the so-called nuclear stalemate by the simile of two scorpions in a bottle ignores the all-important fact that if the two great antagonists annihilate each other they will also kill off the human race. Yet this fact embraces the entire significance of the situation we face.

This fact draws a line between the nuclear antagonists and the rest of humanity, making pariahs of the nuclear powers.

Logically the nuclear stalemate should provide a guarantee against race suicide. But the history of man does not follow the course of logic. History is written more by accident than design, often by the wholly irrational acts of madmen.

Fear is the great enemy of reason. Fear lest the madman, Hitler, produce an atomic weapon led the Anglo-Saxon democracies to open the Pandora's Box of atomic weaponry. Fear drove Stalin to desperate efforts to break the American monopoly. Fear produced the American H-bomb and its Soviet counterpart.

There is no answer to fear except in the realm of the spirit. Where moral conscience is submerged by materialistic expediency, fear inevitably creates hatred and the impulse toward aggression; and the desire to kill an enemy creates the need to believe that the enemy is so wholly evil that he deserves to be killed in the name of righteousness. There is no older story than this in the history of Western Man. Only now the conventional ending is no longer possible. Murder has become automatically punishable by suicide.

We know all this, and so do the Russians. Yet the scorpions are twisting and turning in the bottle.

Soviet leadership cherishes the illusion that the banning of nuclear weapons could restore the old order, in which the communists' massive conventional armaments would leave them supreme. Western leadership chases the mirage of a "limited nuclear war"—a war in which the Russians would graciously permit us to use just enough nuclear weapons to offset their conventional superiority. Each in its own way is trying to turn back the clock of history and thus to obtain an advantage over the other.

But history refuses to be reversed. Inventions cannot be uninvented. *The price which history demands for a safe-conduct into the atomic age is not the limitation and control of armaments but the abolition of war.*

Meanwhile, mankind trembles in apprehension, looking with mounting incomprehension and resentment at the two irresponsible antagonists. Soon China, with one quarter of the world's population, will enter upon the scene as a third and wholly unpredictable element.

The world knows that we of the West began this madness and looks to us to end it. This is easier said than done, but it must be done if the human race is to survive. *How* it can be done is one of the major topics to be discussed in this study.

IV

The cold war is essentially a struggle for the allegiance of the majority of mankind—a struggle between two different concepts of the nature of man and of man's relationship to his fellow man, to his country, and to the universe. It is true that this conflict involves a clash of social-economic theories, but the antithesis between "capitalism" and "socialism" is more apparent than real. The West is no longer capitalist in the Marxist sense, and certainly the communist system is nearer to state capitalism than to socialism. Nor can the struggle be accurately described as a conflict between democracy and dictatorship. The communist orbit provides certain elements of freedom not hitherto enjoyed by its inhabitants. The West has its enclaves of tyranny and dictatorship.

The real essence of the conflict is between two kinds of governments —between governments which foster revolutionary change in what they conceive to be their nations' interests without regard to any concept of international morality, and governments whose policies and actions in support of the *status quo* are limited and guided—no matter how imperfectly—by the moral concept of their peoples.

This antithesis remains obscured so long as both sides pursue the morally indefensible policy of threatening nuclear war.

Such a policy is perhaps consistent with the Marxist-Leninist philosophy, in which violence is sanctioned as an instrument of promoting revolution. It is wholly inconsistent with the professed philosophy of the West.

The Western policy of nuclear deterrence assumes that the risks of nuclear war are preferable to any substantial further expansion of the Sino-Soviet orbit. Underlying this assumption is a tacit belief that race suicide is preferable to a communist conquest of the world. Apart from the fact that this attitude poses a wholly false choice of alternatives, what right have we of the West to make any such choice for all of humanity? Even if we assume that most of the English-speaking peoples and some of the European and Latin-American peoples would find life intolerable under communist dictatorship, how true is this of those great masses of humanity who have never had a taste of freedom? By what moral authority are we entitled to threaten nuclear war—which means extinction for most if not all of humanity—in order to prevent the communists from seizing two little islands off the coast of Asia?

Until the West recaptures its lost moral sensibility, its struggle against communism will remain all but meaningless to the majority of mankind.

V

When and if the threat of race suicide is removed, it will become apparent that the real tension in the world exists not so much between Western Man and Sino-Soviet Man as between the privileged and underprivileged—between the peoples seeking to preserve what they possess and the peoples seeking change for the better.

Except for certain enclaves of poverty, notably in Latin America, the peoples of the Western world live in relative comfort and abundance, while the vast majority of the human race exists in varying degrees of misery. In the past this has been taken more or less for granted, much as the supposedly immutable fate of "the poor" was until recent times taken for granted within Western society.

If the world is saved from destruction, it will no longer be a world in which gross inequality and injustice will be tolerated. The hitherto underprivileged peoples are on the march.

If Western Man wishes to survive, he will have to learn—and learn very quickly—how to live in and with a world which has forever escaped from his control—a world suddenly freed from the fetters of ignorance and released from the coercion of superior physical power.

Western Man will have to do more than endeavor to compete successfully with the communist dictatorships in extending aid to the emerging peoples. He will have to give humanistic meaning to the material assistance he offers. He will have to recapture his belief in the brotherhood of man and rediscover the forgotten teachings of love and compassion. He will have to devote his resources and his ingenuity to the establishment of world-wide social justice as an end in itself—not as a measure of defense against a communist adversary.

Without a reawakening of Western morality, it is extremely doubtful whether Western Man can, in fact, compete successfully with the communists.

The communists' power of attraction derives from their nearness to poverty—from the fact that they have only recently lifted themselves out of illiteracy and squalid backwardness. Thus they have set an example which seems to the emerging peoples relevant to their own predicament and capable of emulation, whereas the high living standards and the accouterments of Western civilization seem out of reach and irrelevant.

Western Man can offset this disadvantage only by greater empathetic understanding of the needs and aspirations of peoples on the march toward what they hope will be a better future, by greater concern for universal social justice as well as for political freedom, by greater respect for divergent belief and opinion—in short, by making love and concern for humanity the operative factors in place of retentiveness and fear.

If our civilization is overrun and submerged by the global revolution of the underprivileged, it will be chiefly because we have failed to learn humility—because we have failed to recognize that we of the West are in no intrinsic sense superior or entitled to special privilege. This is going to be a difficult lesson for Western Man to learn. Notions such as "white supremacy" or *la mission civilisatrice* do not die easily; nor do the habits of greed, possessiveness, and lust for power.

VI

If this is the nature of the crisis of Western Man, we must ask ourselves several questions:

Why have we been sleepwalking into disaster?

How has this crisis come upon us?

What is it that our enemies seek to destroy and that we wish to preserve and defend?

In answer to the last question, most inhabitants of the Western world would probably reply:

"Political freedom, economic freedom, and freedom of worship." The order in which these three elements would be stated as well as the words used to describe them might vary, but the essence of the answer would remain the same.

If asked to define the existing threat or threats to these cherished attributes of Western civilization, most inhabitants of the Western world would probably think at once of an external menace. The simplest and most likely answer would be: "Communism."

The main thesis of this book is that, while the external threat exists, the mortal danger to Western civilization is not the enemy without but the enemy within the gates; that the political and economic systems of the West are being eroded from within; and that the external threat to Western civilization arises less from the strength of its would-be destroyers than from the weakness of its defenders. . . .

Finally, if this study conveys any compressible "message," it is that the foreign policy of a nation or group of nations is conditioned less by the "decisions" of those in high office than by the internal nature and behavior of the societies which those in high office represent; and that the survival or demise of Western civilization will be determined more by such internal matters as the regulation of monopolies, the treatment of minorities, and the nature of the educational system than by the arts of external diplomacy.

The decline of the West is undeniable, but in the writer's opinion it is by no means irreversible. The renaissance of Western civilization must begin within Western society. The key element in Western society is Individual Man.

ᶜᵒ⁰⁰⁰

The Task of Ethics*

P. H. NOWELL-SMITH

P. H. Nowell-Smith (1914-   ) is professor of philosophy at the University of Leicester, England. He has taught at Harvard University and at Trinity College, Oxford. His writings are in the fields of ethics, politics, and the nature and task of philosophy in general.

I

A broad distinction may be drawn between theoretical and practical sciences. The purpose of the former is to enable us to understand the nature of things, whether the things be stars, chemical substances, earthquakes, revolutions, or human behaviour. These sciences consist in answers to such questions as "What is an acid?," "What are the laws of planetary motion?," "How do bees find their way about?," "Why does wood float and iron sink?," "What are the marriage laws of the

* From *Ethics* (Baltimore: Penguin Books, 1954), pp. 11-14, 17.

Arapesh?." The answers take the form of statements, descriptions, gen-eralizations, explanations, and laws. I shall call such discourse "theo-retical," "fact-stating" or "descriptive" discourse; but it must not be supposed that every sentence in such discourse is a theory or states a fact or describes something. Newton's laws belong to descriptive dis-course, but they do not *describe* anything.

Practical discourse, on the other hand, consists of answers to practical questions, of which the most important are "What shall I do?" and "What ought I to do?." If I put these questions to myself the answers are decisions, resolutions, expressions of intention, or moral principles. If I put them to someone else his answer will be an order, injunction, or piece of advice, a sentence in the form "Do such and such." The central activities for which moral language is used are choosing and advising others to choose.

Traditionally, moral philosophy has always been regarded as a prac-tical science, a "science" because it was a systematic inquiry the goal of which was knowledge, and "practical" because the goal was practical knowledge, knowledge of what to do rather than knowledge of what is the case.

The words "morals" and "ethics" are derived from words meaning "custom" or "behaviour"; but the role of the moral philosopher was never conceived to be that of describing or explaining the customs or behaviour of men. That is the task of the psychologist, sociologist, anthropologist, historian, dramatist, and novelist. Moral philosophers set out to perform different tasks. The first was to answer practical ques-tions, the second to criticize, evaluate, or appraise customs and be-haviour. They claimed, not to tell you what men do, but to tell you which of the things that men do are good and which are bad. This second type of judgement, which is expressed in verdicts or appraisals, seems closer to theoretical than to practical discourse. To say that Jones is a good man is not—on the face of it—to tell anyone what to do, but rather to tell you what sort of man Jones is. It states a fact and from its grammatical form alone we should conclude that it is more like "Jones is a tall man" than like "Do what Jones does."

But the great philosophers of the past always treated questions of appraisal as subordinate to practical questions. They assumed—and who would not?—that the point of telling you that Jones is a good or a bad man is that you should imitate or not imitate Jones, that you should or should not give Jones the job or do whatever else might be in question. When they depicted the Good Life they would have thought it very odd if someone had said: "You have told me what the Good Life is and I agree with everything you say. Now tell me what I ought to do." Such a man has obviously misunderstood the philosopher's talk about the Good Life. For this talk was never intended to be a description of anything; it was from the start assumed to be an injunction to do something, to adopt this or that course, to subscribe to this or that moral code.

Moral philosophers did not, of course, undertake to give detailed practical advice as to how you should behave on this or that occasion. A philosopher is not a parish priest or Universal Aunt or Citizens' Advice Bureau. As we shall shortly see, different philosophers held very different views as to the way in which moral philosophy can help you to answer practical questions. But they all agreed that the goal of moral philosophy is practical knowledge, not that we should know what goodness is but that we should become good. From Plato, Aristotle, and Epicurus, from Hobbes, Spinoza, and Butler you can learn how, in their opinion, you ought to live.

And these philosophers were agreed also on another important point. They take for granted the fact that men have certain aims, purposes, and desires which they wish to achieve, fulfil, and satisfy. The achievement of these aims is variously called "The Good Life," "The Good for Man," "Happiness," and "Felicity"; and the task of the moral philosopher was to depict this state in broad outline and to tell you how you can achieve it. Although Plato starts his most elaborate treatise on moral philosophy with the question "What is Justice?," the principal question with which he is concerned is "Which of the two (justice or injustice) will bring happiness to its possessor?." The notion of duty does not play the central role in traditional that it plays in modern ethics and the notion of doing one's duty for duty's sake hardly appears before Kant. Earlier philosophers thought it quite sensible to ask "Why should I do my duty?"; the obligation to do one's duty needs justifying and can only be justified by showing that doing his duty is, in the short or long run, advantageous to the agent; indeed the classic treatises on the subject might be said to be mainly concerned with this justification. This point of view is called "teleological" and is opposed to that called "deontological," according to which duty rather than purpose is the fundamental concept of ethics.

If we turn to the great religious systems of the world we find the same emphasis on the practical nature of moral questions, the same assumption that life has a goal, be it the Christian or the Moslem Paradise or the Buddhist Nirvana, and the same assumption that the rules we are enjoined to live by are rules for achieving this state. This assumption is of the greatest antiquity. The Egyptians had a word "Ma'at" which is translated in three different ways. It means (a) "being straight, level, or even," (b) "order, conformity, regularity," and (c) "truth, justice, righteousness." It has obvious affinities to our word "right." Now the earliest moral document we possess is a manual of instruction on good behaviour to budding civil servants. In this the aspiring official is enjoined to follow the rules of Ma'at, but only because, by so doing, he will get on in the world. In later times the fruits of Ma'at were thought to lie in the next world rather than in this, but the basic conception is the same. We are to practise virtue because, in the short or long run, it pays.

In Christian ethics we find the same basic assumptions. "What shall I do," asks the lawyer, "to inherit eternal life?" The difference between this question and Plato's is simply that felicity is now thought to lie in the next world, not in this. No question is raised as to whether the lawyer wants to inherit eternal life; this is treated as a datum of the problem. Still less is there any question as to whether he ought to want this or ought not rather to have some other aim. In Christian, as in Greek ethics, there is no suggestion that moral rules ought to be obeyed irrespective of any purpose which will be served by obeying them. The answer does indeed take the form: "What is written in the law? How readest thou?." But this would not be an answer at all if it were not assumed that the rules contained in the law are to be obeyed because obedience is conducive to what the lawyer wants to achieve. Without this assumption the answer is simply irrelevant to the lawyer's problem.

But to say that moral rules are rules for achieving happiness or the Good Life does not tell us much. In what does happiness consist? How can we tell a good life from a bad one? How do we know whether obedience to the proffered rules is really going to lead to happiness? It was to these very general questions that the great philosophers mainly devoted themselves. In order to answer them they had to range over a wide field. Since man is a social animal, the Good Life must be life in society and politics must be discussed; indeed ethics and politics were, for these philosophers, one subject. Since it is idle to tell men what they ought to do unless we know what men are, psychology also comes into the picture, and philosophers spent much time analysing the human soul. It is also, for reasons to be given later, necessary to study logic; though this was more apparent to some philosophers than to others. . . .

There are a few fundamental rules of conduct that have never changed and probably never will; indeed it is difficult to imagine what life in society would be like if we abandoned them. The more we study moral codes the more we find that they do not differ on major points of principle and that the divergencies that exist are due partly to different opinions about empirical facts, for example about the effects of certain types of conduct, and partly to differences in social and economic organization that make it appropriate to apply the fundamental rules now in one way, now in another. Thus all codes agree that we have a duty to requite good with good; but obedience to this rule will involve behaving in ways that will differ according to the view that a society takes of what it is to do good to someone. In some societies it is rude for a guest to eat everything on his plate, in others it is rude for him not to do so; but both agree in enjoining that we should not be rude to our hosts.

It is not enough to know the general, unchanging rules; we must also know how to apply them. And it is for this reason that moral rules, like the law, cannot be codified for all time. One of the main tasks of the lawyer is to apply well-tried and stable general principles to cases that could not have arisen in an earlier age simply because the facts involved could not have arisen. New social and economic relations between man and man give rise to new rights and duties that could not have been contemplated by the authors of a particular moral or legal code.

The idea of a "scientific morality"—if it means anything more than the laudable recommendation to make use of discoveries in psychology when we are thinking about means—is as chimerical as the ideal which inspired the *Code Napoléon*. A detailed moral code, a sort of handbook to which we might turn for the answer to every moral problem, cannot help us, because difficulties will always arise about the application of the rules to new cases and because the cases in which the need for practical thinking is particularly acute are just those which are new and those in which we suspect that there is some good reason for breaking the accepted code. The need to think afresh about moral problems is ever present and particularly great in a period of rapid economic and social change and rapid advance in knowledge of human nature. Most of our detailed rules were evolved in societies very different from our own and by people who knew far less about human nature than we now do. . . .

FOR FURTHER STUDY

Frankena, William K. *Ethics*. Englewood Cliffs: Prentice-Hall, 1963, Ch. 1 "Morality and Moral Philosophy."

Garbett, Cyril. *In An Age of Revolution*. New York: Oxford U. Press, 1952. Part I, Chs. 1, 3.

Moskin, J. Robert. "Morality USA," *Look*, 27 (September 24, 1963): 74-78, 81-82.

Mumford, Lewis. *The Conduct of Life*. New York: Harcourt, Brace, 1951. (Harvest ed., 1960.)

Nevins, Allan. "What Has Happened to Our Morality?" *New York Times Magazine*, June 10, 1962, pp. 12, 32, 34, 36, 38, 40, 43.

Nowell-Smith, P. H. *Ethics*. Oxford: Basil Blackwell, 1957, Part 1, "Theory and Practice."

Schweitzer, Albert. *The Philosophy of Civilization*. New York: Macmillan, 1949, Part 1, "The Decay and Restoration of Civilization."

CHAPTER 2

THE DEVELOPMENT
OF MORALITY

∼∽∼∽∼∽∼∽∼∽∼∽∼∽∼∽∼∽∼∽∼∽∼∽∼∽∼∽∼∽∼∽

The Range of Moral Differences*

MAY EDEL
AND
ABRAHAM EDEL

May Edel (1909-   ) is an anthropologist who has taught at a number of schools including the New School for Social Research and Rutgers University (Newark College). Her writings include *The Story of Our Ancestors.*

Abraham Edel (1908-   ) has taught philosophy since 1931 at City College, New York. His writings include *Ethical Judgment,* 1955, and *Method in Ethical Theory,* 1963.

There is, of course, some sense in which we all know what we are talking about when we talk about morality. But this is not adequate for comparative study. How can we be sure that what we have in mind is what we find in other peoples; or that translation in familiar moral terms is true to their language? By what mark shall we know "the moral"? . . .

* From *Anthropology and Ethics,* 1959, pp. 7-10, 19-32 with omissions. Courtesy of Charles C Thomas, Publisher, Springfield, Illinois.

The diversity of trends in assigning the mark of the moral may fruitfully be put into two broad categories, which we shall call Ethics Wide and Ethics Narrow. These seem to involve divergent broad hypotheses about the place of moral phenomena in human life.

Ethics Wide assumes that moralities are part and parcel of the whole field of human endeavor and striving. It poses inquiry conceptually in terms of the search, either by the individual or the group, for man's *good* in the sense of what he aims at, what goals he finds worth while, what values appear and are stabilized in his experience. There are all sorts of human "values"—any interest, any pleasure, any conception of the desired and the desirable, anything fitting or attractive or serviceable may come to rank as a value for human beings. Moral values constitute simply one part of the field. They may be differentiated by their reference to personal character, and their special relevance to desirable forms of interpersonal relations or social organization. Or they may be the values that play an organizing role in the whole field. Or they may have no particular unity beyond some broad servicing role in the achievement and maintenance of fundamental individual and social well-being.

Ethics Wide, therefore, stresses the investigation of the widest possible context. It expects that accounts of virtues, obligations, sanctions, feelings and so forth, will be geared in the long run to descriptions of human values and modes of achieving or realizing them. It sets no initial barrier to the domains into which one may have to go in tracking down the nature and tasks of ethics. Any account of man, whether it comes from biology or theology, may present itself as a candidate for providing insight into morality.

Ethics Narrow, on the other hand, limits the scope of inquiry into moral phenomena. Conceptually it pushes to the fore the idea of *obligation* or *duty*. Values, it says, are far too broad, far too promiscuous. Only those that *ought to be* or *ought to be realized* come within the scope of morality. Beyond, there may be questions of interest, even of importance for human needs and goals, but these are not morality. Descriptively, Ethics Narrow focusses on the moral experience, moral judgment, moral feelings, of the individual. It wants a systematic picture of these sentiments and responses. At times this has meant construing man's moral feelings as complex sympathy reactions, at times as finely-drawn conscience-responses. Ethics Narrow is more prone than Ethics Wide to insist on a unique defining mark or characteristic of the moral in terms of personal consciousness—though there has been no agreement on exactly what this mark is to be. . . .

The impact of anthropology has been felt very sharply on our ordinary thinking about morality. It has become a matter of common knowledge that people's standards, their actual moral rules and ideas about good and bad behavior, vary enormously. Just as our more or less literate children today all know that the Eskimo rub noses as a sign of greeting and affection, so we—their more sophisticated elders—know that Eskimo ideas of marital fidelity are different from our own, that they exchange their wives freely, lending bed and wife with equal hospitality to visiting friends. We know that such contravention of our attitudes—to adultery, or truth-telling or killing or toward virtually any rule we accept—are extremely common among the peoples of different cultures of the world. We know that not all people are shocked and indignant at the things which shock us. A little less confidently, we realize that they may instead be shocked at some aspects of our behavior which seem to us either desirable, or "natural" and morally neutral—like our failing to share our daily bread with all our needy friends and neighbors, or allowing old people to waste away of painful diseases.

The actual range of the differences anthropology has discovered is enormous, and we cannot even begin to chart it here. There are societies in which it is required that you eat your deceased friend or brother to show your respect for him; others in which a cannibal feast on an enemy is an everyday event, and supplying this special game for the larder a required mark of adult status. There are societies where to eat your own crops, grown in your own garden, or the game bagged by your own hunting efforts, is out of the question, wrong in all the ways in which stealing is wrong in our own morality—offensive to gods and men, indicative of a generally bad character, ringed around with evil consequences both social and supernatural—in short, a form of wickedness so wrong that for the average man it is not usually even an admitted temptation. And there are other societies where a man will die of some compound of shame, guilt, remorse or fear if he finds that he has carelessly eaten a guinea hen with a forbidden pattern of markings on its feathers. There are societies where the young are permitted far more sexual freedom than we would allow, but where no man may decently eat in the presence of anyone but a very close relative. And others where extramarital sex relations between mature adults are ordinarily of no moral import whatsoever—matters entirely of the desires and preferences of the parties involved—but become horrifying scandals if they are engaged in at some disapproved time or place.

The same kind of variety that is found in peoples' rules of behavior is found in their ideals of character, in their concepts of virtue and vice and in their goals of life. Anger and shouting may be offensive, abominable to the gods and dangerous; or they may be an admired demonstration of strength of character, pointed to for children to emulate as a model of respected masculine behavior. Plains Indian honors go to the young warrior brave enough to go through the lines of an enemy encampment to steal a tethered horse. To a warrior in another part of the world that would be foolhardy; his own bravery can include ambush, or sudden treachery, and most certainly the good sense of running away from danger. Others abhor fighting altogether and do all they can to minimize it. Among the Trobriand islanders of the South Pacific a basic code of mutual obligation is so ingrained that a man will abandon a day's highly paid pearl diving for a puzzled white trader in order to do a day's fishing for an inland neighbor in return for a few yams or other farm produce, because the obligations to a trading partner must always be fulfilled. But their neighbors from the nearby island of Dobu who also live by a complicated system of trade relations, consider any cheating one can actually get away with as a mark of the greatest shrewdness, an admired stepping-stone to success. To have enough to eat, to have sons, and to die in respected old age on one's own ancestral land, is the conscious goal of some peoples' striving, while others are concerned with wealth or glory or power, and will see such pursuits as the proper aim of a good life.

Anthropologists have found that differences go far beyond these matters of specific rules and regulations, or even goals and values. They reach into any and every part of the phenomena and structure of morality. There are different kinds of sanctions to support moral codes. In one society shame and ridicule may be open weapons, and public opinion a highly charged deterrent pressure, while in another a man's neighbors will be very little concerned with his breaches of the moral code, shrugging them off with "Well, what can you do? That's just the kind of man he happens to be." There are differences in the systematizations, the justifications and rationalizations which people use, and in the basic values and world attitudes which underlie or elaborate their codes. Some people have gods who are malicious, and unconcerned with human morals, while others worship supernaturals who have the same kind of concern with men's behavior that we traditionally consider appropriate. For some people moral issues are explicit, verbalized, central, for others seldom the conscious center in decision situations. The structure of conscience itself, it now begins to appear, may not be quite the same for all people; perhaps some mechanisms of pure fear, and prudence, a total lack of concern with any internal goals and standards may be the picture for at least some of the societies in the world.

We shall concern ourselves later with more detailed examination of some of these areas of difference, and their significance for ethical theory. Meanwhile, however, we must note that this picture of sweeping differences to be found in any part of the moral field to which the student set his sights was one of the first contributions anthropology made to the pool of knowledge of the developing human sciences during the early part of the twentieth century. Of course it was not really a new discovery. The ancients had known it all along, and any careful thinking about European morals over the centuries from classic times through the middle ages and the rise of modern times had perforce to note that there had been great changes in moral standards—from the condemnation of usury to the elevation of finance capitalism, from status-acceptance (the idea of filling the station to which one had been "called") to the ideal of competitive individual success. The ethical theories of the western world also reveal a vast array of differences. The good life of Aristotle, with its harmonious balance, would seem insipid to a Nietzschean in his pursuit of the heroic; stoical inner peace, in the sense of playing one's role whatever the cost, would seem folly to a Hobbesian who sees man's morality as a compromise in the predatory quest for power, wealth and prestige. The rational temper of Socratic virtue contrasts markedly with the pious humility of the Christian, the loyalty and gratitude attitudes of the feudal order, the sobriety and thrift of the early Protestant ethic, or the industriousness, prudence, and often calculating beneficence of the Benthamite.

But somehow the significance of differences in moral standards did not deeply color modern thought until recently. The philosophical differences were obscured by the fact that each morality in turn claimed to be the true one, and each theory the correct one. Eighteenth century thinking was concerned with establishing the natural rights and properties of men. Rousseau, for example, had written of a romanticized "noble savage" who had our virtues undistorted by the corruption of civilization. The nineteenth century, more inclined to see the differences, tended to disregard them, either holding the "savage" to be altogether outside the domain of moral and religious feelings until the missionary came to convert him; or, in its more reflective expressions, assuming that he was somehow at a lower evolutionary stage.

In any case, the shock effect of the anthropological writings with their emphasis on the sweep and range of cultural differences, coupled with the insistence that these data were relevant to any thinking about human nature and human society, was very great. It was felt in sociology, in psychology, in the whole field of the social sciences. Sumner's thinking (1906)—"the standards are in the mores," and "the mores can make anything right"—a complete kind of cultural relativism, became pretty pervasive. Anthropologists wrote of different "patterns of culture" and textbooks of social psychology threw out their lists of instincts to write instead of the differences between the Zuni Indians, or the Kwakiutl, and ourselves. Popular attitudes to morality, at that time in a state of flux, seized upon and reflected these positions. If different people are angry and disapproving about different things, what validity can there be about any one of them? Why bother to be angry or disapproving about anything? If chastity is not a universal value, why value it at all? If the Samoans practise premarital promiscuity, why should we not experiment with it too?

Clearly anthropology was not uniquely responsible for the recasting of the various disciplines in these relativist terms. The mutual influence among the human sciences which were carving out their respective areas and charting their positions in the study of man was, of course, great, and it all tended in this direction. Behaviorist psychology in an extreme form was making a very parallel point, discarding human nature as a theoretical construct, and starting instead with a concept of each person beginning as a perfectly clean slate, a being who must learn all that he would ever know, including the shape of all his feelings and sentiments, through rather mechanical learning experiences, particularly repetitive association. At the same time, philosophy was expressing a sharp positivist trend, discarding as metaphysical nonsense a great part of traditional abstraction, and consigning all value assertions to the domain of simple emotional expression. Sociology was going through a similar phase of new discovery, a process of housecleaning marked more by a tearing down than a building up. All together contributed to a growing picture of mankind and his ways as the result of chance historical circumstances, largely random and whimsical, perhaps even unintelligible.

Of course this is not the only, nor necessarily the most sensible way to look at differences. The discovery that there are other ways than our own, and that these seem pretty well grounded in other peoples' attitudes and habits, need not make us say "Our ways, if not absolute and obvious, are no good, and neither for that matter are any one else's." We might instead say, "Whatever other peoples' different views, our own are best." This, as a matter of fact, is a view that some among us have always held to. And it is the reaction in most other cultures to the awareness of differences. Or we might take the more sophisticated view so well expressed by a Hopi Indian in his auto-biographical discourse: "I could see that the old people were right when they said that Jesus Christ might do for modern Whites in a good climate, but that the Hopi gods had brought success to us in the desert ever since the world began." In short, each people has different ways, and does best to stick to its own. That indeed was the path anthropology tended to take for a while, emphasizing the need to respect different cultures' varying ways as "equally valid patterns of life." Or we might take the most difficult path of all: critical assessment.

We cannot here examine the conditions in our own culture that made the general revolt against absolutes so appealing in the earlier part of the present century. Moral rigidities and changed social conditions, the disillusionment of the generation that followed World War I, a sense of the failure of dominant institutions to ensure progress, the rapid growth of knowledge casting doubt on many a cherished belief—all of these no doubt played a part. In similar fashion, the extremes of economic depression, the conflict with the Nazi world view, the failure to achieve peace after World War II and the intensity of ideological issues since that time, coupled with the menace of atomic warfare, have provoked an insecurity that has become a base for a renewed search for absolutes. This has had its effect on the popular scene in a trend toward conformity and a search for safe anchors for ethics. In the sciences of man there has also been a renewed interest in looking for uniformities, for some common human that lies beyond the differences. The possibly wishful aspect in this new direction of inquiry does not invalidate the search—for the prior emphasis on differences may very well have been excessive—but it does suggest the need that it be conducted with great care. And indeed there is a greater sophistication about it which suggests the possibilities of a sober reckoning rather than a purely pendular swing.

In this renewed inquiry the sciences of man have profited jointly by the advances in their various branches. The psychologist who has discarded his outmoded lists of specific instincts takes up his search for the common human at the level of common dynamic processes and potentialities, rather than simple uniformities of behavior. He works to integrate historically conditioned, learned ways of thinking, feeling and wanting into his accounts of human nature. The anthropologist and sociologist too, while still interested in differences, emphasize the "common denominators" of culture and "invariant properties of social interaction." They are engaged in renewed attempts to understand the trends of culture history and the causal and functional principles that operate in it. In morality particularly, many are reasserting the common meanings and common goals that may be seen beneath the differences in moral codes and moral patterns.

This is of course not altogether a new approach. Franz Boas himself, often presented as the arch-demon of relativism in anthropology—largely because of his supreme distaste for making generalizations in history that were too sweeping to be supported by verifiable evidence—pointed out that the ethics of the in-group provided a kernel of common moral motivation beneath the surface variety of behaviors. For, he wrote, "social obligations that develop in intimate family life . . . may be observed everywhere." Despite differences in the way groups treat outsiders, "the standard of ethical behavior toward members of one's own group is regulated by subordination of the individual to group interests and by recognition of the rights of other members of the group." And Ruth Benedict, certainly steeped in a relativist perspective, wrote, "Mankind has always preferred to say, 'It is morally good,' rather than 'It is habitual' and the fact of this preference is matter enough for a virtual science of ethics." And she went on to say, "It is quite possible that a modicum of what is considered right and what wrong could be disentangled that is shared by the whole human race."

This kind of view is now moving to a position of central interest and concern. Although some anthropologists—Melville Herskovits, for example—are sceptical of the very quest for a common human morality, as itself culture-bound, many do share the view that some common base can be found. A few have even tried to pinpoint some actual areas of common content. Linton, for example, has argued that "societies everywhere have moral principles in common but with different emphases." All societies, he says, "deplore incest and rape," demand "loyalty to some social group," and hold "disloyalty a vice," control aggression to some extent, expect truth in certain situations, as when oaths are taken, and expect people to meet obligations involved in exchange of goods and services. And Kluckhohn in a similar vein writes, "Every culture has a concept of murder . . . The notions of incest and other regulations upon sexual behavior, of prohibitions upon untruth under defined circumstances, of restitution and reciprocity, of mutual obligations between parents and children—these and many other moral concepts are altogether universal."

Others, working in related disciplines, have also looked in various ways for common moral bases. Macbeath, approaching anthropological data as a philosopher, does not believe that one finds specific moral rules or principles that all societies have in common, but he does claim that one can see, in the varying "operative ideals" which act as guides to conduct in the world's varying cultures, a common "formal ideal," a striving for a very general common human goal of satisfaction or fulfillment. And Morris Ginsberg analyzes some of the ways in which differences in moralities may be reduced by recognizing that they are often different means to similar ends, different weightings assigned to common principles, or based on differences in social contexts. However, he maintains that there are some fundamental differences that remain, differences in levels of moral sensitivity, in the "conception of the human person as such," and total rejection of cruelty per se, which are emergent developments of recent social history, rather than merely wider applications of older principles.

Similarly, Karl Duncker, examining moral experience from the perspective of Gestalt psychology, postulates the existence of common human valuations, which can be discovered by probing under the variations in the meaning and institutional settings of acts. People who condone or require infanticide, he maintains, are not disagreeing about the wrongness of killing babies. They just do not consider what they are doing as baby-killing. For them, the new-born are not human until they have breathed, or undergone some ritual treatment; or a malformed infant is held to be an evil spirit. Anthropologists have seen too much variety in human moral attitudes to accept such uniform moral perceptions as established. They agree, of course, that one must look for varying meanings and interpretations; contextual interpretation is their basic methodological stock in trade. But they are sceptical of finding behind *every* cannibal rite some moral altruism, behind every sadistic practice an offering to a—regrettably—demanding god, behind every war the feeling of a holy cause. There are such cases, of course, but they are inclined to wonder if this does not prove merely that man is prone to paint himself in pleasant colors, to disguise cruelty rather than abjure its practice, in short that man is, perhaps, less moral than moralizing.

The anthropologist then does not find it fruitful at this point to look for common moral perceptions and instinctive moral reactions. Instead, in looking for universal moral rules and for an understanding of differences, he pursues a mode of analysis which combines psychological with biosocial and historical factors. His general argument is somewhat as follows. The patterns of human social interaction, however deep their biological and psychological roots, are not simply direct instinctual expression, or the playing out of a built-in psychological drama. They are, as Kluckhohn puts it, "somewhat distinct answers to essentially the same questions posed by human biology and by the generalities of the human situation." They are complex answers, ways which have been built up over time, "experiments in living," to use Macbeath's telling phrase, that different cultures have worked out, in the course of which new and varying needs have themselves been generated. There is room for wide variety in the kinds of lives men build for themselves, but certain minimal standards must be met if these "experiments" are to be successful at all. Each culture must provide patterns of motor habits, social relations, knowledge and beliefs, such that it will be possible for men to survive. Everywhere there must be techniques for making a living, patterns of mating, of mutual help, ways of defining who is a friend and who a foe, and of dealing with each, ways of coping with sickness and old age and death—and means for learning all of these ways. And there are not only common requirements imposed by common problems, but common psychological processes and mechanisms through which they operate and on which they react. Birth and death, love and sorrow and fear are the lot of all men; all are capable of desires and dreams, and use symbolic thinking, identification, reaction-formation. This common human nature sets limits to the forms that any experiments in living can take, to the possible techniques of motivation, the scope of sympathy, the effectiveness of sanctions.

Common needs, common social tasks, common psychological processes, are bound to provide some common framework for the wide variety of human behaviors that different cultures have developed. And part of this framework includes the need for a certain measure of cooperation and conformity in the behavior of the members of any society. Those who live and work together must go along the paths charted by the customs and expectations of the group not just through external coercive pressures but through motivations which are to some degree built into their habits and attitudes. The members of a society must share some common values and accept some bondage to their common goals and goods. "No man is an island" nor can be, for to survive means to have grown up and to live in society, to share its pressures and to share in the "direct experience of the inevitability of interdependence between men in society." And so it is not unreasonable to expect nor surprising to find that among all men, amid all the historically developed cultural diversity, there is not only a nuclear family and some extended kinship, work and dancing, art and religion —but also *morality*. And morality includes common structural patterns, common mechanisms, and, where social institutions are parallel, some detailed similarity in content.

Such a general approach as we have been describing is not so much a particular hypothesis as what has sometimes been called a hypothesis-schema. It does not give us a quick touchstone for discovering common moral traits, nor for understanding all moral differences; it is, rather, a suggestive guide to formulating hypotheses about morality in relation to human needs. The anthropologist working in a sophisticated vein from such a perspective would not start with a ready-made check-list of biosocial demands. He knows that such a list would need to be constantly revised, both because of our increasing knowledge about the nature of man,—as in the increasing evidence of the role of emotional factors in health and disease,—and because new developments in technology or group living and population aggregation change the structure of human needs—as in the past land-space demands changed with the abandonment of a hunting economy, or irrigation agriculture posed new problems about access to water. The anthropologist knows that he has to study the actual, and changing, character of such needs, not merely to assume them. Nor can he assume any specific fixed role in the moral domain for needs of different sorts. He knows that the same end may be sought through differing means, and the pursuit of the same means may represent different goals; that men's actual paths of life may be compromises or resultants of the convergence of values whose subtle interplay may not easily be read off from the observed results; and that he must understand his data in a context of possible change, rather than permanent stability. How malleable different needs may actually prove to be; how they will intermesh with each other, and with the historically-developed institutions and goals; whether their respective sweep in affecting moral development will be vast or small, determining, limiting, or merely exacting of a high price if violated, are empirical questions to be investigated, not prejudged. It is such questions which this general approach suggests as problems to be formulated for empirical research. . . .

FOR FURTHER STUDY

Albert, Ethel M. "Social Science Facts and Philosophical Values," *The Antioch Review*, 17 (Winter 1957-1958): 406-420.

Benedict, Ruth. *Patterns of Culture*. Boston: Houghton Mifflin, 1934. (Pelican Books, 1946.)

Edel, May, and Edel, Abraham. *Anthropology and Ethics*. Springfield: Charles C Thomas, 1959.

Heard, Gerald. *Morals Since* 1900. London: Andrew Dakers, 1950.

Hobhouse, L. T. *Morals in Evolution*. New York: Holt, 1923, Ch. 8, "The Line of Ethical Development."

Macbeath, A. *Experiments in Living*. London: Macmillan, 1952, Ch. 1, "Anthropology and Ethics."

McCown, Chester C. *Man, Morals and History: Today's Legacy from Ancient Times and Biblical Peoples*. New York: Harper, 1958.

Tsanoff, Radoslav A. *Ethics*. New York: Harper, 1955, Ch. 2, "The Beginnings and the Development of Morals in Early Societies."

CHAPTER 3

HUMAN NATURE
AND HUMAN CONDUCT

ᴫᴫᴫᴫᴫᴫᴫᴫᴫᴫᴫᴫᴫᴫᴫᴫᴫᴫᴫᴫᴫᴫᴫᴫ

Can Human Nature Be Changed?*

HAROLD KELMAN
FREDERICK A. WEISS
PAUL TILLICH
KAREN HORNEY

In this Symposium, Harold Kelman (1906-   ), M.D., president of the American Institute for Psychoanalysis and editor of its journal, Frederick A. Weiss (1898-   ), M.D., lecturer at the American Institute for Psychoanalysis, Dr. Paul Tillich (1886-   ), noted theologian of Union Theological Seminary and Harvard University, and Karen Horney (1885-1952), M.D. who was Dean of the American Institute for Psychoanalysis, discuss the nature of human nature.

Discussion by Harold Kelman, M.D.

Human nature can change. This affirmative proposition prompts many questions and to them a host of possible answers. What is human nature, essentially? We do not assert that man by nature is inherently

* From "Human Nature Can Change: A Symposium," *American Journal of Psychoanalysis*, 12 (1952): 62-68 with brief omissions. Used by permission.

destructive and only secondary constructive. Nor do we agree that innately he is both good and bad. Rather do we believe that in all human beings there is the potentiality, as a lifelong tendency and direction, to realize and to fulfill his possibilities as a human being and as a particular human being, as circumstances permit.

What has changed? Our knowledge of the psychological, emotional, physical and social nature of man has increased and been revised so that we now hold this optimistic philosophy regarding human beings. What can and have we changed? As physicians of the body and the soul we have helped many individuals to become less sick and more healthy in their relations to themselves and in their social relations. And through these efforts we have helped individuals in the environment of persons analytically treated to change the direction of their life patterns. The trend toward increased sickness has been slowed and even reversed. And the younger members have been helped toward straighter growing to the end of more joyously and productively assuming their responsible places as citizens of a world in which they will live. In short, we have helped potentiality become actuality.

What has essentially changed in human beings as we study man on the canvas of human history? Here again there are many evidences of the change of potentiality into actuality. From a nomadic existence man has changed to community living. From a pathetic reliance on magic to appease or to master physical and animal nature as well as possible malevolent haunting presences inside and outside of himself, man has attained a greater self-confidence and self-dignity through understanding and co-operating with all the aspects of nature. From isolated family groupings, through the sequence of tribes, nations, empires and through the cycles of rise, decline and decay, we now face the prospect of world unity.

How have these changes come about? Through the expression of certain essential human attributes—to name two, conflict and co-operation. Conflict and co-operation are an essential part of life and are essential to living. Looked at this way we do not overfocus on the fact that there have always been wars but also see in proportionate perspective that there have also been periods of peace.

That the world will become one is in the nature of the human evolutionary process. How it will be unified is a matter of the future; whether under a Communist dictatorship, whether under the rest of the world which might become equally totalitarian to accomplish this unification or whether through a long process of hot and cold wars and arbitration ending in a more truly democratic world than we have yet envisaged.

How can we help make this third potentiality an actuality? By work, faith, and understanding our own essential individual human nature and the nature of others; through conflict and co-operation; through a fuller expression of our agreements and differences while fundamentally agreeing that "Life is worth living." . . .

Discussion by Frederick A. Weiss, M.D.

Modern man has changed nature; he has transformed atoms into tremendous sources of energy, wide areas of water into land, barren deserts into fertile soil. But when it comes to man himself, time and again we hear the statement, "You cannot change human nature."

To be sure, his powerful changes of outer nature have not transformed the inner nature of man. They cannot and will not do so; and the magic expectations of those who wish to believe that leads only to an inertia which perpetuates their present condition and makes mankind itself more and more the mere passive object of mechanization and dehumanization. No, the magic solution does not work—not for individual man, and not for mankind as a whole.

Are we then to believe that human nature cannot change at all? This thesis may sound scientific, but it is pseudoscientific; it misuses and misinterprets biological and psychological facts. I think it is characteristic that this statement about the unchangeability of human nature is most often heard in connection with some evidence that seems to deny the very essence of human nature. When people are confronted with acts by which men exploit, hurt or destroy other men; when arrogant, vindictive leaders dominate masses of self-effacing automatons; when demagogues bent on the pursuit of power make scapegoats of other races or nations; then we hear this slogan of defeat and resignation, that "human nature cannot change." It is used to defend their inertia by those whom Lewis Mumford most aptly called the "Society for the Prevention of Change." Had human history been governed by this maxim, cannibalism, head-hunting and slavery might never have been abolished and our treatment of mental illness might still consist of burning witches and exorcising the devil.

Modern psychology and education, while fully aware of the role of genetic and constitutional factors, have clearly demonstrated the plasticity of human nature and its capacity for change. Children who in an authoritarian social climate are hostile, or inert and paralyzed, become friendly, co-operative and constructive in a democratic climate. Adults are able to change when their motivations shift from goals that are externally, or internally imposed upon them to goals which they really want for their own growth and self-realization.

Psychoanalysis has taught us not only that human nature can and does change, but also how it changes. Freud discovered the tremendous power of unconscious emotions and showed how anxiety and inner conflicts interfere with the free development of human beings. But his assumption that these unconscious, driving forces in man were only "libido" and the "death instinct"—which would leave us only the choice of destroying others or ourselves—resulted in a deeply pessimistic concept of human nature.

Our concept of human nature is a different one. We are convinced of man's inherent potentiality to be human—rather, let us say, to become human—which means to realize himself and to form constructive relationships with his fellow men. Potentiality, however, is not yet realization. Self-realization requires self-awareness and self-transformation.

Pearl Buck recently stated her belief in human nature:

> My knowledge of people compels me to believe that the normal human heart is born good. That is, it is born sensitive and feeling. . . . It neither wishes to be killed nor to kill. If through circumstances it is overcome by evil, it never becomes entirely evil. There remain in it elements of good, however recessive, which continue to hold the possibility of restoration. I believe in human beings, but my faith is without sentimentality. I know that in environments of uncertainty, fear and hunger, the human being is dwarfed and shaped without his being aware of it, just as the plant struggling under a stone does not know its own condition. Only when the stone is removed can it spring up freely into the light. But the power to spring up is inherent.[1]

We fully share Pearl Buck's faith in the constructive forces of human nature, and we want to help in removing the stone that hinders human growth. But our analytic experience has shown that it is not enough merely to release a human being from this outer pressure; he must also become freed from the stone within himself. Thus we try to halt the process of inner petrification which makes people rigid, frozen, lifeless and numb; which anesthetizes them to what they really feel about themselves and others, and what they really do to themselves and others. It

[1] "Roll Away the Stone," in *This I Believe*, ed. Edward R. Murrow (New York: Simon and Schuster, 1952), Vol. I.

is this inner petrification that causes people to perpetuate what they believe to be their "unlucky fate."

Freud observed that some persons seemed to repeat earlier experiences all their lives. "Their stories," he said, "give the impression of a pursuing fate. . . . One knows people with whom every human relationship ends in the same way: . . . men with whom every friendship ends in treachery; . . . others who again and again invest some other persons with authority, then overthrow this authority after a given time, only to replace it by a new one; lovers whose tender relationship with women, each and all, come to the same end."

There can be no doubt that these observations are true to life. We all know people whose lives present such perpetual repetition of experiences destructive to themselves and to others. But is this any proof that human nature cannot change? According to Freud the repetition compulsion, a demonic force far stronger than ourselves, induces us to repeat over and over again the patterns of our childhood. To a large extent, it is true, we do create our own "fate," and often this fate appears highly repetitious. But this is not because we are forced forever to repeat infantile experiences, but because we are unconsciously driven by compulsive, neurotic needs. The protective shelter which we built up in childhood as a defense against basic anxiety has become a self-made prison that restrains our freedom and stunts our growth. Yet we are not doomed by our past if we learn to understand its dynamic meaning. Earlier experiences are important, but to delve into the past is by no means constructive if it merely leads the patient to blame all his misery on others—say, on a domineering father or an overprotective mother—it is constructive only in the degree in which it reveals to him the hidden leitmotifs of his life and helps him to change. . . .

What is needed for real change is that emotional insight which stirs us to the very depths of our being and which tells us: "I am no longer doomed by what others once did to me, if I can feel and understand, now, what I myself am doing to my real self and to others. Do I need to be well liked by everyone, like Willy Loman in *Death of a Salesman*? Is it my only goal to dominate and triumph over others, like Willie Stark in *All the King's Men*? Am I relentlessly driven towards success and prestige, without consideration for the rights and life of others, as is Clyde Griffith in *An American Tragedy*? Do I sacrifice the growth of my real self in the service of pride? Do I tear down my real self because it fails to measure up to my idealized image? Do I externalize my own self-hate by degrading others, particularly members of other racial groups?"

The time we live in has become an era of mass anesthesia. Unable or unwilling to face themselves, people seek to anesthetize themselves by their compulsive participation in the race after success and glory, by compulsive eating and drinking, compulsive television, the compulsive use of barbiturates, and compulsive demands for any kind of therapy that will further diminish their self-awareness—hypnosis, narcoanalysis, and shock therapy.

Indeed, a kind of shock therapy is needed. But this need, in "neurotic personalities of our time," is not for any shock treatment which by physical or chemical means *lessens* the awareness of our human feelings. Rather, it is for that deep, emotional shock through which our innermost human nature is powerfully *made aware*, both of our present inhumanity and of our inherent potentiality—and responsibility—to become human. Then, human nature can change.

Discussion by Paul Tillich

The question raised in my mind by the subject of the symposium is the question of human nature, generally. I do not ask whether human beings, individuals or groups can be changed by external events. This, it seems to me, is beyond any doubt. And the questions to be asked, in this respect, are only how deep do such changes go, how can a transitory and a permanent change be distinguished and how can such changes be brought about? It is the daily task of two other members of the forum to work for such changes. Therefore it is quite fit that they deal predominantly with this side of the problem.

But behind their problem a more general problem is waiting for a solution—if there is a solution. This is the problem of "man changeable and unchangeable," which is the title of a very exciting book by my friend, the philosopher at the New School, Professor Kurt Riezler. In this title the question of human nature is clearly and sharply expressed. And this is the subject to which I want to address myself.

The first thing to be emphasized is that human nature could not change if there were not something unchangeable in it. This is easy to understand: absolute change is an impossible notion, because without a subject of which we can say that *it* changes we neither could notice nor measure a change. In our case this "it" which changes is *man*. We do not ask: has man replaced another being or will he be replaced by another being, but we ask: can this nature change, which we call human, and which remains human nature before and after the change? Our question now can be formulated in a precise way: Which are the changeable and which are the unchangeable elements in that which makes man, man?

Those philosophers, anthropologists, sociologists, and psychologists who are inclined to deny anything unchangeable in man usually point to history and the amazing changes in human behavior in every period. They claim that history has already proved the unlimited possibilities of change in human nature. But there is an obvious fallacy in this arguing. They speak of the changes which have happened and still happen in human history: that is, they presuppose in all historical changes that being called man which *has* history. In the context of our experience man is the only being which has history; he is the only being to whose nature it belongs to act and to change within history. If we go back to our animal ancestors, or go ahead to our angelic descendants, both man and history disappear and with them the problem of our forum. But if we remain within human history as we experience it in our own historical existence we can say something about the unchangeable element in human nature. It is that unity of freedom and destiny, of which we are aware in every moment in which we act as men. I do not refer to the obsolete discussion about the freedom of the will but I point to the immediate experience that we are able to transcend that which is given to us in ourselves and in our world. In a somewhat paradoxical formula we could say: the unchangeable element in man is his freedom to change himself and his world. It is not an unlimited freedom. It is embedded in his historical and personal destiny, in the consequences of his past, the given and the self-made ones, in the structure of reality as a whole. In other words: man is finite and his freedom is finite. But as a *finite* being he *has* freedom. Man can be called in the shortest condensation of all his possibilities and impossibilities, "finite freedom." In this basic structure both the unchangeable and the changeable elements are rooted.

Unchangeable is his having a centered self which has a world to which it belongs and at which it looks at the same time. This unchangeable structure gives him freedom from both himself and his world and therefore the power of transforming both in the process which we call history. *Unchangeable* is his capability of transcending every given situation by asking questions and receiving demands, by making tools and creating language. Every universal, used in the most primitive language, is an expression of man's universality. It liberates him from the bondage to the concrete situation which, on the other hand, is his destiny. And again it is just this unchangeable structure which makes it possible that man builds a world of tools beyond the given world, that he uses that which is given to him for the creation of cultures and civilizations within the ever-changing process of history in which he creates the new.

Unchangeable is man's ability to deliberate and to decide, to receive a stimulus, to take it into the center of the self and to respond in freedom, that is, *through* the center of the self. This gives him the experience of the ought-to-be and of his responsibility for the realization of what ought-to-be. And it is just this unchangeable structure which makes possible the infinite difference of character and the changes of personality structure. The many personality structures are rooted in the *one* structure of personality.

Unchangeable is man's freedom to contradict his own nature, to fall away from what he essentially is and ought to be, to try to escape from himself and his true being into sickness in body and mind, into the narrowness of compulsive self-seclusion, into imaginary worlds, into what everybody does and everybody thinks, into self-estrangement and hostility. *Unchangeable* is a voice which reminds him of the split between what he is and what he ought to be, a voice in him which speaks in a thousand voices and sometimes silently, calling him back to himself, producing in him the anxiety of guilt and sometimes the desperate desire to get rid of himself. But equally *unchangeably* he experiences healing powers, coming from the nature in him and around him, from individual helpers and social forces, from the deepest levels of his own being and from the ground of all being.

But here a mistake must be avoided. To heal man does not mean to change the unchangeable in his nature. It does not mean to deprive him of his freedom to contradict himself. It was the fallacy of the progressivistic interpretation of history that it forgot that man remains finite freedom on every level of civilization and that, therefore, he can use the results of progress to destroy them and to destroy himself with them. The risk implied in finite freedom can never be removed, as long as men are neither animals nor angels. In every newborn child freedom gets a new center, life a new chance and spirit a new risk. Neither social institutions, nor education, nor psychological help can change this central element of human nature. Social institutions of the totalitarian type try to transform men into things through terror; education of the adjustment type tries to transform men into easily manageable citizens, psychotherapy of the mechanistic type tries to transform men into well-functioning homunculi or artificial men. But none of them works permanently. On every level freedom breaks through managed perfection. On every level there are people who enter, to use Karen Horney's term, a devil's pact. And the higher the institutional, moral and educational level on which it is done, the more refined are the conditions of this pact. *You can liberate man only to his freedom.* More than this would be less. For man has the unchangeable structure of finite freedom.

It always remains *finite* freedom. *Unchangeably,* man is finite and aware of his finitude. He anticipates his end and this anticipation, which is present in every moment of his life and in every cell of his body, is what one should call his basic anxiety. It is the anxiety which belongs to human nature and which cannot be removed because man's finitude cannot be removed. Man can be liberated from senseless fears and misplaced anxieties. He can take his anxiety upon himself in a courage which says yes to life, in spite of guilt and finitude. Man can be healed, he can be saved. But it is *man* who is healed and saved. It is that being which is both free and finite, and whose greatness and dignity is unchangeably his power of changing himself and of endangering and risking himself in this change.

Discussion by Karen Horney, M.D.

Those people who are convinced that human nature cannot change usually have not only a static but a pessimistic view of man. In simple terms, their conviction is that man has always been and will always be greedy, envious, cruel, vindictive, and destructive. They usually contend that those who disagree with this viewpoint merely lack the courage to face unpleasant truth, and try to cover it up by a rosy haze of flattering self-deception. Many others consider this a one-sided view. In short, they see in human nature the possibility for good and evil, the latter being expressed in Christian terminology in the symbol of the original sin.

Being in the position to study human beings intimately, we as analysts agree with this latter viewpoint. We see clearly both possibilities, but with one significant distinction. The constructive and destructive possibilities do not stem from the same forces; they are not on the same level; we cannot put them side by side. They are different in origins and different in kind. Briefly, our belief is that the constructive possibilities stem from man's essential nature, from the core of his being, from what we call his real self. Conversely, we believe that man turns unconstructive or destructive only if he cannot fulfill himself—that it is an unfulfilled life which makes him barren or destructive. This belief is not mere speculation, but is based on evidence of three kinds.

1. The first kind can be seen by anyone who keeps his eyes open— it has to do with a child's development. Just as a tree needs certain

conditions for its growth, so does a child. If the environmental conditions are favorable, a child develops whatever particular potentials he has. He does so because, like every other living organism, he has the innate urge to grow. These observations are supported by educators and anthropologists.

However, under conditions unfavorable to his growth, his development can easily go astray. Then he may become wary, hostile, withdrawn or overdependent. If, however, his environmental conditions, in the sense of human relationships, change for the better in early years, he loses his wariness, suspiciousness and resumes or embarks upon healthy growth. If the unfavorable conditions persist, a developmental process sets in—which we call neurotic—which is complicated and essentially unconscious. As a *result* of this neurotic process he develops all kinds of unconstructive or destructive attitudes, the main features of which are pride and conceit, unconscious pretenses and irrational hostility in its many forms like suspiciousness, egocentric callousness, vindictiveness, ruthless ambition.

The conditions under which such a process sets in are manifold but describable. You could not call the results of this process his essential nature, any more than you would do so with a tree. If a tree, because of storms, too little sun, or too poor soil, becomes warped and crooked, you would not call this its essential nature.

2. The most convincing evidence for our belief stems from our clinical experiences. We see that a person who is power- or prestige-ridden, or who is arrogant and vindictive, or who is compliant to the degree of meaningless self-sacrifices, is *driven* toward such attitudes or pursuits by powerful or unconscious forces. He cannot but be aggressive or appeasing: he develops anxiety if he cannot be that way. The drivenness is what we call compulsive and what in medieval terms was called being possessed by demons—which means, in other words, it is not what he wants to, but what he must be or do, determined by inexorable inner necessities, the nature of which are unconscious. To put it differently and make it more concrete: we see that a person who is dominating, irritable, and vindictive has become that way and remains so because, and as long as, he experiences life this way because of all the factors that have driven him toward a devious development.

3. The third kind of evidence is in the changes that occur during psychoanalytical therapy. As such a hostile person, for instance, recognizes how he has hitherto experienced life; as he experiences his drive for power or his vindictiveness or his using others as means to an end; as he experiences the compulsive nature and the intrinsic futility of his

drives or attitudes, he begins to change. The change I am referring to does not consist in better controlling or channeling these drives. It is far more radical. It involves the giving up of irrational, ultimately destructive drives and of functioning in an increasingly more human and healthy way in the direction of self-realization.

FOR FURTHER STUDY

Barker, Roger G. (ed.) *The Stream of Behavior: Explorations of Its Structure and Content*. New York: Appleton-Century-Crofts, 1963.

Cassirer, Ernst. *Essay on Man: An Introduction to a Philosophy of Human Culture*. Garden City: Doubleday Anchor Book, 1955.

Doniger, Ernst (ed.). *The Nature of Man in Theological and Psychological Perspective*. New York: Harper, 1962.

Kramer, Leonard J. (ed.). *Man Amid Change in World Affairs*. New York: Friendship Press, 1964.

Krutch, Joseph Wood. *Human Nature and the Human Condition*. New York: Random House, 1959.

Mascal, Eric L. *The Importance of Being Human*. New York: Columbia U. Press, 1958.

Montagu, Ashley. *On Being Human*. New York: Schuman, 1950.

Rostand, Jean. *Can Man Be Modified?* Trans. from the French by Jonathan Griffin. New York: Basic Books, 1959.

CHAPTER 4

WHY RIGHT IS RIGHT

The Nature of the Right and the Good*

CLARENCE IRVING LEWIS

Clarence Irving Lewis (1883-   ) has had a distinguished career as professor of philosophy at Harvard
University. His main writings include *Mind, and the
World Order*, and his Carus Lectures, *An Analysis
of Knowledge and Valuation*.

In all the world and in all of life there is nothing more important to
determine than what is right. Whatever the matter which lies before us
calling for consideration, whatever the question asked or the problem
to be solved, there is some settlement of it which will meet the situation
and is to be sought as well as various other ways in which it might be
fronted which would fail to satisfy the requirements. . . . What is right
is thus the question of all questions; and the distinction of right and
wrong extends to every topic of reflection and to all that human self-
determination of act or attitude may affect. . . .

Whatever is decidable or can be determined by deliberation is right
or wrong. This distinction extends to all that reflects the possible self-
government of agents like ourselves, but does not extend to what lies

* From *The Ground and Nature of the Right* (New York: Columbia U. Press,
1955), pp. 3, 4, 20, 39, 47-52, 58-61, 64-66, 74-77, 93, 97. Used by permission of the
publisher.

beyond our control. The significant words here are "responsible," "justified" or "unjustified," "correct" or "incorrect." . . .

Rightness in concluding and believing is, perhaps, principally important to ourselves. Even if what we think should be finally significant only by affecting what we do, still the thinking is a separate activity, often carried out at some other time than the doing to which it is pertinent, and we have come to attach to truth and to the rightness of our thinking an importance distinct from that of any doing our beliefs may serve to guide. It is the rightness of our doing, however, with which other people are directly concerned. Whatever a man thinks, if his thinking it never moves him to do anything, or to refrain from doing, it will work no harm to others at least—nor produce any good. Ethics, being preeminently concerned with right and wrong in relation to others, is primarily directed upon the question of rightness in what we do. But ethics is not the only study so concerned: every art and every branch of technology also turns critical attention upon doing—as directed to those desirable ends to which this art or technique is addressed. . . .

Oftentimes, especially in ethics, intentions and consequences are contrasted. Sometimes theories of ethics are spoken of as if they were divisible into two classes, according as it is the intentions of acts or the consequences of them upon which moral rightness is conceived to turn. But if the distinction be so put, then it must be ill-expressed at least. What the intention of an act comprises is simply that total body of consequences which the doer expects in taking this commitment. Whether a particular result is one the doer desired or merely one he foresaw but was indifferent to, or even one he accepted regretfully for the sake of other results, it will in any case be correct to say that he brought it about intentionally if he expected it to happen as result of his commitment. If we need a narrower word for what is both expected and desired, we may use "purpose": the purpose of an act comprises the expected result or results for the sake of which it is adopted. Intentions and purposes do not, then, contrast with consequences; the pertinent distinction is merely between expected (intended) consequences and actual consequences which may coincide with or overlap or quite diverge from those expected. And intentions are right or wrong and criticizable only as the bringing about of what it is *intended to do* is right or wrong.

That manner of rightness which is attributable to an act if, and only if, it is rightly judged that its consequences are such as it will be right to bring about, may be called objective rightness. But let us note that the rightness of the judgment is a rightness of the kind which is ascribable to beliefs and judgments of fact. But a fact so judged is the property of the possible consequences of action—their being such as are right to bring about. What makes it right to bring about the consequences of an act, is one thing. What makes the judgment that a contemplated act is one having such consequences a right judgment, is another thing—the same sort of thing that makes any judgment of fact right; namely the weight of the evidence and correctness in drawing the conclusion from that evidence. It takes both these things to make an act objectively right. That is, an act is objectively right if it is judged that its consequences are such as it will be right to bring about *and* that judgment is correct. What may stand in contrast to such objective rightness, and can be called subjective rightness, is the rightness of any act which the doer *thinks* will have consequences which it is right to bring about—whether his so thinking is a correct judgment or not. In other words, an act is subjectively right if the doer *thinks* it is *objectively* right, whether his so thinking is justified or not. One who *thinks* that what he does (the consequences he expects to bring about) is right to do, has "good intentions," though his judgment in so thinking may be unjustified and wrong. And if he has such good (right) intentions in doing, his act is subjectively right. But it is objectively right only if his intentions are right *and* his judgment in taking these intentions is right or correct judgment.

The distinction between objective rightness and subjective rightness is brought to our attention by contrasting ethical theories, some of which, like Kant's, emphasize intentions as what is determinative of the moral rightness of actions, and others, like utilitarianism, emphasize the kind of consequences which follow from these acts—e.g., the greatest good of the greatest number.

Let us note in passing that this distinction of subjective from objective rightness is not confined to moral judgment of acts but extends also to any mode in which acts can be judged right or wrong—to their prudential rightness or their technical rightness as well as to their character as just or unjust to others. The main points of this distinction are the same, whatever mode of right and wrong doing is in question. If we speak here mainly of ethics and moral rightness, what is said can be extended, in an obvious way, to the other modes of right and wrong doing as well.

One importance of this distinction of objectively right from subjectively right lies in the fact that, for any mode of the critique of doing, there are two kinds of problems upon which it may be directed.

One is that of answering the question what it will be right to do in a given case; and the other is that of assigning praise and blame to doers, and perhaps of meting out reward or punishment for what is done. The first of these is the problem of any right-minded doer called upon to decide what he shall do. And it is a point to note that any doer who so deliberates his choice of action will hold himself responsible for *right thinking* as well as for conforming to what he thinks is right. Thus the problem of any deliberation of what it will be right or wrong to do is the question of the objective rightness of the doing.

But there is also a different kind of question about right and wrong doing; the question, namely, of praise and blame. How far, and on what grounds, shall we hold ourselves responsible if our well-intended act turns out badly? And what will others deserve, at our hands, when their intentions are good but their judgment of what acts should be done, in view of their consequences, is not so good? We have misgivings about both the practical effectiveness and the justice of punishing people for misjudging the results of what they do. And on other grounds, we have misgivings about penalizing others because they hold basically different convictions concerning the standards of right and wrong. The question what we shall blame and punish others for, or praise and reward them for, is a question *we* must settle because it is a question of *our own* conduct. On that question, sensible and civilized people decide that there is no justification for punishing honest errors of judgment. They are also likely to insist upon the privilege of each to do the right as it is given him to see the right, conceiving that this is something to be cherished and socially safeguarded. Somewhat similar considerations may affect our retrospective judgment of our own past doing, and of our past decisions as to right and wrong in doing, if later we recant them. We are all subject to errors of deliberation and conclusion, and the best that any of us can do is what he thinks is right at the time when decision of action is called for. Whoever does that is blameless. However, let us emphasize once more that whoever *thinks* his act right, thinks it *objectively* right; if he did not, then his doing it would not even be subjectively right. And if there were no objective rightness of action to be thought about, there would be no subjective rightness of it either.

Any adequate ethical theory must observe subjective rightness as well as objective rightness—if for no other reason, because retributive justice is a continuing social problem. But any ethics which fails to recognize the question of objective rightness also, or confuses the two, must be a fundamentally unsound theory. There is much which should be ob-

served on just this point concerning various historical and contemporary theories of ethics, but we can note here only one way in which
such inadequacy or confusion may arise.

In the first place, an ethical theory may be premised upon the conception that the primary concern of ethics is with the moral integrity
of the doer and his final responsibility. The perfect judge will not blame
us for errors we cannot help. The best we can do is to act from right
intentions. Therefore, the rightness of our intentions should be our
moral preoccupation; a rightly motivated act is morally right, and whatever a man thinks right is morally right for him to do. That is, it is possible to define the word "moral" by restricting it to the matter of intentions, and hence to the subjective rightness of action. And if this manner
of interpreting the adjective "moral" is not explicit but introduced as
something to be taken for granted, that merely makes it more difficult
to untangle the inevitable complexities. There is, indeed, a highly important character of men which may be called their right-mindedness. This
preparedness to do whatever they are convinced is right, is indeed the
moral attitude. But is that the sole problem of ethics or even its major
problem? Or is the main question justifying the study of our conduct
the question what it is that right-minded men should do? If the only
question which is material for right doing were "Do I think this contemplated action right to do; will my intention in doing it be good?"
it would appear to be a rather simple matter to determine. Nobody can
escape knowing what he *thinks* at the moment it is right to do. Indeed
the subjective moralists have sometimes emphasized just that: "Every
man can know his duty." But some of us have real trouble over that
point—perhaps more trouble in being sure what, as right-minded men,
we ought to do than in struggling against our original and perennial
tendency to deliberate wrong doing. At least there is this other problem
of the objectively right to do, and we are probably safe in thinking that
this is not only the major moral problem but also the problem most
students of ethics recognize as the first and foremost question they
address. . . .

Antecedently to any inquiry, it is obvious that there must be some
essential connection between the right and the good. No act would be
called right if nothing but bad results could be expected from it; and
to condemn as wrong an act which could not possibly lead to anything
but good would surely be a puritanical conception which we should
reject. Also, if there were nothing good or bad which could come about,
and life were in no wise subject to enjoyment or to suffering, it seems
plain that the distinction of right and wrong would disappear along with

that of good and bad. Any ethical theory, though its main business is delimitation of the morally right, must also deal with the subject of the good—perhaps under title of the *summmum bonum*—and with this question of the manner in which what is right depends on what is good.

However, before the right and the good are to be related they must first be distinguished, and the distinction of them is at least as difficult as finding precisely the essential connection between the two.

In the broad, the requirement of this distinction may be plain enough. The achievement of the good is desirable but conformity to the right is imperative. And second, nothing is strictly right or wrong except some possible activity or the manner of it, whereas in an equally strict sense anything under the sun may be good or bad. But what it signifies to speak of the imperative, is none too clear. And the fact that good and bad are attributable to things of diverse categories includes the fact that, amongst other things, actions and decisions may be good or bad as well as right or wrong. Add to this the consideration that, by the general metonymy affecting the use of language, terms applied originally and strictly to one class of things may come to be extended to whatever else is commonly associated with things of that class, and the difficulties of marking off the right from the good, the wrong from the bad, become extreme.

It does not help in this connection, but hinders, that ethicists frequently speak as if moral rightness were the only category of the right, thus obscuring the question whether the essential relation we must seek is one which holds between moral rightness and moral (or social) good, or between moral rightness and the good at large, or between the right in general and the good in general. Also it does not help, but hinders, that those who concern themselves with value-theory sometimes take value as comprehending both the good and the right, thus construing judgments of the right as one type of valuations and making the term "value" significant of the normative in general.

Let us do no more violence to idiom than is necessary, but let us first seek out those *root* senses of "right" and of "good" in terms of which the distinction of these may become clear. When we have done that, perhaps we can also find out what connects the two.

As we have seen, "right" and "wrong" can only be applied to acts by specifying consequences of the commitment; and in result we can hardly say that an act is right without implying that predictable consequences of it are right to bring about. But let us note that when we say that certain consequences of action are "right to bring about" or "wrong to bring about," the rightness or wrongness is attributed to the act which brings them about, and not to the consequences as happenings or states of affairs apart from relation to a commitment of doing. What we should observe, in this connection, is the syntactic ambiguity of statements of the form, "A is right to bring about": the adjective "right" here modifies the infinitive "to bring about," though it may appear to modify the subject "A." Mistake over this small point of idiomatic usage could obscure a most important problem of ethics.

For example, if we give directions to a stranger by telling him, "Cedar Street will be right for you to take," we do not predicate any property of rightness to Cedar Street: the rightness is attributed to his choice of it; to his decision or act of taking it. In less idiomatic but more precise English; "To take Cedar Street will be right for you" or "Your taking Cedar Street will be right." This idiom is not confined to instances in which it is rightness or wrongness which is attributed. When, for example, the cook says, "Sponge cake is hard to make," the hardness is attributed to the making, not to the sponge cake—though the cake may be hard too, in a different sense. What she means is, "To make sponge cake is hard"; "Making sponge cake is hard."

The similar remark applies wherever consequences of action, or expected consequences, appear to be spoken of as right or wrong: "That consequence is right to bring about" means, "It is right to bring about that consequence"; "The bringing about of that consequence is right." It is the decision to aim at these consequences, or the act of bringing them about, which will be right or wrong; there is no implication that the consequences themselves have any property of rightness or wrongness, just as there is no implication that a sponge cake which is hard to make will be a hard sponge cake. . . .

Solution of the central problem of ethics requires us to determine what character of the consequences of action it is by reference to which one act will be right and another wrong. Our tentative suggestion is that this distinguishing property of the consequences is their goodness or their badness. The present point is merely that it could not be their rightness or wrongness: results of action, taken by themselves, could not be either right or wrong; they *could* have, and *do* have, the property of goodness or badness independently of any doer's decision or commitment to bring them about. . . .

The root of goodness and badness in life lies in the fact that humans, like other animals, enjoy and suffer and find the quality of experience as it comes to them gratifying or grievous. And the root senses of "good" and "bad," "value" and "disvalue," reflect that fact. There is indeed nothing which is desirable or undesirable for its own sake and entirely without reference to anything beyond itself except that quality of passages of experience by which he who experiences them finds them satisfying and such as he would prolong, or dissatisfying and such as he would terminate or avoid. Using the adjective "intrinsic" in this sense of "for its own sake," the only kind of thing thus intrinsically good or bad is experience itself or the content of it. But humans, if not other creatures as well, learn to identify objects and happenings in the external world as causative agencies, productive of these qualities of our experience. And "good" and "bad" and other value-terms are extended to those objective things and events and to those characters of them which we identify as causing such good or bad experience. In consequence, the generic value-terms, as well as others which are more specific, come to have two distinguishable senses: (1) as applying to experience directly and signifying the gratifying or grievous quality of it, and (2) as applied to objective things of various kinds and signifying potentialities of them for producing or conducing to experiences which have these qualities. . . .

Such duality of reference—to experience and the quality of it, or to objects as causing experience of that quality—is one ambiguity which affects value-terms, and it is to be dispelled by asking, "What are you talking about?" When one stands in front of a picture and says, "Good," is he talking about his experience of the moment or is he talking about the picture? If he is talking about his experience, then he is reporting an immediate quality of it, about which he could hardly be mistaken. But if he is talking about the picture, then this quality of his experience may be *evidence* that this is a good picture, but it doesn't prove it. For proof, one would better wait and see whether he still finds the picture pleasing after it has hung on his wall for a while, or ask other persons whether they find it pleasing, or offer it for sale and see what someone will pay for it.

However, this particular ambiguity of value-terms is not one which can be dispelled by deciding in favor of one of these two modes of their meaning and discarding the other. Both are required if we are to make any sense of valuations at all. We might be inclined to disregard direct value-findings in transitory experience as merely subjective and trivial. But if so, then we should remind ourselves that, though the experience is transitory, the occurrence of it with just this value-quality is a fact—is indeed that kind of fact in the absence of which there would be no meaningful distinction of good and bad at all. When we ascribe a value to the picture or to any other presentable object we are attributing to it an objective quality by reason of which it is capable of giving

rise to just this kind of experience, on the part of ourselves and
others. . . .

. . . [W]ithout something operative in the manner of a rule or principle, no weighing of good or bad consequences of action will determine any act as right or wrong in any sense—unless, as is altogether
unlikely, we can determine the act as having *no* bad consequences, or
none which are good.

On the other hand, no rule, by itself, can forthwith determine any
act as right or wrong to do except as the specification of the act considered includes circumstances by reason of which the rule is pertinent.
Indeed, for a rule to apply to an act, it will be necessary both that the
rule be, explicitly or implicitly, such as will indicate its relevance to
cases of a certain kind, and that the act be so understood as to make
clear that the rule applies. The rule and the act must, so to say, have
a term in common, like a major and a minor premise, in order that a
conclusion as to rightness of the act, under this rule, should be derivable.

We have observed, however, that there hardly could be a rightness
or wrongness of any species which attaches to any act, without reference to some mode of goodness or badness with which consequences
of the act, as predicted, will be affected. Where there should be no
goodness or badness involved, there could be no question of what it is
right or wrong to bring about; and the question what it is which is to
be brought about is the question what act it is which is under consideration. It would appear then, prima facie, that, explicitly or implicitly,
some import of goodness or badness represents the middle term which
is common to any rule of right doing and any case to be decided under
that rule. The Golden Rule, for example, makes no explicit mention of
good or bad but, by setting as the criterion what we should wish to
realize at the hands of another, it plainly implies goodness of the consequences to other individuals as essential to rightness of our acts affecting them.

It takes two things, then, to determine the rightness of action: a rule
or directive of right doing, or something operative in the manner of a
rule, and a judgment of goodness to be found in the consequences of
the act in question. Characteristically, we should think of the judgment
of good consequences as determining the sanction of this act by the
rule, and of the rule itself as sanctioning acts of this class; as a general
directive extending to this case.

Observation that it takes both these things to constitute an act right
is, I think, often overlooked, and one or the other of them may be cited
as if it alone were a sufficient ground of such rightness. Possibly that

helps to explain the opposition between those who emphasize goodness and consequences and those who emphasize conformity to principles and moral perfection. Insofar as this is the explanation of such opposition, we should observe that the opposition itself is a mistake: each of these emphases represents a half-truth which needs the other as its supplement. The *proximate* determination of an act as right will be by way of assessment of its consequences as good. But that is the minor premise of the moral syllogism; the major premise is some valid rule or principle conveying the general sanction of acts of this class and having such consequences. Either one of the two being given or presumed, it is the other which "makes the act right to do," but without presumption of the other, neither will be sufficient to determine rightness in a particular instance.

However, if it is the imperativeness of any act which is in question, or if it is the ground of any species of rightness which engages us, then we shall look to the rule or principle; it is the rule which carries the sense of a directive; and what consequences an act has, or what kind of consequences, is simply a matter of empirical fact. Also, it is the rule which, by its generality, may have that kind of significance normally looked for in matters of "explanation" or questions of "ground." For the same reason, we seek the general and high-level kind of rules commonly connoted by the word "principle," rather than "rules of thumb," "maxims," or rules themselves derivative from or presupposing others which are more fundamental.

Even such high-level rules, extending to some whole category of the right, may still be quite diverse from one another in the nature of the directives which they convey. Also, there is that most important difference of all: some are "right rules," "really rules," really binding in some connection or in general, and some are merely precepts or directives mistakenly accepted or even wrongly and perversely adopted or promulgated. Some general directives are valid and some which may be proposed are not. The question so raised, of what distinguishes a rule or principle as valid and itself right, is, of course, the deepest-going and the most difficult of all questions concerning right and wrong. . . .

The basic imperative for individuals in their relations to one another, is simply the socially significant counterpart of what we have observed already: the dictate to govern one's activities affecting other persons, as one would if these effects of them were to be realized with the poignancy of the immediate—hence, in one's own person. The dictate is to respect other persons as the realities we representationally recognize them to be—as creatures whose gratifications and griefs have the same poignant factuality as our own; and as creatures who, like ourselves, find it imperative to govern themselves in the light of the cognitive apprehensions vouchsafed to them, by decisions which they themselves reach, and by reference to values discoverable to them.

Perhaps we should divide this most general of moral principles into two. It has one part which turns only upon recognition of other creatures as being, like ourselves, subject to enjoyment and suffering. The dictate so derived may be called the Law of Compassion. And this same general principle of objectivity has another part or bearing which is relevant only in the case of other creatures who are like us also in their cognitive capacities and, in consequence, in the necessity of governing their own behavior by deliberation, and of acting under constraint of the imperatives of rationality. The dictate which is correlative here, we may call the Law of Moral Equality.

It is plain that the Law of Compassion extends not only to other humans but to all conscious beings in measure of that sentience we attribute to them as the capacity to find their experience satisfying or feel pain. Indeed this dictate of compassion is peculiarly in point in relation to those who are not our peers, but may lie within our power to help or harm in ways in which they cannot equally help themselves, or defend themselves against our intentions toward them. . . .

. . . [The] principle of Equality before the Moral Law must be stated in terms which will sound pedantic: Take no decision of action which is member of any class of decisions of doing all members of which you would call upon others to avoid. That is, I think, the intent of recognizing our own acts as right to do toward others only if we likewise acknowledge them as right when done to us. The particular points here are two: first, that rightness under rule is a matter of the classification or modes of acts; and second, that an act is right only if it falls in no class interdicted by rule. It is not sufficient that it exhibit *some* justifiable mode of action—be classified as doing of *some* sort, or acting in *some* way, which is morally permissible. What is essential is that it *not* be doing of *any* sort or acting in *any* way which is morally forbidden. . . .

If, in conclusion, we look briefly to the general character of any ethic which should conform to the general conclusions here reached, we may observe that it would be of that type usually called naturalistic, so far as it is classified by reference to the thesis that no act can be determined as right or wrong without reference to consequences of it as good or bad. Also, it would be naturalistic in its interpretation of good and bad as matters of empirical fact and as significant, at bottom, of naturally found qualities of experience. It would, however, have a character frequently taken to be antithetic to naturalism; namely, in the thesis that right and wrong are nevertheless indeterminable except by reference of rules or principles—principles themselves including reference to the good or bad as essential to determining what specifically they dictate. It would likewise be liable to classification as antithetic to naturalism in its conclusion that these imperatives of right, and the validity of them, have no other determinable and final ground than that character of human nature by which it is called rational. However, if a view incorporating both sets of these features can be consistently maintained, then what so appears is that ethical naturalism and ethical rationalism (if "rationalism" is the right word here) are not in fact antithetic but complementary. Perhaps they are antithetic only for a naturalism which connotes nature short of human nature, or for a rationalism which interprets rationality as non-natural and significant of some transcendent world.

FOR FURTHER STUDY

Frankena, William K. "C. I. Lewis on the Ground and Nature of the Right," *Journal of Philosophy*, 61 (September 17, 1964): 489-496.

Garnett, A. Campbell. *The Moral Nature of Man*. New York: Ronald, 1952, Ch. 5, "What Ought We to Do?"

Johnson, Oliver A. *Rightness and Goodness*. The Hague: Martinus Nijhoff, 1959, Essay VI.

Lewis, Clarence Irving. *The Ground and Nature of the Right*. New York: Columbia U. Press, 1955.

Maclagan, W. G. "Respect for Persons as a Moral Principle," *Philosophy*, I, 35 (July 1960): 193-217; II, 35 (October 1960): 289-305.

Moore, G. E. *Principia Ethica*. New York: Macmillan, 1930.

Ross, W. D. *The Right and the Good*. London: Oxford U. Press, 1930.

Vivas, Eliseo. *The Moral Life and the Ethical Life*. Chicago: U. of Chicago Press, 1950.

Weiss, Paul, "Some Neglected Ethical Questions," in *Moral Principles of Action*, ed. Ruth Nanda Anshen. New York: Harper, 1952.

PART TWO

THE SEARCH FOR
A MORAL STANDARD

CHAPTER 5

MORAL STANDARDS
AND HOW WE TEST THEM

An Example of Ethical Thinking*

WILLIAM K. FRANKENA

William K. Frankena (1908-   ) is professor of philosophy at the University of Michigan. He has written a considerable number of articles and is a contributor in *Philosophical Analysis*, edited by Max Black, and *Essays in Moral Philosophy*, edited by A. I. Melden.

Suppose that all your life you have been trying to be a good person, doing your duty as you see it and seeking to do what is for the good of your fellowmen. Suppose, also, that many of your fellowmen dislike you and what you are doing and even regard you as a danger to society, although they cannot really show this to be true. Suppose, further, that you are indicted, tried, and condemned to death by a jury of your peers, all in a manner which you correctly consider to be quite unjust. Suppose, finally, that while you are in prison awaiting execution, your friends arrange an opportunity for you to escape and go into exile with your family. They argue that they can afford the necessary bribes and will not be endangered by your escaping; that if you escape, you will enjoy a longer life; that your wife and children will be better off; that

* From *Ethics*, pp. 1-5. © 1963, by permission of Prentice-Hall, Inc., Englewood Cliffs, New Jersey.

your friends will still be able to see you; and that people generally will think that you should escape. Should you take the opportunity?

An Example of Ethical Thinking (Socrates)

This is the situation Socrates, the patron saint of moral philosophy, is in at the opening of Plato's dialogue, the *Crito*. The dialogue gives us his answer to our question and a full account of his reasoning in arriving at it. It will, therefore, make a good beginning for our study. Socrates first lays down some points about the approach to be taken. (1) We must not let our decision be affected by our emotions, but must examine the question and follow the best reasoning. We must try to get our facts straight and to keep our minds clear. Questions like this can and should be settled by reason. (2) We cannot answer such questions by appealing to what people generally think. They may be wrong. We must try to find an answer we ourselves can regard as correct. We must think for ourselves. (3) We ought never to do what is morally wrong. The only question we need answer is whether what is proposed is right or wrong, not what will happen to us, what people will think of us, or how we feel about what has happened.

Having said this, Socrates goes on to give, in effect, a threefold argument to show that he ought not to break the laws by escaping. (1) We ought never to harm anyone. Socrates' escaping would harm the state, since it would violate and show disregard for the state's laws. (2) If one remains living in a state when one could leave it, one tacitly agrees to obey its laws; hence, if Socrates were to escape he would be breaking an agreement, which is something one should not do. (3) One's society or state is virtually one's parent and teacher, and one ought to obey one's parents and teachers.

In each of these arguments Socrates appeals to a general moral rule or principle which, upon reflection, he and his friend Crito accept as valid: (1) that we ought never to harm anyone, (2) that we ought to keep our promises, and (3) that we ought to obey or respect our parents and teachers. In each case he also uses another premise which involves a statement of fact and applies the rule or principle to the case in hand: (1) if I escape I will do injury to society, (2) if I escape I will be breaking a promise, and (3) if I escape I will be disobeying my parent and teacher. Then he draws a conclusion about what he should do in his particular situation. This is a typical pattern of reasoning in moral matters and is nicely illustrated here.

It happens that Socrates thinks his three principles all lead to the same conclusion. But sometimes when two or more rules apply to the same case, this is not true. In fact, most moral problems arise in situations where there is a "conflict of duties," that is, where one moral principle pulls one way and another pulls the other way. Socrates is represented in Plato's *Apology* as saying that if the state spares his life on condition that he no longer teach as he has been doing he will not obey, because (4) he has been assigned the duty of teaching by the god, Apollo, and (5) his teaching is necessary for the true good of the state. He would then be involved in a conflict of duties. His duty to obey the state applies, but so do two other duties, (4) and (5), and these he judges to take precedence over his duty to obey the commands of the state. Here, then, he resolves the problem, not just by appealing to rules, for this is not enough, but by deciding which rules take precedence over which others. This is another typical pattern of reasoning in ethics.

To return to the *Crito*, Socrates completes his reasoning by answering his friend's arguments in favor of escaping by contending that he will not really be doing himself, his friends, or even his family any good by becoming an outlaw and going into exile; he also asserts that death is not an evil to an old man who has done his best, whether there is a hereafter or not. In other words, he maintains that there are no good moral grounds on the other side and no good prudential ones—which would count only if moral considerations were not decisive—either.

All this is interesting because it illustrates two kinds of moral problems and how one reflective and serious moral agent went about solving them. It also shows us much of Socrates' working ethics: principles (1) to (5) plus the second-order principle that (4) and (5) take precedence over the duty to obey the state. This duty to obey the state, by the way, is for him a *derivative* rule which rests on (1), (2), and (3), which are more *basic*. One can find out one's own working ethics by seeing how one would answer these two problems oneself, or others like them. This is a good exercise. Suppose that in doing this you disagree with Socrates' answer to the *Crito* problem. You might then challenge his principles, which Crito did not do. You might ask Socrates to justify his regarding (1), (2), and (3) as valid, and Socrates would have to try to answer you, since he believes in reason and argument in ethics, and wants knowledge, not just true opinion.

At this point Socrates might argue that (2), for example, is valid because it follows from a still more basic principle, say, (4) or (5). That is, he might maintain that we should keep promises because it is commanded by the gods or because it is necessary for the general welfare. But, of course, you might question his more basic principle, if you have any good reason for doing so (if you question without reason, you are not really entering into the dialogue). At some point you or he will almost inevitably raise the question of how ethical principles, especially the most *basic* ones, are to be justified anyway; and this is likely to lead to the further question of what is meant by saying that something is right, good, virtuous, just, and the like, a question which Socrates in fact often raises in other dialogues. (In the *Euthyphro*, for example, he argues in effect, that "right" does not mean "commanded by the gods.")

The Nature of Ethics or Moral Philosophy

When this happens the discussion has developed into a full-fledged philosophical one. Ethics is a branch of philosophy; it is *moral philosophy* or philosophical thinking about morality, moral problems, and moral judgments. What this involves is illustrated by the sort of thinking Socrates was doing in the *Crito* and *Apology*, supplemented as we have supposed it to be. Such philosophical thinking will now be explained more fully.

Moral philosophy arises when, like Socrates, we pass beyond the stage in which we are directed by traditional rules and even beyond the stage in which these rules are so internalized that we can be said to be inner-directed, to the stage in which we think for ourselves in critical and general terms (as the Greeks were beginning to do in Socrates' day) and achieve a kind of autonomy as moral agents. We may, however, distinguish three kinds of thinking which relate to morality in one way or another.

1. There is descriptive empirical inquiry, historical or scientific, such as is done by anthropologists, historians, psychologists, and sociologists. Here, the goal is to describe or explain the phenomena of morality or to work out a theory of human nature which bears on ethical questions.

2. There is normative thinking of the sort that Socrates was doing in the *Crito* or that anyone does who asks what is right, good, or obligatory. This may take the form of asserting a normative judgment like

"I ought not to try to escape from prison,"

"Knowledge is good," or

"It is always wrong to harm someone,"

and giving or being ready to give reasons for this judgment. Or it may take the form of debating with oneself or with someone else about what is good or right in a particular case or as a general principle, and then forming some such normative judgment as a conclusion.

3. There is also "analytical," "critical," or "meta-ethical" thinking.

This is the sort of thinking we imagined that Socrates would have come to if he had been challenged to the limit in the justification of his normative judgments. He did, in fact, arrive at this sort of thinking in other dialogues. It does not consist of empirical or historical inquiries and theories, nor does it involve making or defending any normative or value judgments. It does not try to answer either particular or general questions about what is good, right, or obligatory. It asks and tries to answer logical, epistemological, or semantical questions like the following: What is the meaning or use of the expressions "(morally) right" or "good"? How can ethical and value judgments be established or justified? Can they be justified at all? What is the nature of morality? What is the distinction between the moral and the nonmoral? What is the meaning of "free" or "responsible"?

ᴑᴖᴑᴖᴑᴖᴑᴖᴑ

Two Tests of Ethical Principles:
Consistency and Generality*

RICHARD B. BRANDT

Richard B. Brandt (1910-   ) taught philosophy at Swarthmore College for many years and is now at the University of Michigan. Among his writings are *The Philosophy of Schleiermacher* and *Hopi Ethics*.

The basic task of critical ethics or metaethics . . . is twofold. First, it must discover and state the properties an ethical statement or belief, or a system of these, must have in order to be acceptable or valid or

* From *Ethical Theory: The Problems of Normative and Critical Ethics*, pp. 16-20. © 1959, by permission of Prentice-Hall, Inc., Englewood Cliffs, N. J.

tenable. (To state such properties is in effect to state what are good or justified methods of reasoning in support of ethical statements.) Second, it must *justify* its conclusion about what these properties are (or about what proper methods of ethical reasoning are), in some way or other.

We begin with this task. To begin here seems to be making a start at a point very far removed indeed from the practical problems of decision and evaluation. However, there is a decisive reason for beginning with these problems: If we have not faced them, we have no standard for our assessment of ethical principles. How are we to know what to look for, to determine whether a particular ethical principle is valid, until we have thought through the question of when, in principle, an ethical statement is justified? Our foundation would surely be unsteady if we were to recommend an ethical principle for various reasons, without having understood why these reasons are sufficient for thinking a principle to be adequate, correct, or justified.

In this chapter, we shall argue that there are two important tests that ethical statements or principles must pass in order to be tenable: consistency and generality. These are not the only tests, but if a person's statements or beliefs fail them, they are open to objection and a revision must be made.

1. Consistency

Inconsistency in an ethical statement or principle, or in a group of them, is a fatal defect. If someone uncovers an inconsistency in our ethical views, we feel he has made a mortal thrust; something must then be changed. A person's ethical conviction or convictions, then, must be consistent. Indeed, this is one point on which perhaps everyone in the history of ethical theory has agreed.

Nevertheless, a curious person might ask: *Why* should this be? Fortunately, the answer to this question can be simple: Insofar as a person's principle or principles are inconsistent, he *has* no principle (or conviction) at all.

In order to see that this is so, it is helpful to look at some parallel cases. Suppose someone made this statement: "I have just had my house painted. Every bit of it is both white and yellow." What description has this person given us of the color of his house? What *is* it like? Obviously he has told us nothing at all about the color. Or suppose someone gives us an order: "Both open and don't open the door!" What *is* he directing us to do? What could we do that would constitute obedience to his order? It is not possible to answer. Or suppose a father with ten children read them a lesson on table behavior as follows: "Every one of you is to eat heartily at every meal; but never help yourself first—always help yourself only after one of your brothers and sisters!" What are the poor children to do?

Inconsistent ethical statements are like these. They do not set forth any definite statement about what kind of thing or conduct is desirable or right. Such statements can serve no purpose. Something must be changed if there is to be before us some intelligible proposal about what is justifiably desired, condemned, and so on.

It will be agreed, then, we assume, that a person's ethical views must be consistent.

This demand, however, may seem not to take us very far. This "test" for ethical convictions, one may think, is valid but rather toothless. Surely, only fools have had inconsistent principles! But *is* the test so toothless? If we consider it, we can see that it has some important lessons for us.

Consider the Ten Commandments. One of them reads: "Remember the Sabbath day, to keep it holy. . . . In it thou shalt not do any work." Another reads: "Honour thy father and thy mother." These rules, which we assume may be taken as ethical statements (for example, "It is always wrong not to honour your father and mother."), are doubtless rather vague. There is one point, though, on which they are not vague: It seems that there is something we are *always* to do. This fact leads to difficulties. Suppose my father calls me on the phone on a Sunday morning, tells me that a storm has blown off a piece of his roof the previous evening, and invites me to come and help him repair it before there is another rain. I seem not to be "honouring" my father if I refuse; I am breaking the rule about the Sabbath if I comply. (At least there will be some type of case for which this will be true, if the rules are definite.) As the rules stand, they make contradictory statements about what I am to do, if honouring my father requires that I work on Sunday. In order to be consistent, the Ten Commandments need a commentary-supplement, giving instructions about which rules have priority in case of conflict.

A difficulty like this is inherent in *any* set of moral rules of the form, "Always do. . . ." Any such set requires revision. We have suggested that such a set may be saved from inconsistency by a supplement, giving directives about priority in case of conflict. (Of course, then, the original principles must be modified to something like "Always do . . . except when some other principle takes priority, as hereinafter specified.") However, there are other ways in which consistency may be maintained. For instance, instead of having principles of the form "Always do . . . !" we might have moral rules of this form: "There is always a *strong obligation* to do. . . ." Then the rules themselves will not specify which rule is to have priority in case of conflict, leaving this decision to individual judgment. In this case, one's set of moral rules does not give specific instructions for all cases; it offers only signposts, as it were. We shall return to this matter later. Evidently, however, the requirement of consistency is more important than we might at first suppose.

Our examples of inconsistency have illustrated a special type of case: general principles that have clashing implications for possible cases.[1] Another type of inconsistency, doubtless one that seldom occurs in practice and causes few difficulties, is the failure of particular statements to agree with a person's general ones (for example, "This lie happens to be all right" does not agree with "Lies are always wrong"). There is a further type of inconsistency, however, that we are less likely to notice. This is the failure of comparative statements to have the property of "transitivity." For instance, suppose one's daughter says: "Angel food cake with white frosting is better than yellow cake with chocolate frosting. And yellow cake with chocolate frosting is better than devil's-food cake with butterscotch frosting. And devil's-food cake with butterscotch frosting is better than angel's food cake with white frosting." One thing is clear about these statements: they will never give her a clear directive about which one of the three kinds of cake to pick, if she has to make a choice among all three. Whichever she picks, there is always another piece that she says is better. Her statements are properly classified as inconsistent.

Our conclusion, then, is that ethical statements, to be acceptable, must be consistent (both *self*-consistent and consistent with all other statements one accepts). Although we conclude, however, that this requirement has some importance, we must concede that it does not take us very far, for there are many different ways of being consistent. Perhaps the Devil is perfectly consistent, but all his ethical principles are incorrect. All we can say is: *in*consistent ethical convictions cannot be accepted—at least, not all of them as they stand. On the other hand, a consistent set is not necessarily valid either; consistency is not enough.

---

[1] Strictly, there is inconsistency only if we admit that some situations engage *both* principles. Thus, "Do A in situation B" and "Do C (something incompatible with A) in situation D" are inconsistent only if we add, "Some situations are both B and D."

Incidentally, a person can avoid inconsistency by confining his ethical beliefs to noncomparative statements about individual cases, such as "This action is right" and "That action is wrong." We shall argue in a moment that to stop with statements of this sort and refuse to go on to espouse general principles is also unacceptable. But it is unacceptable on grounds other than that of the requirement of consistency.

2. Generality

The second test (by itself, again, not a sufficient or complete test) we shall call the test of "generality." It is a test that applies *only* to particular ethical statements, but it applies to particular ethical statements with all kinds of predicates (for example, "desirable," "wrong," "obligatory," and so on).

It can be understood most easily by considering a line of reasoning we all tend to adopt when we are confronted with some particular ethical statement with which we do not agree. Roughly, the line of reasoning consists in a demand for general ethical principles to support the particular judgment. Let us take an example. Suppose someone says, "Mrs. K. oughtn't to be seeking a divorce." We are doubtful, and ask, "Why not?" The reply is apt to be: "The children are too young and need both a father and a mother." If we are both pertinacious and unimaginative, we shall go on to ask, "Why is that fact relevant?" To this the speaker will reply, if he hopes to silence us, "Because parents should make at least modest personal sacrifices if these are required for the basic welfare of the children." The speaker has now taken us to a *general* ethical statement. It is evident that this general statement, if one combines it with some factual statements about the ages of the children and the effects of a divorce, will lead by a formal argument to the particular statement, "Mrs. K. shouldn't seek a divorce."

By a "general" ethical statement, we mean two things. First, it is universal, in the sense that it is a statement about *every* case of a certain sort, or about *everybody*. Thus, in our case the general statement is about what *all* parents should do. Second, it makes no reference to individuals, but is concerned only with properties. In our example, there is no mention of Mrs. K. or any other person; the statement is about those who have a certain property, that of being parents. One way of putting this that will be familiar to students of logic is to say that general ethical statements may contain only variables and the names of abstract properties—meaning by an "abstract property" the kind of property that might be contained in a scientific law, and the meaning of whose name could be explained without referring to any particular persons or things. Thus, the following statement is *not* general: "Anyone who is the son of Queen Elizabeth should receive special police protection." But a very similar statement *is* general: "Anyone who is in the direct line of succession to the throne of an important country should receive special police protection."

Any particular ethical statement that is valid *can be supported by a valid general principle* in the foregoing sense of "general." (To be "supported" by a general principle means that the general principle, combined with true statements of fact, logically implies the particular ethical statement.) This fact permits us to have a "test" of generality for a particular ethical statement. The test of generality, however, is not quite to demand that a particular ethical statement be supported by a valid general principle. The test is rather simply that one must be prepared to specify a supporting general statement on which one is ready to rest the validity of the particular statement. One's particular statement fails the test of generality if one cannot specify one's supporting general principle at all. The "test of generality" then is this: A particular ethical judgment is valid only if it can be supported by a general principle (and of course the principle must be valid, but this is another matter.)

It does not follow from this "test" that a particular ethical statement is invalid unless someone can actually cite, at the time, a general statement which supports it. This is far from true. Very often we are convinced—and rightly, as it turns out in the end—that a particular ethical judgment is valid but, if the corresponding general principle is demanded, we are nonplussed and unable to specify it. There can very well be a valid general principle that supports a particular ethical statement, even if we are not able to formulate the general principle. Thus, a person is not conclusively refuted if he fails to meet our demand for a general statement supporting his particular one. Nevertheless, his failure is a weakness in his case. We can notice that people, when they are seriously in doubt about a particular judgment, do try to formulate the general principles supporting it. Also, if a person simply refuses to try to formulate such a principle and shows no interest in doing so when his particular statement is sincerely questioned, we have good reason to doubt his sincerity.

FOR FURTHER STUDY

Edel, Abraham. *Ethical Judgment, The Uses of Science in Ethics.* Glencoe: Free Press, 1955.

Johnson, Oliver A. *Rightness and Goodness, A Study in Contemporary Ethical Theory*. The Hague: Martinus Nijhoff, 1959.

Mandelbaum, Maurice H. *The Phenomenology of Moral Experience*. Glencoe: Free Press, 1955.

Sharp, F. E. "Is There a Universally Valid Moral Standard?," *Ethics*, 1927.

Singer, Marcus George. *Generalization in Ethics*. New York: Knopf, 1961.

Urmson, J. O. "On Grading" in *Mind*, 59 (April 1950): 145-169.

Warnock, Mary. *Ethics Since 1900* (Home University Library of Modern Knowledge). Oxford: Oxford U. Press, 1960.

CHAPTER 6

CUSTOM, LAW, AND APPEALS TO MORAL AUTHORITY

On the Diversity of Morals*

MORRIS GINSBERG

Morris Ginsberg (1889-   ) has taught and lectured
in the fields of philosophy and sociology. He was
professor of sociology at the University of London,
1929-1954. He is the author of many books and
papers including the three-volume *Essays in Sociology and Social Philosophy*. The following is from
the Huxley Memorial Lecture, 1953.

. . . I have been impressed by the increasing attention now being
given by anthropologists—after a period of indifference—to ethical problems. Two sets of circumstances have, I think, contributed to this re-
vival of interest, and both are highly relevant to my theme. Firstly,
the fact that anthropologists are now often employed by governments
and other agencies as advisers or consultants has made it very difficult
for them to live up to the doctrine of ethical neutrality on which they,
in common with other social scientists, used to pride themselves. It is
becoming clear to them that in helping to shape policy they cannot

* From *Essays in Sociology and Social Philosophy*, Vol. 1, *On the Diversity
of Morals* (New York: The Macmillan Company, 1956), pp. 97-126 with omissions. Used by permission of The Macmillan Company and Heinemann Educational Books Ltd.

confine themselves to a cold estimate of the consequences likely to follow from the various possible lines of action. They are bound, whether they like it or not, to take into consideration the worthiness of the ends to be pursued, and they soon find that ends and means cannot be dissevered and that it is not possible to abide by a division of labour which leaves the former to the statesman and the latter to the "scientist." In the second place, the attack on humanitarian values made by the Nazis has made the doctrines of ethical relativity, adopted more or less unreflectively by many anthropologists, emotionally untenable, and has forced them, as it has forced psycho-analysts and others who approach ethics from a naturalistic point of view, to examine their attitude to ethical problems afresh. Like other relativists they have to face the question whether it can really be the case that there is no rational way of deciding between the ethics of a Roosevelt and the ethics of a Hitler, and whether the moral indignation aroused by Nazi atrocities can really be intellectually on the same level as the contempt which the Nazis felt for what to them seemed the maudlin sentimentality of their opponents. . . . [I]t might be argued that the diversity of moral judgments affords no more proof of their subjectivity than the diversity of judgments regarding matters of fact throws any doubt on the possibility of valid scientific judgments about them. . . .

. . . It seems to me that comparative study justifies the conclusion that the diversity in the actual content of morals is consistent with a measure of similarity in certain generic ethical relationships and with a certain unity of direction recognizable in the historical development of morality. Morality is universal in the formal sense that everywhere we find rules of conduct prescribing what is to be done or not to be done, or some conception of a good going beyond what is desired at the moment, in the light of which immediate impulse or desire is controlled. Behind this similarity of form there is considerable diversity of content. I would suggest that the variations may be provisionally grouped as follows:

1. Variations in the range of persons to whom moral rules are held to be applicable.
2. Variations arising from differences of opinion or knowledge regarding the non-moral qualities of acts or their consequences.
3. Variations due to the different moral import of the "same" acts in different social situations and institutional contexts.
4. Variations due to difference in emphasis or balance of the different elements in the moral life.

5. Variations arising from the possibility of alternative ways of satisfying primary needs.

6. Variations due to differences of moral insight and general level of development, moral and intellectual.

In what follows, I propose to give examples under each of these heads.

Firstly, there seems to be general agreement that within the primary group there is everywhere what Tylor called a "natural solidarity," i.e., a measure of mutual forbearance, helpfulness and trust. Elementary duties, positive and negative, arising out of this solidarity are thus found to be everywhere recognized. On the other hand, the rules do not apply outside the group. As Tylor pointed out, "a man knew his duty to his neighbour, but all men were not his neighbours," or, as T. H. Green later put it, "It is not the sense of duty to a neighbour, but the practical answer to the question, 'Who is my neighbour?' that has varied." Tylor remarks that "In this simple contrast between one's own people and strangers, the student will find a clue to the thought of right and wrong running through ancient history, and slowly passing into a larger and nobler view." Some, indeed, like Boas are led by these facts to deny the reality of any fundamental change in moral ideas. All that has happened, it is asserted, is that the same fundamental duties have been gradually extended to larger groups. But this hardly does justice to the history of moral universalism and especially to the ideas of equality and the intrinsic value of the individual as such. The quantitative extension of moral rules to wider groups is parallel with a change in the conception of the human person himself. . . .

I agree with Hobhouse that it is not true to say that there have been no discoveries in the ethical field. The notion of equality before the law in the sense of the impartial application of rules and in the sense of the equality of rights themselves, the various efforts that have been made to define rights and to universalize them, and the experiments that have been tried out to reconcile freedom with order represent achievements which should rank high in the history of thought. The embodiment of these ideals in a world order, overriding differences of race, nationality or class, is the work of the future. But that real progress has been made in this direction cannot be denied and the change in scale involves, it seems to me, a qualitative change in the moral consciousness.

The second group of moral variations comprises all those differences which are connected with the growth of knowledge or changes of opinion about the nature of acts and their consequences. Thus in our own time we find that the discovery of new facts gives rise to the application of recognized duties to situations hitherto not known as coming within their scope. For example, the discovery of the part played by microbes in generating disease extends our obligations of cleanliness and hygiene. Again, the Christian attitude to birth control may be changed by new knowledge of the conditions affecting maternal and infant health, or of the laws of heredity and the eugenic considerations arising therefrom, or by a fuller realization of the economic aspects of population policy. Another example may be given from the attitude to vaccination which may vary according to the answer given to the question whether vaccination does or does not prevent smallpox. In these and similar cases the moral differences depend mainly on differences of opinion about the facts and not about fundamental moral principles. In other instances the changes in moral outlook may be deeper in nature and give rise to genuine moral divergences difficult to resolve. The growth of psychological insight into the nature of personality has, for example, deeply affected our views of responsibility and this change, in turn, has been connected with real differences of opinion regarding the ethical basis of punishment, which will no doubt for long remain a matter of dispute.

Especially important in this connexion is the influence of religious beliefs. That this can be exercised in very different ways for both good and ill has been very fully shown by Westermarck and by Lecky among others. Here only a few examples can be given. The moral attitude to suicide was deeply affected by Catholic teaching, which brought it under the category of murder, and even declared it to be the worst form of murder. The act was considered as a particularly heinous defiance of God's will, aggravated by the fact that the individual deprives himself of opportunity to expiate it by repentance. Lecky points out that the influence of Catholicism was seconded by Muhammadanism, which on this as on many other points, borrowed its teaching from the Christian Church and even intensified it. Theological doctrines concerning the duties of resignation, the penal nature of death and the destinies of the soul thus brought about an attitude to suicide markedly different from that which prevailed in the non-Christian world. The treatment of the insane affords another instance of the influence of religious and magical beliefs on moral attitudes. Thousands were burnt as witches or heretics or else treated as criminals. In Europe it was not until the eighteenth century that their treatment began seriously to be humanized. We must agree with Westermarck that "whatever share indifference to human suffering may have had in all these atrocities and all this misery, it is likely that thoughtlessness, superstition and ignorance have had a much larger share."

The history of religious persecution affords another very interesting example. Leaving aside social and political factors, there can be no doubt that the doctrine of the guilt of error and of its infectious nature, together with the doctrine of the infallibility of the Church, served to justify acts of persecution which now seem the gravest moral aberration. In this case, as Lecky points out, a moral inference was drawn from propositions now unacceptable, but then assumed as theologically beyond doubt, namely that to hold certain beliefs is not only a heinous crime but one which by infection is liable to cause the eternal damnation of others. Granted these propositions, there was no moral difficulty in drawing the conclusion that the heretic should be put to death. The effect of the dogma of infallibility was to stifle and to pervert moral insight. The fact, however, that moral insight can be perverted no more establishes the impossibility of genuine insight in the sphere of morals, than the fact that such dogmas as infallibility were once unquestioned shows the impossibility of valid thought in other spheres of knowledge.

In the third group that I have distinguished I include variations attributable to differences in the general framework of life as between different peoples or periods of time, or within the same social system to differences in circumstances, which may give a different moral import to what at first sight appear to be the "same" acts. In comparing moral codes we are apt to look for such rules as "no fraud," "no lying," "no sexual excess," "no aggression," "no parental neglect," and the like. But it is obvious that such rules cannot be defined with precision or applied in practice without reference to context or situation. What is theft in one system of property, for example, will not be such in another. Such rules refer to the direct tendency of a class of acts considered in abstraction or isolation. When applied to a complex situation allowance has to be made for other tendencies which come under other rules. Thus to attack first is "aggression" in peaceful conditions, but "self-defence" to ward off suspected violence; to speak falsely to an invalid is not "lying" if deemed necessary to avoid dangerous shock, and so forth. In these and similar cases we recognize, as we say, that "circumstances alter cases." But we are apt to forget this in comparing different peoples. Thus infanticide and senicide are "murder" in our own society but may not be so regarded in the circumstances of primitive life. What is "usury" at certain levels of economic development is "legitimate interest" at another. So again self-redress is condemned in societies which possess a system of public justice but may be considered a duty where there is no regular public machinery for obtaining redress. In all such cases apparently similar acts have a different moral import if considered in their context. It should be added that there is often a lag in development, so that practices persist despite changes in the circumstances. . . .

I come now to the variations which arise from a difference in the emphasis placed on different elements in the good life or the urgency of different duties. In essentials the moral systems of the world show striking similarities. A list of virtues or duties drawn up by a Buddhist would not differ very greatly from one drawn up by a Christian, a Confucianist, a Muhammadan, or a Jew. Formally all the ethico-religious systems are universalist in scope, and their insistence on sincerity and the inward nature of virtue implies that for them goodness consists in doing what is right because it is believed to be right. But the formal resemblance is deceptive. The universalism is never thorough-going and is variously limited. Doing right because it is believed to be right may mean in one case because it is the will of God and that will may well be considered inscrutable; or it may mean because of the love of God, or because of the love of men, not so much because they are worthy of it, but because they are the objects of divine love and ennobled by the Incarnation; or again for prudential reasons because it would lead to beatitude in this or another world.

In content there are differences of balance or stress. Self-control may deviate into asceticism; the search for inward peace may lead to detachment from and contempt for the things of this world; the stress on love may mean that insufficient attention is given to justice; personal salvation may be sought at the expense of social well-being. Above all, moral systems differ enormously in the clarity with which they distinguish between ethical rules proper and ritual or ceremonial rules. . . .

I come now to a further group of variations in morals which, I suggest, may be due to the fact that first order values may be combined in different ways to constitute second order values and that the same values may be thought to be attainable in different ways. Of this type of variations, sex morals afford interesting examples. In modern Western societies a number of values are implicitly or explicitly appealed to in justifying the monogamous family and the rules of sex morals associated with it. They include at least the following: the association of sex with enduring companionship and the fusion of sex with tenderness, the enhancement of the parental relationship through the common interest in the well-being and love of their children, the value to children of a stable affection and the feeling of security engendered thereby, the recognition of the partners as each an end in himself, and the value consequently attached to a form of union based on reciprocity and freed from possessiveness. These values are held to justify the monogamous family and the restrictions on extra-marital relations associated with it. In other societies, however, the primary values involved may well be recognized but in different combinations or clusters. "Indeed, in Bantu society," we are told, "physical attraction, affection and companionship usually follow quite different channels, a man desiring his wife, loving his sister and seeking companionship among his male relations and friends." Among the Bemba, Dr. Audrey Richards tells us, "the pattern of married relations is one of economic and sex partnership, not of close companionship. In fact intimacy between husband and wife is laughed at." . . .

If these considerations are borne in mind, it would appear that some of the variations in sex morals do not rest upon any radical differences in what I have called first order valuations. There need be no disagreement about the values of affection or companionship or the well-being of children, though there may well be different views about the way in which these values may be combined or about the regulations needed to achieve them. . . .

Our discussion so far suggests that amidst variations moral codes everywhere exhibit striking similarities in essentials. There are no societies without rules of conduct backed by the general approval of the members. There are none which do not regard that which contributes to the needs and survival of the group as good, none which do not condemn conduct interfering with the satisfaction of common needs and threatening the stability of social relations. Indeed, the similarities are so great that they have led many investigators to doubt whether a case can be made out for moral development. . . .

In dealing with arguments of this sort, the practical difficulty of isolating the distinctively moral factor in social development must be admitted. Everything concerned with the satisfaction of human needs and the ordering of human relations comes within the scope of morals which must therefore be affected by the general advance in knowledge and the problems set to it by changes in social relations. From this point of view the history of morals is part of the general theme of the changes in human culture. Yet, does not the argument cut both ways, can we not recognize the operation of moral factors in intellectual development itself? It was the moral attitude to authority and tradition that limited freedom of inquiry in the Middle Ages. Equally, the self-sacrifice and determination with which at the beginning of the modern epoch scientists defied authority implied a moral change in the attitude to truth. No doubt the intellectual virtues were recognized in the ancient world, but the full moral implications of the search for truth—disinterestedness, self-criticism, respect for evidence and the determination to follow it wherever it leads however unpalatable the conclusions—were not realized until the modern period. Again the combination of the scientific outlook with the humanitarian spirit has brought into prominence the conception of rational self-determination and inspired the belief that man can by taking thought shape the course of future development. This has led to the recognition of a new duty—consideration for posterity. . . . In short, new knowledge and new circumstances may help to generate new ethical demands, and on the other hand, ethical advance may be a factor in the growth of new knowledge.

It seems to me beyond dispute that despite a certain similarity in what may be called elementary rights and obligations moral codes differ very widely in the clarity with which the rights and obligations are conceived, the sanctions by which they are upheld and the area of conduct which they cover. In all these respects we may distinguish levels of development and in doing so we cannot escape value judgments, we cannot help regarding some as better than others. Whatever may be the case in dealing with other forms of social development, to describe moral development is to evaluate.

. . . The variations in my second, third, and fifth groups lend no support to the relativist view. They turn not upon any difference of moral principle but upon the application of the same moral principles to different situations, whether due to changes in circumstances or to changes in knowledge of the non-moral qualities of acts; or, in the case of the fifth group, on the fact that primary moral requirements may be satisfied in different ways, or through different social institutions.

The remaining classes of variations, on the other hand, point to genuinely moral differences. In dealing with them, it should be pointed out that on the assumption that universally valid moral principles are discoverable such differences are to be expected. It would be very strange if a Congo pygmy, whose experience of social relations is limited to a group of about thirty or forty individuals, living in conditions of isolation, had the same insight into the nature and conditions of freedom as a modern European, or if a Trobriand philosopher—were one such· to arise—showed the same skill in analysing the rules of reciprocity he finds in his society as that shown by Sidgwick in disentangling the moral axioms implicit in the common-sense morality of our own day.

It is not a question of innate differences in intellectual faculty, but of the range of experience and knowledge and command of method, which must tell in dealing with moral as with other matters.

The variations included in my first group, namely those connected with the expansion of the range of persons to whom moral rules are held to apply, were held by Westermarck to support his view of the emotional nature of moral judgments. This expansion cannot in his view be attributed to any process of reasoning or refinement of moral insight, but to a widening of the altruistic sentiment due to the expansion of the social unit and the increasing intercourse between different societies. There can be no doubt, I think, that sympathy, in the sense of imaginative identification with others, has played an important part in the growth of moral universalism. Sympathy, however, is not a matter of feeling only but requires imagination, the power of seeing oneself in the place of the other and recognizing that the other is a person like oneself, and therefore includes a cognitive element. In any case, moral universalism cannot depend on kindliness or benevolence, which, I suppose, is psychologically always limited and discriminatory. One cannot love anybody and everybody with the same intensity, but one can recognize that there are certain things to which men are entitled whether we love them or not. This is a matter of moral intuition, which, however, can be deepened by enlargement of experience and increased insight into the essentials of human relations.

Next, it is not to be denied that opinions differ about the comparative worth of different goods or about their relations to each other. But this is to be expected. Our moral knowledge is not derived by deduction from some single certain principle. It grows with the growth of our moral experience and insight into the grounds of our choices and preferences, approvals and disapprovals. We learn slowly about human needs and capacities and the values attaching to their satisfaction or fulfilment. We certainly have not solved the problem of the comparability or commensurability of moral values. But this does not justify the conclusion that there are no standards of value or that our preferences are arbitrary or dependent on individual or racial constitution.

Finally, there are the variations in morals due to differences in the general level of mental development. The concept of levels of moral development is extremely vague and I shall try later to give it some precision. Here I confine myself to some observations on the relations between intellectual and moral development. Westermarck was of the opinion that, compared with the progress of scientific knowledge, the changes of moral ideas appeared very small, and he gave as the reason for this that "the changes of moral ideas have been no discoveries at all but have only been due to the more or less varying reactions of the moral emotions." I wonder how psychology, anthropology, sociology, and political science would fare if judged by a similar test. The question is important because moral judgments necessarily contain factual components, and it may quite well be that advance in ethical thought has been hindered by the comparative failure of the social sciences to throw light on the relevant facts.

It is true that gifted seers have in the past penetrated to some of the essentials of man's moral nature by direct insight or intuition and may do so again in the future. But their maxims are, as we have seen, imprecise and require to be corrected and systematized, and this cannot be done without more pedestrian inquiry into human needs and the laws of social interaction. "That ye love one another" will not solve the problems of war or economic depression; it may not even suffice to enable people to understand one another. The really difficult problems are those in which facts and values are interwoven. We may agree that to use violence against others is *pro tanto* evil, but this will not help us to determine the limits within which force may be rightly used. To do this we need to know whether the ends sought *can* be attained by force and cannot be attained in any other way. This leads to further inquiries into the efficiency of the appeal to reason, the indirect effects of repression, the importance of freedom for social cooperation. Very often in political morality the most perplexing problems are those which arise from the fact that the ends we set ourselves change in the process of their realization, and are apt to be distorted or perverted by the means used in attaining them. In dealing with questions of this sort, it is extremely difficult to isolate the purely moral factors, and further progress depends as much on fuller grasp or more refined analysis of the relevant facts as upon improved moral insight. In popular morality differences of attitude are often rooted in ignorance and distortion both of the relevant facts and the values and in confusions between them. Examples can readily be found in the attitudes towards race equality or sex equality. In both cases it is as difficult to obtain agreement about the facts as about the values.

The conclusions that emerge from this survey of the main types of variations in moral opinion and sentiment may be now briefly summarized. Firstly, morality is universal in the sense that everywhere we find a recognition, implicit or explicit, that conduct has to be controlled or guided by reference to principle. Secondly, in content moral systems vary greatly but the variations are far from arbitrary. The recognition that there must be rules does not suffice to tell us what the rules should be. These are arrived at slowly and gropingly and embody judgments of good and evil, ultimately traceable to primary experiences of value. These judgments are made at very different levels of insight and experience. The primary valuations may be combined in various ways to form higher order valuations and different peoples may find different ways of achieving similar ends. Hence it is not at all surprising that there should be considerable variation in the content of morals. But, thirdly, there is evidence of development in the sense of growth of insight into the nature and conditions of well-being made possible by a wider experience of human needs and capacities and of the conditions of social co-operation. Especially important in this connexion is the discovery of methods of reflection and analysis. This has made possible efforts at systematization and a measure of self-criticism and self-direction which are almost completely absent in the earlier phases of the history of morals. It follows from these considerations that in comparing different moral systems we should have, firstly, to elicit the primary experiences of value on which they are based. Since these relate to basic human needs, bodily and mental, they would probably be found much the same everywhere. We should have, secondly, to inquire how these primary values are combined to form higher order values and how these are embodied in the institutional framework. Here we should expect to find, and easily do find, much variation. Thirdly, in considering these variations we cannot but recognize differences of level. I doubt whether anybody seriously believes that all cultures are "equally valid." The question is what we mean by differences of level.

I think that the above discussion throws some light on the direction in which an answer is to be sought. It points to a number of characteristics which we probably have in mind obscurely in estimating differences of level.

To begin with, moral systems differ in the range or area of persons who come within the scope of the common good. As far as doctrine is concerned, the decisive step is taken by the higher religions which at their best are all universalist in outlook. The injunction to love all men, however, rarely means all men; and in any case, the general goodwill does not pervade the specific rules of behaviour, which are always limited in range of application. The rise of what may be called an international conscience as distinguished from a vague philanthropy, it has been well said, is a new thing on the earth. The extent to which universalism has entered into the working codes of morality is therefore a good indication of the level of moral development.

In the second place, moral systems differ widely in the range or comprehensiveness of the experience which they embody. Morality changes with growing knowledge of human needs and capacities and experience of conflicts and their adjustment. Especially varied is the history of the way in which men learn to balance control and spontaneity, self-denial and self-fulfilment, personal good and social good, and in the adventurousness they show in the search for new values. In this connexion it is difficult, as we have seen, to isolate knowledge of fact from moral insight. But I do not see how anyone can deny that in both fields there has been advance both in range and depth of experience.

In the third place, moral codes differ in the extent to which the principles underlying them are brought to light, and in the degree of coherence and systematic connectedness between the parts. The study of any system of morals always reveals inconsistencies and contradictions, as is shown for example by Sidgwick's analysis of the "commonsense morality" of his day. Philosophers, of course, have given a good deal of attention to the general principles of morals. But the disrepute into which "casuistry" has fallen has brought it about that little attention is given to the "middle principles" and to the ways in which these are applied to the detail of life. The result is that the systematization of morals compares very unfavourably with that achieved in the sphere of law. In this respect, too, there must be differences between different systems of morals.

A fourth point in defining level of development is the differentiation of morals from religion and law. The way in which the sphere of law is demarcated from the sphere of morals is of special importance, since it involves an answer to the question, what can be left to the individual and what requires enforcement by the machinery of the law. The extent to which societies resort to coercion seems to me to be perhaps the best general index of the level of moral development.

Finally, moral systems may be judged by the extent to which they permit or encourage self-criticism and self-direction. In the more complex societies social forces are deliberately manipulated and change is consciously directed. Hence, from the ethical point of view, the part that is played by objective and disinterested thought in the shaping of public policy is of the greatest importance. Could we but find a way of estimating the influence of changes in moral outlook upon legislation in different societies, we should have an important index of the level of development.

In all this I have assumed a rationalist ethic. The tests that I have employed—comprehensiveness, systematic connexion, articulation of principles and assumptions, objectivity, and disinterestedness—are tests of rationality in general. They would no doubt be considered inappropriate by those who consider that morality is outside the domain of reason. Those who take this view would, however, have to dismiss the concept of levels of development as devoid of meaning. . . .

In conclusion, I should like to make a few further comments on the notion of levels of moral development. In connexion with the first of the criteria that I suggested above, namely the expansion of the range of the persons to whom moral rules are held to apply, it should be remembered that the test is not intended to be purely quantitative. It is not only a question of the number of persons belonging to other groups than one's own who come within the scope of the rules, but also of the kind of consideration that is given to their needs and claims. This can be estimated not only by the degree of readiness to respond to the cry of distress anywhere in the world, but by changes in the moral character of political relations, e.g., in the attitude to the "right" of conquest, in the willingness to resort to arbitration in case of disputes, or to bear in mind the needs of would-be migrants in considering laws restricting immigration.

The test of coherence and systematic connectedness has to be applied in conjunction with the test of comprehensiveness. For a system may be internally coherent and yet clash with other systems. In such a case the conflict can only be resolved within a wider system which includes and reconciles the claims and interests of both systems.

The test of differentiation of morals from religion and law may raise doubts. As regards religion, I have in mind mainly the distinction between moral rules and ritual rules, which as far as I can see has everywhere been connected with deepening of moral insight. As to law, the important point is the emergence of the distinction between inward and outward sanctions. Systems in which law, religion, and morals are fused tend to regulate every detail of life and thus to leave little scope to individual initiative.

Finally, the part played by objective and disinterested thought in the shaping of policy and the remoulding of institutions is a test which in a sense includes all the others. For objective thought necessarily involves appeal to the test of comprehensiveness, systematic connexion, and articulation of principles and assumptions, and cannot proceed far without self-criticism and the ability to distinguish between subjective and objective factors of belief. The value of a moral system depends not only on the clarity and objectivity of the concepts it uses, but on the extent to which objective and disinterested thought is allowed to influence conduct in the various spheres of economic and political life. Judged in this way, there are unmistakable differences of level as between the pre-literate societies and the societies of the ancient and modern world, and as between the different societies within the modern world. The concept of levels of development involves a distinction between higher and lower and it is the higher that decide that they are the higher. But this, I fear, cannot be helped.

FOR FURTHER STUDY

Benedict, Ruth. *Patterns of Culture*. Boston: Houghton Mifflin, 1934. (Pelican Book, 1946.)

Brinton, Crane. *A History of Western Morals*. New York: Harcourt, Brace, 1959.

Carnes, John R. "Why Should I Obey the Law?" *Ethics*, 71 (October 1960): 14-26.

Piddington, Ralph. "An Anthropologist's Viewpoint," *Year Book of Education, 1951*, ed. J. A. Larowerys and N. Hans. London: Evan Brothers, 1951.

Roche, John P., and Gordon, Milton M. "Can Morality Be Legislated?" *New York Times Magazine*, May 22, 1955, pp. 10, 42, 44, 47, 49.

Sumner, William G. *Folkways*. Boston: Ginn, 1940.

CHAPTER 7

INDIVIDUALISM AND RELATIVISM IN MORALS

Naive Subjectivism*

PAUL EDWARDS

Paul Edwards (1923–   ) has taught philosophy at
a number of schools and has been with New York
University since 1948, where he teaches at Washington Square College. His books and articles include
The Moral Judgment. He is general editor of a series
of books on the problems of philosophy and editor-
in-chief of *The Encyclopedia of Philosophy* (1966).

1. Correct and Misleading Formulations of Subjectivism

Naive subjectivism . . . is the theory that moral judgments are subjective—they are statements to the effect that the person who makes the
judgment has or tends to have a certain feeling or attitude towards a
certain object.

Naive subjectivists have differed among themselves as to what attitude or feeling moral judgments refer to. Westermarck and Hume
claimed that the feelings were mainly those of approval and disapproval
while Russell for the most part holds that moral judgments refer to the
speaker's desire, frequently his desire for other people to have certain

* Reprinted with permission of The Free Press from *The Logic of Moral
Discourse*, pp. 49-65 with omissions, by Paul Edwards. Copyright 1955 by The
Free Press, a corporation.

desires. There is no reason why a naive subjectivist should not hold a combination of these theories, i.e., that some moral judgments, e.g., those involving the words "good" and "evil," refer to approval and disapproval, while others, e.g., those involving "ought," refer to the speaker's desires.

It is worth observing that, according to naive subjectivism, ethical predicates cannot be defined "in isolation," meaning by this, that no phrase can be substituted for any of them, without changes being made in other parts of the sentence. They can only be given what is called a definition in use. "Good" or any of the other ethical predicates is *not* synonymous on this view with "approved" or "desired," but sentences containing the former phrase are analyzable into sentences containing the latter. If a man, A, says, "cruelty is evil" this, on Westermarck's view for instance, does not mean "cruelty is disapproved." It means, rather, "I, A, have a tendency to disapprove of cruelty." Not only has the word "good" been eliminated, but the subject of the sentence too has changed. Naive subjectivism has often been misrepresented by philosophers who paid no attention to this point.

According to naive subjectivism, moral judgments *refer* to and do not merely *express* feelings or attitudes on the part of the person who makes the moral judgment. According to it, therefore, moral judgments *are* true or false. It follows from naive subjectivism that if a person really has the attitude whose existence he is asserting by means of the moral judgment, then the moral judgment is true, while if he does not really have that attitude, his judgment is false. Westermarck, unlike some other supporters of naive subjectivism, is quite content to admit this consequence. . . . Russell is not prepared to admit this consequence. " 'I ought to do so,' " he says in one place, "primarily means, 'this is the act towards which I feel the emotion of approval.' "[1] But he also says: "I see no property analogous to truth that belongs or does not belong to an ethical judgment."[2] . . .

2. The Arguments for Naive Subjectivism

According to Moore, "nothing whatever" can be said for naive subjectivism, "except that so many philosophers have been absolutely convinced that it is true. None of them seem to me to have succeeded in bringing forward a single argument in favor of their view."[3] This sug-

[1] *Outline of Philosophy*, p. 234.
[2] *The Philosophy of Bertrand Russell*, p. 723.
[3] *Philosophical Studies*, p. 331.

gests that the writings of naive subjectivists are full of nothing but dogmatic pronouncements. This is far from being the case. Several arguments are commonly advanced by them and I now wish to consider those I believe to be the most important.

(i) First, there is the argument from the widespread differences of opinion on moral questions. This argument is more commonly advanced in support of public subjectivism. But it has also been used to back naive subjectivism. The argument, briefly, is this: We find enormously widespread differences on practically all moral questions. In one culture polygamy is considered right and natural, in another it is considered highly immoral; in one society burning widows is considered a duty while in another it is believed to be utterly wrong. Moreover, even within the same culture or society there are frequently very widespread differences of opinion on moral questions. Thus many people in our society regard the segregation of Negroes as shameful while others consider equality of treatment reprehensible. Some think that cruelty to animals is justified in the interests of science while others do not. Countless other instances could be cited. All this, it is said, shows that moral judgments are merely "subjective."

This argument, by itself, proves absolutely nothing. For it rests on a major premise which is quite certainly false. The major premise is this: on *any* topic on which there is widespread difference of opinion the statements of both parties are only about their own attitudes or states of mind. This is simply not so. There are very widespread differences of opinion as to whether there are slave labor camps in the Soviet Union, but the *subject matter* of both of the sentences, "there is plenty of slave labor in the Soviet Union" and "there is no slave labor in the Soviet Union" are not attitudes or feelings on the part of the speakers. Again, there is very widespread disagreement on the cause of neurosis and psychosis and on the efficacy of different types of treatment. But statements like "the cause of neurosis is the patient's emotional isolation" are quite plainly objective in the only relevant sense.

(ii) It is very commonly maintained by subjectivists that moral judgments must be merely subjective since moral disputes are undecidable in the sense that nothing can be done to prove the views of one side and disprove those of the other. If moral judgments were objective claims this would not be so. . . .

There is a two-fold reply to this. Firstly, even if the premises of this argument were true, this would not necessarily prove the conclusion. The fact, if it is a fact, that moral disputes are undecidable is compatible with several other theories concerning the nature of moral judgments, e.g., with the theory that moral judgments *express* the speaker's attitude, or with the theory that moral judgments are objective claims but that the parties do not use ethical terms in the same senses. Secondly, the premise of the argument has been questioned on the ground that no *actual* moral dispute is ever a dispute concerning the "intrinsic" value of anything and that no *actual* moral judgment, occurring in a living context, is ever an "intrinsic" or "ultimate" moral judgment. . . .

(iii) It is sometimes argued, among others by Westermarck, that since moral judgments are caused by emotions on their author's part, since they are thus "colored" by, "shot-through-and-through" with the speaker's feelings, they cannot have any claim to objective validity. Their emotional origin proves that they are merely subjective.

Now, it may readily be granted, as Hume emphasized again and again, that if human beings had no desires and never felt approval or disapproval, moral judgments would never have been made. It may be granted that emotions such as fear and envy play a very large part in the causation of the most formidable body of moral judgments, namely, those relating to sexual behavior. But all this in no way proves that the *subject matter* of moral judgments is the speaker's own attitude. The major premise implied in this argument—any statement which is the result of emotion is *about* the speaker's own feeling or attitude—is plainly false. Thus supposing X is a young philosopher who has been extremely successful and who is admired by most philosophers, young and old. Supposing, further, that I am an intensely ambitious person with small gifts and that I am full of envy towards X. My envy may then cause me to start spreading vicious rumors about him. I might say, "He does not write his own books but engages me to write them for him. He seduces all the pretty girls in his classes. He got his present position because he married his Chairman's daughter whom nobody else wanted to take. He works for the FBI in his spare time and other philosophers tremble in his presence for fear he will pass in derogatory reports about them. He gives high grades to students who lavishly entertain him at fashionable restaurants." Supposing all these statements are complete fabrications due to nothing but my insane envy of X. In spite of this, they are *about* X and not about me. In the only relevant sense they are objective claims.

Furthermore, the fact that an objective claim is the result of emotion, even of pathological emotion, does not show that it is or is likely to be false. A great deal of what Nietzsche and Schopenhauer said about human beings and especially about their contemporaries was undoubtedly the outcome of their own diseased emotions. But a great deal of what they said was true. An unhappy man may wish everybody else to be unhappy also and this wish may cause him to say that X and Y and Z are miserable. Since most people are unhappy, he will frequently be right: in fact, his desire that everybody else be unhappy, is likely to make him perceive a great many things beneath the surface which a person not having his desire might miss.

The fact, therefore, that moral judgments have an emotional origin—itself not to be accepted without several qualifications—does nothing to show that they are merely subjective claims or that, if objective, they are likely to be false.

(iv) I finally come to what seems the strongest argument for naive subjectivism. Careful observation of the way in which people use language, it might be said, shows that very frequently, maybe always, when they make a moral judgment, they would quite willingly substitute for it a subjective claim. In fact, often they *actually* do so. Thus supposing a man has given a lecture on the "Justification of Mercy-Killing." He might conclude with the sentence, "For these reasons, ladies and gentlemen, I approve of mercy-killing in the circumstances I describe." Or we might ask a man who knew the late Homer Lane: "What sort of a man was he?" The answer might be, "Lane was a profoundly good man" or it might be, "I admired Lane very profoundly." The speaker would be as ready to say the one thing as the other, and we, too, would, in most circumstances, consider the two sentences to be saying the same thing.

I hope to show later that this argument too, although it proves *something*, does not prove naive subjectivism. However, it is impossible at this stage to make any useful comments upon it. . . .

3. The Arguments against Naive Subjectivism

We shall now consider the most powerful arguments against naive subjectivism. (i) If two sentences, e.g., "Jones is a father" and "Jones is a male parent," are synonymous in the sense of having the same referent, then the facts which make one of them true ipso facto make the other one true and the facts which make one of them false ipso facto make the other one false also. Conversely, if there are facts which are sufficient to prove one sentence—e.g., "X is a father"—but are not sufficient to prove another—e.g., "X is an old man"—then the two sentences cannot be synonymous in the sense in question.

Let m_1 be a typical moral judgment made by a person whom we

shall call Gangle. m_1 is the sentence, "Mercy-killing is always wrong."
Let a_1 be the sort of subjective statement which has frequently been
claimed to be the correct translation of judgments like m_1. Let a_1 then
be the sentence, "I, Gangle, disapprove of mercy-killing under all
circumstances." A naive subjectivist, now, would maintain that m_1 and
a_1 are synonymous, that they have the same referent. And this assertion
is open to the following fatal objection. For Gangle to prove a_1 it
would be sufficient for him to produce certain data *concerning himself*, e.g., the fact that he is a Catholic, that he demanded the death
sentence for Dr. Sanders, that he regularly sends donations to the
Society Against the Legalization of Euthanasia, etc. But neither he
nor anybody else would consider this proof or indeed any kind of
relevant evidence for m_1. In other words: the facts which make a_1 true
do not make m_1 true. Again, a_1 could be disproven if it turned out
that Gangle made the statement, "I disapprove of mercy-killing in all
circumstances" only because his boss, a fanatical Catholic, happened to
be in the company, but that he secretly works for the Euthanasia Society of America, that he sent money to the defense fund for Dr.
Sanders, and so forth. But neither he nor anybody else would regard
this as being a disproof of or any sort of evidence against m_1. In other
words: the facts which make a_1 false do not make m_1 false.

Many people who hear this argument for the first time get the feeling
that it is somehow unfair. I shall try to represent how an intelligent
sympathizer with naive subjectivism might express this feeling: "You
misunderstand and misrepresent naive subjectivism in this argument.
According to naive subjectivism the question, 'Is mercy-killing ever
right?' is incomplete as it stands and cannot therefore be answered. It
has to be further qualified. It can be answered when it is completed,
e.g., to read, 'Is mercy-killing ever right according to Sanders?' or,
'Is mercy-killing ever right according to Horn?' or, 'Is mercy-killing
ever right according to Bertrand Russell?' Naive subjectivism does not
deal with incomplete statements like 'Mercy-killing is always wrong.'
It deals with statements like 'Mercy-killing is always wrong, according
to me,' as made by some specific individual. Your argument only shows
that the former statements are not synonymous with subjective claims.
It in no way proves that the latter are not synonymous with subjective
statements."

This answer [may be] disposed of [by giving] attention to the two
very different functions of such phrases as "I think" or "I believe" or "It
is my opinion." In one context they serve merely as indications of the
degree of assuredness with which an objective claim is asserted by the

speaker. In another context they determine the subject matter of the statement. . . . In the sentence, "It is my conviction that war will break out within the next six months," as uttered by a political analyst at a public meeting, "It is my conviction" functions as an indication of the man's assuredness. The sentence itself is clearly an objective claim—a statement about the course of the world during the following six months. The same sentence . . . when uttered to a psychiatrist in a clinical context is a subjective claim and there the "It is my conviction" does help to indicate the subject matter of the statement. For the rest of this discussion we shall underline phrases like "I think" or "It is my opinion" in sentences which they make into subjective statements. In those sentences in which they occur but which are objective claims, we shall underline the words which give us the real subject matter and we shall put the autobiographical phrase in brackets. The concluding sentence of the political lecture we shall write as:

"(It is my conviction that) *war will break out within six months*."

The statement to the psychiatrist we shall write as:

"*It is my conviction* that war will break out within six months."

Keeping this distinction in mind, let us now look at the following three statements, each made by Gangle:

(i) Mercy-killing is always wrong.

(ii) (According to me) *mercy-killing is always wrong*.

(iii) *According to me* mercy-killing is always wrong.

Now, (i) and (ii) are clearly synonymous in the same way as "War will break out within six months" is synonymous with "It is my conviction that *war will break out within six months*." But (iii) is not synonymous with either of them, any more than "*It is my conviction* that war will break out within six months" is synonymous with "War will break out within six months" or with "It is my conviction that *war will break out within six months*." Furthermore, (iii) is not really a moral judgment at all since "wrong" is not really its predicate, the sentence being synonymous with "*In me there exists* the belief that mercy-killing is always wrong."

To tell us something of interest concerning the meaning or function of moral judgments, naive subjectivism must be a theory about statements like (i) and (ii) and not about statements like (iii). In showing that in m_1 and a_1 in the above example are not synonymous I was therefore arguing to the point. If naive subjectivism maintains merely that sentences like (iii) are synonymous with subjective claims many objectivists would agree with this. My argument would then be irrelevant, but the theory itself would cease to be a metaethic in our sense.

Granting for the moment that a_1 is a correct translation of "*According to me*, mercy-killing is always wrong," as asserted by Gangle, the argument against naive subjectivism may also be expressed in this way: m_1—i.e., "Mercy-killing is always wrong"—is not synonymous with "*According to me*, mercy-killing is always wrong." The facts which make the latter sentence true do not ipso facto make the former one true. By the way, a person who has been lecturing against mercy-killing and concludes with the sentence, "In view of these considerations mercy-killing is always wrong" would not at all be willing to substitute for it the sentence, "In view of these considerations, mercy-killing is always wrong according to me," if the emphasis were placed on the phrase "according to me."

(ii) What is substantially the same argument may also be expressed in this way: If two sentences—e.g., "Jones is a father" and "Jones is a male parent"—really have the same referent, then the combination "Since Jones is a male parent, he is a father" is a tautology. If such a combination of two sentences does not produce a tautology then the two sentences cannot have the same referent. E.g., "Since Jones is an old man he is a father" is not a tautology and the sentences "Jones is a father" and "Jones is an old man" do not have the same referent. Now the appropriate combination of a_1 and m_1 is the sentence "Since I, Gangle, disapprove of mercy-killing under all circumstances, it is always wrong." This, so far from being a tautology, is "a piece of gross conceit." . . .

(iv) The next objection I wish to consider is due to Sir David Ross.

> If something, without changing its nature, at some moment aroused for the first time the feeling in some mind, we should clearly judge not that the object had then first become good, but that its goodness had then first been apprehended.[4]

Again:

> If I judge that Brutus did wrong in assassinating Caesar, I certainly do not think that his act first acquired his wrongness when I began to experience disapproval of it, or will cease to be wrong when I have ceased to do so.[5]

The same argument has also been advanced in several places by Brand Blanshard. Thus he writes:

> Suppose that when we are away from home a pet dog gets caught in a trap, struggles long and vainly to get free, and is found dead on

[4] *The Right and the Good*, p. 11, also pp. 82 ff.
[5] *The Foundations of Ethics*, pp. 23-24.

our return. We look back on what he must have gone through and put it down as a very bad thing that he should have suffered so. But according to the theory, the suffering was not bad at all, and all we are doing when we say it was bad is expressing our present feelings about it. Nothing in fact was bad until we came home and said our say; and if the dog had remained undiscovered, nothing bad would have happened at all; for it is only as people take up attitudes that good or bad comes into being. And if people could manage to delight in the suffering, once they discovered it, then it would be good. This conclusion has actually been held by able men; but it does small credit either to their heads or their hearts.[6]

Substantially the same argument is also contained in Moore's famous contrast of the exceedingly beautiful world with "the ugliest world you can imagine,"[7] where he argues that the former would be better than the latter even if no conscious being ever contemplated either world.

Maybe the following illustration will show what a very powerful objection this is. Like many other people, I believe that the Fair Employment Practices Bill, which had the support of President Truman but which Congress has for several years been refusing to consider, is a thoroughly just piece of legislation. Now whatever I actually mean by saying that the F.E.P.C. is a just piece of legislation, I do not mean anything which implies that if I suddenly died the F.E.P.C. would cease to be a just piece of legislation. I also do not mean anything which implies that if all people who believe that the F.E.P.C. is a just policy were exterminated and if no converts were ever again made to this belief, the F.E.P.C. would cease to be just.

Westermarck admits all of this but insists that it does not refute naive subjectivism:

> I agree with Dr. Ross that if, for instance, some one were to become aware of an act of self-denial and admire it, he might "pronounce it had been good even when no one had been admiring it," inasmuch as he might attribute to himself a tendency to admire or, as I should say, approve of it, and consequently to the object a tendency to arouse in him the emotion of approval.[8]

The substitution of "A has a tendency to approve of x" for "A in fact approves of x" does not get at the heart of Ross' objection. When I say that the F.E.P.C. is a just bill I do not mean anything which implies that it would cease to be just once I died. This shows that I

---

[6] "Personal Ethics," in *Preface to Philosophy* (ed. W. P. Tolley), pp. 126-127.
[7] *Principia Ethica*, pp. 83-85.
[8] *Ethical Relativity*, pp. 144-45.

mean neither "I approve of the F.E.P.C." *nor* "I have a tendency to approve of the F.E.P.C." In the second part of Westermarck's reply we have another of his many shifts—this time to the theory we are calling "causal subjectivism."[9]

(v) I should like to mention, without discussing it, one further objection. Ross has stated it in the following words:

> When I consider this emotion (the emotion of moral disapproval) it appears to me that it is not just a feeling which arises in us, we know not why, when we contemplate a right action. It seems to presuppose some insight into the nature of the action, as, for instance, that it is an action likely to redound to the general good, or a fulfilment of promise. It seems to be an intellectual emotion, presupposing the thought that the action is right, and right as being of a certain recognized character. And if this contention is correct, if the emotion of moral approval presupposes the thought that the action is right, it follows that we cannot mean by calling the action right that it awakes this emotion, since in order to have the emotion we must already be thinking of the action as right.[10]

I believe this objection to be substantially valid. I am also not aware of any place where a naive subjectivist has offered an intelligible answer to it. . . .

4. Conclusions

It will be convenient to list here some of the conclusions to which we have been led in the discussions of this chapter:

1. Statements of the form, "X *is good* (according to me)" are by no means synonymous with statements of the form, "X is good, *according to me*." Even if the latter are synonymous with statements asserting the existence of the speaker's attitude towards X, the former are not.

2. When a person makes a statement of the form, "This morality is higher than that one" he does not mean or he does not merely mean, "I prefer this morality to that" or, "This is *my* morality, the other one is not."

3. When we say of something that it is right or good or ought to be done, whatever we do mean, we do not mean anything which

---

[9] It should be observed that this objection is without force against a "dispositional" form of subjectivism. Richard Brandt's view that "X is wrong" (roughly) means, "If I had all the facts about X clearly in mind and were ethically consistent, I would disapprove of X," is an example of such a theory.

[10] *The Foundations of Ethics*, p. 23; cf. also *The Right and the Good*, p. 131.

implies that the object in question would cease to be good or right if we ceased to believe this.

4. Moral approval is an intellectual emotion in the sense that it presupposes beliefs of one kind or another concerning the nature of the object approved.

5. People *are* frequently, if not always, ready to substitute sentences such as "I cannot approve of this" or "I favor that" for moral judgments.

It may seem at first sight that conclusions 1. and 5. are mutually contradictory. I hope to show eventually that this is not so. In any case, it seems to me that an adequate metaethic must be able, among other things, to account for all the facts summarized in this section.

FOR FURTHER STUDY

Blanshard, Brand. "The New Subjectivism in Ethics," *Philosophy and Phenomenological Research*, 9 (March 1949): 504-511.

———. *Reason and Goodness*. New York: Macmillan, 1961, Ch. 1, "The Tension Between Reason and Feeling in Western Ethics," Ch. 5 "Subjectivism."

Burlingame, Roger. *The American Conscience*. New York: Knopf, 1957.

Frankena, William K. *Ethics*. Englewood Cliffs: Prentice-Hall, 1963, Ch. 6.

Faurit, J. H. "The Question of Conscience," *The Personalist*, 41 (Spring 1960): 133-147.

Fromm, Erich, "Conscience" in *Moral Principles of Action*, ed. Ruth Nanda Anshen. New York: Harper, 1952.

McGuire, Martin C. "On Conscience," *Journal of Philosophy*, 60 (May 9, 1963): 253-263.

MacIver, R. M. *Integrity and Compromise: Problems of Public and Private Conscience*. New York: Harper, 1957.

Peterfreund, Sheldon P. "The Status of Contemporary Meta-Ethics," *The Personalist*, 45 (Spring 1964): 207-213.

Rader, Melvin, *Ethics and the Human Community*. New York: Holt, Rinehart and Winston, 1964, Ch. 9, "Cultural Relativism," Ch. 10, "Subjectivism."

Rice, Philip Blair. *On the Knowledge of Good and Evil*. New York: Random House, 1955, Chs. 1, 2, 3, 13.

Smith, T. V., *Beyond Conscience*. New York: McGraw-Hill, 1934.

CHAPTER 8

KANT AND THE
SEARCH FOR STANDARDS

∿∿∿∿∿∿∿∿∿∿∿∿∿∿∿∿∿∿∿∿∿∿∿

*The Supreme Principle of Morality**

IMMANUEL KANT

Immanuel Kant (1724-1804), who taught philosophy
at the University of Königsberg, Germany, is one of
the great intellects in the history of Western philosophy. His influence has been widespread in the fields
of epistemology, metaphysics, and ethics. His moral
philosophy is one of the few great ethical systems
studied today.

As my concern here is with moral philosophy, I limit the question
suggested to this: whether it is not of the utmost necessity to construct
a pure moral philosophy, perfectly cleared of everything which is only
empirical, and which belongs to anthropology? For that such a philosophy must be possible is evident from the common idea of duty
and of the moral laws. Everyone must admit that if a law is to have
moral force, that is, to be the basis of an obligation, it must carry with
it absolute necessity; that, for example, the precept, "Thou shalt not
lie," is not valid for men alone, as if other rational beings had no need
to observe it; and so with all the other moral laws properly so called;

* From "Fundamental Principles of the Metaphysic of Morals," in *Critique of
Practical Reason and Other Works on the Theory of Ethics*, trans. Thomas
Kingsmill Abbott (London: Longmans, Green, 1909), pp. 9-46 with omissions.

that, therefore, the basis of obligation must not be sought in the nature of man, or in the circumstances in the world in which he is placed, but *a priori* simply in the conceptions of pure reason; and although any other precept which is founded on principles of mere experience may be in certain respects universal, yet in as far as it rests even in the least degree on an empirical basis, perhaps only as to a motive, such a precept, while it may be a practical rule, can never be called a moral law.

Thus not only are moral laws with their principles essentially distinguished from every other kind of practical knowledge in which there is anything empirical, but all moral philosophy rests wholly on its pure part. When applied to man, it does not borrow the least thing from the knowledge of man himself (anthropology), but gives laws *a priori* to him as a rational being. No doubt these laws require a judgment sharpened by experience, in order, on the one hand, to distinguish in what cases they are applicable, and, on the other, to procure for them access to the will of the man, and effectual influence on conduct; since man is acted on by so many inclinations that, though capable of the idea of a practical pure reason, he is not so easily able to make it effective *in concreto* in his life.

A metaphysic of morals is therefore indispensably necessary, not merely for speculative reasons, in order to investigate the sources of the practical principles which are to be found *a priori* in our reason, but also because morals themselves are liable to all sorts of corruption as long as we are without that clue and supreme canon by which to estimate them correctly. For in order that an action should be morally good, it is not enough that it *conform* to the moral law, but it must also be done *for the sake of the law*, otherwise that conformity is only very contingent and uncertain; since a principle which is not moral, although it may now and then produce actions conformable to the law, will also often produce actions which contradict it. . . .

The present treatise is, however, nothing more than the investigation and establishment of *the supreme principle of morality*, and this alone constitutes a study complete in itself, and one which ought to be kept apart from every other moral investigation. . . .

Transition from the Common Rational Knowledge of Morality to the Philosophical

Nothing can possibly be conceived in the world, or even out of it, which can be called good without qualification, except a *good will*.

Intelligence, wit, judgment, and the other *talents* of the mind, however they may be named, or courage, resolution, perseverance, as qualities of temperament, are undoubtedly good and desirable in many respects; but these gifts of nature may also become extremely bad and mischievous if the will which is to make use of them, and which, therefore, constitutes what is called *character*, is not good. It is the same with the *gifts of fortune*. Power, riches, honor, even health, and the general well-being and contentment with one's condition which is called *happiness*, inspire pride, and often presumption, if there is not a good will to correct the influence of these on the mind, and with this also to rectify the whole principle of acting, and adapt it to its end. The sight of a being who is not adorned with a single feature of a pure and good will, enjoying unbroken prosperity, can never give pleasure to an impartial rational spectator. Thus a good will appears to constitute the indispensable condition even of being worthy of happiness.

There are even some qualities which are of service to this good will itself, and may facilitate its action, yet which have no intrinsic unconditional value, but always presuppose a good will, and this qualifies the esteem that we justly have for them, and does not permit us to regard them as absolutely good. Moderation in the affections and passions, self-control, and calm deliberation are not only good in many respects, but even seem to constitute part of the intrinsic worth of the person; but they are far from deserving to be called good without qualification, although they have been so unconditionally praised by the ancients. For without the principles of a good will, they may become extremely bad; and the coolness of a villain not only makes him far more dangerous, but also directly makes him more abominable in our eyes than he would have been without it.

A good will is good not because of what it performs or effects, not by its aptness for the attainment of some proposed end, but simply by virtue of the volition—that is, it is good in itself, and considered by itself is to be esteemed much higher than all that can be brought about by it in favor of any inclination, nay, even of the sum-total of all inclinations. Even if it should happen that, owing to special disfavor of fortune, or the niggardly provision of a step-motherly nature, this will should wholly lack power to accomplish its purpose, if with its greatest efforts it should yet achieve nothing, and there should remain only the good will (not, to be sure, a mere wish, but the summoning of all means in our power), then, like a jewel, it would still shine by its own light, as a thing which has its whole value in itself. Its usefulness or fruitlessness can neither add to nor take away anything from this value. It would be, as it were, only the setting to enable us to handle it the more conveniently in common commerce, or to attract to it the attention of those who are not yet connoisseurs, but not to recommend it to true connoisseurs, or to determine its value. . . .

In the physical constitution of an organized being, that is, a being adapted suitably to the purposes of life, we assume it as a fundamental principle that no organ for any purpose will be found but what is also the fittest and best adapted for that purpose. Now in a being which has reason and a will, if the proper object of nature were its *conservation*, its *welfare*, in a word, its *happiness*, then nature would have hit upon a very bad arrangement in selecting the reason of the creature to carry out this purpose. For all the actions which the creature has to perform with a view to this purpose, and the whole rule of its conduct, would be far more surely prescribed to it by instinct, and that end would have been attained thereby much more certainly than it ever can be by reason. . . .

And, in fact, we find that the more a cultivated reason applies itself with deliberate purpose to the enjoyment of life and happiness, so much the more does the man fail of true satisfaction. . . . And this we must admit, that the judgment of those who would very much lower the lofty eulogies of the advantages which reason gives us in regard to the happiness and satisfaction of life, or who would even reduce them below zero, is by no means morose or ungrateful to the goodness with which the world is governed, but that there lies at the root of these judgments the idea that our existence has a different and far nobler end, for which, and not for happiness, reason is properly intended, and which must, therefore, be regarded as the supreme condition to which the private ends of man must, for the most part, be postponed.

For as reason is not competent to guide the will with certainty in regard to its objects and the satisfaction of all our wants (which it to some extent even multiplies), this being an end to which an implanted instinct would have led with much greater certainty; and since, nevertheless, reason is imparted to us as a practical faculty, that is, as one which is to have influence on the *will*, therefore, admitting that nature generally in the distribution of her capacities has adapted the means to the end, its true destination must be to produce a *will*, not merely good as a *means* to something else, but *good in itself*, for which reason was absolutely necessary. This will then, though not indeed the sole and complete good, must be the supreme good and the condition of every other, even of the desire of happiness. Under these circumstances, there is nothing inconsistent with the wisdom of nature in the fact that the cultivation of the reason, which is requisite for the first and uncondi- tional purpose, does in many ways interfere, at least in this life, with the attainment of the second, which is always conditional—namely, happiness. Nay, it may even reduce it to nothing, without nature thereby failing of her purpose. . . .

We have then to develop the notion of a will which deserves to be highly esteemed for itself, and is good without a view to anything further. . . . In order to do this, we will take the notion of duty, which includes that of a good will, although implying certain subjective restrictions and hindrances. . . .

I omit here all actions which are already recognized as inconsistent with duty, although they may be useful for this or that purpose, for with these the question whether they are done *from duty* cannot arise at all, since they even conflict with it. I also set aside those actions which really conform to duty, but to which men have *no* direct *inclination*, performing them because they are impelled thereto by some other inclination. For in this case we can readily distinguish whether the action which agrees with duty is done *from duty* or from a selfish view. It is much harder to make this distinction when the action accords with duty, and the subject has besides a *direct* inclination to it. For example, it is always a matter of duty that a dealer should not overcharge an inexperienced purchaser; and wherever there is much commerce the prudent tradesman does not overcharge, but keeps a fixed price for everyone, so that a child buys of him as well as any other. Men are thus *honestly* served; but this is not enough to make us believe that the tradesman has so acted from duty and from principles of honesty; his own advantage required it; it is out of the question in this case to suppose that he might besides have a direct inclination in favor of the buyers, so that, as it were, from love he should give no ad- vantage to one over another. Accordingly the action was done neither from duty nor from direct inclination, but merely with a selfish view.

On the other hand, it is a duty to maintain one's life; and, in addition, everyone has also a direct inclination to do so. But on this account the often anxious care which most men take for it has no intrinsic worth, and their maxim has no moral import. They preserve their life *as duty requires*, no doubt, but not *because duty requires*. On the other hand, if adversity and hopeless sorrow have completely taken away the relish for life, if the unfortunate one, strong in mind, indignant at his fate rather than desponding or dejected, wishes for death, and yet preserves his life without loving it—not from inclination or fear, but from duty—then his maxim has a moral worth.

To be beneficent when we can is a duty; and besides this, there are many minds so sympathetically constituted that, without any other motive of vanity or self-interest, they find a pleasure in spreading joy around them, and can take delight in the satisfaction of others so far as it is their own work. But I maintain that in such a case an action of this kind, however proper, however amiable it may be, has nevertheless no true moral worth, but is on a level with other inclinations, for example, the inclination to honor, which, if it is happily directed to that which is in fact of public utility and accordant with duty, and consequently honorable, deserves praise and encouragement, but not esteem. For the maxim lacks the moral import, namely, that such actions be done *from duty*, not from inclination. Put the case that the mind of that philanthropist was clouded by sorrow of his own, extinguishing all sympathy with the lot of others, and that while he still has the power to benefit others in distress, he is not touched by their trouble because he is absorbed with his own; and now suppose that he tears himself out of this dead insensibility and performs the action without any inclination to it, but simply from duty, then first has his action its genuine moral worth. Further still, if nature has put little sympathy in the heart of this or that man, if he, supposed to be an upright man, is by temperament cold and indifferent to the sufferings of others, perhaps because in respect of his own he is provided with the special gift of patience and fortitude, and supposes, or even requires, that others should have the same—and such a man would certainly not be the meanest product of nature—but if nature had not specially framed him for a philanthropist, would he not still find in himself a source from whence to give himself a far higher worth than that of a good-natured temperament could be? Unquestionably. It is just in this that the moral worth of the character is brought out which is incomparably the highest of all, namely, that he is beneficent, not from inclination, but from duty.

To secure one's own happiness is a duty, at least indirectly; for discontent with one's condition, under a pressure of many anxieties and amidst unsatisfied wants, might easily become a great *temptation to transgression of duty*. But here again, without looking to duty, all men have already the strongest and most intimate inclination to happiness, because it is just in this idea that all inclinations are combined in one total. But the precept of happiness is often of such a sort that it greatly interferes with some inclinations, and yet a man cannot form any definite and certain conception of the sum of satisfaction of all of them which is called happiness. It is not then to be wondered at that a single inclination, definite both as to what it promises and as to the time within which it can be gratified, is often able to overcome such a fluctuating idea, and that a gouty patient, for instance, can choose to enjoy what he likes, and to suffer what he may, since, according to his calculation, on this occasion at least, he has [only] not sacrificed the enjoyment of the present moment to a possibly mistaken expectation of a happiness which is supposed to be found in health. But even in this case, if the general desire for happiness did not influence his will, and supposing that in his particular case health was not a necessary element in this calculation, there yet remains in this, as in all other cases, this law—namely, that he should promote his happiness not from inclination but from duty, and by this would his conduct first acquire true moral worth.

It is in this manner, undoubtedly, that we are to understand those passages of Scripture also in which we are commanded to love our neighbor, even our enemy. For love, as an affection, cannot be commanded, but beneficence for duty's sake may, even though we are not impelled to it by any inclination—nay, are even repelled by a natural and unconquerable aversion. This is *practical* love, and not *pathological* —a love which is seated in the will, and not in the propensions of sense— in principles of action and not of tender sympathy; and it is this love alone which can be commanded.

The second proposition is: That an action done from duty derives its moral worth, *not from the purpose* which is to be attained by it, but from the maxim by which it is determined, and therefore does not depend on the realization of the object of the action, but merely on the *principle of volition* by which the action has taken place, without regard to any object of desire. It is clear from what precedes that the purposes which we may have in view in our actions, or their effects regarded as ends and springs of the will, cannot give to actions any unconditional or moral worth. In what, then, can their worth lie if it is not to consist in the will and in reference to its expected effect? It cannot lie anywhere but in the *principle of the will* without regard to the ends which can be attained by the action. . . .

The third proposition, which is a consequence of the two preceding, I would express thus: *Duty is the necessity of acting from respect for the law.* I may have *inclination* for an object as the effect of my proposed action, but I cannot have *respect* for it just for this reason that it is an effect and not an energy of will. Similarly, I cannot have respect for inclination, whether my own or another's; I can at most, if my own, approve it; if another's, sometimes even love it, that is, look on it as favorable to my own interest. It is only what is connected with my will as a principle, by no means as an effect—what does not subserve my inclination, but overpowers it, or at least in case of choice excludes it from its calculation—in other words, simply the law of itself, which can be an object of respect, and hence a command. . . .

Thus the moral worth of an action does not lie in the effect expected from it, nor in any principle of action which requires to borrow its motive from this expected effect. For all these effects—agreeableness of one's condition, and even the promotion of the happiness of others—could have been also brought about by other causes, so that for this there would have been no need of the will of a rational being; whereas it is in this alone that the supreme and unconditional good can be found. The pre-eminent good which we call moral can therefore consist in nothing else than *the conception of law* in itself, *which certainly is only possible in a rational being*, in so far as this conception, and not the expected effect, determines the will. This is a good which is already present in the person who acts accordingly, and we have not to wait for it to appear first in the result.

But what sort of law can that be the conception of which must determine the will, even without paying any regard to the effect expected from it, in order that this will may be called good absolutely and without qualification? As I have deprived the will of every impulse which could arise to it from obedience to any law, there remains nothing but the universal conformity of its actions to law in general, which alone is to serve the will as a principle, that is, I am never to act otherwise than so *that I could also will that my maxim should become a universal law*. Here, now, it is the simple conformity to law in general, without assuming any particular law applicable to certain actions, that serves the will as its principle, and must so serve it if duty is not to be a vain delusion and a chimerical notion. The common reason of men in its practical judgments perfectly coincides with this, and always has in view the principle here suggested. Let the question be, for example: May I when in distress make a promise with the intention not to keep it? I readily distinguish here between the two significations which the question may have: whether it is prudent or whether it is right to make a false promise? The former may undoubtedly often be the case. I see clearly indeed that it is not enough to extricate myself from a present difficulty by means of this subterfuge, but it must be well considered whether there may not hereafter spring from this lie much greater inconvenience than that from which I now free myself, and as, with all my supposed *cunning*, the consequences cannot be so easily foreseen but that credit once lost may be much more injurious to me than any mischief which I seek to avoid at present, it should be considered whether it would not be more *prudent* to act herein according to a universal maxim, and to make it a habit to promise nothing except with the intention of keeping it. But it is soon clear to me that such a maxim will still only be based on the fear of consequences. Now it is a wholly different thing to be truthful from duty, and to be so from apprehension of injurious consequences. In the first case, the very notion of the action already implies a law for me; in the second case, I must first look about elsewhere to see what results may be combined with it which would affect myself. For to deviate from the principle of duty is beyond all doubt wicked; but to be unfaithful to my maxim of prudence may often be very advantageous to me, although to abide by it is certainly safer. The shortest way, however, and an unerring one, to discover the answer to this question whether a lying promise is consistent with duty, is to ask myself, Should I be content that my maxim (to extricate myself from difficulty by a false promise) should hold good as a universal law, for myself as well as for others; and should I be able to say to myself, "Every one may make a deceitful promise when he finds himself in a difficulty from which he cannot otherwise extricate himself"? Then I presently become aware that, while I can will the lie, I can by no means will that lying should be a universal law. For with such a law there would be no promises at all, since it would be in vain to allege my intention in regard to my future actions to those who would not believe this allegation, or if they overhastily did so, would pay me back in my own coin. Hence my maxim, as soon as it should be made a universal law, would necessarily destroy itself. . . .

Now all *imperatives* command either *hypothetically* or *categorically*. The former represent the practical necessity of a possible action as means to something else that is willed (or at least which one might possibly will). The categorical imperative would be that which represented an action as necessary of itself without reference to another end, that is, as objectively necessary.

Since every practical law represents a possible action as good, and on this account, for a subject who is practically determinable by reason as necessary, all imperatives are formulae determining an action which is necessary according to the principle of a will good in some respects. If now the action is good only as a means *to something else*, then the imperative is *hypothetical*; if it is conceived as good *in itself* and consequently as being necessarily the principle of a will which of itself conforms to reason, then it is *categorical*. . . .

When I conceive a hypothetical imperative, in general I do not know beforehand what it will contain until I am given the condition. But when I conceive a categorical imperative, I know at once what it contains. For as the imperative contains besides the law only the necessity that the maxims shall conform to this law, while the law contains no conditions restricting it, there remains nothing but the general statement that the maxim of the action should conform to a universal law, and it is this conformity alone that the imperative properly represents as necessary.

There is therefore but one categorical imperative, namely, this: *Act only on that maxim whereby thou canst at the same time will that it should become a universal law.*

Now if all imperatives of duty can be deduced from this one imperative as from their principle, then, although it should remain undecided whether what is called duty is not merely a vain notion, yet at least we shall be able to show what we understand by it and what this notion means.

Since the universality of the law according to which effects are produced constitutes what is properly called *nature* in the most general sense (as to form)—that is, the existence of things so far as it is determined by general laws—the imperative of duty may be expressed thus: *Act as if the maxim of thy action were to become by thy will a universal law of nature.*

We will now enumerate a few duties, adopting the usual division of them into duties to ourselves and to others, and into perfect and imperfect duties.

1. A man reduced to despair by a series of misfortunes feels wearied of life, but is still so far in possession of his reason that he can ask himself whether it would not be contrary to his duty to himself to take his own life. Now he inquires whether the maxim of his action could become a universal law of nature. His maxim is: From self-love I adopt it as a principle to shorten my life when its longer duration is likely to bring more evil than satisfaction. It is asked then simply whether this principle founded on self-love can become a universal law of nature. Now we see at once that a system of nature of which it should be a law to destroy life by means of the very feeling whose special nature it is to impel to the improvement of life would contradict itself, and therefore could not exist as a system of nature; hence that maxim

cannot possibly exist as a universal law of nature, and consequently would be wholly inconsistent with the supreme principle of all duty.

2. Another finds himself forced by necessity to borrow money. He knows that he will not be able to repay it, but sees also that nothing will be lent to him unless he promises stoutly to repay it in a definite time. He desires to make this promise, but he has still so much conscience as to ask himself: Is it not unlawful and inconsistent with duty to get out of a difficulty in this way? Suppose, however, that he resolves to do so, then the maxim of his action would be expressed thus: When I think myself in want of money, I will borrow money and promise to repay it, although I know that I never can do so. Now this principle of self-love or of one's own advantage may perhaps be consistent with my whole future welfare; but the question now is, Is it right? I change then the suggestion of self-love into a universal law, and state the question thus: How would it be if my maxim were a universal law? Then I see at once that it could never hold as a universal law of nature, but would necessarily contradict itself. For supposing it to be a universal law that everyone when he thinks himself in a difficulty should be able to promise whatever he pleases, with the purpose of not keeping his promise, the promise itself would become impossible, as well as the end that one might have in view in it, since no one would consider that anything was promised to him, but would ridicule all such statements as vain pretenses.

3. A third finds in himself a talent which with the help of some culture might make him a useful man in many respects. But he finds himself in comfortable circumstances and prefers to indulge in pleasure rather than to take pains in enlarging and improving his happy natural capacities. He asks, however, whether his maxim of neglect of his natural gifts, besides agreeing with his inclination to indulgence, agrees also with what is called duty. He sees then that a system of nature could indeed subsist with such a universal law, although men (like the South Sea islanders) should let their talents rest and resolve to devote their lives merely to idleness, amusement, and propagation of their species— in a word, to enjoyment; but he cannot possibly *will* that this should be a universal law of nature, or be implanted in us as such by a natural instinct. For, as a rational being, he necessarily wills that his faculties be developed, since they serve him, and have been given him, for all sorts of possible purposes.

4. A fourth, who is in prosperity, while he sees that others have to contend with great wretchedness and that he could help them, thinks: What concern is it of mine? Let everyone be as happy as Heaven pleases,

or as he can make himself; I will take nothing from him nor even envy him, only I do not wish to contribute anything to his welfare or to his assistance in distress! Now no doubt, if such a mode of thinking were a universal law, the human race might very well subsist, and doubtless even better than in a state in which everyone talks of sympathy and good-will, or even takes care occasionally to put it into practice, but, on the other side, also cheats when he can, betrays the rights of men, or otherwise violates them. But although it is possible that a universal law of nature might exist in accordance with that maxim, it is impossible to *will* that such a principle should have the universal validity of a law of nature. For a will which resolved this would contradict itself, inasmuch as many cases might occur in which one would have need of the love and sympathy of others, and in which, by such a law of nature, sprung from his own will, he would deprive himself of all hope of the aid he desires. . . .

If now we attend to ourselves on occasion of any transgression of duty, we shall find that we in fact do not will that our maxim should be a universal law, for that is impossible for us; on the contrary, we will that the opposite should remain a universal law, only we assume the liberty of making an *exception* in our own favor or (just for this time only) in favor of our inclination. Consequently, if we considered all cases from one and the same point of view, namely, that of reason, we should find a contradiction in our own will, namely, that a certain principle should be objectively necessary as a universal law, and yet subjectively should not be universal, but admit of exceptions. As, however, we at one moment regard our action from the point of view of a will wholly conformed to reason, and then again look at the same action from the point of view of a will affected by inclination, there is not really any contradiction, but an antagonism of inclination to the precept of reason, whereby the universality of the principle is changed into a mere generality, so that the practical principle of reason shall meet the maxim half way. Now, although this cannot be justified in our own impartial judgment, yet it proves that we do really recognize the validity of the categorical imperative and (with all respect for it) only allow ourselves a few exceptions which we think unimportant and forced from us. . . .

If then there is a supreme practical principle or, in respect of the human will, a categorical imperative, it must be one which, being drawn from the conception of that which is necessarily an end for everyone because it is *an end in itself*, constitutes an *objective* principle of will, and can therefore serve as a universal practical law. The foundation of this principle is: *rational nature exists as an end in itself*. Man necessarily conceives his own existence as being so; so far then this is a *subjective* principle of human actions. But every other rational being regards its existence similarly, just on the same rational principle that holds for me; so that it is at the same time an objective principle from which as a supreme practical law all laws of the will must be capable of being deduced. Accordingly the practical imperative will be as follows: *So act as to treat humanity, whether in thine own person or in that of any other, in every case as an end withal, never as means only.*

FOR FURTHER STUDY

Broad, Charlie D. *Five Types of Ethical Theory*. New York: Harcourt, Brace, 1930, Ch. 5.

Jensen, O. C. "Kant's Ethical Formalism," *Philosophy*, IX (April 1934): 195-208.

Johnson, Oliver A. *Rightness and Goodness, A Study in Contemporary Ethical Theory*. The Hague: Martinus Nijhoff, 1959.

Paton, Herbert James. *The Categorical Imperative; a Study in Kant's Moral Philosophy*. Chicago: U. of Chicago Press, 1948.

Schilpp, Paul Arthur. *Kant's Pre-Critical Ethics*. Evanston: Northwestern U. Press, 1938.

Swakey, William Curtis. *Ethical Theory: From Hobbes to Kant*. New York: Philosophical Library, 1961, Ch. 12, "Kant."

Werkmeister, W. H. *Theories of Ethics*. Lincoln: Johnsen, 1961, Ch. 8, "The Morality of Freedom and Human Dignity."

CHAPTER 9

HAPPINESS AS
THE END OF LIFE

Epicurus to Menoeceus*

EPICURUS

Epicurus (342-270 B. C.), after teaching in various
communities in Asia Minor, moved to Athens (about
306 B. C.) and purchased a garden that became the
famous Garden of Epicurus. Here he expounded his
views to his disciples and students, but unfortunately
only portions of his writings have come down to us.

Let no one when young delay to study philosophy, nor when he is
old grow weary of his study. For no one can come too early or too
late to secure the health of his soul. And the man who says that the age
for philosophy has either not yet come or has gone by is like the man
who says that the age for happiness is not yet come to him, or has
passed away. Wherefore both when young and old a man must study
philosophy, that as he grows old he may be young in blessings through
the grateful recollection of what has been, and that in youth he may be
old as well, since he will know no fear of what is to come. We must
then meditate on the things that make our happiness, seeing that when
that is with us we have all, but when it is absent we do all to win it.

The things which I used unceasingly to commend to you, these do

* From *Epicurus: The Extant Remains* by Cyril Bailey. By permission of the
Clarendon Press, Oxford.

and practise, considering them to be the first principles of the good life. First of all believe that god is a being immortal and blessed, even as the common idea of a god is engraved on men's minds, and do not assign to him anything alien to his immortality or ill-suited to his blessedness: but believe about him everything that can uphold his blessedness and immortality. For gods there are, since the knowledge of them is by clear vision. But they are not such as the many believe them to be: for indeed they do not consistently represent them as they believe them to be. And the impious man is not he who denies the gods of the many, but he who attaches to the gods the beliefs of the many. For the statements of the many about the gods are not conceptions derived from sensation, but false suppositions, according to which the greatest misfortunes befall the wicked and the greatest blessings the good by the gift of the gods. For men being accustomed always to their own virtues welcome those like themselves, but regard all that is not of their nature as alien.

Become accustomed to the belief that death is nothing to us. For all good and evil consists in sensation, but death is deprivation of sensation. And therefore a right understanding that death is nothing to us makes the mortality of life enjoyable, not because it adds to it an infinite span of time, but because it takes away the craving for immortality. For there is nothing terrible in life for the man who has truly comprehended that there is nothing terrible in not living. So that the man speaks but idly who says that he fears death not because it will be painful when it comes, but because it is painful in anticipation. For that which gives no trouble when it comes, is but an empty pain in anticipation. So death, the most terrifying of ills, is nothing to us, since so long as we exist, death is not with us; but when death comes, then we do not exist. It does not then concern either the living or the dead, since for the former it is not, and the latter are no more.

But the many at one moment shun death as the greatest of evils, at another yearn for it as a respite from the evils in life. But the wise man neither seeks to escape life nor fears the cessation of life, for neither does life offend him nor does the absence of life seem to be any evil. And just as with food he does not seek simply the larger share and nothing else, but rather the most pleasant, so he seeks to enjoy not the longest period of time, but the most pleasant.

And he who counsels the young man to live well, but the old man to make a good end, is foolish, not merely because of the desirability of life, but also because it is the same training which teaches to live well and to die well. Yet much worse still is the man who says it is good not to be born, but "once born make haste to pass the gates of Death."

[Theognis, 427]

For if he says this from conviction why does he not pass away out of life? For it is open to him to do so, if he had firmly made up his mind to this. But if he speaks in jest, his words are idle among men who cannot receive them.

We must then bear in mind that the future is neither ours, nor yet wholly not ours, so that we may not altogether expect it as sure to come, nor abandon hope of it, as if it will certainly not come.

We must consider that of desires some are natural, others vain, and of the natural some are necessary and others merely natural; and of the necessary some are necessary for happiness, others for the repose of the body, and others for very life. The right understanding of these facts enables us to refer all choice and avoidance to the health of the body and the soul's freedom from disturbance, since this is the aim of the life of blessedness. For it is to obtain this end that we always act, namely, to avoid pain and fear. And when this is once secured for us, all the tempest of the soul is dispersed, since the living creature has not to wander as though in search of something that is missing, and to look for some other thing by which he can fulfil the good of the soul and the good of the body. For it is then that we have need of pleasure, when we feel pain owing to the absence of pleasure; but when we do not feel pain, we no longer need pleasure. And for this cause we call pleasure the beginning and end of the blessed life. For we recognize pleasure as the first good innate in us, and from pleasure we begin every act of choice and avoidance, and to pleasure we return again, using the feeling as the standard by which we judge every good.

And since pleasure is the first good and natural to us, for this very reason we do not choose every pleasure, but sometimes we pass over many pleasures, when greater discomfort accrues to us as the result of them: and similarly we think many pains better than pleasures, since a greater pleasure comes to us when we have endured pains for a long time. Every pleasure then because of its natural kinship to us is good, yet not every pleasure is to be chosen: even as every pain also is an evil, yet not all are always of a nature to be avoided. Yet by a scale of comparison and by the consideration of advantages and disadvantages we must form our judgement on all these matters. For the good on certain occasions we treat as bad, and conversely the bad as good.

And again independence of desire we think a great good—not that we may at all times enjoy but a few things, but that, if we do not possess many, we may enjoy the few in the genuine persuasion that those have the sweetest pleasure in luxury who least need it, and that all that is natural is easy to be obtained, but that which is superfluous is hard. And so plain savours bring us a pleasure equal to a luxurious diet, when all the pain due to want is removed; and bread and water produce the highest pleasure, when one who needs them puts them to his lips. To grow accustomed therefore to simple and not luxurious diet gives us health to the full, and makes a man alert for the needful employments of life, and when after long intervals we approach luxuries, disposes us better towards them, and fits us to be fearless of fortune.

When, therefore, we maintain that pleasure is the end, we do not mean the pleasures of profligates and those that consist in sensuality, as is supposed by some who are either ignorant or disagree with us or do not understand, but freedom from pain in the body and from trouble in the mind. For it is not continuous drinkings and revellings, nor the satisfaction of lusts, nor the enjoyment of fish and other luxuries of the wealthy table, which produce a pleasant life, but sober reasoning, searching out the motives for all choice and avoidance, and banishing mere opinions, to which are due the greatest disturbance of the spirit.

Of all this the beginning and the greatest good is prudence. Wherefore prudence is a more precious thing even than philosophy: for from prudence are sprung all the other virtues, and it teaches us that it is not possible to live pleasantly without living prudently and honourably and justly, nor, again, to live a life of prudence, honour, and justice without living pleasantly. For the virtues are by nature bound up with the pleasant life, and the pleasant life is inseparable from them. For indeed who, think you, is a better man than he who holds reverent opinions concerning the gods, and is at all times free from fear of death, and has reasoned out the end ordained by nature? He understands that the limit of good things is easy to fulfil and easy to attain, whereas the course of ills is either short in time or slight in pain: he laughs at destiny, whom some have introduced as the mistress of all things. He thinks that with us lies the chief power in determining events, some of which happen by necessity and some by chance, and some are within our control; for while necessity cannot be called to account, he sees that chance is inconstant, but that which is in our control is subject to no master, and to it are naturally attached praise and blame. For, indeed, it were better to follow the myths about the gods than to become a slave to the destiny of the natural philosophers: for the former suggests a hope of placating the gods by worship, whereas the latter involves a necessity which knows no placation. As to chance, he does not regard it as a god as most men do (for in a god's acts there is no disorder), nor as an uncertain cause of all things: for he does not believe that good and evil are given by chance to man for the framing of a blessed life, but that opportunities for great good and great evil are afforded by it. He therefore thinks it better to be unfortunate in reasonable action than to prosper in unreason. For it is better in a man's actions that what is well chosen should fail, rather than that what is ill chosen should be successful owing to chance.

Meditate therefore on these things and things akin to them night and day by yourself, and with a companion like to yourself, and never shall you be disturbed waking or asleep, but you shall live like a god among men. For a man who lives among immortal blessings is not like to a mortal being.

Morals and Legislation*

JEREMY BENTHAM

Jeremy Bentham (1748-1832), an Englishman with a strong interest in political and social reforms, is sometimes called the father or founder of utilitarianism. He tried to put the happiness theory on a quantitative or mathematical basis.

Chapter I—Of the Principle of Utility

I. Nature has placed mankind under the governance of two sovereign masters, *pain* and *pleasure*. It is for them alone to point out what we ought to do, as well as to determine what we shall do. On the one hand the standard of right and wrong, on the other the chain of causes and effects, are fastened to their throne. They govern us in all we do, in

* From *An Introduction to the Principles of Morals and Legislation* (1823), Chapters I and IV with omissions.

all we say, in all we think: every effort we can make to throw off our
subjection, will serve but to demonstrate and confirm it. In words a
man may pretend to abjure their empire: but in reality he will remain
subject to it all the while. The *principle of utility* recognises this subjection, and assumes it for the foundation of that system, the object of
which is to rear the fabric of felicity by the hands of reason and of law.
Systems which attempt to question it, deal in sounds instead of sense,
in caprice instead of reason, in darkness instead of light.

But enough of metaphor and declamation: it is not by such means
that moral science is to be improved.

II. The principle of utility is the foundation of the present work: it
will be proper therefore at the outset to give an explicit and determi-
nate account of what is meant by it. By the principle of utility is meant
that principle which approves or disapproves of every action whatsoever, according to the tendency which it appears to have to augment
or diminish the happiness of the party whose interest is in question: or,
what is the same thing in other words, to promote or to oppose that
happiness. I say of every action whatsoever; and therefore not only of
every action of a private individual, but of every measure of government.

III. By utility is meant that property in any object, whereby it tends
to produce benefit, advantage, pleasure, good, or happiness, (all this
in the present case comes to the same thing) or (what comes again to
the same thing) to prevent the happening of mischief, pain, evil, or
unhappiness to the party whose interest is considered: if that party be
the community in general, then the happiness of the community: if a
particular individual, then the happiness of that individual.

IV. The interest of the community is one of the most general expressions that can occur in the phraseology of morals: no wonder that
the meaning of it is often lost. When it has a meaning, it is this. The
community is a fictitious *body*, composed of the individual persons
who are considered as constituting as it were its *members*. The interest
of the community then is, what?—the sum of the interests of the several
members who compose it.

V. It is in vain to talk of the interest of the community, without
understanding what is the interest of the individual. A thing is said
to promote the interest, or to be *for* the interest, of an individual, when
it tends to add to the sum total of his pleasures: or, what comes to the
same thing, to diminish the sum total of his pains.

VI. An action then may be said to be conformable to the principle
of utility, or, for shortness sake, to utility (meaning with respect to

the community at large), when the tendency it has to augment the happiness of the community is greater than any it has to diminish it.

VII. A measure of government (which is but a particular kind of action, performed by a particular person or persons) may be said to be conformable to or dictated by the principle of utility, when in like manner the tendency which it has to augment the happiness of the community is greater than any which it has to diminish it.

VIII. When an action, or in particular a measure of government, is supposed by a man to be conformable to the principle of utility, it may be convenient, for the purposes of discourse, to imagine a kind of law or dictate, called a law or dictate of utility: and to speak of the action in question, as being conformable to such law or dictate.

IX. A man may be said to be a partizan of the principle of utility, when the approbation or disapprobation he annexes to any action, or to any measure, is determined by and proportioned to the tendency which he conceives it to have to augment or to diminish the happiness of the community: or in other words, to its conformity or unconformity to the laws or dictates of utility.

X. Of an action that is conformable to the principle of utility one may always say either that it is one that ought to be done, or at least that it is not one that ought not to be done. One may say also, that it is right it should be done; at least that it is not wrong it should be done: that it is a right action; at least that it is not a wrong action. When thus interpreted, the words *ought*, and *right* and *wrong*, and others of that stamp, have a meaning: when otherwise, they have none.

XI. Has the rectitude of this principle been ever formally contested? It should seem that it had, by those who have not known what they have been meaning. Is it susceptible of any direct proof? it should seem not: for that which is used to prove every thing else, cannot itself be proved: a chain of proofs must have their commencement somewhere. To give such proof is as impossible as it is needless.

XII. Not that there is or ever has been that human creature breathing, however stupid or perverse, who has not on many, perhaps on most occasions of his life, deferred to it. By the natural constitution of the human frame, on most occasions of their lives men in general embrace this principle, without thinking of it: if not for the ordering of their own actions, yet for the trying of their own actions, as well as of those of other men. There have been, at the same time, not many, perhaps, even of the most intelligent, who have been disposed to embrace it purely and without reserve. There are even few who have not taken some occasion or other to quarrel with it, either on account of their not understanding always how to apply it, or on account of some prejudice or other which they were afraid to examine into, or could not bear to part with. For such is the stuff that man is made of: in principle and in practice, in a right track and in a wrong one, the rarest of all human qualities is consistency.

XIII. When a man attempts to combat the principle of utility, it is with reasons drawn, without his being aware of it, from that very principle itself. His arguments, if they prove any thing, prove not that the principle is *wrong*, but that, according to the applications he supposes to be made of it, it is *misapplied*. Is it possible for a man to move the earth? Yes; but he must first find out another earth to stand upon. . . .

Chapter IV—Value of a Lot of Pleasure or Pain,
How to Be Measured

I. Pleasures then, and the avoidance of pains, are the *ends* which the legislator has in view: it behoves him therefore to understand their *value*. Pleasures and pains are the *instruments* he has to work with: it behoves him therefore to understand their force, which is again, in other words, their value.

II. To a person considered *by himself*, the value of a pleasure or pain considered *by itself*, will be greater or less, according to the four following circumstances:

1. Its *intensity*.
2. Its *duration*.
3. Its *certainty* or *uncertainty*.
4. Its *propinquity* or *remoteness*.

III. These are the circumstances which are to be considered in estimating a pleasure or a pain considered each of them by itself. But when the value of any pleasure or pain is considered for the purpose of estimating the tendency of any *act* by which it is produced, there are two other circumstances to be taken into the account; these are,

5. Its *fecundity*, or the chance it has of being followed by sensations of the *same* kind: that is, pleasures, if it be a pleasure: pains, if it be a pain.

6. Its *purity*, or the chance it has of *not* being followed by sensations of the *opposite* kind: that is, pains, if it be a pleasure: pleasures, if it be a pain.

These two last, however, are in strictness scarcely to be deemed properties of the pleasure or the pain itself; they are not, therefore, in strictness to be taken into the account of the value of that pleasure or that pain. They are in strictness to be deemed properties only of the act, or other event, by which such pleasure or pain has been produced; and accordingly are only to be taken into the account of the tendency of such act or such event.

IV. To a *number* of persons, with reference to each of whom the value of a pleasure or a pain is considered, it will be greater or less, according to seven circumstances: to wit, the six preceding ones; *viz.*

1. Its *intensity*.
2. Its *duration*.
3. Its *certainty* or *uncertainty*.
4. Its *propinquity* or *remoteness*.
5. Its *fecundity*.
6. Its *purity*.

And one other; to wit:

7. Its *extent*; that is, the number of persons to whom it *extends*; or (in other words) who are affected by it.

V. To take an exact account then of the general tendency of any act, by which the interests of a community are affected, proceed as follows. Begin with any one person of those whose interests seem most immediately to be affected by it: and take an account,

1. Of the value of each distinguishable *pleasure* which appears to be produced by it in the *first* instance.

2. Of the value of each *pain* which appears to be produced by it in the *first* instance.

3. Of the value of each pleasure which appears to be produced by it *after* the first. This constitutes the *fecundity* of the first *pleasure* and the *impurity* of the first *pain*.

4. Of the value of each *pain* which appears to be produced by it after the first. This constitutes the *fecundity* of the first *pain*, and the *impurity* of the first pleasure.

5. Sum up all the values of all the *pleasures* on the one side, and those of all the pains on the other. The balance, if it be on the side of pleasure, will give the *good* tendency of the act upon the whole, with respect to the interests of that *individual* person; if on the side of pain, the *bad* tendency of it upon the whole.

6. Take an account of the *number* of persons whose interests appear to be concerned; and repeat the above process with respect to each. *Sum up* the numbers expressive of the degrees of *good* tendency, which the act has, with respect to each individual, in regard to whom the tendency of it is *good* upon the whole: do this again with respect

to each individual, in regard to whom the tendency of it is *bad* upon the whole. Take the *balance*; which, if on the side of *pleasure*, will give the general *good tendency* of the act, with respect to the total number or community of individuals concerned; if on the side of pain, the general *evil tendency*, with respect to the same community.

VI. It is not to be expected that this process should be strictly pursued previously to every moral judgment, or to every legislative or judicial operation. It may, however, be always kept in view: and as near as the process actually pursued on these occasions approaches to it, so near will such process approach to the character of an exact one.

VII. The same process is alike applicable to pleasure and pain, in whatever shape they appear: and by whatever denomination they are distinguished: to pleasure, whether it be called *good* (which is properly the cause or instrument of pleasure) or *profit* (which is distant pleasure, or the cause or instrument of distant pleasure), or *convenience*, or *advantage, benefit, emolument, happiness,* and so forth: to pain, whether it be called *evil* (which corresponds to *good*), or *mischief*, or *inconvenience*, or *disadvantage*, or *loss*, or *unhappiness*, and so forth.

VIII. Nor is this a novel and unwarranted, any more than it is a useless theory. In all this there is nothing but what the practice of mankind, wheresoever they have a clear view of their own interest, is perfectly conformable to. An article of property, an estate in land, for instance, is valuable, on what account? On account of the pleasures of all kinds which it enables a man to produce, and what comes to the same thing the pains of all kinds which it enables him to avert. But the value of such an article of property is universally understood to rise or fall according to the length or shortness of the time which a man has in it: the certainty or uncertainty of its coming into possession: and the nearness or remoteness of the time at which, if at all, it is to come into possession. As to the *intensity* of the pleasures which a man may derive from it, this is never thought of, because it depends upon the use which each particular person may come to make of it; which cannot be estimated till the particular pleasures he may come to derive from it, or the particular pains he may come to exclude by means of it, are brought to view. For the same reason, neither does he think of the *fecundity* or *purity* of those pleasures.

Thus much for pleasure and pain, happiness and unhappiness, in *general*.

The Greatest Happiness Principle*

JOHN STUART MILL

John Stuart Mill (1806-1873), an English empiricist, was an outstanding defender of tolerance, freedom and nineteenth-century liberalism. Along with Jeremy Bentham, he was a great advocate of the moral philosophy of utilitarianism.

Chapter II—What Utilitarianism Is

A passing remark is all that needs be given to the ignorant blunder of supposing that those who stand up for utility as the test of right and wrong use the term in that restricted and merely colloquial sense in which utility is opposed to pleasure. An apology is due to the philosophical opponents of utilitarianism for even the momentary appearance of confounding them with anyone capable of so absurd a misconception; which is the more extraordinary, inasmuch as the contrary accusation, of referring everything to pleasure, and that, too, in its grossest form, is another of the common charges against utilitarianism: and, as has been pointedly remarked by an able writer, the same sort of persons, and often the very same persons, denounce the theory "as impracticably dry when the word 'utility' precedes the word 'pleasure,' and as too practicably voluptuous when the word 'pleasure' precedes the word 'utility.'" Those who know anything about the matter are aware that every writer, from Epicurus to Bentham, who maintained the theory of utility meant by it, not something to be contradistinguished from pleasure, but pleasure itself, together with exemption from pain; and instead of opposing the useful to the agreeable or the ornamental, have always declared that the useful means these, among other things. Yet the common herd, including the herd of writers, not only in newspapers and periodicals, but in books of weight and pretension, are perpetually falling into this shallow mistake. Having caught up the word "utilitarian," while knowing nothing whatever about it but its sound, they habitually express by it the rejection or the neglect

* From *Utilitarianism* (1863), Chapters II and IV with omissions.

of pleasure in some of its forms: of beauty, of ornament, or of amusement. Nor is the term thus ignorantly misapplied solely in disparagement, but occasionally in compliment, as though it implied superiority to frivolity and the mere pleasures of the moment. And this perverted use is the only one in which the word is popularly known, and the one from which the new generation are acquiring their sole notion of its meaning. Those who introduced the word, but who had for many years discontinued it as a distinctive appellation, may well feel themselves called upon to resume it if by doing so they can hope to contribute anything toward rescuing it from this utter degradation.

The creed which accepts as the foundation of morals "utility" or the "greatest happiness principle" holds that actions are right in proportion as they tend to promote happiness; wrong as they tend to produce the reverse of happiness. By happiness is intended pleasure and the absence of pain; by unhappiness, pain and the privation of pleasure. To give a clear view of the moral standard set up by the theory, much more requires to be said; in particular, what things it includes in the ideas of pain and pleasure, and to what extent this is left an open question. But these supplementary explanations do not affect the theory of life on which this theory of morality is grounded—namely, that pleasure and freedom from pain are the only things desirable as ends; and that all desirable things (which are as numerous in the utilitarian as in any other scheme) are desirable either for pleasure inherent in themselves or as means to the promotion of pleasure and the prevention of pain.

Now such a theory of life excites in many minds, and among them in some of the most estimable in feeling and purpose, inveterate dislike. To suppose that life has (as they express it) no higher end than pleasure—no better and nobler object of desire and pursuit—they designate as utterly mean and groveling, as a doctrine worthy only of swine, to whom the followers of Epicurus were, at a very early period, contemptuously likened; and modern holders of the doctrine are occasionally made the subject of equally polite comparisons by its German, French, and English assailants.

When thus attacked, the Epicureans have always answered that it is not they, but their accusers, who represent human nature in a degrading light, since the accusation supposes human beings to be capable of no pleasures except those of which swine are capable. If this supposition were true, the charge could not be gainsaid, but would then be no longer an imputation; for if the sources of pleasure were precisely the same to human beings and to swine, the rule of life which is good enough for the one would be good enough for the other. The comparison of the Epicurean life to that of beasts is felt as degrading, precisely because a beast's pleasures do not satisfy a human being's conceptions of happiness. Human beings have faculties more elevated than the animal appetites and, when once made conscious of them, do not regard anything as happiness which does not include their gratification. I do not, indeed, consider the Epicureans to have been by any means faultless in drawing out their scheme of consequences from the utilitarian principle. To do this in any sufficient manner, many Stoic, as well as Christian, elements require to be included. But there is no known Epicurean theory of life which does not assign to the pleasures of the intellect, of the feelings and imagination, and of the moral sentiments a much higher value as pleasures than to those of mere sensation. It must be admitted, however, that utilitarian writers in general have placed the superiority of mental over bodily pleasures chiefly in the greater permanency, safety, uncostliness, etc., of the former—that is, in their circumstantial advantages rather than in their intrinsic nature. And on all these points utilitarians have fully proved their case; but they might have taken the other and, as it may be called, higher ground with entire consistency. It is quite compatible with the principle of utility to recognize the fact that some kinds of pleasure are more desirable and more valuable than others. It would be absurd that, while in estimating all other things quality is considered as well as quantity, the estimation of pleasure should be supposed to depend on quantity alone.

If I am asked what I mean by difference of quality in pleasures, or what makes one pleasure more valuable than another, merely as a pleasure, except its being greater in amount, there is but one possible answer. Of two pleasures, if there be one to which all or almost all who have experience of both give a decided preference, irrespective of any feeling of moral obligation to prefer it, that is the more desirable pleasure. If one of the two is, by those who are competently acquainted with both, placed so far above the other that they prefer it, even though knowing it to be attended with a greater amount of discontent, and would not resign it for any quantity of the other pleasure which their nature is capable of, we are justified in ascribing to the preferred enjoyment a superiority in quality so far outweighing quantity as to render it, in comparison, of small account.

Now it is an unquestionable fact that those who are equally acquainted with and equally capable of appreciating and enjoying both do give a most marked preference to the manner of existence which employs their higher faculties. Few human creatures would consent to be changed into any of the lower animals for a promise of the fullest allowance of a beast's pleasures; no intelligent human being would consent to be a fool, no instructed person would be an ignoramus, no person of feeling and conscience would be selfish and base, even though they should be persuaded that the fool, the dunce, or the rascal is better satisfied with his lot than they are with theirs. They would not resign what they possess more than he for the most complete satisfaction of all the desires which they have in common with him. If they ever fancy they would, it is only in cases of unhappiness so extreme that to escape from it they would exchange their lot for almost any other, however undesirable in their own eyes. A being of higher faculties requires more to make him happy, is capable probably of more acute suffering, and certainly accessible to it at more points, than one of an inferior type; but in spite of these liabilities, he can never really wish to sink into what he feels to be a lower grade of existence. We may give what explanation we please of this unwillingness; we may attribute it to pride, a name which is given indiscriminately to some of the most and to some of the least estimable feelings of which mankind are capable; we may refer it to the love of liberty and personal independence, an appeal to which was with the Stoics one of the most effective means for the inculcation of it; to the love of power or to the love of excitement, both of which do really enter into and contribute to it; but its most appropriate appellation is a sense of dignity, which all human beings possess in one form or other, and in some, though by no means in exact, proportion to their higher faculties, and which is so essential a part of the happiness of those in whom it is strong that nothing which conflicts with it could be otherwise than momentarily an object of desire to them. Whoever supposes that this preference takes place at a sacrifice of happiness—that the superior being, in anything like equal circumstances, is not happier than the inferior—confounds the two very different ideas of happiness and content. It is indisputable that the being whose capacities of enjoyment are low has the greatest chance of having them fully satisfied; and a highly endowed being will always feel that any happiness which he can look for, as the world is constituted, is imperfect. But he can learn to bear its imperfections, if they are at all bearable; and they will not make him envy the being who is indeed unconscious of the imperfections, but only because he feels not at all the good which those imperfections qualify. It is better to be a human being dissatisfied than a pig satisfied; better to be Socrates dissatisfied than a fool satisfied. And if the fool, or the pig, are of a different opinion, it is because they only know their own side of the question. The other party to the comparison knows both sides.

It may be objected that many who are capable of the higher pleasures occasionally, under the influence of temptation, postpone them to the lower. But this is quite compatible with a full appreciation of the intrinsic superiority of the higher. Men often, from infirmity of character, make their election for the nearer good, though they know it to be the less valuable; and this no less when the choice is between two bodily pleasures than when it is between bodily and mental. They pursue sensual indulgences to the injury of health, though perfectly aware that health is the greater good. It may be further objected that many who begin with youthful enthusiasm for everything noble, as they advance in years, sink into indolence and selfishness. But I do not believe that those who undergo this very common change voluntarily choose the lower description of pleasures in preference to the higher. I believe that, before they devote themselves exclusively to the one, they have already become incapable of the other. Capacity for the nobler feelings is in most natures a very tender plant, easily killed, not only by hostile influences, but by mere want of sustenance; and in the majority of young persons it speedily dies away if the occupations to which their position in life has devoted them, and the society into which it has thrown them, are not favorable to keeping that higher capacity in exercise. Men lose their high aspirations as they lose their intellectual tastes, because they have not time or opportunity for indulging them; and they addict themselves to inferior pleasures, not because they deliberately prefer them, but because they are either the only ones to which they have access or the only ones which they are any longer capable of enjoying. It may be questioned whether anyone who has remained equally susceptible to both classes of pleasures ever knowingly and calmly preferred the lower, though many, in all ages, have broken down in an ineffectual attempt to combine both.

From this verdict of the only competent judges, I apprehend there can be no appeal. On a question which is the best worth having of two pleasures, or which of two modes of existence is the most grateful to the feelings, apart from its moral attributes and from its consequences, the judgment of those who are qualified by knowledge of both, or, if they differ, that of the majority among them, must be admitted as final. And there needs be the less hesitation to accept this judgment respecting the quality of pleasures, since there is no other tribunal to be referred to even on the question of quantity. What means are there of determining which is the acutest of two pains, or the intensest of two pleasurable sensations, except the general suffrage of those who are familiar with both? Neither pains nor pleasures are homogeneous, and pain is always heterogeneous with pleasure. What is there to decide whether a particular pleasure is worth purchasing at the cost of a particular pain, except the feelings and judgment of the experienced? When, therefore, those feelings and judgment declare the pleasures derived from the higher faculties to be preferable *in kind*, apart from the question of intensity, to those of which the animal nature, disjoined from the higher faculties, is susceptible, they are entitled on this subject to the same regard. . . .

Chapter IV—Of What Sort of Proof the Principle of Utility Is Susceptible

It has already been remarked that questions of ultimate ends do not admit of proof, in the ordinary acceptation of the term. To be incapable of proof by reasoning is common to all first principles, to the first premises of our knowledge, as well as to those of our conduct. But the former, being matters of fact, may be the subject of a direct appeal to the faculties which judge of fact—namely, our senses and our internal consciousness. Can an appeal be made to the same faculties on questions of practical ends? Or by what other faculty is cognizance taken of them?

Questions about ends are, in other words, questions [about] what things are desirable. The utilitarian doctrine is that happiness is desirable, and the only thing desirable, as an end; all other things being only desirable as means to that end. What ought to be required of this doctrine, what conditions is it requisite that the doctrine should fulfill—to make good its claim to be believed?

The only proof capable of being given that an object is visible is that people actually see it. The only proof that a sound is audible is that people hear it; and so of the other sources of our experience. In like manner, I apprehend, the sole evidence it is possible to produce that anything is desirable is that people do actually desire it. If the end which the utilitarian doctrine proposes to itself were not, in theory and in practice, acknowledged to be an end, nothing could ever convince any person that it was so. No reason can be given why the general happiness is desirable, except that each person, so far as he believes it to be attainable, desires his own happiness. This, however, being a fact, we have not only all the proof which the case admits of, but all which it is possible to require, that happiness is a good, that each person's happiness is a good to that person, and the general happiness, therefore, a good to the aggregate of all persons. Happiness has made out its title as *one* of the ends of conduct and, consequently, one of the criteria of morality.

But it has not, by this alone, proved itself to be the sole criterion. To do that, it would seem, by the same rule, necessary to show, not only that people desire happiness, but that they never desire anything else. Now it is palpable that they do desire things which, in common language, are decidedly distinguished from happiness. They desire, for example, virtue and the absence of vice no less really than pleasure and the absence of pain. The desire of virtue is not as universal, but it is as authentic a fact as the desire of happiness. And hence the opponents of the utilitarian standard deem that they have a right to infer that there are other ends of human action besides happiness, and that happiness is not the standard of approbation and disapprobation.

But does the utilitarian doctrine deny that people desire virtue, or maintain that virtue is not a thing to be desired? The very reverse. It maintains not only that virtue is to be desired, but that it is to be desired disinterestedly, for itself. Whatever may be the opinion of utilitarian moralists as to the original conditions by which virtue is made virtue, however they may believe (as they do) that actions and dispositions are only virtuous because they promote another end than virtue, yet this being granted, and it having been decided, from considerations of this description, what *is* virtuous, they not only place virtue at the very head of the things which are good as means to the ultimate end, but they also recognize as a psychological fact the possibility of its being, to the individual, a good in itself, without looking to any end beyond it; and hold that the mind is not in a right state, not in a state conformable to utility, not in the state most conducive to the general happiness, unless it does love virtue in this manner—as a thing desirable in itself, even although, in the individual instance, it should not produce those other desirable consequences which it tends to produce, and on account of which it is held to be virtue. This opinion is not, in the smallest degree, a departure from the happiness principle. The ingredients of happiness are very various, and each of them is desirable in itself, and not merely when considered as swelling an aggregate. The principle of utility does not mean that any given pleasure, as music, for instance, or any given exemption from pain, as for example health, is to be looked upon as means to a collective something termed happiness, and to be desired on that account. They are desired and desirable in and for themselves; besides being means, they are a part of the end. Virtue, according to the utilitarian doctrine, is not naturally and originally part of the end, but it is capable of becoming so; and in those who love it disinterestedly it has become so, and is desired and cherished, not as a means to happiness, but as a part of their happiness.

To illustrate this further, we may remember that virtue is not the only thing originally a means, and which if it were not a means to anything else would be and remain indifferent, but which by association with what it is a means to comes to be desired for itself, and that too with the utmost intensity. What, for example, shall we say of the love of money? There is nothing originally more desirable about money than about any heap of glittering pebbles. Its worth is solely that of the things which it will buy; the desires for other things than itself, which it is a means of gratifying. Yet the love of money is not only one of the strongest moving forces of human life, but money is, in many cases, desired in and for itself; the desire to possess it is often stronger than the desire to use it, and goes on increasing when all the desires which point to ends beyond it, to be compassed by it, are falling off. It may, then, be said truly that money is desired not for the sake of an end, but as part of the end. From being a means to happiness, it has come to be itself a principal ingredient of the individual's conception of happiness. The same may be said of the majority of the great objects of human life: power, for example, or fame, except that to each of these there is a certain amount of immediate pleasure annexed, which has at least the semblance of being naturally inherent in them—a thing which cannot be said of money. Still, however, the strongest natural attraction, both of power and of fame, is the immense aid they give to the attainment of our other wishes; and it is the strong association thus generated between them and all our objects of desire which gives to the direct desire of them the intensity it often assumes, so as in some characters to surpass in strength all other desires. In these cases the means have become a part of the end, and a more important part of it than any of the things which they are means to. What was once desired as an instrument for the attainment of happiness has come to be desired for its own sake. In being desired for its own sake it is, however, desired as *part* of happiness. The person is made, or thinks he would be made, happy by its mere possession; and is made unhappy by failure to obtain it. The desire of it is not a different thing from the desire of happiness any more than the love of music or the desire of health. They are included in happiness. They are some of the elements of which the desire of happiness is made up. Happiness is not an abstract idea but a concrete whole; and these are some of its parts. And the utilitarian standard sanctions and approves their being so. Life would be a poor thing, very ill provided with sources of happiness, if there were not this provision of nature by which things originally indifferent, but conducive to, or otherwise associated with, the satisfaction of our primitive desires, become in themselves sources of pleasure more valuable than the primitive pleasures, both in permanency, in the space of human existence that they are capable of covering, and even in intensity.

Virtue, according to the utilitarian conception, is a good of this description. There was no original desire of it, or motive to it, save its conduciveness to pleasure, and especially to protection from pain. But through the association thus formed it may be felt a good in itself, and desired as such with as great intensity as any other good; and with this difference between it and the love of money, of power, or of fame—that all of these may, and often do, render the individual noxious to the other members of the society to which he belongs, whereas there is nothing which makes him so much a blessing to them as the cultivation of the disinterested love of virtue. And consequently, the utilitarian standard, while it tolerates and approves those other acquired desires, up to the point beyond which they would be more injurious to the general happiness than promotive of it, enjoins and requires the cultivation of the love of virtue up to the greatest strength possible, as being above all things important to the general happiness.

It results from the preceding considerations that there is in reality nothing desired except happiness. Whatever is desired otherwise than as a means to some end beyond itself, and ultimately to happiness, is desired as itself a part of happiness, and is not desired for itself until it has become so. Those who desire virtue for its own sake desire it either because the consciousness of it is a pleasure, or because the consciousness of being without it is a pain, or for both reasons united; as in truth the pleasure and pain seldom exist separately, but almost always together—the same person feeling pleasure in the degree of virtue attained, and pain in not having attained more. If one of these gave him no pleasure, and the other no pain, he would not love or desire virtue, or would desire it only for the other benefits which it might produce to himself or to persons whom he cared for.

We have now, then, an answer to the question, of what sort of proof the principle of utility is susceptible. If the opinion which I have now stated is psychologically true—if human nature is so constituted as to desire nothing which is not either a part of happiness or a means of happiness—we can have no other proof, and we require no other, that these are the only things desirable. If so, happiness is the sole end of human action, and the promotion of it the test by which to judge of all human conduct; from whence it necessarily follows that it must be the criterion of morality, since a part is included in the whole.

FOR FURTHER STUDY

Bentham, Jeremy. *An Introduction to the Principles of Morals and Legis-lation.* New York: Doubleday, 1935. (Doubleday Series in Philosophy, Volume III.)

Broad, Charlie D. *Five Types of Ethical Theory.* New York: Harcourt, Brace, 1954, Ch. 1.

Hill, Thomas English. *Contemporary Ethical Theories.* New York: Mac-millan, 1950, Ch. 12, "Hedonistic and Related Theories."

Hyde, William De Witt. *The Five Great Philosophies of Life.* New York: Macmillan, 1927, Ch. 1, "The Epicurean Pursuit of Pleasure." (Collier Book, 1961.)

Mill, John Stuart. *Utilitarianism.* New York: Dutton, Everyman's Library, 1910.

Moore, George E. *Ethics.* New York: Holt, 1912, Chs. 1 and 2. (Home University Library of Modern Knowledge.)

Pratt, James Bissett. *Reason in the Art of Living.* New York: Macmillan, 1950, Ch. 10, "Egoistic Hedonism," Ch. 11, "The Hedonistic Philosophy," Ch. 12, "Altruistic Hedonism."

Schilpp, Paul Arthur. "The Place of Pleasure in the Good Life" in *The Student Seeks an Answer,* ed. John A. Clark. Waterville: Colby College Press, 1960.

CHAPTER 10

EVOLUTIONARY ETHICS

Human Nature as a Product
of Evolution*

THEODOSIUS DOBZHANSKY

Theodosius Dobzhansky (1900-   ) is a professor
of zoology at Columbia University. Among his writings are *Evolution, Genetics, and Man* and *Mankind
Evolving.*

A century ago, in 1858, Darwin and Wallace showed that the
world of life did not suddenly spring into existence in the state in
which we observe it today. Instead, life is the outcome of perhaps
more than two billion years of evolutionary development. Darwin's
work *The Descent of Man* appeared in 1871. It showed that man is
a part of nature and one of the products of the evolutionary process.

Man is a zoological species. But this species has evolved properties
so unique and unprecedented on the animal level that in man the
biological evolution has transcended itself. Over and over again, some

* From *New Knowledge of Human Values*, ed. Abraham H. Maslow (New
York: Harper, 1959), pp. 75-85. Reprinted with the permission of Harper & Row,
Publishers.

The author wishes to acknowledge his obligations to his colleagues and friends
for discussions which have helped to clarify some of the ideas presented in this
article, particularly to Drs. J. A. Beardmore, L. C. Birch, L. C. Dunn, and G. L.
Stebbins.

biologists made themselves ridiculous by urging solutions of human social and political problems based on the assumption that man is nothing but an animal. How dangerous may be such false keys to human riddles is shown by the fruits of one of these errors—the race theory. We have seen it being used under Hitler to justify murder on an unprecedented scale, and it contributes to the unhappiness of human beings from South Africa to Arkansas.

Biological and Historical Development

Human nature has been molded by evolutionary forces which were basically the same as those which operated in the living world at large. Man has certainly not freed himself from all the shackles of his animal frame. Yet, in man the evolutionary forces have formed a pattern so singular that man has reached heavenward and acquired powers which no other organism even remotely approached. Man's powers now include the power to destroy himself if he so chooses. But they include also the knowledge which may permit man to direct the further evolution of his nature along the paths which he will select. We must avoid the vulgar error of mistaking the biological man for the whole man. Nevertheless, human nature cannot be adequately understood except as a product of its historical development, which is in part biological development.

It is not my purpose here to set forth in any detail the unique features of the human biological nature and of human evolution. I can only attempt to indicate in broad lines the evolutionary forces which impinge upon man, particularly in the formation of his conscience. Two general characteristics of the evolutionary process must be kept in mind in any discussion of the origins of human nature. First, evolution is utilitarian. Secondly, it is opportunistic. Evolution is utilitarian because the main directing force of evolutionary change is natural selection. The action of natural selection is usually to maintain or to enhance the adaptedness of life to its environments. Evolution is opportunistic because natural selection lacks a prescience of the future. The evolution of life and of man has not been planned in advance; it is a natural creative process which contains an element of freedom but also a risk of failure. The biological nature of man, like that of any other living species, has been shaped as it has because it enabled mankind to go on living and to spread to populate the earth. But, unless evolution is consciously managed, it is appallingly myopic. At any given time it tends to make the species successful in the environment which prevails at that particular time, quite regardless of the future needs. Hence the apparent paradox: living species change almost always in the direction of a greater adaptedness, and yet most of them end sooner or later by becoming extinct.

By any reasonable criteria of biological achievement, man is thus far the most successful product of organic evolution. Mankind has not only increased rapidly in numbers but spread to all parts of the world. Man has adapted himself to his environments not only by making his biological nature conform to the environments, but also by forcing the environments to conform to his nature. He has controlled, or will soon be able to control, all other organisms which could conceivably compete with him or to prey on him. The chances of extinction of man as a species are negligible, except through his own folly.

Man's biological success certainly does not mean that his biological nature is free from faults and flaws. Far from this; man is a paradoxical creature full of internal contradictions. On the one hand, he is being endowed with reason and compassion. Although we no longer share the happy assurance of the Age of Enlightenment that men would naturally lead virtuous lives if only certain political and educational reforms will be made, most of us still believe that democracy may be the least imperfect method to achieve some degree of happiness for most people. On the other hand, we often witness the sorry spectacle of apparently enlightened and contented people behaving in most unlovely ways. And Freud and his followers persuade us that we are born with a confused host of desires which can only with greatest difficulty be brought in accord with the requirements of living in any human society, and then mostly by means of suppression or of sublimation. It would seem that the most vengeful believers in original sin and damnation held opinions about human nature which were hardly less favorable than those held by some of the Freudians.

Now, a mixture of excellence and taint in human nature is what could be expected on biological grounds. For one thing, a species living in a rapidly changing environment is necessarily adapted best to the conditions which have lapsed, and is only in the process of adaptation to the present conditions. Civilized as well as so-called primitive people carry genes which were implanted by natural selection acting when men lived under conditions very different from those in which they now live. Coon believes that the human biological equipment took essentially its present form during the paleolithic hunting stage, but only very few of the carriers of this equipment now live by hunting.

The Evolutionary Advantage—Intelligence

Another consideration is still more pertinent. The opportunism inherent in biological evolution results in defects and imperfections being tolerated, provided that the handicaps imposed by them are compensated for by a superiority in other qualities. The biological success of the human species became a reality notwithstanding the fact that man is, for his bulk, neither particularly strong nor particularly agile nor resistant to inclement weather. Man became a winner in the evolutionary race because of the powers of his brain, not those of his body. Natural selection cannot improve the strength, or the resistance, or the intelligence separately from other qualities. It is the man as a whole who survives or dies, raises a family or remains childless. A supple intellect may offset the drawbacks of a relatively flabby body. Natural selection gives therefore even less assurance of an all-round perfection of the biological organization of a species than of its continued existence.

The unique human quality which has brought about the biological ascendancy of our species is the ability to think in terms of symbols and abstractions. This ability has permitted the development of the peculiarly human mode of communication, by means of symbolic languages. Such languages are only faintly foreshadowed on the animal level. Communication by speech, and later by writing, has enabled man to evolve a stock of learned traditions and skills which constitute culture. The transmission of biological heredity is a process vastly less efficient than that of culture. The former is transferred exclusively from parents to children and other direct descendants by the genes in the sex cells. The latter is passed by teaching and training, in principle to any normal human being willing to receive it, and, after the invention of writing and printing, potentially independently of distance in space and in time. Acquired bodily characteristics are not inherited; acquired cultural traits can be transmitted together with the traditional ones, and thus added to the cultural patrimony. The genetic equipment of mankind endows it with a capacity of cardinal importance, that to acquire and to transmit from generation to generation the knowledge and the skills to control the environment. Every succeeding generation can, if it so chooses, stand on the shoulders of the preceding ones and aspire to ever greater attainments. The emergence of this genetic equipment was the evolutionary masterstroke which placed our species at the summit of the living world.

Interesting attempts have been made to understand the origin of human values as a part of the genetic equipment of our species. In recent years, Julian Huxley has been the most active protagonist of this view. Indeed, it is reasonably safe to assume that certain urges related to the world of values are genetically conditioned. Man is a mammal, and one of the characteristic adaptations in mammals is parental care of the progeny. Parental love rises from the depths of human nature. Since man is a social animal, he usually profits more from amicable than from pugnacious disposition and behavior. Natural selection may have implanted in us dispositions suitable for living in organized groups. It is, however, difficult to account on this basis for the systems of values which we find in human societies. Many ways of behavior which are regarded as ethical or praiseworthy enhance neither the chances of survival nor of reproductive success of the persons so behaving. And yet, the selective value of a genetic equipment is measured precisely by the contribution which its carriers make to the succeeding generations. The "surviving fittest" is, according to this view, nothing more spectacular than the parent of the largest number of surviving children and grandchildren. The origin of human values through natural selection is an over-simplification which can hardly be sustained. Human values are a part of our cultural heritage; they have been forged in the fires of cultural, not of biological, evolution. Their dependence on biological underpinnings of our nature is very real but indirect.

Reference has already been made to the cheerful creed of the Age of Enlightenment. The celebrated *tabula rasa* theory of John Locke asserted that the human mind is formed entirely by experience and education. But this equality of identical blankness at birth would, according to Rousseau, make everybody good—"Man is naturally good and only by institutions is he made bad." The natural man is a noble savage, untouched by the evil influences of civilization. Nowadays the belief in noble savagery has fallen in disuse, but the confidence in natural goodness of man is ably defended by Ashley Montagu. "It is not evil babies who grow up into evil human beings, but an evil society which turns good babies into disordered adults, and it does so on a regimen of frustration. Babies are born good and desirous of continuing to be good."

The *tabula rasa* theory can just as easily be combined with the belief that man is naturally bad. The classical example is Hobbes' view that the natural state of man is "*bellum omnium contra omnes*," perpetual war of all against all. This sounds very much like Darwin's inexorable struggle for existence. The so-called social Darwinism, which Darwin himself would probably have repudiated with disgust, is a cleverly contrived hodgepodge of Hobbes, Malthus, Darwin, and biological racism. Far from being a *tabula rasa* at birth, the personality is determined by our genes, and every one of us is born with genes different from everybody else. Moreover, the racists, from Gobineau to Darlington, claim that some people are born good or superior, while others are predestined by their heredities to be evil, or inferior, or both. Environment and education are powerless to change the qualities set by the genes. By a singular coincidence, the racist himself almost always belongs to the group of people who are genetically the best and most superior.

That human cultural evolution is conditioned by the genetic endowment of our species is evident enough. A person acquires his cultural traits by learning, beginning with the process of socialization in infancy. But the possession of normal human genes is necessary for receptivity to the socializing influences of the human social milieu. The genes of a microcephalic idiot make learning impossible. An ape, a monkey, a parrot, or a dog can learn many different things, but not many of these which a human child learns easily. The evolution of culture became possible only when some basis for it had been blocked out in biological evolution. However, culture reacted back on biology, and the chief trend in the biological development of mankind has been to give full play to the cultural development.

The autonomy of cultural evolution does not mean that an impenetrable wall separates our culture from our genes. The autonomy of culture means that while the genes make it possible they do not determine its contents. Similarly, human genes determine the capacity of speech, but they do not determine what is said. The evidence of autonomy comes from the radical cultural changes which many human societies underwent without apparent genetic alterations. The ancestors of most of us were, a hundred or even less generations ago, rude barbarians eking out precarious existence from the niggardly nature of the forest zone of Europe. The industrial revolution has altered the occupations and the modes of life of many millions of people within very few generations. It is most probable that some genetic changes are taking place at all times in all human populations. But there is no reason to believe that the differences between our cultural state and those of our ancestors two, or twenty, or a hundred generations ago are to an appreciable degree due to differences between our genes.

Again and again, attempts have been made to postulate genetic changes that could be supposed to be responsible for the vicissitudes of human history. The decline of Rome has been ascribed to the alleged dysgenic practices of the latter-day Romans. Disintegration of our own civilization has been confidently predicted because of the high birth rates of the economically less fortunate classes. A detailed discussion of these matters is obviously impossible here, but it is not unfair to say that none of the above attempts have given fully convincing results. The state of the genetic equipment of human populations must be carefully watched, especially if many people try to insure their security by sowing more atomic bombs. Meanwhile, enormous improvements of the human lot may be expected from amelioration of the environment.

Genes or Culture?

The ability of man to undergo acculturation, to change his occupations, his whole mode of life, and even his beliefs, hopes, and desires without corresponding genetic change is biologically most extraordinary. Organisms other than man are usually specialized for a single or for a few alternative modes of life; adaptation to new environments is possible only by way of evolutionary changes in the genetic equipment of the species. Man can adapt to new environments by changing his culture, or by changing the environments by means of his culture. This is one of the most fundamental properties of human biological nature. The *tabula rasa* theory seemed to follow from the everyday observation that people can, more or less easily, at least in comparison with animals, adjust themselves to new circumstances and new tasks.

The observation is correct but the conclusion drawn from it is false. The crucial fact is that human social and cultural environments are singularly inconstant, both in terms of an individual's life, and even more in terms of the destinies of families, tribes, and races. Biological heredity is simply too rigid, and biological evolution is too slow to serve as mechanisms of adaptation to the restlessly variable human environments. The cultural heritage is, as pointed out above, both more flexible and vastly more easily transmissible. This is in itself a sufficient reason why the genes which facilitated the transmission of the cultural heritage were established by natural selection in human evolution. They yielded an adaptive mechanism of an overwhelming potency, which worked especially well under the unique and biologically unprecedented conditions of the human estate. The ability of the organism to compensate for changes in its external environments in such ways that its normal functioning proceeds undisturbed is known as homeostasis. Human ability to profit by experience, learning and education is a singularly efficient homeostatic mechanism.

The doctrine of *tabula rasa* seemed useful to those who believed that all men have been created equal. Equality is, however, an ethical and not a biological concept. It is an outcome of the cultural, not of the biological, evolution. Equality is not predicated upon biological identity. As a matter of fact, no two persons in the world, identical twins excepted, carry the same genes. It does not follow from this that men are "free and unequal." Human personality development is remarkably responsive to variations in the cultural environments. The followers of the *tabula rasa* doctrine took this for evidence that people are really all alike. Precisely the reverse conclusion is warranted. The plasticity of the human developmental pattern is a method of making people different, depending upon the conditions in which they live. People are diverse but equal.

Methods of Adaptation

Man is proficient in controlling his physical surroundings. Thanks to advances of technology, the physical conditions under which people live in different climes are now less diverse than they would have been had all of us remained in primitive cultural states. Conversely, civilization increases enormously the range of vocations, functions, and roles which people are called upon to assume. In what ways could the evolutionary process make provisions for adaptation to this virtually infinite variety of functions? Biologically, two methods are possible. The first is genetic specialization. This may be illustrated by an analogy with breeds of dogs, horses, or other domesticated forms. There are hunting dogs, watch dogs, and dogs to captivate the heart of a superannuated spinster. The second method is homeostasis and developmental plasticity. To give a zoological example—a Drosophila fly coming from a well-fed larva may weigh three times as much as one from a starved larva. A fly larva faced with a food scarcity does not die, it merely gives an undersized adult.

Man's adjustment to his sociocultural environments makes use of both methods. Moreover, these methods are not alternative, as they are often imagined to be. They are complementary. Modification by experience and training is conjoined with genetic diversity. True, the developmental plasticity is, by and large, the more important of the two methods. Its progressive refinement has been, as pointed out above, adaptively the most significant feature of human evolution. The demands which human society makes on the individual are too diversified, and, most important, too rapidly changing with time to make genetic specialization alone competent to insure the perpetuation of our species, at least in its civilization stage. Genetic diversity yields, however, an additional increment of adaptive potentialities.

The genetic equipments of the human species do not make all men inherently good or irrevocably bad, virtuous or wicked, clever or stupid, cheerful or morose. They rather provide man with a range of potentialities, to be realized according to circumstances. Moreover, there is no such thing as a genetic equipment common to all, or even to all "normal" men. The variety of genetic equipment is very great, almost coextensive with the numbers of men who live, have lived, and will live. Every person is a carrier of an unprecedented and non-recurrent gene pattern. Human natures are diverse, and so are their outlooks on life.

To quote George Sarton:

> Men understand the world in different ways. The main difference lies in this, that some men are more abstract-minded, and they naturally think first of unity and of God, of wholeness, of infinity and other such concepts, while the minds of other men are concrete and they cogitate about health and disease, profit and loss. They invent gadgets and remedies; they are less interested in knowing anything than in applying whatever knowledge they may already have to practical problems; they try to make things work and pay, to heal and teach. The first are called dreamers; the second kind are recognized as practical and useful. History has often proved the shortsightedness of the practical men and vindicated the "lazy" dreamers; it has also proved that the dreamers are often mistaken.

Unfortunately, we do not know to what extent the differences between the "dreamers" and the "practical men" are caused by variations in their genes and in their environments. Both are probably involved to some extent. In any case, a society which has some dreamers and some practical men is better off than a community of dreamers alone or exclusively of practical men. Human societies, and especially civilized societies, thrive on diversity, whether environmentally or genetically induced, because human societies have so many different functions to be served. The evolution of man has, indeed, provided the biological foundations for educability and occupational versatility on one hand, and for genetic diversity on the other. The great riddle is how best to make use of the diversity of men equal in rights to secure the greatest happiness of the greatest number. Who is bold enough to claim that he has fully solved this riddle?

FOR FURTHER STUDY

Adams, E. M. *Ethical Naturalism and the Modern World View*. Chapel Hill: U. of North Carolina Press, 1960.

Darwin, Charles. *The Descent of Man*. New York: Warne, 1930. (Thinker's Library, No. 12.)

————. *Origin of the Species by Means of Natural Selection*. New York: Dutton, Everyman's Library, 1928.

Dewey, John. *Influence of Darwin on Philosophy, and Other Essays in Contemporary Thought*. New York: Holt, 1910.

Hill, Thomas English. *Contemporary Ethical Theories*. New York: Macmillan, 1950, Ch. 8, "Evolutionary Theories."

Huxley, Julian S. *Evolutionary Ethics*. London: Oxford U. Press, 1943.

Jaspers, Karl. "Nature and Ethics" in *Moral Principles in Action*, ed. Ruth Nanda Anshen. New York: Harper, 1952, Ch. 3.

Maritain, Jacques. "Natural Law and Moral Law" in *Moral Principles in Action*, ed. Ruth Nanda Anshen. New York: Harper, 1952, Ch. 4.

Montagu, Ashley. *Darwin, Competition and Co-operation*. New York: Schuman, 1952.

Ross, Herbert H. *A Synthesis of Evolutionary Theory*. Englewood Cliffs: Prentice-Hall, 1962.

CHAPTER 11

THE FULFILLMENT OF THE INDIVIDUAL IN SOCIETY

๛๛๛๛๛๛๛๛๛๛๛๛๛๛๛๛๛

The Vision of the Good*

PLATO

Plato (c. 427-347 B.C.) was a student of Socrates and
a teacher of Aristotle. The Academy that he founded
endured for more than nine centuries. Few, if any,
philosophers have had greater influence on the course
of Western thought. He wrote many dialogues of
high literary quality, including the *Apology*, the
Symposium, and the *Republic*, from which we quote.

Next, said I, here is a parable to illustrate the degrees in which our
nature may be enlightened or unenlightened. Imagine the condition of
men living in a sort of cavernous chamber underground, with an
entrance open to the light and a long passage all down the cave. Here
they have been from childhood, chained by the leg and also by the
neck, so that they cannot move and can see only what is in front of
them, because the chains will not let them turn their heads. At some
distance higher up is the light of a fire burning behind them; and
between the prisoners and the fire is a track with a parapet built along
it, like the screen at a puppet-show, which hides the performers while
they show their puppets over the top.

* From *The Republic of Plato*, trans. Francis MacDonald Cornford (New York:
Oxford U. Press, 1945), pp. 227-232. Used by permission of the publisher.

I see, said he.

Now behind this parapet imagine persons carrying along various arti-ficial objects, including figures of men and animals in wood or stone or other materials, which project above the parapet. Naturally, some of these persons will be talking, others silent.

It is a strange picture, he said, and a strange sort of prisoners.

Like ourselves, I replied; for in the first place prisoners so confined would have seen nothing of themselves or of one another, except the shadows thrown by the fire-light on the wall of the Cave facing them, would they?

Not if all their lives they had been prevented from moving their heads.

And they would have seen as little of the objects carried past.

Of course.

Now, if they could talk to one another, would they not suppose that their words referred only to those passing shadows which they saw?

Necessarily.

And suppose their prison had an echo from the wall facing them? When one of the people crossing behind them spoke, they could only suppose that the sound came from the shadow passing before their eyes.

No doubt.

In every way, then, such prisoners would recognize as reality nothing but the shadows of those artificial objects.

Inevitably.

Now consider what would happen if their release from the chains and the healing of their unwisdom should come about in this way. Suppose one of them set free and forced suddenly to stand up, turn his head, and walk with eyes lifted to the light; all these movements would be painful, and he would be too dazzled to make out the objects whose shadows he had been used to see. What do you think he would say, if someone told him that what he had formerly seen was meaningless illu-sion, but now, being somewhat nearer to reality and turned towards more real objects, he was getting a truer view? Suppose further that he were shown the various objects being carried by and were made to say, in reply to questions, what each of them was. Would he not be per-plexed and believe the objects now shown him to be not so real as what he formerly saw?

Yes, not nearly so real.

And if he were forced to look at the fire-light itself, would not his eyes ache, so that he would try to escape and turn back to the things which he could see distinctly, convinced that they really were clearer than these other objects now being shown to him?

Yes.

And suppose someone were to drag him away forcibly up the steep and rugged ascent and not let him go until he had hauled him out into the sunlight, would he not suffer pain and vexation at such treatment, and, when he had come out into the light, find his eyes so full of its radiance that he could not see a single one of the things that he was now told were real?

Certainly he would not see them all at once.

He would need, then, to grow accustomed before he could see things in that upper world. At first it would be easiest to make out shadows, and then the images of men and things reflected in water, and later on the things themselves. After that, it would be easier to watch the heavenly bodies and the sky itself by night, looking at the light of the moon and stars rather than the Sun and the Sun's light in the day-time.

Yes, surely.

Last of all, he would be able to look at the Sun and contemplate its nature, not as it appears when reflected in water or any alien medium, but as it is in itself in its own domain.

No doubt.

And now he would begin to draw the conclusion that it is the Sun that produces the seasons and the course of the year and controls everything in the visible world, and moreover is in a way the cause of all that he and his companions used to see.

Clearly he would come at last to that conclusion.

Then if he called to mind his fellow prisoners and what passed for wisdom in his former dwelling-place, he would surely think himself happy in the change and be sorry for them. They may have had a practice of honouring and commending one another, with prizes for the man who had the keenest eye for the passing shadows and the best memory for the order in which they followed or accompanied one another, so that he could make a good guess as to which was going to come next. Would our released prisoner be likely to covet those prizes or to envy the men exalted to honour and power in the Cave? Would he not feel like Homer's Achilles, that he would far sooner "be on earth as a hired servant in the house of a landless man" or endure anything rather than go back to his old beliefs and live in the old way?

Yes, he would prefer any fate to such a life.

Now imagine what would happen if he went down again to take his former seat in the Cave. Coming suddenly out of the sunlight, his eyes would be filled with darkness. He might be required once more to deliver his opinion on those shadows, in competition with the prisoners who had never been released, while this eyesight was still dim and unsteady; and it might take some time to become used to the darkness. They would laugh at him and say that he had gone up only to come back with his sight ruined; it was worth no one's while even to attempt the ascent. If they could lay hands on the man who was trying to set them free and lead them up, they would kill him.

Yes, they would.

Every feature in this parable, my dear Glaucon, is meant to fit our earlier analysis. The prison dwelling corresponds to the region revealed to us through the sense of sight, and the fire-light within it to the power of the Sun. The ascent to see the things in the upper world you may take as standing for the upward journey of the soul into the region of the intelligible; then you will be in possession of what I surmise, since that is what you wish to be told. Heaven knows whether it is true; but this, at any rate, is how it appears to me. In the world of knowledge, the last thing to be perceived and only with great difficulty is the essential Form of Goodness. Once it is perceived, the conclusion must follow that, for all things, this is the cause of whatever is right and good; in the visible world it gives birth to light and to the lord of light, while it is itself sovereign in the intelligible world and the parent of intelligence and truth. Without having had a vision of this Form no one can act with wisdom, either in his own life or in matters of state.

So far as I can understand, I share your belief.

Then you may also agree that it is no wonder if those who have reached this height are reluctant to manage the affairs of men. Their souls long to spend all their time in that upper world—naturally enough, if here once more our parable holds true. Nor, again, is it at all strange that one who comes from the contemplation of divine things to the miseries of human life should appear awkward and ridiculous when, with eyes still dazed and not yet accustomed to the darkness, he is compelled, in a law-court or elsewhere, to dispute about the shadows of justice or the images that cast those shadows, and to wrangle over the notions of what is right in the minds of men who have never beheld Justice itself.

It is not at all strange.

No; a sensible man will remember that the eyes may be confused in two ways—by a change from light to darkness or from darkness to light; and he will recognize that the same thing happens to the soul. When he sees it troubled and unable to discern anything clearly, instead of laughing thoughtlessly, he will ask whether, coming from a brighter existence, its unaccustomed vision is obscured by the darkness, in which case he will think its condition enviable and its life a happy one; or whether, emerging from the depths of ignorance, it is dazzled by excess of light. If so, he will rather feel sorry for it; or, if he were inclined to laugh, that would be less ridiculous than to laugh at the soul which has come down from the light.

That is a fair statement.

If this is true, then, we must conclude that education is not what it is said to be by some, who profess to put knowledge into a soul which does not possess it, as if they could put sight into blind eyes. On the contrary, our own account signifies that the soul of every man does possess the power of learning the truth and the organ to see it with; and that, just as one might have to turn the whole body round in order that the eye should see light instead of darkness, so the entire soul must be turned away from this changing world, until its eye can bear to contemplate reality and that supreme splendour which we have called the Good.

ance of the perjury." They voted for the side that seemed to tell fewer lies.

Juries might get at the truth if counsel researched cases scientifically. When two research men investigate causes of cancer they make a hypothesis and check it with an open mind. They may pursue different courses but they clear their findings with each other.

Not so in criminal trial practice. According to the late eminent attorney, Charles P. Curtis, the counsel who sets out to build evidence "will waste a lot of time if he goes with an open mind." Unlike a scientist, he will not sit down with his opposite number and say, "Here is what I found. What did you find? We are both after the same thing—truth. What can we agree on, in the interest of justice?" Instead, he squirrels away his evidence, citations, and arguments—his putative "facts"—hoping his opponent will be overwhelmed by them in the courtroom.

An attorney told a Bar Association audience: "Of course surprise elements should be hoarded. Your opponent should not be educated as to matters concerning which you believe he is still in the dark. Obviously, the traps should not be uncovered. Indeed, you may cast a few more leaves over them so that your adversary will step more boldly on the low ground believing it is solid."

The leaves over the low ground are yellowed pages of musty law books containing ancient trial decisions, which serve as precedents. Precedents are hallowed. What was good enough for great-great-grandpappy is all the better today because it is aged-in-the-book. The contemporary counselor who has a talent for digging these vintage morsels becomes a scholar in the law, highly respected and extravagantly paid. More important, he gains an advantage. The older a precedent, the less likely it is his adversary will find it, too. In court, before an amused jury, the opposing lawyer is trapped and the victory may go to the legal scholar.

What makes such tactics more deplorable is that the precedents often fail to go to the heart of a matter. They award a decision, not on the essence of a case—that is, whether the defendant is guilty or not—but more frequently on mere technicality. If, as happened in one Florida case, the judge simply has to leave the bench to answer the call of nature while counsel is summing up for the jury, the opposing lawyer will make no demur. He has an early precedent up his sleeve that holds if a judge has to go, the trial should be recessed, even though all the evidence is in and only summation is in progress. Then, if the verdict is against his side, the lawyer will jostle the precedent loose and demand a new trial.

The Nature of the Good*

ARISTOTLE

Aristotle (384-322 B.C.), a student of Plato, founded
the Lyceum near Athens. His works have had a profound influence on philosophical and scientific thinking in Western civilization. His *Nicomachean Ethics*
was the first systematic treatise on ethics.

In this book Aristotle discusses the good for man.
It is generally agreed to be happiness, he says; but
what is happiness? Is it pleasure? honor? wealth?
contemplation? Is it an Idea universally predicable
of all good things or an Idea with independent existence? Having rejected each of these alternatives,
Aristotle resumes the search.

We may now return to the Good which is the object of our search,
and try to find out what exactly it can be. For good appears to be one
thing in one pursuit or art and another in another: it is different in
medicine from what it is in strategy, and so on with the rest of the arts.
What definition of the Good then will hold true in all the arts? Perhaps
we may define it as that for the sake of which everything else is done.
This applies to something different in each different art—to health in
the case of medicine, to victory in that of strategy, to a house in architecture, and to something else in each of the other arts; but in every
pursuit or undertaking it describes the end of that pursuit or undertaking, since in all of them it is for the sake of the end that everything
else is done. Hence if there be something which is the end of all the
things done by human action, this will be the practicable Good—or if
there be several such ends, the sum of these will be the Good. Thus by
changing its ground the argument has reached the same result as before.
We must attempt however to render this still more precise.

Now there do appear to be several ends at which our actions aim;

* Reprinted by permission of the publishers from *The Nicomachean Ethics*,
trans. H. Rackham (Cambridge, Mass.: Harvard U. Press, 1934).

but as we choose some of them—for instance wealth, or flutes, and instruments generally—as a means to something else, it is clear that not all of them are final ends; whereas the Supreme Good seems to be something final. Consequently if there be some one thing which alone is a final end, this thing—or if there be several final ends, the one among them which is the most final—will be the Good which we are seeking. In speaking of degrees of finality, we mean that a thing pursued as an end in itself is more final than one pursued as a means to something else, and that a thing never chosen as a means to anything else is more final than things chosen both as ends in themselves and as means to that thing; and accordingly a thing chosen always as an end and never as a means we call absolutely final. Now happiness above all else appears to be absolutely final in this sense, since we always choose it for its own sake and never as a means to something else; whereas honour, pleasure, intelligence, and excellence in its various forms, we choose indeed for their own sakes (since we should be glad to have each of them although no extraneous advantages resulted from it), but we also choose them for the sake of happiness, in the belief that they will be a means to our securing it. But no one chooses happiness for the sake of honour, pleasure, etc., nor as a means to anything whatever other than itself.

The same conclusion also appears to follow from a consideration of the self-sufficiency of happiness—for it is felt that the final good must be a thing sufficient in itself. The term self-sufficient, however, we employ with reference not to oneself alone, living a life of isolation, but also to one's parents and children and wife, and one's friends and fellow citizens in general, since man is by nature a social being. On the other hand a limit has to be assumed in these relationships; for if the list be extended to one's ancestors and descendants and to the friends of one's friends, it will go on ad infinitum. But this is a point that must be considered later on; we take a self-sufficient thing to mean a thing which merely standing by itself alone renders life desirable and lacking in nothing, and such a thing we deem happiness to be. Moreover, we think happiness the most desirable of all good things without being itself reckoned as one among the rest; for if it were so reckoned, it is clear that we should consider it more desirable when even the smallest of other good things were combined with it, since this addition would result in a larger total of good, and of two goods the greater is always the more desirable.

Happiness, therefore, being found to be something final and self-sufficient, is the End at which all actions aim.

To say however that the Supreme Good is happiness will probably

appear a truism; we still require a more explicit account of what constitutes happiness. Perhaps then we may arrive at this by ascertaining
what is man's function. For the goodness or efficiency of a flute-player
or sculptor or craftsman of any sort, and in general of anybody who
has some function or business to perform, is thought to reside in that
function; and similarly it may be held that the good of man resides in
the function of man, if he has a function.

Are we then to suppose that, while the carpenter and the shoemaker
have definite functions or businesses belonging to them, man as such has
none, and is not designed by nature to fulfill any function? Must we
not rather assume that, just as the eye, the hand, the foot and each of
the various members of the body manifestly has a certain function of
its own, so a human being also has a certain function over and above
all the functions of his particular members? What then precisely can
this function be? The mere act of living appears to be shared even by
plants, whereas we are looking for the function peculiar to man; we
must therefore set aside the vital activity of nutrition and growth. Next
in the scale will come some form of sentient life; but this too appears
to be shared by horses, oxen, and animals generally. There remains
therefore what may be called the practical life of the rational part of
man. (This part has two divisions, one rational as obedient to principle,
the other as possessing principle and exercising intelligence.) Rational
life again has two meanings; let us assume that we are here concerned
with the active exercise of the rational faculty, since this seems to be
the more proper sense of the term. If then the function of man is the
active exercise of the soul's faculties in conformity with rational principle, or at all events not in dissociation from rational principle, and if
we acknowledge the function of an individual and of a good individual
of the same class (for instance, a harper and a good harper, and so
generally with all classes) to be generically the same, the qualification
of the latter's superiority in excellence being added to the function in
his case (I mean that if the function of a harper is to play the harp, that
of a good harper is to play the harp well): if this is so, and if we declare
that the function of a man is a certain form of life, and define that form
of life as the exercise of the soul's faculties and activities in association
with rational principle, and say that the function of a good man is to
perform these activities well and rightly, and if a function is well performed when it is performed in accordance with its own proper excellence—from these premises it follows that the Good of man is the active
exercise of his soul's faculties in conformity with excellence or virtue,

or if there be several human excellences or virtues, in conformity with the best and most perfect among them.

Moreover, this activity must occupy a complete lifetime; for one swallow does not make summer, nor does one fine day; and similarly one day or a brief period of happiness does not make a man supremely blessed and happy. . . .

It is this that gives rise to the question whether happiness is a thing that can be learnt, or acquired by training, or cultivated in some other manner, or whether it is bestowed by some divine dispensation or even by fortune. (1) Now if anything that men have is a gift of the gods, it is reasonable to suppose that happiness is divinely given—indeed of all man's possessions it is most likely to be so, inasmuch as it is the best of them all. This subject however may perhaps more properly belong to another branch of study. Still, even if happiness is not sent us from heaven, but is won by virtue and by some kind of study or practice, it seems to be one of the most divine things that exist. For the prize and end of virtue must clearly be supremely good—it must be something divine and blissful. (2) And also on our view it will admit of being widely diffused, since it can be attained through some process of study or effort by all persons whose capacity for virtue has not been stunted or maimed. (3) Again, if it is better to be happy as a result of one's own exertions than by the gift of fortune, it is reasonable to suppose that this is how happiness is won; inasmuch as in the world of nature things have a natural tendency to be ordered in the best possible way, and the same is true of the products of art, and of causation of any kind, and especially the highest. Whereas that the greatest and noblest of all things should be left to fortune would be too contrary to the fitness of things.

Light is also thrown on the question by our definition of happiness, which said that it is a certain kind of activity of the soul; whereas the remaining good things are either merely indispensable conditions of happiness, or are of the nature of auxiliary means, and useful instrumentally. This conclusion moreover agrees with what we laid down at the outset; for we stated that the Supreme Good was the end of the political science, but the principal care of this science is to produce a certain character in the citizens, namely to make them virtuous, and capable of performing noble actions. . . .

Now of everything that is continuous and divisible, it is possible to take the larger part, or the smaller part, or an equal part, and these parts may be larger, smaller, and equal either with respect to the thing itself or relatively to us; the equal part being a mean between excess and deficiency. By the mean of the thing I denote a point equally distant from either extreme, which is one and the same for everybody; by the mean relative to us, that amount which is neither too much nor too little, and this is not one and the same for everybody. For example, let 10 be many and 2 few; then one takes the mean with respect to the thing if one takes 6, since $6 - 2 = 10 - 6$; this is the mean according to arithmetical proportion. But we cannot arrive by this method at the mean relative to us. Suppose that 10 lb. of food is a large ration for anybody and 2 lb. a small one: it does not follow that a trainer will prescribe 6 lb., for perhaps even this will be a large ration, or a small one, for the particular athlete who is to receive it; it is a small ration for a Milo, but a large one for a man just beginning to go in for athletics. And similarly with the amount of running or wrestling exercise to be taken. In the same way then an expert in any art avoids excess and deficiency, and seeks and adopts the mean—the mean, that is, not of the thing but relative to us. If therefore the way in which every art or science performs its work well is by looking to the mean and applying that as a standard to its productions (hence the common remark about a perfect work of art, that you could not take from it nor add to it— meaning that excess and deficiency destroy perfection, while adherence to the mean preserves it)—if then, as we say, good craftsmen look to the mean as they work, and if virtue, like nature, is more accurate and better than any form of art, it will follow that virtue has the quality of hitting the mean. I refer to moral virtue, for this is concerned with feelings and actions, in which one can have excess or deficiency or a due mean. For example, one can be frightened or bold, feel desire or anger or pity, and experience pleasure and pain in general, either too much or too little, and in both cases wrongly; whereas to feel these feelings at the right time, on the right occasion, towards the right people, for the right purpose and in the right manner, is to feel the best amount of them, which is the mean amount—and the best amount is of course the mark of virtue. And similarly there can be excess, deficiency, and the due mean in actions. Now feelings and actions are the objects with which virtue is concerned; and in feelings and actions excess and deficiency are errors, while the mean amount is praised, and constitutes success; and to be praised and to be successful are both marks of virtue. Virtue, therefore, is a mean state in the sense that it is able to hit the mean. Again, error is multiform (for evil is a form of the unlimited, as in the old Pythagorean imagery, and good of the limited), whereas success is possible in one way only (which is why it is easy to fail and difficult to succeed—easy to miss the target and difficult to hit it); so this is another reason why excess and deficiency are a mark of vice, and observance of the mean a mark of virtue:

Goodness is simple, badness manifold.

Virtue then is a settled disposition of the mind as regards the choice of actions and emotions, consisting essentially in the observance of the mean relative to us, this being determined by principle, that is, as the prudent man would determine it.

And it is a mean state between two vices, one of excess and one of defect. Furthermore, it is a mean state in that whereas the vices either fall short of or exceed what is right in feelings and in actions, virtue ascertains and adopts the mean. Hence while in respect of its substance and the definition that states what it really is in essence virtue is the observance of the mean, in point of excellence and rightness it is an extreme.

Not every action or emotion however admits of the observance of a due mean. Indeed the very names of some directly imply evil, for instance malice, shamelessness, envy, and, of actions, adultery, theft, murder. All these and similar actions and feelings are blamed as being bad in themselves; it is not the excess or deficiency of them that we blame. It is impossible therefore ever to go right in regard to them— one must always be wrong; nor does right or wrong in their case depend on the circumstances, for instance, whether one commits adultery with the right woman, at the right time, and in the right manner; the mere commission of any of them is wrong. One might as well suppose there could be a due mean and excess and deficiency in acts of injustice or cowardice or profligacy, which would imply that one could have a medium amount of excess and of deficiency, an excessive amount of excess and a deficient amount of deficiency. But just as there can be no excess or deficiency in temperance and justice, because the mean is in a sense an extreme, so there can be no observance of the mean nor excess nor deficiency in the corresponding vicious acts mentioned above, but however they are committed, they are wrong; since, to put it in general terms, there is no such thing as observing a mean in excess or deficiency, nor as exceeding or falling short in the observance of a mean.

We must not however rest content with stating this general definition, but must show that it applies to the particular virtues. In practical philosophy, although universal principles have a wider application, those covering a particular part of the field possess a higher degree of truth; because conduct deals with particular facts, and our theories are bound to accord with these.

Let us then take the particular virtues from the diagram.

The observance of the mean in fear and confidence is Courage. The man that exceeds in fearlessness is not designated by any special name (and this is the case with many of the virtues and vices); he that exceeds in confidence is Rash; he that exceeds in fear and is deficient in confidence is Cowardly. In respect of pleasures and pains—not all of them, and to a less degree in respect of pains—the observance of the mean is Temperance, the excess Profligacy. Men deficient in the enjoyment of pleasures scarcely occur, and hence this character also has not been assigned a name, but we may call it Insensible. In regard to giving and getting money, the observance of the mean is Liberality; the excess and deficiency are Prodigality and Meanness, and these exceed and fall short in opposite ways: the prodigal exceeds in giving and is deficient in getting, whereas the mean man exceeds in getting and is deficient in giving. For the present then we describe these qualities in outline and summarily, which is enough for the purpose in hand; but they will be more accurately defined later.

There are also other dispositions in relation to money, namely, the mode of observing the mean called Magnificence (the magnificent man being different from the liberal, as the former deals with large amounts and the latter with small ones), the excess called Tastelessness or Vulgarity, and the defect called Shabbiness. These are not the same as Liberality and the vices corresponding to it; but the way in which they differ will be more accurately defined later. . . .

Enough has now been said to show that moral virtue is a mean, and in what sense this is so, namely that it is a mean between two vices, one of excess and the other of defect; and that it is such a mean because it aims at hitting the middle point in feelings and in actions. This is why it is a hard task to be good, for it is hard to find the middle point in anything: for instance, not everybody can find the centre of a circle, but only someone who knows geometry. So also anybody can become angry—that is easy, and so it is to give and spend money; but to be angry with or give money to the right person, and to the right amount, and at the right time, and for the right purpose, and in the right way— this is not within everybody's power and is not easy; so that to do these things properly is rare, praiseworthy, and noble.

Hence the first rule in aiming at the mean is to avoid that extreme which is the more opposed to the mean, as Calypso advises—
    Steer the ship clear of yonder spray and surge.
For of the two extremes one is a more serious error than the other. Hence, inasmuch as to hit the mean extremely well is difficult, the sec-

ond best way to sail, as the saying goes, is to take the least of the evils; and the best way to do this is the way we enjoin.

The second rule is to notice what are the errors to which we are ourselves most prone (as different men are inclined by nature to different faults)—and we shall discover what these are by observing the pleasure or pain that we experience—then we must drag ourselves away in the opposite direction, for by steering wide of our besetting error we shall make a middle course. This is the method adopted by carpenters to straighten warped timber.

Thirdly, we must in everything be most of all on our guard against what is pleasant and against pleasure; for when pleasure is on her trial we are not impartial judges. The right course is therefore to feel towards pleasure as the elders of the people felt towards Helen, and to apply their words to her on every occasion; for if we roundly bid her be gone, we shall be less likely to err.

These then, to sum up the matter, are the precautions that will best enable us to hit the mean. But no doubt it is a difficult thing to do, and especially in particular cases: for instance, it is not easy to define in what manner and with what people and on what sort of grounds and how long one ought to be angry; and in fact we sometimes praise men who err on the side of defect in this matter and call them gentle, sometimes those who are quick to anger and style them manly. However, we do not blame one who diverges a little from the right course, whether on the side of the too much or of the too little, but one who diverges more widely, for his error is noticed. Yet to what degree and how seriously a man must err to be blamed is not easy to define on principle. For in fact no object of perception is easy to define; and such questions of degree depend on particular circumstances, and the decision lies with perception.

Thus much then is clear, that it is the middle disposition in each department of conduct that is to be praised, but that one should lean sometimes to the side of excess and sometimes to that of deficiency, since this is the easiest way of hitting the mean and the right course. . . .

Now we stated that happiness is not a certain disposition of character; since if it were it might be possessed by a man who passed the whole of his life asleep, living the life of a vegetable, or by one who was plunged in the deepest misfortune. If then we reject this as unsatisfactory, and feel bound to class happiness rather as some form of activity, as has been said in the earlier part of this treatise, and if activities are of two kinds, some merely necessary means and desirable only for the sake of something else, others desirable in themselves, it is clear that happiness is to be classed among activities desirable in themselves, and not among those desirable as a means to something else; since happiness lacks nothing, and is self-sufficient. . . .

But if happiness consists in activity in accordance with virtue, it is reasonable that it should be activity in accordance with the highest virtue; and this will be the virtue of the best part of us. Whether then this be the intellect, or whatever else it be that is thought to rule and lead us by nature, and to have cognizance of what is noble and divine, either as being itself also actually divine, or as being relatively the divinest part of us, it is the activity of this part of us in accordance with the virtue proper to it that will constitute perfect happiness; and it has been stated already that this activity is the activity of contemplation.

And that happiness consists in contemplation may be accepted as agreeing both with the results already reached and with the truth. For contemplation is at once the highest form of activity (since the intellect is the highest thing in us, and the objects with which the intellect deals are the highest things that can be known), and also it is the most continuous, for we can reflect more continuously than we can carry on any form of action. And again we suppose that happiness must contain an element of pleasure; now activity in accordance with wisdom is admittedly the most pleasant of the activities in accordance with virtue: at all events it is held that philosophy or the pursuit of wisdom contains pleasures of marvellous purity and permanence, and it is reasonable to suppose that the enjoyment of knowledge is a still pleasanter occupation than the pursuit of it. Also the activity of contemplation will be found to possess in the highest degree the quality that is termed self-sufficiency: for while it is true that the wise man equally with the just man and the rest requires the necessaries of life, yet, these being adequately supplied, whereas the just man needs other persons towards whom or with whose aid he may act justly, and so likewise do the temperate man and the brave man and the others, the wise man on the contrary can also contemplate by himself, and the more so the wiser he is; no doubt he will study better with the aid of fellow-workers, but still he is the most self-sufficient of men. Also the activity of contemplation may be held to be the only activity that is loved for its own sake: it produces no result beyond the actual act of contemplation, whereas from practical pursuits we look to secure some advantage, greater or smaller, beyond the action itself. Also happiness is thought to involve leisure; for we do business in order that we may have leisure, and carry on war in order that we may have peace. Now the practical virtues are exercised in politics or in warfare; but the pursuits of politics and war seem to be unleisured—those of war indeed entirely so, for no one desires to be at war for the sake of being at war, nor deliberately takes steps to cause a war: a man would be thought an utterly blood-thirsty character if he declared war on a friendly state for the sake of causing battles and massacres. But the activity of the politician also is unleisured, and aims at securing something beyond the mere participation in politics—positions of authority and honour, or, if the happiness of the politician himself and of his fellow-citizens, this happiness conceived as something distinct from political activity (and in fact we are investigating it as so distinct). If then among practical pursuits displaying the virtues, politics and war stand out pre-eminent in nobility and grandeur, and yet they are unleisured, and directed to some further end, not chosen for their own sakes: whereas the activity of the intellect is felt to excel in serious worth, consisting as it does in contemplation, and to aim at no end beyond itself, and also to contain a pleasure peculiar to itself, and therefore augmenting its activity: and if accordingly the attributes of this activity are found to be self-sufficiency, leisuredness, such freedom from fatigue as is possible for man, and all the other attributes of blessedness: it follows that it is the activity of the intellect that constitutes complete human happiness—provided it be granted a complete span of life, for nothing that belongs to happiness can be incomplete.

Such a life as this however will be higher than the human level: not in virtue of his humanity will a man achieve it, but in virtue of something within him that is divine; and by as much as this something is superior to his composite nature, by so much is its activity superior to the exercise of the other forms of virtue. If then the intellect is something divine in comparison with man, so is the life of the intellect divine in comparison with human life. Nor ought we to obey those who enjoin that a man should have man's thoughts and a mortal the thoughts of mortality, but we ought so far as possible to achieve immortality, and do all that man may to live in accordance with the highest thing in him; for though this be small in bulk, in power and value it far surpasses all the rest.

It may even be held that this is the true self of each, inasmuch as it is the dominant and better part; and therefore it would be a strange thing if a man should choose to live not his own life but the life of some other than himself. . . .

FOR FURTHER STUDY

Aristotle. *The Nicomachean Ethics*. Trans. H. Rackham. Cambridge: Harvard U. Press, 1926. Book I. (Loeb Classical Library.) Also in *The Works of Aristotle*. Trans. under the editorship of W. D. Ross. New York: Oxford U. Press, 1925, Volume IX.

Hill, Thomas English. *Contemporary Ethical Theories*. New York: Macmillan, 1950, Ch. 16, "Self-Realization Theories."

Hyde, William De Witt. *The Five Great Philosophies of Life*. New York: Macmillan, 1930, Ch. 3, "The Platonic Subordination of Lower to Higher," Ch. 4, "The Aristotelian Sense of Proportion." (Collier Book 1962).

Joachim, Harold Henry. *Aristotle: The Nicomachean Ethics; A Commentary*, ed. D. A. Rees. Oxford: The Clarendon Press, 1951.

Montague, William Pepperell. "The Good as the Abundant Life" in *Moral Principles of Action*. ed. Ruth Nanda Anshen. New York: Harper, 1952, Ch. 11.

Plato. *The Republic*. Trans. with an Introduction and Notes by Francis Macdonald Cornford. New York: Oxford U. Press, 1945.

Veatch, Henry B. *Rational Man: A Modern Interpretation of Aristotelian Ethics*. Bloomington: Indiana U. Press, 1962.

CHAPTER 12

VALUES, RIGHTS,
AND OBLIGATIONS

~~~~~~~~~~~~~~~~~~~~~~~~~~~~~~~~~~~

A Growing Recognition of
*the 'Rights of Man**

The Universal Declaration of Human Rights is not a law. It is not a treaty. . . . Like our own Bill of Rights, the Declaration grew out of public demand. In 1945, at the birth of the UN, people of many nations spoke up. They wanted an international bill of rights. To foster its observance, they wanted a commission, a permanent international body. Let this be made clear, they said: We have seen enough of bloodshed caused by contempt for the individual and his sacred rights.

So it came about that in the Charter of the UN, the Member States pledged themselves to promoting "respect for human rights and fundamental freedoms for all without distinction as to race, sex, language or religion."

The Commission on Human Rights was established by the UN in 1946 and held its first session in February 1947. Its members represented 15 nations. Its first chairman was Mrs. Franklin D. Roosevelt, Representative from the United States. The vice chairmen were Dr. P. C. Chang of China and Professor René Cassin of France.

The Commission's initial job was to write the Universal Declaration

* From *Human Rights: A Guidebook for Community Action,* prepared by an editorial committee, Ethel C. Phillips, The American Jewish Committee, chairman, and sponsored by over thirty nongovernmental organizations on the initiative of the U. S. National Commission for UNESCO (New York: American Association for the United Nations, Inc., 1962).

of Human Rights. Almost two years of drafting and debate finally brought the Declaration to the UN General Assembly. There was no dissenting vote, although South Africa, Saudi Arabia and the Communist countries abstained. None rejoiced more on that December night in 1948 than the ten members of the U.S. delegation who had crusaded for the Declaration from the start.

Since its initial appearance in print, the Universal Declaration has been translated into 74 languages and dialects. It reads the way people speak and describes the way people have a right to live. The rights it sets forth may be described in four categories:

First, personal rights—those that make it possible to live one's private life without capricious interference from other people or the government. These include freedom of conscience and the right to "manifest religion or belief in teaching, practice, worship and observance"; liberty and security of person; privacy of home, family life and personal correspondence; the right to marry and raise children, with a free choice of one's marriage partner; the right to travel without hindrance within a country and to leave a country.

Second, economic rights—freedom from slavery and servitude; the right to a job, with fair working conditions and pay; to form and join a labor union; to own property; to enjoy a fair standard of living; to have rest and leisure.

Third, political and social rights. These include the right to take part in government and vote for representatives who govern; to assemble peacefully with others and join—or refrain from joining—any legitimate organization or group; to receive equal protection under the law; to be granted a fair public trial, including the presumption that one is innocent until proved guilty; to enjoy a full cultural life in accordance with one's artistic, literary or scientific inclinations.

Finally, there are certain across-the-board rights:

—Freedom of opinion and expression, including the right "to hold opinions without interference and to seek, receive and impart information and ideas through any media and regardless of frontiers . . ."

—The right to education "directed to the full development of the human personality and to the strengthening of respect for human rights and fundamental freedoms . . ."

—The right to equal opportunity in all areas of life, "without distinction of any kind, such as race, color, sex, language, religion, political or other opinion, national or social origin, property, birth or other status . . ."

Although not in itself a law, the Declaration has evoked from the law-makers of the world a spontaneous and far-reaching response. Its influence is evident in numerous national statutes, in decisions of national courts, in the new constitutions of more than 30 countries in Africa, Asia, Europe and South America, and in new international agreements, or conventions, which many governments have voluntarily accepted as law.

To the half-billion people who have gained political independence in the last 20 years, the Declaration stands as the embodiment of their aspirations. Devotion to its principles is expressly affirmed in the constitutions of 16 African nations.

In Europe, almost all the free countries are bound in a legal compact—the Convention for the Protection of Human Rights and Fundamental Freedoms—which embraces the most important civil and political rights in the Declaration. Adopted in 1950 by the 15 member governments of the Council of Europe, this was the first comprehensive international measure cementing human rights into law.

Following this regional pattern, the Organization of American States, which adopted a Declaration of the Rights and Duties of Man in 1948, is drafting an Inter-American Convention on Human Rights. . . .

Many nations have ratified a series of international conventions. Some are meant to enforce specific rights of specific groups—the rights of refugees and stateless persons, the political rights of women, the nationality rights of married women, the rights of workers to organize and bargain collectively, the rights of men and women to receive equal pay for work of equal value. Others are designed to end specific wrongs—slavery, forced labor, traffic in women and children, discrimination in employment, discrimination in education.

Several more conventions, still in various stages of completion, apply to freedom of information, the reduction of statelessness, and the protection of women in marriage through guarantees of free consent, minimum age and registration. In addition, in December 1962, the General Assembly asked that the Human Rights Commission be charged with preparing two comprehensive conventions—one "on the elimination of all forms of racial discrimination," the other "on the elimination of all forms of religious intolerance." Declarations on these subjects also were called for.

For several years, two all-embracing covenants drafted by the Human Rights Commission—on civil and political rights, and on economic, social and cultural rights—have been before the General Assembly for approval. These covenants, which would be legally binding on the ratifying states, have encountered many obstacles, but they are moving gradually toward completion. . . .

In 1959, the Commission laid before the General Assembly a Declaration of the Rights of the Child, which was unanimously adopted. It sets forth the principle that "mankind owes the child the best it has to give"—the right to "develop in a healthy and normal manner and in conditions of freedom and dignity"; to have his health protected with adequate food, housing, recreation and medical care; to receive an education that equips him to become a useful member of society, able and willing to understand and serve his fellow men.

Here is a declaration of responsibilities that no member of the human race can deny. For the one abiding interest that transcends all disinterests, all divisive ideologies, is the child. A doctrine may be embraced or rejected, defended or denounced; but not a child. He is not debatable. He stands unchallenged as the cherished common concern of mankind.

Yet can the world's children be protected in time? Can we save them from growing up contaminated—not by nuclear fallout alone, but also by noxious prejudices which perpetuate discrimination, injustice, misery and conflict?

ʌɔ·ːʌ·ːʌ·ːʌɔ

The United States Bill of Rights

AMENDMENTS I TO X TO THE CONSTITUTION OF THE UNITED STATES

ARTICLE I

Congress shall make no law respecting an establishment of religion, or prohibiting the free exercise thereof; or abridging the freedom of speech, or of the press; or the right of the people peaceably to assemble, and to petition the Government for a redress of grievances.

ARTICLE II

A well regulated Militia, being necessary to the security of a free State, the right of the people to keep and bear Arms, shall not be infringed.

ARTICLE III

No Soldier shall, in time of peace be quartered in any house, without the consent of the Owner, nor in time of war, but in a manner to be prescribed by law.

ARTICLE IV

The right of the people to be secure in their persons, houses, papers, and effects, against unreasonable searches and seizures, shall not be violated, and no Warrants shall issue, but upon probable cause, supported by Oath or affirmation, and particularly describing the place to be searched, and the persons or things to be seized.

ARTICLE V

No person shall be held to answer for a capital, or otherwise infamous crime, unless on a presentment or indictment of a Grand Jury, except in cases arising in the land or naval forces, or in the Militia, when in actual service in time of War or public danger; nor shall any person be subject for the same offense to be twice put in jeopardy of life or limb; nor shall be compelled in any criminal case to be a witness against himself, nor be deprived of life, liberty, or property, without due process of law; nor shall private property be taken for public use, without just compensation.

ARTICLE VI

In all criminal prosecutions, the accused shall enjoy the right to a speedy and public trial, by an impartial jury of the State and district wherein the crime shall have been committed, which district shall have been previously ascertained by law, and to be informed of the nature and cause of the accusation; to be confronted with the witnesses against him; to have compulsory process for obtaining witnesses in his favor, and to have the Assistance of Counsel for his defense.

ARTICLE VII

In suits at common law, where the value in controversy shall exceed twenty dollars, the right of trial by jury shall be preserved, and no fact tried by a jury, shall be otherwise re-examined in any Court of the United States, than according to the rules of the common law.

ARTICLE VIII

Excessive bail shall not be required, nor excessive fines imposed, nor cruel and unusual punishments inflicted.

ARTICLE IX

The enumeration in the Constitution, of certain rights, shall not be construed to deny or disparage others retained by the people.

ARTICLE X

The powers not delegated to the United States by the Constitution, nor prohibited by it to the States, are reserved to the States respectively, or to the people.

Universal Declaration of Human Rights

ADOPTED BY THE GENERAL ASSEMBLY OF THE UNITED NATIONS, DECEMBER 10, 1948

PREAMBLE

WHEREAS recognition of the inherent dignity and of the equal and inalienable rights of all members of the human family is the foundation of freedom, justice and peace in the world,

WHEREAS disregard and contempt for human rights have resulted in barbarous acts which have outraged the conscience of mankind, and the advent of a world in which human beings shall enjoy freedom of speech and belief and freedom from fear and want has been proclaimed as the highest aspiration of the common people,

WHEREAS it is essential, if man is not to be compelled to have recourse, as a last resort, to rebellion against tyranny and oppression, that human rights should be protected by the rule of law,

WHEREAS it is essential to promote the development of friendly relations between nations,

WHEREAS the peoples of the United Nations have in the Charter re-affirmed their faith in fundamental human rights, in the dignity and worth of the human person and in the equal rights of men and women and have determined to promote social progress and better standards of life in larger freedom,

WHEREAS Member States have pledged themselves to achieve, in co-operation with the United Nations, the promotion of universal respect for and observance of human rights and fundamental freedoms,

WHEREAS a common understanding of these rights and freedoms is of the greatest importance for the full realization of this pledge,

Now, therefore, *The General Assembly proclaims* THIS UNIVER-SAL DECLARATION OF HUMAN RIGHTS as a common standard of achievement for all peoples and all nations, to the end that every indi-vidual and every organ of society, keeping this Declaration constantly in mind, shall strive by teaching and education to promote respect for these rights and freedoms and by progressive measures, national and international, to secure their universal and effective recognition and observance, both among the peoples of Member States themselves and among the peoples of territories under their jurisdiction.

ARTICLE 1

All human beings are born free and equal in dignity and rights. They are endowed with reason and conscience and should act towards one another in a spirit of brotherhood.

ARTICLE 2

(1) Everyone is entitled to all the rights and freedoms set forth in this Declaration, without distinction of any kind, such as race, color, sex, language, religion, political or other opinion, national or social origin, property, birth or other status.

(2) Furthermore, no distinction shall be made on the basis of the political, jurisdictional or international status of the country or terri-tory to which a person belongs, whether it be independent, trust, non-self-governing or under any other limitation of sovereignty.

ARTICLE 3

Everyone has the right to life, liberty and security of person.

ARTICLE 4

No one shall be held in slavery or servitude; slavery and the slave trade shall be prohibited in all their forms.

ARTICLE 5

No one shall be subjected to torture or to cruel, inhuman or degrading treatment or punishment.

ARTICLE 6

Everyone has the right to recognition everywhere as a person before the law.

ARTICLE 7

All are equal before the law and are entitled without any discrimination to equal protection of the law. All are entitled to equal protection against any discrimination in violation of this Declaration and against any incitement to such discrimination.

ARTICLE 8

Everyone has the right to an effective remedy by the competent national tribunals for acts violating the fundamental rights granted him by the constitution or by law.

ARTICLE 9

No one shall be subjected to arbitrary arrest, detention or exile.

ARTICLE 10

Everyone is entitled in full equality to a fair and public hearing by an independent and impartial tribunal, in the determination of his rights and obligations and of any criminal charge against him.

ARTICLE 11

(1) Everyone charged with a penal offense has the right to be presumed innocent until proved guilty according to law in a public trial at which he has had all the guarantees necessary for his defense.

(2) No one shall be held guilty of any penal offence on account of any act or omission which did not constitute a penal offence, under national or international law, at the time when it was committed. Nor shall a heavier penalty be imposed than the one that was applicable at the time the penal offence was committed.

ARTICLE 12

No one shall be subjected to arbitrary interference with his privacy, family, home or correspondence, nor to attacks upon his honour and reputation. Everyone has the right to the protection of the law against such interference or attacks.

ARTICLE 13

(1) Everyone has the right to freedom of movement and residence within the borders of each state.

(2) Everyone has the right to leave any country, including his own, and to return to his country.

ARTICLE 14

(1) Everyone has the right to seek and to enjoy in other countries asylum from persecution.

(2) This right may not be invoked in the case of prosecutions genuinely arising from non-political crimes or from acts contrary to the purposes and principles of the United Nations.

ARTICLE 15

(1) Everyone has the right to a nationality.

(2) No one shall be arbitrarily deprived of his nationality or denied the right to change his nationality.

ARTICLE 16

(1) Men and women of full age, without any limitation due to race, nationality or religion, have the right to marry and to found a family. They are entitled to equal rights as to marriage, during marriage and at its dissolution.

(2) Marriage shall be entered into only with the free and full consent of the intending spouses.

(3) The family is the natural and fundamental group unit of society and is entitled to protection by society and the State.

ARTICLE 17

(1) Everyone has the right to own property alone as well as in association with others.

(2) No one shall be arbitrarily deprived of his property.

ARTICLE 18

Everyone has the right to freedom of thought, conscience and religion; this right includes freedom to change his religion or belief, and freedom, either alone or in community with others and in public or private, to manifest his religion or belief in teaching, practice, worship and observance.

ARTICLE 19

Everyone has the right to freedom of opinion and expression; this right includes freedom to hold opinions without interference and to seek, receive and impart information and ideas through any media and regardless of frontiers.

ARTICLE 20

(1) Everyone has the right to freedom of peaceful assembly and association.

(2) No one may be compelled to belong to an association.

ARTICLE 21

(1) Everyone has the right to take part in the government of his country, directly or through freely chosen representatives.

(2) Everyone has the right of equal access to public service in his country.

(3) The will of the people shall be the basis of the authority of government; this will shall be expressed in periodic and genuine elections which shall be by universal and equal suffrage and shall be held by secret vote or by equivalent free voting procedures.

ARTICLE 22

Everyone, as a member of society, has the right to social security and is entitled to realization, through national effort and international co-operation and in accordance with the organization and resources of each State, of the economic, social and cultural rights indispensable for his dignity and the free development of his personality.

ARTICLE 23

(1) Everyone has the right to work, to free choice of employment, to just and favorable conditions of work and to protection against unemployment.

(2) Everyone, without any discrimination, has the right to equal pay for equal work.

(3) Everyone who works has the right to just and favorable remuneration insuring for himself and his family an existence worthy of human dignity, and supplemented, if necessary, by other means of social protection.

(4) Everyone has the right to form and to join trade unions for the protection of his interests.

ARTICLE 24

Everyone has the right to rest and leisure, including reasonable limitation of working hours and periodic holidays with pay.

ARTICLE 25

(1) Everyone has the right to a standard of living adequate for the health and well-being of himself and of his family, including food, clothing, housing and medical care and necessary social services, and the right to security in the event of unemployment, sickness, disability, widowhood, old age or other lack of livelihood in circumstances beyond his control.

(2) Motherhood and childhood are entitled to special care and assistance. All children, whether born in or out of wedlock, shall enjoy the same social protection.

ARTICLE 26

(1) Everyone has the right to education. Education shall be free, at least in the elementary and fundamental stages. Elementary education shall be compulsory. Technical and professional education shall be made generally available and higher education shall be equally accessible to all on the basis of merit.

(2) Education shall be directed to the full development of the human personality and to the strengthening of respect for human rights and fundamental freedoms. It shall promote understanding, tolerance and friendship among all nations, racial or religious groups, and shall further the activities of the United Nations for the maintenance of peace.

(3) Parents have a prior right to choose the kind of education that shall be given to their children.

ARTICLE 27

(1) Everyone has the right freely to participate in the cultural life of the community, to enjoy the arts and to share in scientific advancement and its benefits.

(2) Everyone has the right to the protection of the moral and material interests resulting from any scientific, literary or artistic production of which he is the author.

ARTICLE 28

Everyone is entitled to a social and international order in which the rights and freedoms set forth in this Declaration can be fully realized.

ARTICLE 29

(1) Everyone has duties to the community in which alone the free and full development of his personality is possible.

(2) In the exercise of his rights and freedoms, everyone shall be subject only to such limitations as are determined by law solely for the purpose of securing due recognition and respect for the rights and freedoms of others and of meeting the just requirements of morality, public order and the general welfare in a democratic society.

(3) These rights and freedoms may in no case be exercised contrary to the purposes and principles of the United Nations.

ARTICLE 30

Nothing in this Declaration may be interpreted as implying for any State, group or person any right to engage in any activity or to perform any act aimed at the destruction of any of the rights and freedoms set forth herein.

Declaration of the Rights
of the Child

PREAMBLE

WHEREAS, the peoples of the United Nations have, in the Charter, reaffirmed their faith in fundamental human rights, and in the dignity and worth of the human person, and have determined to promote social progress and better standards of life in larger freedom,

WHEREAS the United Nations has, in the Universal Declaration of Human Rights, proclaimed that everyone is entitled to all the rights and freedoms set forth therein, without distinction of any kind, such as race, color, sex, language, religion, political or other opinion, national or social origin, property, birth or other status,

WHEREAS the child, by reason of his physical and mental immaturity, needs special safeguards and care, including appropriate legal protection, before as well as after birth,

WHEREAS the need for such special safeguards has been stated in the Geneva Declaration of the Rights of the Child of 1924, and recognized in the Universal Declaration of Human Rights and in the statutes of specialized agencies and international organizations concerned with the welfare of children,

WHEREAS mankind owes to the child the best it has to give,

NOW THEREFORE,

The GENERAL ASSEMBLY proclaims

This DECLARATION OF THE RIGHTS OF THE CHILD to the end that he may have a happy childhood and enjoy for his own good and for the good of society the rights and freedoms herein set forth, and calls upon parents, upon men and women as individuals and upon voluntary organizations, local authorities and national governments to recognize these rights and strive for their observance by legislative and other measures progressively taken in accordance with the following principles:

PRINCIPLE 1

The child shall enjoy all the rights set forth in this Declaration. All children, without any exception whatsoever, shall be entitled to these rights, without distinction or discrimination on account of race, color, sex, language, religion, political or other opinion, national or social origin, property, birth or other status, whether of himself or of his family.

PRINCIPLE 2

The child shall enjoy special protection, and shall be given opportunities and facilities, by law and by other means, to enable him to develop physically, mentally, morally, spiritually and socially in a healthy and normal manner and in conditions of freedom and dignity. In the enactment of laws for this purpose the best interests of the child shall be the paramount consideration.

PRINCIPLE 3

The child shall be entitled from his birth to a name and a nationality.

PRINCIPLE 4

The child shall enjoy the benefits of social security. He shall be entitled to grow and develop in health; to this end special care and protection shall be provided both to him and to his mother, including adequate pre-natal and post-natal care. The child shall have the right to adequate nutrition, housing, recreation and medical services.

PRINCIPLE 5

The child who is physically, mentally or socially handicapped shall be given the special treatment, education and care required by his particular condition.

PRINCIPLE 6

The child, for the full and harmonious development of his personality, needs love and understanding. He shall, wherever possible, grow up in the care and under the responsibility of his parents, and in any case in an atmosphere of affection and of moral and material security; a child of tender years shall not, save in exceptional circumstances, be separated from his mother. Society and the public authorities shall have the duty to extend particular care to children without a family and to those without adequate means of support. Payment of state and other assistance toward the maintenance of children of large families is desirable.

PRINCIPLE 7

The child is entitled to receive education, which shall be free and compulsory, at least in the elementary stages. He shall be given an education which will promote his general culture, and enable him on a basis of equal opportunity to develop his abilities, his individual judgment, and his sense of moral and social responsibility, and to become a useful member of society.

The best interests of the child shall be the guiding principle of those responsible for his education and guidance; that responsibility lies in the first place with his parents.

The child shall have full opportunity for play and recreation, which should be directed to the same purposes as education; society and the public authorities shall endeavor to promote the enjoyment of this right.

PRINCIPLE 8

The child shall in all circumstances be among the first to receive protection and relief.

PRINCIPLE 9

The child shall be protected against all forms of neglect, cruelty and exploitation. He shall not be the subject of traffic, in any form.

The child shall not be admitted to employment before an appropriate minimum age; he shall in no case be caused or permitted to engage in any occupation or employment which would prejudice his health or education, or interfere with his physical, mental or moral development.

PRINCIPLE 10

The child shall be protected from practices which may foster racial, religious and any other form of discrimination. He shall be brought up in a spirit of understanding, tolerance, friendship among peoples, peace and universal brotherhood and in full consciousness that his energy and talents should be devoted to the service of his fellow men.

Human Rights

A POLICY STATEMENT OF THE NATIONAL COUNCIL OF THE CHURCHES OF CHRIST IN THE UNITED STATES OF AMERICA

ADOPTED BY THE GENERAL ASSEMBLY
DECEMBER 6, 1963

A responsible society, according to our Christian faith, is one in which freedom is practiced by men who acknowledge responsibility to justice and public order, and where those who hold political authority or economic power are responsible for its exercise to God and to the people whose welfare is affected by it.

In accord with these principles we set forth certain of the more specific rights which we believe are due to all persons and will make for the building of the responsible society. Among the rights that are due to all persons without discrimination as to creed, race, color, sex, birth, nationality, or economic status, are the following:

General Rights Due To All Persons

General rights due to all persons because of their personal worth and inherent dignity include:

Freedom of religion and conscience, embracing rights to hold and to change faith, to express it in worship and practice, to teach and persuade others by the sharing of viewpoints in mutual respect, and to conduct religious education of children.

Freedom to marry by mutual consent and the right to protections of a minimum age of consent and a registered marriage.

Freedom of speech, press, inquiry, including expression of economic, political and social opinions.

Freedom of peaceable association, assembly, and demonstration.

Freedom to petition government for redress of grievances.

Freedom from arbitrary arrest, arbitrary or secret imprisonment, police brutality, mob violence, intimidation, cruel or unusual punishment, and from any attempts to manipulate or tamper with human personality through drugs, hypnosis, isolation, duress, or other means of "brainwashing."

Political and Civic Rights

The right to full participation of the person in political and civic life, including the opportunity:

To vote by secret ballot, with alternative choices;

To organize peaceful political activity;

To be a candidate for public office;

To participate in any branch of government; to serve without discrimination in the Armed Forces, or on grounds of conscience to be excused from such service;

To receive such benefits of social welfare, health, community and other services as are provided by governments at all levels;

To enjoy equality before the law, including protection by the police; the right of an accused person to a prompt, fair, and public trial; the right of counsel; the right to be confronted with written indictment, evidence, and witnesses against him; the right to present evidence and witnesses on his own behalf and to cross-examine other witnesses; the right to have the judgment of his actions depend on an evaluation of facts in the light of law, by due process, such as by impartial judges or an impartial jury of his peers.

Economic Rights

The right to participate in the economic life of the community, including the opportunity:

To earn a standard of living adequate to promote the welfare and security of the individual and family; to work in decent and healthful conditions, and to have free choice of employment, for just compensation, with protection against unemployment;

To receive, when absence of opportunity for work or other unavoidable causes prevent employment, a proper standard of relief payments from public sources;

To obtain employment solely on the basis of ability and character;

To acquire vocational, professional, or job training or apprenticeship solely on the basis of ability and character;

To receive equal pay for equal work;

To gain promotion in employment in accord with ability, experience, and character;

To own property;

To engage in an individual business enterprise or a profession;

To form voluntary economic organizations such as corporations, cooperatives, and labor unions;

To engage in social action on economic issues.

Social and Cultural Rights

The right to take part in the social and cultural life of the community, including the opportunity:

To have wholesome living space, necessary for the health and welfare of persons and families;

To move within a country and to leave and return to one's country;

To obtain education and training;

To make use of cultural and recreational opportunities and facilities;

To enjoy privacy, protected against invasion of personal or family life by unreasonable searches or seizures, such as wire-tapping, interception of mail, electronic eavesdropping, or other forcible or surreptitious interference;

To enjoy freedom of association with other persons regardless of racial or other distinctions;

To have access to social welfare, health and other community services;

To share equally in the use of public transportation;

To receive equal service from businesses and persons serving the public—such as stores, theaters, hotels, and restaurants.

FOR FURTHER STUDY

Albert, Ethel M. "Social Science Facts and Philosophical Values," *The Antioch Review*, 17 (Winter, 1957-1958): 406-420. Reprinted in *The Range of Philosophy*, eds. Harold H. Titus and Maylon H. Hepp. New York: American Book, 1964, pp. 250-263.

Brown, Stuart M., Jr. "Inalienable Rights," *Philosophical Review*, 64 (April 1955): 192-211.

Douglas, William O. "The Bill of Rights Is Not Enough," in *The Great Rights*, ed. Edmond Cahn. New York: Macmillan, 1963.

Frankena, William F. "Natural and Inalienable Rights," *Philosophical Review*, 64 (April 1955): 212-232.

Green, Thomas Hill. *Political Theory of T. H. Green*, ed. John R. Rodman. New York: Appleton, 1950.

Hart, H. L. A. "Are There Any Natural Rights?" *Philosophical Review*, 64 (April 1955): 175-191.

Keeton, Morris. *Values Men Live By*. New York: Abingdon, 1960, p. 212.

Lewis, Clarence Irving. *An Analysis of Knowledge and Valuation*. LaSalle: Open Court, 1946, Ch. 12, "Knowing, Doing and Valuing."

Mumford, Lewis. *The Conduct of Life*. New York: Harcourt, Brace, 1951, Ch. 5, "The Basis of Human Development."

Weiss, Paul. *Our Public Life*. Bloomington: Indiana U. Press, 1959, Ch. 2, "Man's Native Rights."

Wieman, Henry N. *The Source of Human Good*. Chicago: U. of Chicago Press, 1946, Ch. 3, "Creative Good."

PART THREE

SPECIFIC PROBLEMS OF PERSONAL AND SOCIAL MORALITY

CHAPTER 13

PHYSICAL AND
MENTAL HEALTH

ᵃᵃᵃᵃᵃᵃᵃᵃᵃᵃᵃᵃᵃᵃᵃᵃᵃᵃᵃᵃᵃᵃᵃ

Physical and Mental Well-Being*

ABRAHAM H. MASLOW

Abraham H. Maslow (1908-   ) is a professor of psychology at Brandeis University. He is the author of articles in professional journals dealing with mental and social problems. His books include *Motivation and Personality*, 1954, and *Toward a Psychology of Being* (1962).

Humanists for thousands of years have attempted to construct a naturalistic, psychological value system that could be derived from man's own nature, without the necessity of recourse to authority outside the human being himself. Many such theories have been offered throughout history. They have all failed for mass purposes exactly as all other value theories have failed. We have about as many scoundrels in the world today as we have ever had, and *many more* neurotic, probably, than we have ever had.

These inadequate theories, most of them, rested on psychological assumptions of one sort or another. Today practically all of these

* From "Psychological Data and Value Theory," in *New Knowledge in Human Values*, Abraham H. Maslow (New York: Harper, 1959), pp. 119-135. Copyright © 1959 by Research Society for Creative Altruism. Reprinted with the permission of Harper and Row, Publishers.

can be shown, in the light of recently acquired knowledge, to be false, inadequate, incomplete, or in some other way lacking. But it is my belief that developments in the science and art of psychology, in the last few decades, make it possible for us for the first time to feel confident that this age-old hope may be fulfilled if only we work hard enough. We know how to criticize the old theories, we know, even though dimly, the shape of the theories to come, and, most of all, we know where to look and what to do in order to fill in the gaps in knowledge, that will permit us to answer the age-old questions, "What is the good life? What is the good man? How can people be taught to desire and prefer the good life? How ought children to be brought up to be sound adults?, etc." That is, we think that a scientific ethic may be possible, and we think we know how to go about constructing it.

The following section will discuss briefly a few of the promising lines of evidence and of research, their relevance to past and future value theories, along with a discussion of the theoretical and factual advances we must make in the near future. Since my space is too short to assay the level of confidence of these various data, I think it safer to judge them all as more or less probable rather than as certain.

Free Choice Experiments: Homeostasis

Hundreds of experiments have been made that demonstrate a universal inborn ability in all sorts of animals to select a beneficial diet if enough alternatives are presented from among which they are permitted free choice. This wisdom of the body is often retained under less usual conditions, e.g., adrenalectomized animals can keep themselves alive by readjusting their self-chosen diet, pregnant animals will nicely adjust their diets to the needs of the growing embryo, etc.

We now know this is by no means a perfect wisdom. These appetites are less efficient, for instance, in reflecting body need for vitamins. Lower animals protect themselves against poisons more efficiently than higher animals and humans. Previously formed habits of preference may quite overshadow present metabolic needs. And most of all, in the human being, and especially in the neurotic human being, all sorts of forces can contaminate this wisdom of the body, although it never seems to be lost altogether.

The general principle is true not only for selection of food but also for all sorts of other body needs, as the famous homeostasis experiments have shown.

It seems quite clear that all organisms are more self-governing, self-regulating, and autonomous than we thought twenty-five years ago. The organism deserves a good deal of trust and we are learning steadily to rely on this internal wisdom of our babies with reference to choice of diet, time of weaning, amount of sleep, time of toilet training, need for activity, and a lot else.

But more recently we have been learning, especially from physically and mentally sick people, that there are good choosers and bad choosers. We have learned, especially from the psychoanalysts, much about the hidden causes of such behavior and have learned to respect these causes.

In this connection we have available a startling experiment, which we have been trying to repeat at Brandeis, that is pregnant with implications for value theory. It turns out that chickens allowed to choose their own diet vary widely in their ability to choose what is good for them. The good choosers become stronger, larger, more dominant than the poor choosers, which means that they get the best of everything. If then the diet chosen by the good choosers is forced upon the poor choosers, it is found that *they* now get stronger, bigger, healthier, and more dominant, although never reaching the level of the good choosers. That is, good choosers can choose better than bad choosers what is better for the bad choosers themselves. If similar findings are made in human beings, as I think they will be, we are in for a good deal of reconstruction of all sorts of theories. So far as human theory is concerned, no theory will be adequate that rests simply on the statistical description of the choices of unselected human beings. To average the choices of good and bad choosers, of healthy and sick people is useless. Only the choices and tastes and judgments of healthy human beings will tell us much about what is good for the human species in the long run. The choices of neurotic people can tell us mostly what is good for keeping a neurosis stabilized, just as the choices of a brain-injured man are good for preventing a catastrophic breakdown, or as the choices of an adrenalectomized animal may keep *him* from dying but would kill a healthy animal.

I think that this is the main reef on which most hedonistic value theories and ethical theories have foundered. Pathologically motivated pleasures cannot be averaged with healthily motivated pleasures.

Furthermore, any ethical code will have to deal with the fact of constitutional differences not only in chickens and rats but also in men, as Sheldon and Morris have shown. Some values are common to all (healthy) mankind, but also some other values will *not* be common to all mankind, but only to some types of people, or to specific individuals. What I have called the basic needs are probably common to all mankind and are therefore shared values. But idiosyncratic needs generate idiosyncratic values.

Constitutional differences in individuals generate preferences among ways of relating to self, and to culture and to the world, *i.e.*, generate values. These researches support and are supported by the universal experience of clinicians with individual differences. This is also true of the ethnological data that make sense of cultural diversity by postulating that each culture selects for exploitation, suppression, approval or disapproval, a small segment of the range of human constitutional possibilities. This is all in line with the biological data and theories and self-actualization theories which show that an organ system presses to express itself, in a word, to function. The muscular person likes to use his muscles, indeed, *has* to use them in order to self-actualize and to achieve the subjective feeling of harmonious, uninhibited, satisfying functioning which is so important an aspect of psychological health. People with intelligence must use their intelligence, people with eyes must use their eyes, people with the capacity to love have the *impulse* to love and the *need* to love in order to feel healthy. Capacities clamor to be used, and cease their clamor only when they *are* used sufficiently. That is to say, capacities are needs, and therefore are intrinsic values as well. To the extent that capacities differ, so will values also differ.

Basic Needs and Their Hierarchical Arrangement

It has by now been sufficiently demonstrated that the human being has, as part of his intrinsic construction, not only physiological needs, but also truly psychological ones. They may be considered as deficiencies which must be optimally fulfilled by the environment to avoid sickness and to avoid subjective ill-being. They can be called basic, or biological, and likened to the need for salt, or calcium or vitamin D because:
1. The person yearns for their gratification persistently.
2. Their deprivation makes the person sicken and wither, or stunts his growth.
3. Gratifying them is therapeutic, curing the deficiency-illness.
4. Steady supplies forestall these illnesses.
5. Healthy people do not demonstrate these deficiencies.

But these needs or values are related to each other in a hierarchical and developmental way, in an order of strength and of priority. Safety is a more prepotent, or stronger, more pressing, earlier appearing, more vital need than love, for instance, and the need for food is usually stronger than either. Furthermore *all* these basic needs may be considered to be simply steps along the time path to general self-actualization, under which all basic needs can be subsumed.

By taking these data into account, we can solve many value problems that philosophers have struggled with ineffectually for centuries. For one thing, it looks as if *there were* a single ultimate value for mankind, a far goal toward which all men strive. This is called variously by different authors self-actualization, self-realization, integration, psychological health, individuation, autonomy, creativity, productivity, but they all agree that this amounts to realizing the potentialities of the person, that is to say, becoming fully human, everything that the person *can* become.

But it is also true that the person himself does not know this. We, the psychologists observing and studying, have constructed this concept in order to integrate and explain lots of diverse data. So far as the person himself is concerned, all *he* knows is that he is desperate for love, and thinks he will be forever happy and content if he gets it. He does not know in advance that he will strive on *after* this gratification has come, and that gratification of one basic need opens consciousness to domination by another, "higher" need. So far as he is concerned, *the* absolute, ultimate value, synonymous with life itself, is whichever need in the hierarchy he is dominated by during a particular period. These basic needs or basic values therefore may be treated *both* as ends and as steps toward a single end-goal. It is true that there is a single, ultimate value or end of life, and *also* it is just as true that we have a hierarchical and developmental system of values, complexly interrelated.

This also helps to solve the apparent paradox of contrast between Being and Becoming. It is true that human beings strive perpetually toward ultimate humanness, which itself is anyway a different kind of Becoming and growing. It's as if we were doomed forever to try to arrive at a state to which we could never attain. Fortunately we now know this not to be true, or at least it is not the only truth. There is another truth which integrates with it. We are again and again rewarded for good Becoming by transient states of absolute Being, which I have summarized as peak-experiences. Achieving basic-need gratifications gives us many peak-experiences, each of which are absolute delights, perfect in themselves, and needing no more than themselves to validate life. This is like rejecting the notion that a

Heaven lies someplace beyond the end of the path of life. Heaven, so to speak, lies waiting for us throughout life, ready to step into for a time and to enjoy before we have to come back to our ordinary life of striving. And once we have been in it, we can remember it forever, and feed ourselves on this memory and be sustained in time of stress.

Not only this, but the process of moment to moment growth is itself intrinsically rewarding and delightful in an absolute sense. If they are not mountain peak-experiences, at least they are foothill-experiences, little glimpses of absolute, self-validative delights, little moments of Being. Being and Becoming are *not* contradictory or mutually exclusive. Approaching and arriving are both in themselves rewarding.

I should make it clear here that I want to differentiate the Heaven ahead (of growth and transcendence) from the "Heaven" behind (of regression). The "high Nirvana" is very different in important ways from the "low Nirvana" even though most clinicians confuse them because they are also similar in some ways.

Self-Actualization: Growth

I have published in another place a survey of all the evidence that forces us in the direction of a concept of healthy growth or of self-actualizing tendencies. This is partly deductive evidence in the sense of pointing out that, unless we postulate such a concept, much of human behavior makes no sense. This is on the same scientific principle that led to the discovery of a hitherto unseen planet that *had* to be there in order to make sense of a lot of other observed data.

There is also some direct evidence, or rather the beginnings of direct evidence which needs much more research, to get to the point of certainty. The only direct study of self-actualizing people I know is the one I made, and it is a very shaky business to rest on just one study made by just one person when we take into account the known pitfalls of sampling error, of wish-fulfillment, of projection, etc. However, the conclusions of this study have been so strongly paralleled in the clinical and philosophical conclusions of Rogers, of Fromm, of Goldstein, of Angyal, of Murray, of C. Bühler, of Horney, Jung, Nuttin, and many others that I shall proceed under the assumption that more careful research will not contradict my findings radically. We can certainly now assert that at least a reasonable, theoretical, and empirical case has been made for the presence within the human being of a tendency toward, or need for, growing in a direction that can be summarized in general as self-actualization, or psychological health or maturation, and specifically as growth toward each and all of the sub-aspects of self-actualization. That is to say, the human being has within him a pressure (among other pressures) toward unity of personality, toward spontaneous expressiveness, toward full individuality and identity, toward seeing the truth rather than being blind, toward being creative, toward being good, and a lot else. That is, the human being is so constructed that he presses toward fuller and fuller being and this means pressing toward what most people would call good values, toward serenity, kindness, courage, knowledge, honesty, love, unselfishness, and goodness.

Few in number though they be, we can learn a great deal from the direct study of these highly evolved, most mature, psychologically healthiest individuals, and from the study of the peak moments of average individuals, moments in which they become transiently self-actualized. This is because they are in very real empirical and theoretical ways, *most fully human*. For instance, they are people who have retained and developed all their human capacities, especially those capacities which define the human being and differentiate him from let us say the monkey. (This accords with Hartman's axiological approach to the same problem of defining the good human being as the one who has more of the characteristics which define the concept "human being.") From a developmental point of view, they are more fully evolved because not fixated at immature or incomplete levels of growth. This is no more mysterious, or *a priori*, or question-begging than the selection of a type specimen of butterfly by a taxonomist or the most physically healthy young man by the physician. They both look for the "perfect or mature or magnificent specimen" for the exemplar, and so have I. One procedure is as repeatable in principle as the other.

Full humanness can be defined not only in terms of the degree to which the definition of the concept "human" is fulfilled, *i.e.*, the species norm. It also has a descriptive, cataloguing, measurable, psychological definition. We now have from a few research beginnings and from countless clinical experiences some notion of the characteristics both of the fully evolved human being and of the well-growing human being. These characteristics are not only neutrally describable; they are also subjectively rewarding, and pleasurable and reinforcing.

Among the objectively describable and measurable characteristics of the healthy human specimen are:

1. Clearer, more efficient perception of reality.

2. More openness to experience.
3. Increased integration, wholeness, and unity of the person.
4. Increased spontaneity, expressiveness; full functioning; aliveness.
5. A real self; a firm identity; autonomy; uniqueness.
6. Increased objectivity, detachment, transcendence of self.
7. Recovery of creativeness.
8. Ability to fuse concreteness and abstractness, primary and secondary process cognition, etc.
9. Democratic character structure.
10. Ability to love, etc.

These all need research confirmation and exploration but it is clear that such researches are feasible.

In addition, there are subjective confirmations or reinforcements of self-actualization or of good growth toward it. These are the feelings of zest in living, of happiness or euphoria, of serenity, of joy, of calmness, of responsibility, of confidence in one's ability to handle stresses, anxieties, and problems. The subjective signs of self-betrayal, of fixation, of regression, and of living by fear rather than by growth are such feelings as anxiety, despair, boredom, inability to enjoy, intrinsic guilt, intrinsic shame, aimlessness, feelings of emptiness, of lack of identity, etc.

These subjective reactions are also susceptible of research exploration. We have clinical techniques available for studying them.

It is the free choices of such self-actualizing people (in those situations where real choice is possible from among a variety of possibilities) that I claim can be descriptively studied as a naturalistic value system with which the hopes of the observer absolutely have nothing to do, *i.e.*, it is "scientific." I do not say "He *ought* to choose this or that" but only "Healthy people, permitted to choose, are *observed* to choose this or that." This is like asking "What *are* the values of the best human beings" rather than "What *should* be their values?" or "What *ought* they do?" (Compare this with Aristotle's belief that "it is the things which are valuable and pleasant to a good man that are really valuable and pleasant.")

Furthermore I think these findings can be generalized to most of the human species because it looks to me (and to others) as if *all* or most people tend toward self-actualization (this is seen most clearly in the experiences in psychotherapy, especially of the uncovering sort), and as if, in principle at least, all people are capable of self-actualization.

If the various extant religions may be taken as expressions of human aspiration, *i.e.*, what people would *like* to become if only they could, then we can see here too a validation of the affirmation that all people yearn toward self-actualization or tend toward it. This is so because our description of the actual characteristics of self-actualizing people parallels at many points the ideals urged by the religions, *e.g.*, the transcendence of self, the fusion of the true, the good and the beautiful, contribution to others, wisdom, honesty and naturalness, the transcendence of selfish and personal motivations, the giving up of "lower" desires in favor of "higher" ones, the easy differentiation between ends (tranquility, serenity, peace) and means (money, power, status), the decrease of hostility, cruelty and destructiveness and the increase of friendliness, gentleness and kindness, etc.

1. One conclusion from all these free choice experiments, from developments in dynamic motivation theory and from examination of psychotherapy is a very revolutionary one that no other large culture has ever arrived at, namely, that our deepest needs are *not*, in themselves, dangerous or evil or bad. This opens up the prospect of resolving the dichotomy between Apollonian and Dionysian, classical and romantic, scientific and poetic, between reason and impulse, work and play, verbal and preverbal, maturity and childlikeness, masculine and feminine, growth and regression.

2. The main social parallel to this change in our philosophy of human nature is the rapidly growing tendency to perceive the culture as an instrument of need-gratification as well as of frustration and control. We can now reject, as a localism, the almost universal mistake that the interests of the individual and of society are *of necessity* mutually exclusive and antagonistic, or that civilization is primarily a mechanism for controlling and policing human instinctoid impulses. All these age-old axioms are swept away by the new possibility of defining the main function of a healthy culture and each of its institutions as the fostering of universal self-actualization.

3. In healthy people only is there a good correlation between subjective delight in the experience, impulse to the experience, or wish for it, and "basic need" for the experience (it's good for him in the long run). Only such people uniformly yearn for what is good for them and for others, and then are able wholeheartedly to enjoy it, and approve of it. For such people virtue is its own reward in the sense of being enjoyed in itself. They spontaneously tend to do right because that is what they *want* to do, what they *need* to do, what they enjoy, what they approve of doing, and what they will continue to enjoy.

It is this unity, this network of positive intercorrelation that falls apart into separateness and conflict as the person gets psychologically sick. Then what he wants to do may be bad for him; even if he does it he may not enjoy it; even if he enjoys it he may simultaneously disapprove of it so that the enjoyment is itself poisoned or may disappear quickly. What he enjoys at first he may not enjoy later. His impulses, desires, and enjoyments then become a poor guide to living. He must accordingly mistrust and fear the impulses and the enjoyments which lead him astray, and so he is caught in conflict, dissociation, indecision; in a word, he is caught in civil war.

So far as philosophical theory is concerned, many historical dilemmas and contradictions are resolved by this finding. Hedonistic theory *does* work for healthy people; it does *not* work for sick people. The true, the good and the beautiful *do* correlate some, but only in healthy people do they correlate strongly.

4. Self-actualization is a relatively achieved "state of affairs" in a few people. In most people, however, it is rather a hope, a yearning, a drive, a "something" wished for but not yet achieved, showing itself clinically as drive toward health, integration, growth, etc. The projective tests are also able to detect these trends as potentialities rather than as overt behavior, just as an X-ray can detect incipient pathology before it has appeared on the surface.

This means for us that that which the person *is* and that which the person *could be* exist simultaneously for the psychologist, thereby resolving the dichotomy between Being and Becoming. Potentialities not only *will* be or could be; they also *are*. Self-actualization values as goals exist and are real even though not yet actualized. The human being is simultaneously that which he is and that which he yearns to be.

Growth and Environment

Man demonstrates *in his own nature* a pressure toward fuller and fuller Being, more and more perfect actualization of his humanness in exactly the same naturalistic, scientific sense than an acorn may be said to be "pressing toward" being an oak tree, or that a tiger can be observed to "push toward" being tigerish, or a horse toward being equine. Man is ultimately *not* molded or shaped into humanness or taught to be human. The role of the environment is ultimately to permit him or help him to actualize *his own* potentialities, not *its* potentialities. The environment does not give him potentialities and capacities; he *has* them in inchoate or embryonic form, just exactly as he has embryonic arms and legs. And creativeness, spontaneity, selfhood, authenticity, caring for others, being able to love, yearning for truth are embryonic potentialities belonging to his species-membership just as much as are his arms and legs and brain and eyes.

This is not in contradiction to the data already amassed which show clearly that living in a family and in a culture are absolutely necessary to *actualize* these psychological potentials that define humanness. Let us avoid this confusion. A mother or a culture does not create a human being. It does not implant within him the ability to love, or to be curious, or to philosophize, or to symbolize, or to be creative. Rather, it permits or fosters or encourages or helps what exists in embryo to become real and actual. The same mother or the same culture, treating a kitten or a puppy in exactly the same way, cannot make it into a human being. The culture is sun and food and water: it is not the seed.

"Instinct" Theory

The group of thinkers who have been working with self-actualization, with self, with authentic humanness, etc., have pretty firmly established their case that man has a tendency to realize himself. By implication he is exhorted to be true to his own nature, to trust, himself, to be authentic, spontaneous, honestly expressive, to look for the sources of his actions in his own deep inner nature.

But, of course, this is an ideal counsel. They do not sufficiently warn that most adults don't know *how* to be authentic and that if they "express" themselves, they may bring catastrophe not only upon themselves but upon others as well. What answer must be given to the rapist or the sadist who asks "Why should I too not trust and express myself?"

These thinkers as a group have been remiss in several respects. They have *implied* without making explicit that if you can behave authentically, you *will* behave well, that if you emit action from within, it will be good and right behavior. What is very clearly implied is that this inner core, this real self, is good, trustworthy, ethical. This is an affirmation that is clearly separable from the affirmation that man actualizes himself, and needs to be separately proven (as I think it will be). Furthermore, these writers as a group very definitely have ducked the crucial statement about this inner core, *i.e.*, that it *must* in some degree be inherited or else everything else they say is so much hash.

In other words, we must grapple with "instinct" theory, or, as I prefer to call it, basic need theory, that is to say, with the study of the original, intrinsic, heredity-determined needs, urges, wishes, and, I may say, values of mankind. We can't play both the biology game and the sociology game simultaneously. We can't affirm *both* that culture does everything and anything and that man has an inherent nature. The one is incompatible with the other.

And of all the problems in this area of instinct, the one of which we know least and should know most is that of aggression, hostility, hatred, and destructiveness. The Freudians claim this to be instinctive: most other dynamic psychologists claim it to be not directly instinctive but rather an ever-present reaction to frustration of instinctoid or basic needs. The truth is that we don't really know. Clinical experience hasn't settled the problem because equally good clinicians come to these divergent conclusions. What we need is hard, firm research.

The Problem of Controls and Limits

Another problem confronting the morals-from-within theorists is to account for the easy self-discipline which is customarily found in self-actualizing, authentic, genuine people and which is *not* found in average people.

In these healthy people we find duty and pleasure to be the same thing, as are also work and play, self-interest and altruism, individualism and selflessness. We know they *are* that way, but not how they *get* that way. I have the clear impression that such authentic, fully human persons are the actualization of what *any* human being could be. And yet we are confronted with the sad fact that so few people achieve this goal, perhaps only one in a hundred, or two hundred. We can be hopeful for mankind because in principle anyone *could* become a good and healthy man. But we must also feel sad because so few actually *do* become good men. If we wish to find out why some do and some don't, then the research problem presents itself of studying the life history of self-actualizing men to find out how they get that way.

We know already that the main prerequisite of healthy growth is gratification of the basic needs, especially in early life. (Neurosis is very often a deficiency disease, like avitaminosis.) But we have *also* learned that unbridled indulgence and gratification has its own dangerous consequences, *e.g.*, psychopathic personality, irresponsibility, inability to bear stress, spoiling, immaturity, certain character disorders. Research findings are rare, but there is now available a large store of clinical and educational experience which allows us to make a reasonable guess that the young child needs not only gratification; he needs also to learn the limitations that the physical world puts upon his gratifications, and he has to learn that other human beings seek for gratifications, too, even his mother and father, *i.e.*, they are not only means to his ends. This means control, delay, limits, renunciation, frustration-tolerance, and discipline. Only to the self-disciplined and responsible person can we say, "Do as you will, and it will probably be all right."

Regressive Forces: Psychopathology

And now we must face the problem of what stands in the way of growth; that is to say, the problems of cessation of growth and evasion of growth, of fixation, regression, and defensiveness, in a word, the attractiveness of psychopathology, or, as other people would prefer to say, the problem of evil.

Why do so many people have no real identity, so little power to make their own decisions and choices?

1. These impulses and directional tendencies toward self-fulfillment, though instinctive, are very weak, so that, in contrast with all other animals who have strong instincts, these impulses are very easily drowned out by habit, by wrong cultural attitudes toward them, by traumatic episodes, by erroneous education. Therefore, the problem of choice and of responsibility is far, far more acute in humans than in any other species.

2. There has been a special tendency in Western culture, historically determined, to assume that these instinctoid needs of the human being, his so-called animal nature, are bad or evil. As a consequence, many cultural institutions are set up for the express purpose of controlling, inhibiting, suppressing and repressing this original nature of man.

3. There are two sets of forces pulling at the individual, not just one. In addition to the pressures forward toward health, there are also regressive pressures backward, toward sickness and weakness. We can either move forward toward a "high Nirvana," or backward to a "low Nirvana."

I think the main factual defect in the value theories and ethical theories of the past and the present has been insufficient knowledge of psychopathology and psychotherapy. Throughout history, learned men have set out before mankind the rewards of virtue, the beauties of goodness, the intrinsic desirability of psychological health and self-fulfillment. It's all as plain as ABC, and yet most people perversely refuse to step into the happiness and self-respect that is offered them. Nothing is left to the teachers but irritation, impatience, disillusionment, alternations between scolding, exhortation, and hopelessness. A good many have thrown up their hands altogether and talked about original sin or intrinsic evil and concluded that man could be saved only by extrahuman forces.

Meanwhile there lies available the huge, rich, and illuminating literature of dynamic psychology and psychopathology, a great store of information on man's weaknesses, and fears. We know much about *why* men do wrong things, *why* they bring about their own unhappiness and their self-destruction, *why* they are perverted and sick. And out of this has come the insight that human evil is largely human weakness, forgivable, understandable and also, in principle, curable.

I find it sometimes amusing, sometimes saddening that so many scholars and scientists, so many philosophers and theologians, who talk about human values, of good and evil, proceed in complete disregard of the plain fact that professional psychotherapists every day, as a matter of course, change and improve human nature, help people to become more strong, virtuous, creative, kind, loving, altruistic, serene. These are only some of the consequences of improved self-knowledge and self-acceptance. There are many others as well that can come in greater or lesser degree.

The subject is far too complex even to touch here. All I can do is draw a few conclusions for value theory.

1. Self-knowledge seems to be the major path of self-improvement, though not the only one.

2. Self-knowledge and self-improvement are very difficult for most people. They usually need great courage and long struggle.

3. Though the help of a skilled professional therapist makes this process much easier, it is by no means the only way. Much that has been learned from therapy can be applied to education, to family life, and to the guidance of one's own life.

4. Only by such study of psychopathology and therapy can one learn a proper respect for and appreciation of the forces of fear, of regression, of defense, of safety. Respecting and understanding these forces makes it much more possible to help oneself and others to grow toward health. False optimism sooner or later means disillusionment, anger and hopelessness.

5. To sum up, we can never really understand human weakness without also understanding human health. Otherwise we make the mistake of pathologizing everything. But also we can never fully understand or help human strength without also understanding human weakness. Otherwise we fall into the errors of overoptimistic reliance on rationality alone.

If we wish to help humans to become more fully human, we must realize not only that they try to realize themselves but that they are also reluctant or afraid or unable to do so. Only by fully appreciating this dialectic between sickness and health can we help to tip the balance in favor of health.

FOR FURTHER STUDY

Barron, Frank. *Creativity and Psychological Health*. New York: Van Nostrand, 1964.

Long, Gladys Engel (ed.). *Mental Health*. New York: Wilson, 1958. (The Reference Shelf, Vol. 30, No. 1; Contains a wide range of selections.)

Lucia, Salvatore Pablo. *Alcohol and Civilization*. New York: McGraw-Hill, 1963.

Phenix, Philip H. *Education and the Common Good*. New York, Harper, 1961, Ch. 10.

Schifferes, Justus J. *Essentials of Healthier Living*. New York: Wiley, 1960.

Smoking and Health: Report of the Advisory Committee of the Surgeon General of the Public Health Service. Washington, D. C.: U. S. Government Printing Office, 1964. (Public Health Service Publication, No. 1103.)

Stearn, Allen E., and Stearn, Esther W. *College Hygiene for Total Health*. Philadelphia: Lippincott, 1961.

CHAPTER 14

FREEDOM OF THOUGHT
AND EXPRESSION

On Liberty*

JOHN STUART MILL

John Stuart Mill (1806-1873), an English empiricist,
here presents one of the classic defenses of freedom
of expression. Mill made important contributions to
nineteenth-century liberalism and to the moral philosophy known as utilitarianism.

Chapter 1—Introductory

The subject of this Essay is not the so-called Liberty of the Will, so
unfortunately opposed to the misnamed doctrine of Philosophical
Necessity; but Civil, or Social Liberty: the nature and limits of the
power which can be legitimately exercised by society over the individual. A question seldom stated, and hardly ever discussed, in general
terms, but which profoundly influences the practical controversies of
the age by its latent presence, and is likely soon to make itself recognized as the vital question of the future. It is so far from being new,
that, in a certain sense, it has divided mankind, almost from the re-
motest ages; but in the stage of progress into which the more civilized
portions of the species have now entered, it presents itself under new
conditions and requires a different and more fundamental treatment. . . .

* From *On Liberty* (1859), Parts I-IV with omissions.

The object of this Essay is to assert one very simple principle, as entitled to govern absolutely the dealings of society with the individual in the way of compulsion and control, whether the means used be physical force in the form of legal penalties, or the moral coercion of public opinion. That principle is, that the sole end for which mankind are warranted, individually or collectively, in interfering with the liberty of action of any of their number, is self-protection. That the only purpose for which power can be rightfully exercised over any member of a civilized community, against his will, is to prevent harm to others. His own good, either physical or moral, is not a sufficient warrant. He cannot rightfully be compelled to do or forbear because it will be better for him to do so, because it will make him happier, because, in the opinions of others, to do so would be wise, or even right. These are good reasons for remonstrating with him, or reasoning with him, or persuading him, or entreating him, but not for compelling him, or visiting him with any evil in case he do otherwise. To justify that, the conduct from which it is desired to deter him, must be calculated to produce evil to some one else. The only part of the conduct of any one, for which he is amenable to society, is that which concerns others. In the part which merely concerns himself, his independence is, of right, absolute. Over himself, over his own body and mind, the individual is sovereign. . . .

But there is a sphere of action in which society, as distinguished from the individual, has, if any, only an indirect interest; comprehending all that portion of a person's life and conduct which affects only himself, or if it also affects others, only with their free, voluntary, and undeceived consent and participation. When I say only himself, I mean directly, and in the first instance: for whatever affects himself, may affect others through himself; and the objection which may be grounded on this contingency will receive consideration in the sequel. This, then, is the appropriate region of human liberty. It comprises, first, the inward domain of consciousness; demanding liberty of conscience, in the most comprehensive sense; liberty of thought and feeling; absolute freedom of opinion and sentiment on all subjects, practical or speculative, scientific, moral, or theological. The liberty of expressing and publishing opinions may seem to fall under a different principle, since it belongs to that part of the conduct of an individual which concerns other people; but, being almost of as much importance as the liberty of thought itself, and resting in great part on the same reasons, is practically inseparable from it. Secondly, the principle requires liberty of tastes and pursuits; of framing the plan of our life to suit our own character; of doing as we like, subject to such consequences as may follow: without impediment from our fellow creatures, so long as what we do does not harm them, even though they should think our conduct foolish, perverse, or wrong. Thirdly, from this liberty of each individual, follows the liberty, within the same limits, of combination among individuals; freedom to unite, for any purpose not involving harm to others: the persons combining being supposed to be of full age, and not forced or deceived.

No society in which these liberties are not, on the whole, respected, is free, whatever may be its form of government; and none is completely free in which they do not exist absolute and unqualified. The only freedom which deserves the name, is that of pursuing our own good in our own way, so long as we do not attempt to deprive others of theirs, or impede their efforts to obtain it. Each is the proper guardian of his own health, whether bodily, or mental and spiritual. Mankind are greater gainers by suffering each other to live as seems good to themselves, than by compelling each to live as seems good to the rest.

Though this doctrine is anything but new, and, to some persons, may have the air of a truism, there is no doctrine which stands more directly opposed to the general tendency of existing opinion and practice. Society has expended fully as much effort in the attempt (according to its lights) to compel people to conform to its notions of personal, as of social excellence. . . .

Apart from the peculiar tenets of individual thinkers, there is also in the world at large an increasing inclination to stretch unduly the powers of society over the individual, both by the force of opinion and even by that of legislation: and as the tendency of all the changes taking place in the world is to strengthen society, and diminish the power of the individual, this encroachment is not one of the evils which tend spontaneously to disappear, but, on the contrary, to grow more and more formidable. The disposition of mankind, whether as rulers or as fellow citizens, to impose their own opinions and inclinations as a rule of conduct on others, is so energetically supported by some of the best and by some of the worst feelings incident to human nature, that it is hardly ever kept under restraint by anything but want of power; and as the power is not declining, but growing, unless a strong barrier of moral conviction can be raised against the mischief, we must expect, in the present circumstances of the world, to see it increase.

It will be convenient for the argument, if, instead of at once entering upon the general thesis, we confine ourselves in the first instance to a single branch of it, on which the principle here stated is, if not fully, yet to a certain point, recognized by the current opinions. This one branch is the Liberty of Thought: from which it is impossible to separate the cognate liberty of speaking and of writing. Although these liberties, to some considerable amount, form part of the political morality of all countries which profess religious toleration and free institutions, the grounds, both philosophical and practical, on which they rest, are perhaps not so familiar to the general mind, nor so thoroughly appreciated by many even of the leaders of opinion, as might have been expected. . . .

Chapter II—Of the Liberty of Thought and Discussion

The time, it is to be hoped, is gone by, when any defense would be necessary of the "liberty of the press" as one of the securities against corrupt or tyrannical government. No argument, we may suppose, can now be needed, against permitting a legislature or an executive, not identified in interest with the people, to prescribe opinions to them, and determine what doctrines or what arguments they shall be allowed to hear. This aspect of the question, besides, has been so often and so triumphantly enforced by preceding writers, that it needs not be specially insisted on in this place. Though the law of England, on the subject of the press, is as servile to this day as it was in the time of the Tudors, there is little danger of its being actually put in force against political discussion, except during some temporary panic, when fear of insurrection drives ministers and judges from their propriety; and, speaking generally, it is not, in constitutional countries, to be apprehended, that the government, whether completely responsible to the people or not, will often attempt to control the expression of opinion, except when in doing so it makes itself the organ of the general intolerance of the public. Let us suppose, therefore, that the government is entirely at one with the people, and never thinks of exerting any power of coercion unless in agreement with what it conceives to be their voice. But I deny the right of the people to exercise such coercion, either by themselves or by their government. The power itself is illegitimate. The best government has no more title to it than the worst. It is as noxious, or more noxious, when exerted in accordance with public opinion, than when in opposition to it. If all mankind minus one, were of one opinion, and only one person were of the contrary opinion, mankind would be no more justified in silencing that one person, than he, if he had the power, would be justified in silencing mankind. Were an opinion a personal possession of no value except to the owner; if to be obstructed in the enjoyment of it were simply a private injury, it would make some difference whether the injury was inflicted only on a few persons or on many. But the peculiar evil of silencing the expression of an opinion is, that it is robbing the human race; posterity as well as the existing generation; those who dissent from the opinion, still more than those who hold it. If the opinion is right, they are deprived of the opportunity of exchanging error for truth: if wrong, they lose, what is almost as great a benefit, the clearer perception and livelier impresssion of truth, produced by its collision with error.

It is necessary to consider separately these two hypotheses, each of which has a distinct branch of the argument corresponding to it. We can never be sure that the opinion we are endeavoring to stifle is a false opinion; and if we were sure, stifling it would be an evil still.

First: the opinion which it is attempted to suppress by authority may possibly be true. Those who desire to suppress it, of course deny its truth; but they are not infallible. They have no authority to decide the question for all mankind, and exclude every other person from the means of judging. To refuse a hearing to an opinion, because they are sure that it is false, is to assume that *their* certainty is the same thing as *absolute* certainty. All silencing of discussion is an assumption of infallibility. Its condemnation may be allowed to rest on this common argument, not the worse for being common.

Unfortunately for the good sense of mankind, the fact of their fallibility is far from carrying the weight in their practical judgment, which is always allowed to it in theory; for while every one well knows himself to be fallible, few think it necessary to take any precautions against their own fallibility, or admit the supposition that any opinion, of which they feel very certain, may be one of the examples of the error to which they acknowledge themselves to be liable. . . . And the world, to each individual, means the part of it with which he comes in contact; his party, his sect, his church, his class of society: the man may be called, by comparison, almost liberal and large-minded to whom it means anything so comprehensive as his own country or his own age. Nor is his faith in this collective authority at all shaken by his being aware that other ages, countries, sects, churches, classes, and parties have thought, and even now think, the exact reverse. . . .

Mankind can hardly be too often reminded, that there was once a man named Socrates, between whom and the legal authorities and public opinion of his time, there took place a memorable collision. Born in an age and country abounding in individual greatness, this man has been handed down to us by those who best knew both him and the age, as the most virtuous man in it; while *we* know him as the head and prototype of all subsequent teachers of virtue, the source equally of the lofty inspiration of Plato and the judicious utilitarianism of Aristotle, "*i maëstri di color che sanno*," the two headsprings of ethical as of all other philosophy. This acknowledged master of all the eminent thinkers who have since lived—whose fame, still growing after more than two thousand years, all but outweighs the whole remainder of the names which make his native city illustrious—was put to death by his countrymen, after a judicial conviction, for impiety and immorality. . . .

But, indeed, the dictum that truth always triumphs over persecution, is one of those pleasant falsehoods which men repeat after one another till they pass into commonplaces, but which all experience refutes. History teems with instances of truth put down by persecution. If not suppressed for ever, it may be thrown back for centuries. . . . It is a piece of idle sentimentality that truth, merely as truth, has any inherent power denied to error, of prevailing against the dungeon and the stake. Men are not more zealous for truth than they often are for error, and a sufficient application of legal or even of social penalties will generally succeed in stopping the propagation of either. The real advantage which truth has, consists in this, that when an opinion is true, it may be extinguished once, twice, or many times, but in the course of ages there will generally be found persons to rediscover it, until some one of its reappearances falls on a time when from favorable circumstances it escapes persecution until it has made such head as to withstand all subsequent attempts to suppress it. . . .

Socrates was put to death, but the Socratic philosophy rose like the sun in heaven, and spread its illumination over the whole intellectual firmament. Christians were cast to the lions, but the Christian church grew up a stately and spreading tree, overtopping the older and less vigorous growths, and stifling them by its shade. . . .

Let us now pass to the second division of the argument, and dismissing the supposition that any of the received opinions may be false, let us assume them to be true, and examine into the worth of the manner in which they are likely to be held, when their truth is not freely and openly canvassed. However unwillingly a person who has a strong opinion may admit the possibility that his opinion may be false, he ought to be moved by the consideration that however true it may be, if it is not fully, frequently, and fearlessly discussed, it will be held as a dead dogma, not a living truth.

There is a class of persons (happily not quite so numerous as formerly) who think it enough if a person assents undoubtingly to what they think true, though he has no knowledge whatever of the grounds of the opinion, and could not make a tenable defense of it against the most superficial objections. Such persons, if they can once get their creed taught from authority, naturally think that no good, and some harm, comes of its being allowed to be questioned. Where their influence prevails, they make it nearly impossible for the received opinion to be rejected wisely and considerately, though it may still be rejected rashly and ignorantly; for to shut out discussion entirely is seldom possible, and when it once gets in, beliefs not grounded on conviction are apt to give way before the slightest semblance of an argument. Waiving, however, this possibility—assuming that the true opinion abides in the mind, but abides as a prejudice, a belief independent of, and proof against, argument—this is not the way in which truth ought to be held by a rational being. This is not knowing the truth. Truth, thus held, is but one superstition the more accidentally clinging to the words which enunciate a truth. . . .

He who knows only his own side of the case, knows little of that. His reasons may be good, and no one may have been able to refute them. But if he is equally unable to refute the reasons on the opposite side; if he does not so much as know what they are, he has no ground for preferring either opinion. . . .

It still remains to speak of one of the principal causes which make diversity of opinion advantageous, and will continue to do so until mankind shall have entered a stage of intellectual advancement which at present seems at an incalculable distance. We have hitherto considered only two possibilities: that the received opinion may be false, and some other opinion, consequently true; or that, the received opinion being true, a conflict with the opposite error is essential to a clear apprehension and deep feeling of its truth. But there is a commoner case than either of these; when the conflicting doctrines, instead of being one true and the other false, share the truth between them; and the nonconforming opinion is needed to supply the remainder of the truth, of which the received doctrine embodies only a part. Popular opinions, on subjects not palpable to sense, are often true, but seldom or never the whole truth. . . .

In politics, again, it is almost a commonplace, that a party of order or stability, and a party of progress or reform, are both necessary elements of a healthy state of political life; until the one or the other shall have so enlarged its mental grasp as to be a party equally of order and of progress, knowing and distinguishing what is fit to be preserved from what ought to be swept away. Each of these modes of thinking derives its utility from the deficiencies of the other; but it is in a great measure the opposition of the other that keeps each within the limits of reason and sanity. . . .

We have now recognized the necessity to the mental well-being of mankind (on which all their other well-being depends) of freedom of opinion, and freedom of the expression of opinion, on four distinct grounds; which we will now briefly recapitulate.

First, if any opinion is compelled to silence, that opinion may, for aught we can certainly know, be true. To deny this is to assume our own infallibility.

Secondly, though the silenced opinion be an error, it may, and very commonly does, contain a portion of truth; and since the general or prevailing opinion on any subject is rarely or never the whole truth, it is only by the collision of adverse opinions that the remainder of the truth has any chance of being supplied.

Thirdly, even if the received opinion be not only true, but the whole truth; unless it is suffered to be, and actually is, vigorously and earnestly contested, it will, by most of those who receive it, be held in the manner of a prejudice, with little comprehension or feeling of its rational grounds. And not only this, but, fourthly, the meaning of the doctrine itself will be in danger of being lost, or enfeebled, and deprived of its vital effect on the character and conduct: the dogma becoming a mere formal profession, inefficacious for good, but cumbering the ground, and preventing the growth of any real and heartfelt conviction, from reason or personal experience. . . .

Chapter III—Of Individuality, as One of the Elements of Well-Being

Such being the reasons which make it imperative that human beings should be free to form opinions, and to express their opinions without reserve; and such the baneful consequences to the intellectual, and through that to the moral nature of man, unless this liberty is either conceded, or asserted in spite of prohibition; let us next examine whether the same reasons do not require that men should be free to act upon their opinions—to carry these out in their lives, without hindrance, either physical or moral, from their fellow men, so long as it is at their own risk and peril. This last proviso is of course indispensable.

No one pretends that actions should be as free as opinions. On the contrary, even opinions lose their immunity, when the circumstances in which they are expressed are such as to constitute their expression a positive instigation to some mischievous act. An opinion that corn-dealers are starvers of the poor, or that private property is robbery, ought to be unmolested when simply circulated through the press, but may justly incur punishment when delivered orally to an excited mob assembled before the house of a corn-dealer, or when handed about among the same mob in the form of a placard. Acts, of whatever kind, which, without justifiable cause, do harm to others, may be, and in the more important cases absolutely require to be, controlled by the unfavorable sentiments, and, when needful, by the active interference of mankind. The liberty of the individual must be thus far limited; he must not make himself a nuisance to other people. But if he refrains from molesting others in what concerns them, and merely acts according to his own inclination and judgment in things which concern himself, the same reasons which show that opinion should be free, prove also that he should be allowed, without molestation, to carry his opinions into practice at his own cost. That mankind are not infallible; that their truths, for the most part, are only half-truths; that unity of opinion, unless resulting from the fullest and freest comparison of opposite opinions, is not desirable, and diversity not an evil, but a good, until mankind are much more capable than at present of recognizing all sides of the truth, are principles applicable to men's modes of action, not less than to their opinions. As it is useful that while mankind are imperfect there should be different opinions, so is it that there should be different experiments of living; that free scope should be given to varieties of character, short of injury to others; and that the worth of different modes of life should be proved practically, when any one thinks fit to try them. It is desirable, in short, that in things which do not primarily concern others, individuality should assert itself. Where (not the person's own character) but the traditions or customs of other people are the rule of conduct, there is wanting one of the principal ingredients of human happiness, and quite the chief ingredient of individual and social progress. . . .

Chapter IV—Of the Limits to the Authority of Society Over the Individual

What, then, is the rightful limit to the sovereignty of the individual over himself? Where does the authority of society begin? How much of human life should be assigned to individuality, and how much to society?

Each will receive its proper share, if each has that which more particularly concerns it. To individuality should belong the part of life in which it is chiefly the individual that is interested; to society, the part which chiefly interests society.

Though society is not founded on a contract, and though no good purpose is answered by inventing a contract in order to deduce social obligations from it, every one who receives the protection of society owes a return for the benefit, and the fact of living in society renders it indispensable that each should be bound to observe a certain line of conduct towards the rest. This conduct consists, first, in not injuring the interests of one another; or rather certain interests, which, either by express legal provision or by tacit understanding, ought to be considered as rights; and secondly, in each person's bearing his share (to be fixed on some equitable principle) of the labors and sacrifices incurred for defending the society or its members from injury and molestation. These conditions society is justified in enforcing at all costs to those who endeavor to withhold fulfilment. Nor is this all that society may do. The acts of an individual may be hurtful to others, or wanting in due consideration for their welfare, without going the length of violating any of their constituted rights. The offender may then be justly punished by opinion, though not by law. As soon as any part of a person's conduct affects prejudicially the interests of others, society has jurisdiction over it, and the question whether the general welfare will or will not be promoted by interfering with it, becomes open to discussion. But there is no room for entertaining any such question when a person's conduct affects the interests of no persons besides himself, or needs not affect them unless they like (all the persons concerned being of full age, and the ordinary amount of understanding). In all such cases there should be perfect freedom, legal and social, to do the action and stand the consequences.

It would be a great misunderstanding of this doctrine to suppose that it is one of selfish indifference, which pretends that human beings have no business with each other's conduct in life, and that they should not concern themselves about the well-doing or well-being of one another, unless their own interest is involved. Instead of any diminution, there is need of a great increase of disinterested exertion to promote the good of others. But disinterested benevolence can find other instruments to persuade people to their good, than whips and scourges, either of the literal or the metaphorical sort. I am the last person to undervalue the self-regarding virtues; they are only second in importance, if even second, to the social. It is equally the business of education to cultivate both. But even education works by conviction and persuasion as well as by compulsion, and it is by the former only that, when the period of education is past, the self-regarding virtues should be inculcated. Human beings owe to each other help to distinguish the better from the worse, and encouragement to choose the former and avoid the latter. They should be for ever stimulating each other to increased exercise of their higher faculties, and increased direction of their feelings and aims towards wise instead of foolish, elevating instead of degrading, objects and contemplations. . . .

*The Freedom to Think**

ZECHARIAH CHAFEE, JR.

Zechariah Chafee, Jr. (1885-1957) was from 1916 to 1956 Professor of Law at Harvard University and an authority on civil liberties and related issues. He wrote many articles and books including *Freedom of Speech and Press*, 1955.

If a man does not keep pace with his companions, perhaps it is because he hears a different drummer. Let him step to the music which he hears, however measured or far away.—THOREAU, *Walden*

If the universities had not recently brought the social sciences into the curriculum, they would have saved themselves a lot of trouble. Their freedom would have been attacked very little in the Twentieth Century. The struggle between the natural sciences and religion ended

* From *The Blessings of Liberty* by Zechariah Chafee, Jr. Copyright 1956 by Zechariah Chafee, Jr. Published by J. B. Lippincott Company.

in an armistice decades ago. Geology no longer battles against Genesis, and evolution can be taught with impunity outside Tennessee and Mississippi. New theories and discoveries in physics, chemistry, and biology are enthusiastically heralded. They may enable us to save sick men by the hundreds or slaughter well men by the hundreds of thousands. They may bring about inventions which will add to our comfort and help the advertising business. As for the humanities, innovation has always been welcome since Homer said, "Men ever love the song that rings newest in the ear." If universities had only stuck to the classics, professors of Latin and Greek might have imparted radicalism to their students by insisting that the Conspiracy of Catiline was a frame-up by Cicero just as the Reichstag Fire was a frame-up by Hitler, or injected Fascist ideas into lectures on the *Republic* of Plato. Most people would not have known what they were talking about and nobody would have cared.

No such obscurity awaits the professor who indulges in heterodox views about economics, government, international affairs, or law. He occupies the front page of newspapers beside bank robbers. Columnists bracket him with spies. The lightning he keeps attracting does not spare the university where he works. If it protects itself from the storm by sending him away, it will often lose the teaching and research of a distinguished scholar, and it will surely demoralize his colleagues and lessen its future power to recruit a strong faculty. Yet if the university dares to retain the unpopular professor, it, too, will become a favorite target for professional patriots. The sources of indispensable funds may perhaps dry up, and many parents of desirable undergraduates, present or potential, will be honestly disturbed. One of the great calamities of these angry attacks on disliked ideas in universities is that they distract the heads of an institution from their vital task of facilitating thought and ask them to stifle thought.

People are inclined to regard the multiplication table as characteristic of all education—something which is just so and not otherwise, which once learned stays with you through life. When a professor expresses to his class ideas about politics or economics with which the critics disagree, they think it just as bad as telling boys and girls that seven times nine is sixty-one. Of course there is a core of indubitable knowledge in education, but most of the teacher's task consists in imparting methods for understanding what is still unknown and for dealing with it wisely. The best kind of education was what Mark Twain got as an apprentice pilot on the Mississippi. After he had learned all the shoals and points in the river from St. Louis to New Orleans, he found that many of them had changed. He had to learn them all over again; and better yet, he had to know how to be perpetually acquiring information through which he could predict those changes. . . .

In the United States today institutions are not frozen, nor are they so anywhere in the free world from which we must seek allies. As the newly independent nations of Asia plan their governments, we ought not to be shocked if they decide to govern themselves in ways which are somewhat unfamiliar to us. The numerous problems the American people face at home or in their relations with other countries call for inventiveness and wisdom on the part of the few who propose solutions and of the many who decide whether to accept or modify or reject them. Devotion to tradition is useless here. The inevitability of change requires our unyielding maintenance of the principle of open discussion, not only for ideas and persons we like but also for those we detest.

This brings me to what I want to say most. The universities of the United States are taking an indispensable share in the work of continuously testing, readjusting, and improving the machinery of human relations, and nobody else can do what they do. Of course, a great deal of this work will always be carried on by the active men in the field such as politicians, journalists, lawyers, judges, and businessmen. They have an experience, a sense of what is possible and other qualities of mind which are rare among professors. Still, no matter how shrewd the practical men are, they are absorbed in a crowded succession of immediate tasks; and this leaves them far less time than professors have for taking long views. Few social problems are wholly novel. One may seem so to the man in the field, but the professor is likely to have encountered something resembling it during his researches. . . .

What I am saying about the indispensable task of a university applies to all universities in the United States, public or endowed, and particularly to the former. As taxes rise, endowed universities lose and state universities gain. The fact that these public universities are ultimately controlled by legislatures ought to be irrelevant to their performance of the indispensable task of supplying long views about the problems of society. The government pays judges, but it does not tell them how to decide. An independent state university is as essential to the community as an independent judiciary. Legislatures make it possible for scholars to think and teach. There the political part in education should end. When he who pays the piper insists on calling the tune, he is not likely to get much good music.

For many decades the American universities have been performing their indispensable task. All of a sudden they are gravely hampered in carrying it out by current fears of radicalism. There is no class of people more injured by repression than teachers. If you confine the teaching in his thinking, what do you leave him? That is his job, to think. Universities should not be transformed, as in Nazi Germany, into loud-speakers for the men who wield political power. If they are deprived of freedom of thought and speech, there is no other place to which citizens can confidently turn for long views about public issues. Here and there some courageous writer or speaker may still make himself known, but such men are no substitute for the present systematic creation and communication of ideas which take place in our universities.

Ye are the salt of the earth: but if the salt have lost his savour, where withal shall it be salted?

Without attempting any exhaustive presentation of current efforts to block the indispensable task of universities, I want to speak of three kinds of attacks on professors who express unwelcome views about the social sciences. Right away let me make it plain that I am not writing about professors who are really Communists. Only a handful of such men have been discovered among university teachers during all the investigations by Congress and state legislatures. Many university presidents have announced that they will not hire or keep a Communist on their faculties. The Federal Bureau of Investigation is well informed about members of the Communist Party. There is plenty of federal legislation to take care of dangerous revolutionaries on or off the campus.

What began years ago as an onslaught on a few Communist scholars has been long since transformed into an onslaught on a great many scholars who are not Communists, but who are suspected of holding views which happen to be unpopular with an influential number of citizens.

Let me give some concrete illustrations. The University of Colorado was urged to dismiss an economist for favoring a Missouri Valley Authority like the TVA. A prominent alumnus of Harvard Law School refused to give any money for its new dormitories unless the leading American astronomer was turned out of Harvard Observatory for presiding over a meeting at the Waldorf of scientists and other thinkers from all over the world, including (with our government's definite sanction) some from the Soviet Union. No evidence was offered that the astronomer was a Communist. The regents of the University of California expressly said that none of the numerous distinguished professors they discharged were Communists. In California, too, a professor's textbook on American history was denounced because he wrote that the Supreme Court reacted to the wishes and thinking of the people when it eventually held New Deal legislation to be constitutional. This, said the critic, was subtly hidden Communist propaganda; in fact the Court decides cases free of such pressures. . . .

The second attack on universities is the rapidly increasing practice of singling out teachers in public and endowed institutions for test oaths and compulsory declarations of loyalty. Thus to regard all professors as potential transgressors is an insult to law-abiding and hard-working men and women. . . .

If we are going to revive the abomination of exculpatory oaths, why stop at one profession and one kind of objectionable behavior? Why not extend the device to other occupations and other offenses? Let us require every Congressman to swear that there were no illegal practices at his election and that he has never accepted a bribe or taken a kickback out of the salary of his secretary. Let us require every lawyer to swear that he has never solicited clients by ambulance-chasing, every doctor that he has never performed an abortion, and every businessman that he has never violated the antitrust laws. Imagine the indignation which these proposals would raise from men who see no harm in teachers' oath laws. Yet these offenses are far more frequent in the respective occupations than disloyalty among teachers, and they are at least as injurious to society. . . .

Lastly, I want to speak of the attack on scholars at the frontiers of the United States. Our government, seven years ago, signed the Universal Declaration of Human Rights, which proclaims "freedom . . . to seek, receive, and impart information and ideas . . . regardless of frontiers." This freedom embodies the experience of centuries. Many notable contributions to the art and literature of the world have been made by men who wrote or published in countries not their own—Dante, Locke, Montesquieu, Voltaire, Rousseau, Heine, and Mazzini. Foreign scholars have enriched thought at universities ever since Erasmus sojourned at Cambridge. Of late years, they have gathered at many international conferences with great benefit to intellectual and practical progress.

The values just described will be hard to obtain if our government continues its present inhospitality to traveling thinkers on the ground of their real or supposed political opinions. Men with original ideas to give the world do not fall into orthodox patterns. If they did, they would probably be unable to tell us anything new. The writer who complies strictly with established views is usually not worth listening to.

We have come a long, long way from Thomas Jefferson, whose name is so frequently invoked by the politicians who have brought about the present laws of the United States. He invited professors from abroad to the University of Virginia, which (he wrote) "will be based on the illimitable freedom of the human mind. For here we are not afraid to follow truth wherever it may lead, nor to tolerate error so long as reason is left free to combat it." Our government is repudiating the spirit of Jefferson just at the time when it is more important than ever before that the free countries of the world should pool their intellectual resources for the sake of preserving their freedom and increasing human welfare. . . .

Anybody who regards this simple procedure as perilously hospitable to "subversive" foreigners ought to remember that Great Britain, France, Italy, and most other countries of free Europe require no visas whatever for a visiting American. He just needs a passport to get in and stay in, so long as he behaves himself. Yet those countries are three thousand miles nearer to the Soviet Union and its satellites than we are. If they are willing to take a chance on our citizens, why are we afraid to take a much smaller chance on theirs?

But that is not the way things are now. Although the situation has become somewhat better than in 1952 and continues to improve, it is still a good deal worse than it ought to be. For example, a conference on High Energy Nuclear Physics was held in Rochester, New York, on January 31, 1955, with the Atomic Energy Commission and the Office of Naval Research among its sponsors. Winners of the Nobel Prize and several other distinguished scientists, whose discoveries were the basis of a large portion of the discussions, were invited but did not come because of visa difficulties. . . .

The real danger to our colleges and universities is not from radical teachers—or conservative teachers—but from uninspiring teachers, men who can't get over the footlights, dispensers of branded canned goods. The greatest need is for teachers who will produce eagerness of spirit among young men and women and the ability to deal in after life with what is around the corner. Such a spirit is best nurtured by a teacher who can have untroubled periods of time when "the wind bloweth where it listeth" and, in the words of Hobbes: "Thoughts run [seeking] as a spaniel ranges in the field, till he finds a scent." Helmholtz, the great scientist, declared on his seventieth birthday: "Happy ideas have never come to me at my working table. They come particularly rapidly during the slow ascent of wooded hills on a sunny day." . . .

To presidents, trustees, regents, alumni, I say, "This is your fight."

Despite proper anxieties about future gifts and student enrollments, I believe a university which proclaims its devotion to freedom and lives up to it will attract farsighted givers and young men and women who are worth teaching. It is easy to underestimate the admiration which American citizens feel toward courage.

The issue is whether the unusual man shall be rigidly controlled by the usual men. . . .

The time has come for the universities of the United States to stop retreating and carry the war into Africa. We ought to educate more than our students. "We must educate our masters"—the legislators and the citizens who in the end make educational institutions possible. We need to persuade them to minimize the dangers of heterodoxy and be ready, as Jefferson was, to take a calculated risk. We need to convince them of what they have forgotten—the importance of intellectual freedom, if we are to have the kind of country most loyal Americans desire. We need to make our fellow-citizens realize that freedom is not safety, but opportunity.

FOR FURTHER STUDY

Barth, Alan. *The Price of Liberty.* New York: Viking, 1961.

Chafee, Zechariah, Jr. *The Blessings of Liberty.* Philadelphia: Lippincott, 1956, Ch. 3, "Forty Years with Freedom of Speech and of the Press."

Commager, Henry Steele. "The Pragmatic Necessity of Freedom," in *Civil Liberties Under Attack,* ed. Clair Wilcox. Philadelphia: U. of Pennsylvania Press, 1951.

Daniels, Walter M. (ed.). *The Censorship of Books.* New York: Wilson, 1954 (The Reference Shelf, Vol. 26, No. 5).

Douglas, William O. *Freedom of the Mind.* Chicago: American Library Association in cooperation with the Public Affairs Committee, 1962.

Gordon, Edward R. *et al. The Students' Right to Read.* Champaign: National Council of Teachers of English, 1962. (Pamphlet)

Muller, Herbert J. *Issues of Freedom.* New York: Harper, 1960, Chs. 1-5.

CHAPTER 15

TRUTHFULNESS
AND OTHER VIRTUES

*American Morality**

WILLIAM PETERS

> William Peters interviews eight outstanding men
> and women on the subject of American morality.
> Those interviewed are Fairfax Cone, Margaret Mead,
> Agnes E. Meyer, Margaret Chase Smith, Learned
> Hand, Phyllis McGinley, Reinhold Niebuhr, and
> Edward R. Murrow.

Last October, after more than two years of investigation, a New
York grand jury returned indictments for perjury against a group of
television quiz contestants. By that time, of course, all America knew
that some of its favorite quiz shows had been "rigged." Meanwhile, the
word "payola" had found a home in the American vernacular after
revelation of payoffs to disc jockeys by record producers. Even as the
quiz contestants were being charged, New York authorities were investigating housing violations by slum landlords, rigged bids by rock
salt suppliers, illegal outside jobs held by city policemen and suspected
bribery of police by tow-truck operators. In Chicago, meanwhile, a
police cleanup to end direct partnerships with criminals was under
way. At about the same time, a retiring Navy admiral was caught

smuggling untaxed liquor into California from Guam in a case labeled "household effects."

In the academic world a 1958 study reported that 75 per cent of the college seniors questioned admitted cheating and that only 13 per cent felt a cheating student was basically dishonest. This knowledge may have prepared some Americans for the more recent exposé of graduate theses ghostwritten for money by professional writers.

When the president of the Chrysler Corporation resigned in 1960 after his profitable connections with suppliers were revealed, the *Wall Street Journal* quoted Chrysler dealers on their lack of concern. "Customers look at this conflict-of-interest mess like payola; they don't like it but they realize they can live with it," said one. "In this business," said another, "it's good to have people talking about you, even if it isn't good talk."

But businessmen presumably felt different about a report that white-collar employees were stealing from their employers at least $1 billion a year, a figure more than double the annual national loss from professional thieves and burglars. A profile of the typical white-collar thief drawn by the U.S. Fidelity and Guaranty Company should have been even more disturbing: "He's 35 years old, has one or two children. He lives in a respectable neighborhood, is probably buying his own home. He drives a low- or medium-priced car, and has been employed by the same firm for three years. He has been stealing for eight months."

When we add to this picture recent evidence of a growth in evasion of income taxes, misuse of business expense accounts and fraudulent insurance claims, the recent public concern over the state of American morality becomes understandable. Many critics have concluded that we are less moral and more dishonest than any previous generation. The more cautious have insisted that we are only more tolerant of personal dishonesty than ever before.

It is impossible to prove either charge, though an increased acceptance of dishonesty would seem to be indicated by the general excusing of the quiz-show frauds as involving "only entertainment," by the Navy admiral's statement that "everybody does it," students' explanations that "when you're graded on a curve, you have to cheat to keep the cheaters from pushing your grades down," and the results of a recent survey in which less than ten per cent of the Americans interviewed felt that honesty was a prime requisite for success.

If there is widespread dishonesty and growing acceptance of it in American life, the questions remain: Why? What does it mean? What are the causes? What should we be doing about it?

This article is the result of an inquiry into these and related questions. Eight outstanding Americans whose professions range over business, politics, religion, the law, the social sciences, the arts, the press, radio and television were interviewed at length. Each interview probed the causes, cures and implications of personal dishonesty and attempted to reach at least tentative conclusions about the nature of the problem.

Most of those interviewed felt that there was more personal dishonesty and more tolerance of it than in previous American generations. Several dated the increase from the years following World War I and specifically blamed Prohibition. Fairfax Cone, chairman of the executive committee of Foote, Cone and Belding, a leading advertising agency, felt that a whole new national attitude toward crime, criminals and the law had sprung up during the 1920s.

"Suddenly," he said, "the people you looked up to as honest—bankers, brokers, doctors and all sorts of business people—not only flouted the law but became part of the machinery of lawlessness. When I first bought whiskey from a bootlegger it would never have occurred to me to rob a bank; yet I knew I was dealing with a criminal and playing into the hands of crooked police, judges, lawyers and politicians. For the first time in America, a vast segment of the people entered into a conspiracy without even stopping to think about the possible consequences.

"By the time Prohibition ended in 1933, we had become accustomed to the idea that certain people we knew were operating illegally and were mixed up in a world in which hijacking, bribery, shooting and killing were almost commonplace.

"After repeal many bootleggers turned to new rackets: gambling, prostitution, protection. And many previously legitimate businesses took on the coloration of rackets. Buying an automobile, and particularly a used car, for example, became an unequal contest between purchaser and dealer—a contest everyone knew was loaded. People today expect to be cheated by easy-credit salesmen for cars, retail furniture, household alterations, heating equipment, real estate and a long list of other high-cost, long-term purchases."

This feeling that some of today's personal dishonesty and our acceptance of it began with Prohibition is shared by Dr. Margaret Mead, anthropologist for the American Museum of Natural History and author of many well-known books. "We have to remember that a whole generation grew up," she says, "watching their parents break the law for their own personal pleasure. That generation of parents and children makes up a large portion of adult Americans today.

"It is peculiarly American to believe that if a system or law appears to be inequitable at any point, we are absolved from loyalty to it. Ours being a predominantly Protestant population, the typically Protestant belief that one should not obey an unjust law is significant too. These concepts have an important place in our national history. The Boston Tea Party demonstrated our refusal to pay what we regarded as an unfair tax. The sit-ins of Negro students in the South are examples of this determination to place a higher value on what is thought to be right than on custom, practice or law.

"Sometimes, of course, the application of this concept can be harmful, as in the case of Prohibition, though there is certainly a difference between defying a bad law and taking the consequences on the one hand and simply cheating on the other.

"Basically, people tend to cheat against things they feel are cheating them. There was little cheating under our wartime sugar-rationing program, for example. Everyone got precisely the same amount and it was felt to be fair. But gasoline rationing attempted to differentiate among people who used cars for different purposes. Many people felt cheated, and a mammoth black market resulted."

The idea that some people tend to cheat when they feel cheated was expressed frequently during the interviews. And when recent examples of dishonesty were examined, it became evident that in nearly every case the cheating was against either a large, impersonal institution or a faceless, anonymous segment of the public. The institutions were many and varied: government, insurance companies, schools, corporations, large department and chain stores.

The segments of the public being cheated were equally impersonal: consumers, slum dwellers, stockholders, television audiences.

Many of the people interviewed felt that honesty between individuals was as strong as ever, that the man who might brag about "making money on the expense account," for example, would be likely to hand back to a neighborhood storekeeper an extra dollar in change. The difference, of course, is that the storekeeper is seen as an individual, familiar and friendly, while the company from which the expense money is taken represents an impersonal institution. An individual obviously can be hurt by dishonesty, but it is an easy—though false—assumption that dishonesty toward an institution hurts no one.

Beyond this, there was agreement that the very institutions that are singled out as fair game for cheating are felt by many Americans to be cheating them in one way or another. Almost everyone pointed to inequities in the income-tax law, and several mentioned the social-security regulation that penalizes people for working after they are 65. One felt that the rise in fraudulent insurance claims was due, at least in part, to a general feeling that insurance companies treat their own customers like suspected cheats. Several felt that exaggerated advertising claims, not to mention outright fraudulent advertising, had led to a feeling that all businesses that advertise are fair marks for cheating right back.

If some of the roots of this problem appear to go back to the Prohibition period, others seem to lie in the experiences of World War II. Writing in 1944 of the uprooting of families, the shattering of home life and other results of the American war effort, Mrs. Agnes E. Meyer, author, journalist and widow of Eugene Meyer, former publisher of the *Washington Post and Times-Herald*, predicted: "It will take the nation three generations to get over the social effects of this chaos."

"Our war effort was totally uncoordinated, terribly uncontrolled," Mrs. Meyer says today in discussing the question of American morality, "and it wasn't just the result of our being unprepared. War intensified our problems; it didn't create them.

"We were a people at drift before the war, and the war effort showed up the gap between our preachments and our practices. For all our talk about love of children, for example, there was a relentless cruelty toward children. With women plunging into war industries, whether from patriotism, a desire to escape the home or the lure of money, children all over America were abandoned to the streets. The children most affected were not the infants; even the worst mother made some provision for her baby's care. But few people realize even today the terrible lack of discipline, of love or care, to which a whole generation of older children was subjected. Few understand that the rise of juvenile delinquency after the war began during the war. Nor was this cruelty solely the fault of parents; the government, the communities and the war industries that urged women to leave the home and men to work under abnormal conditions simply ignored in far too many cases the question of what would happen to the children.

"Truancy rose alarmingly. Child labor laws were flouted as adult workers shifted to war work and juveniles were hired to replace them. Older children, pulled by the lure of easy money and pushed by disintegrating families, left home, frequently for good. Among girls, some of them only eleven or twelve years old, sex delinquency became a major problem.

"Parental behavior was a major cause. Marital upsets and promiscuity among men and women war workers increased. Many women who earned more money than their husbands told them off or invited them to leave. Too often neither parent really wanted the children.

"These wartime conditions had a destructive influence on today's adults, and to a great extent they were unnecessary. A few communities avoided many of them. They were, on the whole, well-organized communities, both economically and socially, with strong school systems. Basically they were communities whose leadership felt a moral commitment to bridge the gap between American ideals and American practices."

United States Senator Margaret Chase Smith, of Maine, was another who pointed to the nation's wartime experience. "Children were certainly affected by the wartime pressures," she said, "and to whatever extent we are raising children today in an atmosphere of tolerance for personal dishonesty we are threatening the national morality in the future, when these children will be adults. But the most important danger to children, I think, is a parental attitude of living only for today which may be passed on to them.

"This is the attitude that far too many parents have taken ever since 1940 and 1941, when they used it to excuse all kinds of behavior in the climate of individual insecurity brought on by the war. We have today a generation between their late teens and early thirties that was brought up under this psychology, a psychology that encourages a mental and moral flabbiness that is the greatest threat to national security and the future of our country.

"Whether we are more or less moral than ever before, I cannot say. There is always a question when we examine specific cases of whether they are the exceptions or the rule. We know from experience that scandals are always well publicized while good works often pass unnoticed.

"Personally, I see no excuse for any kind of lie. Even in the social area there's no place for 'white' lies. I'm often asked, for example, to speak at various affairs, and if there is a doubt that I can appear, I find it much more satisfactory to refuse at the outset than accept and possibly have to cancel the appointment later. I don't like to give evasive answers or brush off difficult questions; I'd far rather refuse any answer.

"There have always been those who have pointed to certain aspects of political life as dishonest, but I think this is mostly a lack of understanding. The question of the honesty of ghostwritten speeches, for instance, becomes more clear as we examine it. I see nothing dishonest in it if the speech represents the speaker's own convictions. Who would expect a President of the United States to write every word of his budget messages?

"Political compromise is another disputed point. What people should remember is that the very art of legislation is compromise, that no law can be one hundred per cent right for one hundred per cent of the people. Nor can any representative possibly hold precisely the same ideas as all of his constituents. If he is to represent them well, he must often compromise his views. There is nothing dishonest in honest compromise."

Alone among all those interviewed, Judge Learned Hand, of New York's Federal Court of Appeals, stressed what he sees as a great increase in certain kinds of morality. "Looking back over great stretches of time," he says, "I think the outlook for morality is very hopeful. We no longer have the barbarities of public execution, the widespread political graft or the wholesale voting frauds we once had. Most Americans have a far more tender conscience toward those in need and are much more sensitive to the problems of the underdog than previously. As far as the law and the courts are concerned, I think the standards of judicial conduct are a good deal better. And I would guess that honesty between individuals has probably improved too.

"But as we have come to expect the community and the government to do more for us, we seem also to have lost much of our former sense of personal responsibility. Social security, old-age pensions, retirement programs and unemployment compensation have had the effect of putting into the law and contract our feelings that we are our brothers' keepers, that we are all responsible for human welfare in general. This, I believe, is good. But as we have set up institutions to carry out our ethical beliefs in these areas, as we have developed a group morality and begun to put it into practice, we seem to have lost the sense of need to exert ourselves individually."

There were others who made this distinction between private and social morality. Phyllis McGinley, well known for her light verse and serious observations and author of the recent book *Times Three*, carried the point further. "What is lacking," she said, "is a sense of personal honor. I think there is just as much honesty between individuals as there ever was, and I feel sure that the corporate conscience of the world is much stronger than ever. But the kind of personal honor that stands between an individual and a private immoral decision seems to have declined. Honor is no longer a fashionable virtue; it has been replaced by tolerance.

"Today, to be a bigot or to hold racial or religious prejudices is the popular evil, and certainly progress in this direction was—and still is—needed. But being tolerant is a comparatively easy virtue; it doesn't require much in the way of action. Furthermore, it has the effect of making us feel virtuous, and a self-satisfied people is hardly a people that comes to real grips with the harder questions of private morality. I think that our increased social morality has given us this feeling of self-satisfaction.

"There is far too little sense of honor instilled in children today; they have no school spirit, no class spirit, few of the minor patriotisms of other generations. Instead of reading stories with a moral point, school children today read about trips to the fire department.

"Boys no longer want to grow up to be heroes; they want to be wealthy and retire early. The one moral lesson in schoolbooks today is tolerance, the idea that we are all brothers. If this works—and it seems to—why don't we again stress the other virtues?

"As we have lost our sense of personal honor we also have lost our feelings of personal responsibility for our actions. The muscles of character, like any others, are weakened by disuse, and the institution that suffers most is marriage and the home. Once a person abdicates responsibility, he decides that what is comfortable for him is best. Marriage is not always comfortable, and when people stop working at it, it fails. A high divorce rate and the mixed-up family life that results from divorce cannot help but contribute to national immorality.

"It is popular now to believe that if you are not hurting someone else, there is nothing wrong with your actions. In such a climate personal morality has no importance, because the feeling of personal responsibility to God is gone. These problems are difficult to solve without religion; but since religion seems to have relaxed its hold on many people, we obviously need something else—a national emergency, well-defined national goals, some sense of urgency—to force us to face up to our need for a sense of personal morality and responsibility."

Dr. Reinhold Niebuhr, professor of Applied Christianity at Union Theological Seminary, touched on this same theme. "Religion is much more popular but much less meaningful in America today," he said. "There has been a gradual loss of spirit in the religious community, and the church has become more a social than a religious institution in recent

years. One of the effects of this has been that religion has become senti-
mentalized and easy.

"The idea of a personal responsibility to God is a strong element in
the Puritan philosophy, and from it came a sort of secular Calvinism,
establishing the qualities of diligence, frugality and honesty as major
middle-class virtues. Benjamin Franklin was a spokesman of this point of
view, and on this foundation we established a society based largely on
the assumption of honesty in others. Our whole intricate system of
credit, of verbal and written contracts, depends on the belief that most
people are honest most of the time.

"But as the Protestant ethic has lost its power, as we have lost much of
this sense of a personal responsibility to God and its secular counterpart,
the society we erected on these beliefs is threatened. You can't have
credit without trust no matter what kind of enforcement there is. And
much of our economy is based now on credit."

What are the signs that these threats to our society are already present? Edward R. Murrow, who as a radio and television commentator
for C.B.S. for years has been a close observer of the American and international scene, sees one of these signs in what he calls "an American
allergy to unpleasant information."

"We can see this in the public's resistance to reporting—and wanting
to know—all the news. Basically, of course, this is dishonesty—an attempt to filter out unpleasant or alarming truths. I think it stems mainly
from fear: fear of controversy; fear of unpopularity; fear of upsetting
the boss, the sponsor, the advertiser, the American public or ourselves.
The temptation is to do a little less than the whole job, to censor ourselves, and the result is that communications in general are more bland
and comforting than they should be. The significant, tough reporting
today is being done in magazines and books, where the audience that
wants to know the truth is self-selecting. Radio, television, motion
pictures, newspapers and even political speeches—all media aimed at
the largest possible audience—have tended to temper the hard facts in
order not to disturb us.

"And this, I think, is part of a larger problem: our current preoccupation with security. There is nothing wrong with trying to make ourselves more secure, whether as a nation against attack or as individuals
against old age. But when a desire for complete security becomes a
major goal, it is little more than a desire to return to the warmth and
comfort of a protected childhood. Because there is no complete security; and in the last analysis our only real security, personal or national,

will lie in our ability to deal with the real world around us. We're not likely to do that if we protect ourselves from it by pretending its unpleasant aspects don't exist."

There were others who felt that this preoccupation with security as an end in itself was a contributing factor to the current moral scene. "Social Security is fine," Mrs. Meyer said, "but it's not enough by itself. A monthly check won't make old age satisfactory. What we need is the security of an orderly society in which people can grow and develop their potentialities even in old age. World War II showed clearly that the basis for such a society was shaky and that an uncontrolled drive for money and 'success' could all but topple it. Our society was sick and we didn't know it; compassion had suffered because of this highly competitive drive for economic status. Democracy depends on good human relations, and a dog-eat-dog race for money destroys good human relations.

"One of the dangers in this worship of money and status is that when it becomes a goal in itself, nothing is more devastating to the individual than to reach his goal and find the hoped-for happiness somewhere else. I talked with war workers who said, in effect, 'We thought if we just had money, all our problems would be solved. Now we have it and we're just as unhappy.' What happened was that the means of getting the money destroyed the setting in which it might provide greater enjoyment; it destroyed family relationships, took the wife and mother out of the home, left the children neglected and undisciplined and crowded the home with paying boarders.

"The pressures are still here, and we face the same kind of disaster unless we realize that the time is long past to begin to make conscious choices. If our women go to work, what about the children? We have to decide what kind of society we want to build. We need increased production, but we must control the society in which we work for it so that we don't make too dangerous a sacrifice to get it."

The sources of this somewhat conflicting drive for security on the one hand and wealth and status on the other lie, Mrs. Meyer believes, in a pervasive sense of insecurity that afflicts a great many Americans. "This insecurity has many roots," she says. "What is missing is a feeling of warmth and belonging. The churches have failed to supply it; the family, which used to be its primary source, has been undermined; and the movement of a whole people to urban industrial and business centers has placed an already insecure people in the most impersonal community setting imaginable."

Edward R. Murrow felt too that the increased impersonality of American life has a good deal to do with present-day morality. "As the nation, our government, business, labor and most of our institutions have become bigger, each of us has been more and more cut off from the kind of individual relationships that used to pervade most areas of our lives," he said. "Employer-employee relationships are highly impersonal; a man can spend his whole life working for a company and never exchange a word with his boss. Often, he has no boss in the old sense but rather a board of directors and thousands of stockholders.

"Even our attitude toward debt has changed under the impact of this new impersonality. Where we used to borrow from relatives or friends or from the banker whom we at least knew slightly, we borrow now from a credit institution. The man who has mortgaged his future for the next fifteen years to various faceless credit organizations has a different attitude toward meeting his debts with honor on a day-to-day basis.

"More important, a feeling of impersonality leaves us feeling far more helpless than ever before. We have lost a good deal of the sense that we as individuals can really do anything effective about the problems that threaten us. We've lost the feeling that national decisions can be influenced by individuals. The helpless feeling of the World War II draftee that he had suddenly been reduced to a cipher, a set of holes punched in an IBM card, that he could be sent anywhere, trained as anything, without regard to his education, experience or preference, by the simple mechanical shuffling of cards in a machine, has become a peacetime nightmare for millions of Americans.

One probable result is that we tend to lash out against the system that has reduced us to this kind of impotence. The knowledge that 'the Bomb' hangs impersonally over all of us may have led to a permanent wartime philosophy of 'let's take what we can get.'

"At the same time, a prosperity that has included more Americans than ever before may well have left many of us feeling cheated because it simply hasn't brought the expected satisfactions. I wonder if much of the cheating that goes on today doesn't reflect the average individual's feeling that he has too little room to maneuver, too few areas in which he can make a personal choice. This may be his way of nibbling away at a system that has denied him a feeling of personal dignity and importance.

"And I have a hunch too that a lot of people who spend hours every week watching Westerns on television are demonstrating a strong, nostalgic longing for the kind of independence that the Western hero displays—a reliance solely on himself and his six-guns. I have a feeling that they see in these heroes the independence of action and ability to change situations that they themselves want so desperately in their new, impersonal worlds."

Mr. Murrow feels strongly that individuals are not nearly as helpless to change the course of events as they may sometimes feel. Dr. Mead makes precisely the same point. "Adults who are active in civic, political and social affairs in their communities know that the individual can have great impact on our institutions and there are great satisfactions to be derived from the effort," she says. "It is vital that we teach our children this lesson as they grow up.

"Instead, there are areas in which we actually teach them that they are powerless. The student governments in most of our schools are shams—pretenses at giving students power when they really have none and know it. The best way to teach children that their acts do matter is to set up situations—like real self-government—in which they can act for themselves and see the results.

"An important factor in our current feeling of helplessness is our postwar habit of bundling together as subversive not merely outright treason and political disloyalty but also neurotic behavior and personal and sexual deviations. This new association we owe to the American ex-Communists who have received so much attention in the postwar years. As Communists they had blamed neuroses and deviations on capitalism; as ex-Communists, they have tended to associate them with their new enemy, Communism; and many Americans have uncritically accepted this new association.

"The result is that many individuals whose patriotism is beyond question have been blackmailed both legally, through loyalty and security investigations, and extralegally, through blacklists and threats of exposure. The inordinate increase in spying, both public and private, that has resulted has naturally increased people's feelings of helplessness.

"These feelings are further abetted by the growth of snooping by advertisers, sociologists, insurance and credit investigators, employers, private detectives and a host of others, all of which leads to a new sense of hidden danger and of someone peering over our shoulders from the cradle to the grave. This was the very thing Americans believed themselves to be particularly free of in their democratic society.

"But the crucial issue—the factor that is basic to our current feeling of impotence—is the sense that we have nothing to say about whether our world is going to blow up or not. Since we seem doomed to live under a thermonuclear cloud for some years to come, it would seem more than usually important for us to do everything possible to remove all the other possible reasons for feeling helpless."

This sense of the urgency of maintaining our national morale and morality pervaded nearly every interview. Phyllis McGinley put it this way: "I am afraid that in the contest with Russia we have become infected with a feeling of need to use Communist weapons—a kind of flagrant flouting of the truth."

To Edward R. Murrow, the danger in an increase in personal dishonesty or its tolerant acceptance by Americans was similar. "If it goes on long enough and deepens," he said, "it will place in jeopardy the very thing that nearly every good foreign observer of our nation has commented on: the American genius for cooperation. It will reduce the trust men place in one another, the very basis both of our economy and our government."

And Dr. Mead added, "I think the acceptance of private immorality is corrosive; it cannot coexist with any kind of real commitment. Occurring at a time when we're in more deadly danger than ever before, it becomes serious. Everything is so urgent today that any diminution of dedication and commitment is dangerous to the whole world."

Where do the solutions lie? "In strengthening community stability through both governmental and voluntary contributions," says Mrs. Meyer, "and in using our tremendous resources of knowledge in the area of human relations to cope with the human-relations problems that confront us." Dr. Mead agrees. "We must bury the cliché that our problems are a result of too rapid strides in the natural sciences and too little progress in the social sciences," she says. "We have tremendous knowledge in the behavioral sciences that is simply not being used. The racial crisis in the South today is in part a result of the fact that people who had the knowledge of what was needed simply were not consulted or were consulted and then ignored."

There was general agreement that discipline must be strengthened. "When both parents work," Fairfax Cone said, "children grow up undisciplined. It's hard to learn self-discipline by yourself. I think enforcement is a key. Honor systems break down because people won't report each other. There's no means of enforcement. If we would only begin enforcing a few things, I think the effect would quickly spread. A drive against illegal parking, for instance, would immediately bring cleaner, safer streets. It would force cities to face up to the problem of providing decent off-the-street parking facilities. I can visualize such a drive spreading into other areas once people saw its good effects."

Judge Learned Hand feels too that unenforced laws have a harmful influence on people's respect for law in general. "Laws must either be enforced or repealed," he says. "Facing up to such a choice would force us to take a good look at some of our laws and decide whether they make sense or not. The confusion of different state laws on divorce, drinking, driving ages and many other subjects is also a serious problem. This and the piling of statute on statute all interpreted by judicial decisions leads to doubt about what the law actually is. In this situation, respect for law can only suffer."

At least equal stress was laid by many of those interviewed on removing the inequities from necessary laws and rules. Unfair income-tax laws, inequitable earning requirements under Social Security, confusion of purpose in business expense accounts, shadowy lines between honest practices and conflicts of interest, unjust grading of students on curves and on strictly objective tests that ignore individual differences, draft regulations that discriminate, unequal application of laws—all these and more were cited as needing rigorous correction.

But of all the neglected needs mentioned, one stood out. "The American people have lacked leadership in all these areas," Mrs. Meyer says. "We need the new values and goals that can only be defined by strong, vigorous and intelligent national leadership. Instead of pursuing individual goals of wealth and security, we need to have our horizons broadened until we can see the far greater importance of freedom and cooperation. Our public leaders must begin using all available scientific knowledge about the modern world and its problems to arrive at an understanding of our proper national goals and then they must begin to talk clearly and honestly to the American people about them."

"People," Phyllis McGinley says, "need to be asked to give more of themselves. I think all human beings need to have demands made of them. All of us yearn to be better than we are, but our leaders have failed to use this human desire to be noble and to contribute. We know that in a grave national emergency, where the goals are clear, people always respond with bravery and nobility beyond all expectations. If a human being can learn to run the mile in less than four minutes, we can learn to improve our capacities for virtue and nobility. But we need to have specific goals set for us."

"No nation was ever great without greatness being demanded of it by its leaders," says Edward R. Murrow. "Americans for years have been asked only to pay their income taxes."

FOR FURTHER STUDY

Bertocci, Peter A., and Millard, Richard M. *Personality and the Good*. New York: McKay, 1963, Ch. 16, "Traits, Virtues, and Personality," Ch. 17, "A Scheme of Virtues."

Cabot, Richard C. *Honesty*. New York: Macmillan, 1938.

Everett, Millard Spencer. *Ideals of Life*. New York: Wiley, 1954, Ch. 8, "Weighing the Consequences—Rules and Exceptions."

Faber, Frederick. *Self-Deceit*. Wallingford: Pendle Hill, 1949. (Pendle Hill Pamphlet, No. 50.)

Isenberg, Arnold, "Deontology and the Ethics of Lying." *Philosophy and Phenomenological Research*, 24 (June 1964): 463-480.

Peck, Robert F., and Havighurst, Robert J. *The Psychology of Character Development*. New York: Wiley, 1960.

Trueblood, David Elton. *Foundations for Reconstruction*. New York: Harper, 1946.

CHAPTER 16

INSTITUTIONAL AND VOCATIONAL ETHICS

The Social Significance
of Professional Ethics*

R. M. MACIVER

R. M. MacIver (1882-   ), after teaching at the
University of Toronto and Barnard College, taught
political philosophy and sociology at Columbia University, 1929-1950. He is the author of many articles
and books, including *Democracy and the Economic
Challenge*. In 1963 he became Acting President of
the New School for Social Research and is now
Chancellor.

The spirit and method of the craft, banished from industry, finds a
more permanent home in the professions. Here still prevail the long
apprenticeship, the distinctive training, the small-scale unit of employment and the intrinsic—as distinct from the economic—interest alike in
the process and the product of the work. The sweep of economic
evolution seems at first sight to have passed the professions by. The
doctor, the lawyer, the architect, the minister of religion, remain individual practitioners, or at most enter into partnerships of two or three

* From *The Annals of the American Academy of Political and Social Science*,
297 (January 1955): 118-124. Used by permission of The Academy and the author.

members. Specialization takes place, but in a different way, for the specialist in the professions does not yield his autonomy. He offers his specialism directly to the public, and only indirectly to his profession. But this very autonomy is the condition under which the social process brings about another and no less significant integration. The limited "corporations" of the business world being thus ruled out, the whole profession assumes something of the aspect of a corporation. It supplements the advantage or the necessity of the small-scale, often the one-man, unit by concerted action to remove its "natural" disadvantage, that free play of uncontrolled individualism which undermines all essential standards. It achieves an integration not of form but of spirit. Of this spirit nothing is more significant than the ethical code which it creates.

There is in this respect a marked contrast between the world of business and that of the professions. It cannot be said that business has yet attained a specific code of ethics, resting on considerations broader than the sense of self-interest and supplementing the minimal requirements of the law. Such a code may be in the making, but it has not yet established itself, and there are formidable difficulties to be overcome. When we speak of business ethics, we generally mean the principles of fair play and honorable dealing which men *should* observe in business. Sharp dealing, "unfair" competition, the exaction of the pound of flesh, may be reprobated and by the decent majority condemned, but behind such an attitude there is no definite code which businessmen reinforce by their collective sense of its necessity and by their deliberate adoption of it as expressly binding upon themselves. There is no general brotherhood of businessmen from which the offender against these sentiments, who does not at the same time overtly offend against the law of the land, is extruded as unworthy of an honorable calling. There is no effective criticism which sets up a broader standard of judgment than mere success.

If we inquire why this distinction should hold between business and professional standards the social significance of the latter is set in a clearer light. It is not that business, unlike medicine or law for example, lacks those special conditions which call for a code of its own. Take, on the one hand, the matter of competitive methods. It is a vital concern of business, leading to numerous agreements of all sorts, but these are mere *ad hoc* agreements of a particular nature, not as yet deductions from a fully established principle which business, as a self-conscious whole, deliberately and universally accepts. Take, on the other hand, such a problem as that of the duty of the employer to his workpeople.

Is not this a subject most apt for the introduction of a special code defining the sense of responsibility involved in that relationship? But where is such a code to be found?

The Ideal of Service

Something more than a common technique and a common occupation is evidently needed in order that an ethical code shall result. We might apply here the significant and much misunderstood comparison which Rousseau drew between the "will of all" and the "general will." In business we have as yet only the "will of all," the activity of businessmen, each in pursuit of his own success, not overridden though doubtless tempered by the "general will," the activity which seeks first the common interest. The latter can be realized only when the ideal of service controls the ideal of profits. We do not mean that businessmen are in fact selfish while professional men are altruistic. We mean simply that the *ideal of the unity of service* which business renders is not yet explicitly recognized and proclaimed by itself. It is otherwise with the professions. They assume an obligation and an oath of service. "A profession," says the ethical code of the American Medical Association, "has for its prime object the service it can render to humanity; reward or financial gain should be a subordinate consideration," and again it proclaims that the principles laid down for the guidance of the profession "are primarily for the good of the public." Similar statements are contained in the codes of the other distinctively organized professions. "The profession," says the proposed code of the Canadian legal profession, "is a branch of the administration of justice and not a mere money-getting occupation." Such professions as teaching, the ministry, the civil service, and social work by their very nature imply like conceptions of responsibility. They imply that while the profession is of necessity a means of livelihood or of financial reward, the devoted service which it inspires is motivated by other considerations.

In business there is one particular difficulty retarding any like development of unity and responsibility. It may safely be said that so long as within the industrial world the cleavage of interest between capital and labor, employer and employee, retains its present character, business cannot assume the aspect of a profession. This internal strife reveals a fundamental conflict of acquisitive interests within the business world and not only stresses that interest in both parties to the struggle but makes it impossible for the intrinsic "professional" interest to prevail. The professions are in general saved from that confusion. Within the profession there is not, as a rule, the situation where one group habitually employs for gain another group whose function, economic interest, and social position are entirely distinct from its own. The professions have thus been better able to adjust the particular interests of their members to their common interest and so to attain a clearer sense of their relationship to the whole community.

Once that position is attained the problem of occupational conduct takes a new form. It was stated clearly long enough ago by Plato in the *Republic*. Each "art," he pointed out, has a special good or service. "Medicine for example, gives us health; navigation, safety at sea, and so on. . . . Medicine is not the art—or profession—of receiving pay because a man takes fees while he is engaged in healing. . . . The pay is not derived by the several 'artists' from their respective 'arts.' But the truth is, that while the 'art' of medicine gives health, and the 'art' of the builder builds a house, another 'art' attends them which is the 'art' of pay." The ethical problem of the profession, then, is to reconcile the two "arts," or, more generally, to fulfill as completely as possible the primary service for which it stands while securing the legitimate economic interest of its members. It is the attempt to effect this reconciliation, to find the due place of the intrinsic and of the extrinsic interest, which gives a profound social significance to professional codes of ethics.

Standards Common, Codes Distinctive

The demarcation and integration of the profession is a necessary preliminary to the establishment of the code. Each profession becomes a functional group in a society whose tendency is to organize itself less and less in terms of territory or race or hereditary status, and more and more in terms of function. Each profession thus acquires its distinctive code. It is important to observe that what is distinctive is the code rather than the standard. The different codes of racial or national groups reveal variant ethical standards, but the different codes of professional groups represent rather the deliberate application of a generally accepted social standard to particular spheres of conduct. Medical ethics do not necessarily differ in quality or level from engineering ethics, nor the ethics of law or of statesmanship from those of architecture. The false old notion that there was for that most ancient and still most imperfectly defined profession of statesmanship a peculiar code which liberated it from the ordinary ethical standards has died very hard. In truth there could be no conflict of ethics and politics, for politics could justify itself only by applying to its own peculiar situations and needs the principles which belong equally to every sphere of life.

Ethics cannot be summed up in a series of inviolate rules or commandments which can be applied everywhere and always without regard to circumstances, thought of consequences, or comprehension of the ends to be attained. What is universal is the good in view, and ethical rules are but the generally approved ways of preserving it. The rules may clash with one another, and then the only way out is to look for guidance to the ideal. The physician may have to deceive his patient in order to save his life. The lawyer, the priest, and the physician may have to observe secrecy and keep confidences under conditions where it might be the layman's duty to divulge them, for the conception of the social welfare which should induce the one to speak out may equally in the peculiar professional relationship compel the other to silence. Every profession has its own problems of conduct, in the interpretation within its own province of the common principles of ethical conduct. The medical man to whom is entrusted, under conditions which usually admit of no appeal save to his own conscience, the safeguarding of the health of his patient, with due consideration for the health of the whole community, has to depend upon a special code applicable to that situation. So with the legal profession which, for example, has to provide professional service for all litigants, irrespective of the popularity or unpopularity of the cause. So with the architect, who has to determine his responsibility alike to the client, to the contractor, to the workmen, to the "quantity surveyor," and to the community. So with the university professor, who has to uphold the necessity of academic freedom against the pressure of prejudice and the domination of controlling interests which care less for truth than for their own success. So with the journalist, in his peculiarly difficult situation as the servant of a propagandist press. So with the engineer, the surveyor, the accountant, or the technician generally, who has to maintain standards of service and of efficiency against the bias of profit making. So with the manager, the secretary, or the officer of a corporation—for here business assumes most nearly the aspect of a profession—who has to reconcile the trust imposed on him by his employers with the duty he owes to himself and to those whose services he in turn controls. Out of such situations develop the written and the unwritten codes of professional ethics.

Responsibility to the Wider Community

We need not assume that these codes originate from altruistic motives, nor yet condemn them because they protect the interest of the profession itself as well as the various interests which it serves. To do so would be to misunderstand the nature of any code. An ethical code is something more than the prescription of the duty of an individual towards others; in that very act it prescribes their duty towards him and makes his welfare too its aim, refuting the false disassociation of the individual and the social. But the general ethical code prescribes simply the duties of the members of a community towards one another. What gives the professional code its peculiar significance is that it prescribes also the duties of the members of a whole group towards those outside the group. It is just here that in the past ethical theory and practice alike have shown the greatest weakness. The group code has narrowed the sense of responsibility by refusing to admit the application of its principles beyond the group. Thereby it has weakened its own logic and its sanction, most notably in the case of national groups, which have refused to apply or even to relate their internal codes to the international world. The attempt of professional groups to co-ordinate their responsibilities, relating at once the individual to the group and the group itself to the wider community, marks thus an important advance.

We must, however, admit that it is in this matter, in the relation of the profession *as a whole* to the community, that professional codes are still weakest and professional ethics least effectively developed. The service to the community they clearly envisage is the service rendered by individual members of the profession to members of the public. The possibility that there may still be an inclusive professional interest—generally but not always an economic one—that at significant points is not harmonized with the community interest is nowhere adequately recognized.

The problem of professional ethics, viewed as the task of co-ordinating responsibilities, of finding, as it were, a common center for the various circles of interest, wider and narrower, is full of difficulty and far from being completely solved. The magnitude and the social significance of this task appear if we analyze on the one hand the character of the professional interest and on the other the relation of that interest to the general welfare.

Character of the Professional Interest

The professional interest combines a number of elements. It includes what we may term the extrinsic interest, that devoted to the economic and social status, the reputation, authority, success, and emoluments attaching to the profession as a body. It includes also the technical

interest directed to the art and craft of the profession, to the maintenance and improvement of its standards of efficiency, to the quest for
new and better methods and processes, and to the definition and promotion of the training considered requisite for the practice of the profession. It may also include a third interest which can be classed as cultural.
To illustrate, in the profession of teaching the technical interest in the
system of imparting knowledge is one thing, and the cultural interest in
the knowledge imparted quite another. Even more obvious is the case
of the minister of religion, whose technique of ministration is as a rule
very simple and whose main interest lies in the significance of the doctrine. The distinction is clear also in the spheres of the sciences and of
the fine arts where the interest in truth or beauty may be discerned
from the interest in the modes of investigation or of expression. In other
professions it may be harder to identify the cultural as distinct from the
technical interest, but if we interpret the term "culture" widely enough
to include, for example, such objects as health and the beauty of work-
manship, it may be maintained that the cultural interest belongs to every
profession and is in fact one of the criteria by which to determine
whether or not a given occupation is to be classed as a profession.

  Now these three strands of interest are usually interwoven in the
general professional interest, but sometimes they are separated and subject to the pull of opposite forces. Thus while the technical and economic interests usually go together and while, for example, the maintenance of standards usually works towards the economic advantage of
the profession, these may be unfortunately disjoined. Better technique
may at points be antagonistic to professional gain. The lawyer may, to
take one instance, lose a source of profits by the introduction of a
simpler and more efficient system of conveyancing. The architect, working on a percentage basis, may find his pecuniary advantage at variance
with his professional duty to secure the best service for the least cost.
Likewise, opposition may arise between the economic and the cultural
interest. The teacher and the preacher may suffer loss from a wholehearted devotion to the spirit of truth as they conceive it. The artist,
the playwright, the author, may have to choose between the ideals of
their art and the more lucrative devices of popularity. Finally, the
technical and the cultural interest may work apart. Routine methods
and processes may dominate the professional mind to the obscuration
of the ends which they should serve. A notable statement of this opposition is given in the valuable investigation into professional organization in England which was published in two supplements of the *New*

Statesman.[1] The investigation points to "the undisguised contempt in which both solicitors and barristers, notably those who have attained success in their profession and control its organization, hold, and have always held, not only all scholarship or academic learning of a professional kind, but also any theoretic or philosophical or scientific treatment of law."

Here, therefore, in the structure of the general professional interest we find a rich mine of ethical problems, still for the most part unworked but into which the growing ethical codes of the professions are commencing to delve. A still greater wealth of the material for ethical reflection is revealed when we turn next to analyze the relation of the professional interest as a whole to that of the community.

Professional Interest and General Welfare

Every organized profession avows itself to be an association existing primarily to fulfill a definite service within the community. Some codes distinguish elaborately between the various types of obligation incumbent on the members of the profession. The lawyer, for example, is declared to have specific duties to his client, to the public, to the court or to the law, to his professional brethren, and to himself. It would occupy too much space to consider the interactions, harmonies, and potential conflicts of such various duties. Perhaps the least satisfactory reconciliation is that relating the interest of the client to the interest of the public, not merely in the consideration of the particular cases as they arise but still more in the adaptation of the service to the needs of the public as a whole as distinct from those of the individual clients. Thus the medical profession has incurred to many minds a serious liability, in spite of the devotion of its service to actual patients, by its failure for so long to apply the preventive side of medicine, in particular to suggest ways and means for the prevention of the needless loss of life and health and happiness caused by the general medical ignorance and helplessness of the poor.

In addition it must suffice to show that the conception of communal service is apt to be obscured alike by the general and by the specific bias of the profession. It is to the general bias that we should attribute such attempts to maintain a vested interest as may be found in the undue restriction of entrants to the profession—undue when determined by such professionally irrelevant considerations as high fees and expensive licenses; in the resistance to specialization, whether of tasks or of men,

[1] April 21 and 28. 1917.

the former corresponding to the resistance to "dilution" in the trade union field; in the insistence on a too narrow orthodoxy, which would debar from professional practice men trained in a different school; in the unnecessary multiplication of tasks, of which a flagrant example is the English severance of barrister and solicitor. Another aspect of the general bias is found in the shuffling of responsibility under the cloak of the code. This is most marked in the public services, particularly the civil service and the army and navy—and incidentally it may be noted that the problem of professional ethics is aggravated when the profession as a whole is in the employ of the state. "An official," says Émile Faguet is one of his ruthless criticisms of officialdom,[2] "is a man whose first and almost only duty is to have no will of his own."

Danger of Specific Group Bias

This last case brings us near to what we have called the specific bias of the profession. Each profession has a limited field, a special environment, a group psychology. Each profession tends to leave its distinctive stamp upon a man, so that it is easier in general to distinguish, say, the doctor and the priest, the teacher and the judge, the writer and the man of science, than it is to discern, outside their work, the electrician from the railwayman or the plumber from the machinist. The group environment creates a group bias. The man of law develops his respect for property at the risk of his respect for personal rights. The teacher is apt to make his teaching an over-narrow discipline. The priest is apt to underestimate the costs of the maintenance of sanctity. The diplomat may overvalue good form and neglect the penalty of exclusiveness. The civil servant may make a fetish of the principle of seniority, and the soldier may interpret morality as mere *esprit de corps*.

All this, however, is merely to say that group ethics will not by themselves suffice for the guidance of the group unless they are always related to the ethical standards of the whole community. This fact has a bearing on the question of the limits of professional self-government, though we cannot discuss that here. Professional group codes are, as a matter of fact, never isolated, and thus they are saved from the narrowness and egotism characteristic of racial group ethics. Their dangers are far more easily controlled, and their services to society, the motive underlying all codes, vastly outweigh what risks they bring. They provide a support for ethical conduct less diffused than that inspired by nationality, less exclusive than that derived from the sense of class, and

[2] *The Dread of Responsibility* (New York: G. P. Putnam's Sons, 1914).

less instinctive than that begotten of the family. As they grow they witness to the differentiation of community. Their growth is part of the movement by which the fulfillment of function is substituted as a social force for the tradition of birth or race, by which the activity of service supersedes the passivity of station. For all their present imperfections these codes breathe the inspiration of service instead of the inspiration of mere myth or memory. As traditional and authoritative ethics weaken in the social process, the ethics formulated in the light of function bring to the general standard of the community a continuous and creative reinforcement.

FOR FURTHER STUDY

For a wide range of articles dealing with the ethical standards of professional and business groups see *The Annals* of the American Academy of Political and Social Science. Philadelphia: The Academy. Vol. 280, *Ethical Standards in American Public Life*, 1952; Vol. 297, *Ethical Standards and Professional Conduct*, 1955; Vol. 343, *Ethics of Business Enterprise*, 1962.

Forrester, W. R. *Christian Vocation*. New York: Scribner, 1951.

Hall, Cameron P. (ed.). *On-the-Job Ethics*. New York: National Council of Churches, 1963.

Kadushin, C. "Social Distance Between Client and Professional," *American Journal of Sociology*, 67 (March 1962): 517-531.

Leys, Wayne A. R. *Ethics for Policy Decisions*. New York: Prentice-Hall, 1952.

Minor, William S. "Public Interest and Ultimate Commitment," in *The Public Interest*, ed. Carl J. Friedrich. New York: Atherton Press, 1962, Ch. 3 (Nomos V).

Richardson, A. P. *Ethics of a Profession*. New York: Hoeber, 1950.

CHAPTER 17

THREE PROFESSIONAL
GROUPS AND THEIR PROBLEMS

Ethical Standards of
*the Medical Profession**

WILLIAM T. FITTS, JR.

AND

BARBARA FITTS

William T. Fitts, Jr. (1915-   ) is professor of
surgery at the Graduate School of Medicine, University of Pennsylvania. He is engaged in teaching,
research, and the practice of surgery. His wife,
Barbara Fitts, edits the University of Pennsylvania
Medical Bulletin.

The ethical standards that have developed around the doctor-patient
relationship are probably the oldest standards of any of the professions,
either in tacit or written form. . . .

The rash of controversy that has broken out recently, both within the
medical profession and outside of it, over fundamental problems of
medical practice—prepayment insurance plans, advertising, the hiring of

* From *The Annals of the American Academy of Political and Social Science*,
297 (January 1955): 17-28 with omissions. Used by permission of The Academy
and the authors.

physicians by institutions, and fee-splitting—would seem to indicate that something fairly serious is happening to the oldest and most pre-eminent of the professions. The present controversy contrasts strongly with the [earlier] complacent picture . . . and at first sight it would seem that the physicians of the country had suddenly abandoned their high standards and disinterested motives in favor of a mercenary concern over fees. The underlying problems go far deeper, however, to a group of factors that have been disturbing the economic and ethical patterns of the profession for some years.

It is our opinion that chief among these factors is the great "splinter-ing of medical knowledge" into specialties, which has made some type of group practice inevitable and thus altered the nature of the doctor-patient relationship. A second factor is the spread of the insurance principle to medicine, which has intruded a third party between the doctor and his patient and has imposed uniform fee scales in a notor-iously nonuniform field. A third factor is the radical treatment of serious disease, which appears, when first applied, to verge dangerously upon human experimentation.

The resulting disturbance to the ethical relationships within the profession—of physician to patient, and of physician to physician—has brought about vigorous attempts to revise the written code of medical ethics established by the American Medical Association and to enforce the code more effectively throughout the country.

AMA and Its Principles of Medical Ethics

The ethical principles of the medical profession of this country were first codified in written form by the American Medical Association in 1848 and were based on Sir Thomas Percival's *Medical Ethics,* written in 1803. The AMA code of ethics has been revised at intervals since that time—1903, 1912, 1940, and 1949—and is still undergoing restudy and revision. The code reflects the consensus of the medical profession in this country because the AMA, by its influence and its organization, is the one all-embracing association for the profession. And much of the current controversy over medical ethics concerns the provisions of the AMA code. . . .

Of the approximately 200,000 physicians in this country, 138,000 are members of the AMA. All physicians who are legally qualified to prac-tice medicine and who agree to conform to the Principles of Ethics are eligible for membership. This means that they must have graduated from an approved medical school, served a hospital internship of at least one year, and passed an examination allowing them to practice medicine in their respective state or territory. Membership in the AMA is required by some hospitals and clinics as prerequisite for staff appointment. . . .

The body within the AMA which decides questions of an ethical or judicial nature is the Judicial Council . . . the Council is charged with interpreting both the Principles of Ethics and the constitution and may make recommendations to the House of Delegates concerning proposed changes in these documents. . . .

AMA PRINCIPLES OF ETHICS

The AMA Principles of Ethics—with the interpretation of which the Judicial Council is charged—is a mixture of general moral principles and specific rules of conduct. The subject matter falls roughly into three categories: the relation of the doctor to society, to the patient, and to other doctors. The specific rules of conduct, especially those concerning the relation of doctor to doctor, are subject to frequent alterations and revisions as customs change, but the general principles embodied in the codes, like the Hippocratic Oath, do not vary greatly except in the wording. "The prime object of the medical profession is to render service to humanity; reward or financial gain is a subordinate consideration."[1]

The principal revisions or additions to the codes since 1922 have concerned groups and clinics, advertising and the giving out of information to the public, rebates (fee-splitting), and contract practice. Many of these changes reflect the intrusion of a third party or parties into the traditional doctor-patient relationship. For an explanation of their meaning we must look to the larger panorama of changing knowledge and a changing economy.

Specialization

The unrest and controversy concerning medical care may result from a number of causes, but specialization is of primary importance. The accumulation of new medical knowledge pouring out of the physical and biological sciences has reached a point where the individual physician cannot encompass it, let alone master the laboratory technics that go with it. He is more and more joined by other physicians in an informal or formal (as the case may be) medical team. Although the

[1] Principles of Medical Ethics of the American Medical Association, December 1953.

general practitioner remains the backbone of medical practice, the types of medical specialists and their total number are increasing with enormous speed. . . .

Since . . . [1922], the splintering of medical knowledge has led to the development of nineteen separately organized specialties and the formation of many subspecialties, each with its trained experts and special tools. The Specialty Boards have had tremendous influence on the practice of medicine because many hospitals and other institutions have made appointments to their staffs contingent on board certification. The requirements for certification are usually three or four years of specialty training following an approved internship, plus an oral and written examination to determine the candidate's proficiency in his specialty. . . .

GROUP PRACTICE

The struggles of the profession to tie its specialties back together are apparent in the number of surgical teams, group practice clinics, diagnostic clinics, and special disease clinics that have appeared in the United States in the past quarter century. The shift from a "single practice" system of medical care to a "multiple practice" arrangement is now reaping its harvest of major readjustments in the relations of physicians to each other and to the patient. It is a process of readjustment which is being felt all along the line—in medical ethics, medical economics, and medical administration. And the two major areas of controversy (which are really two sides of the same coin) are: how to divide responsibility *for* the patient and how to divide fees *from* the patient. Much of the debate over division of fees which has rocked the medical world and the public in recent months arises from problems of multiple practice, and not from any sudden outburst of mercenary motives on the part of the medical profession.

The division of responsibility for the patient varies rather widely, but the referring physician is usually considered "in charge" of the patient, and the specialist takes responsibility for those periods of specialty care that pertain to him. A surgeon, for example, will take responsibility for the operation and for pre- and postoperative care while the patient is in the hospital, but will probably refer the patient back to the original doctor for all but a few checkups.

FEE-SPLITTING

The division of fees should relate to the division of patient responsibility, but fees depend not only on responsibility but on the amount of training of the physician and on the patient's estimate of value received. Each new specialty as it develops has had to establish an approximate scale of fees. Many critics believe that specialists' fees are too high, and the determination to correct an "unfair" distribution of income has led physicians in certain parts of the country to use secret rebates—a practice widely known as fee-splitting. Although the AMA Principles of Medical Ethics forbids fee-splitting, the practice is widespread. . . .

Fee-splitting usually arises in the division of fees between a surgeon and the referring physician who first sees the patient. For example, the surgeon may charge $150 for the removal of an acutely inflamed appendix in the middle of the night and be paid willingly by the patient, who will balk at the $15 charge of the general practitioner who first examined him and made the diagnosis—the general practitioner often spending more time with the patient than the surgeon. The problem then is twofold: how much more should the specialist be paid in a given instance for his more specialized knowledge and (at times) greater responsibility, and should the patient know where his money goes? . . .

GHOST SURGERY

"Ghost surgery" is fee-splitting in reverse, and is not as prevalent as fee-splitting. In ghost surgery, the nonsurgical physician makes the diagnosis and receives the entire fee, which he secretly splits with a "ghost surgeon." The patient either does not know of the existence of the "ghost" or believes him to be a minor assistant at the operation. He credits the operation to his own doctor, who usually supervises all pre- and postoperative care. The danger of ghost surgery lies in the fact that the physician who does the operating usually does not make the diagnosis and may not even examine the patient before he operates.

The American College of Surgeons has conducted a forthright campaign against fee-splitting and ghost surgery, so forthright in fact that the College has been severely criticized for "washing dirty linen in public." In 1951 it removed from its list of hospitals approved for surgical residencies two hospitals in Bloomington, Illinois, whose staffs were engaged in unethical practices. It has encouraged the use of the Columbus Plan, or variations of it, in which groups of surgeons or entire medical societies agree to submit their account books, patient lists, and income tax returns to a certified public accountant at regular intervals for inspection. Variations of this plan have been successfully adopted at the Bloomington hospitals and are now being tried by a group of American College of Surgeons' Fellows in Iowa.

STANDARD FEES

The problem of fees is further complicated by recent tendencies towards a more uniform fee scale for medical services, a trend strengthened by the growth of medical insurance plans. Most companies have standard fees for every service. The Blue Shield plan, for example, pays $150 for removal of a gall bladder whether the operation is done by the most highly skilled surgical specialist or by a general practitioner, or whether the patient is rich or poor. Many in the profession have urged a standard fee scale and many county medical societies publish a list of acceptable fees. Yet it is difficult to standardize such an unstandard service as medical care. For example, the removal of a diseased gall bladder containing stones may vary from a routine and easy operation to a most difficult one, if the gall bladder is acutely inflamed. The patient who demands a "flat fee" for an operation may get "flat" care.

. . . Clearly, a fair division of fees is not easily determined under the present conditions of rapidly varying relationships between physicians.

Application of Insurance Principle to Medical Care

Specialization, with its long training and special laboratory technics, has been accompanied by a substantial increase in medical costs to the patient. Although higher costs are frequently offset by shorter hospital visits and lower mortality, patients do not compare their medical costs with the morbidity and mortality rates of twenty years ago, but with the cost of other goods and services that they buy. In recent years nearly all large items of expense that must come out of the consumer's pocketbook have been put on a prepayment insurance or a credit basis, and medical costs have remained as a large and unexpected drain on the patient's budget. The spread of the prepayment insurance principle to medicine was almost inevitable under the circumstances. Therefore the growth of prepayment plans for medical care has been phenomenal. The Blue Cross, a nonprofit hospitalization plan, now covers nearly one third of the population of the United States, and the coverage rises to 60 and 75 per cent in well-organized areas. Blue Shield, which pays the services of physicians, now covers one fifth of the total population, but may run one third or higher in organized areas. Both plans pay a set fee for service directly to the hospital or physician and allow free choice of a physician. . . .

Problems of Radical Therapy

The remarkable advances of scientific knowledge in medicine have made it possible to carry out many radical measures for the relief of chronic or terminal diseases. For example, procedures have been developed (prefrontal lobotomy) for the treatment of intractable pain, which relieve the pain by destroying that part of the brain responsible for pain perception. Such an operation also changes the patient's personality to some degree. Is this ethical? Surgical technics have been developed to such a point that extensive and deforming operations can be performed with a low mortality rate. These ultraradical operations, performed usually for the treatment of cancer, frequently offer little hope of cure. They prolong life, but often leave the patient wretched and miserable and unable to lead a useful or happy existence. In addition, the surgery is extremely expensive to the patient and his family.

The physician often finds himself hard pressed to know the "ethical" answers to a specific problem. Should "everything possible" be done to effect a cure in an individual patient? One hundred ultraradical operations may yield 5 per cent of cures and many miserable months of life for the remaining patients, whereas a hundred palliative operations may yield no cures but many months of comfort. In Chapter II, Section 2, of the Principles of Medical Ethics is found the statement, "In such instances the physician should act as he would desire another to act toward one of his own family in like circumstances." But does this really answer the ethical problem?

The greatest ethical question arising from radical therapy—euthanasia—has been temporarily put in abeyance by the terrible example of the Nazis during World War II. The pros and cons of "mercy killing" are no longer very seriously argued in medical circles.

One important ethical problem that is currently debated is the question of the controlled "clinical trial" which was recently used on a large scale in this country in the field tests of gamma globulin for poliomyelitis. Is it ethical to withhold medicine from a group of control patients while giving it to a second group of patients for testing? Unquestionably this takes us into the field of human experimentation via the route of statistics. However, any new medicine or treatment is, basically, an experiment on human beings; and the clinical trial is unquestionably a more intelligent evaluation of new medicines than simple trial and error.

Education of Laymen in Medical Affairs

The outpouring of new medical knowledge and new "wonder drugs" could not fail to arouse the interest of laymen. At the same time the medical profession has deliberately fostered public interest in medicine for reasons of its own. It has gradually turned to the public for research funds to help replace the large private contributions that are slowly drying up. It has also promoted informational campaigns about cancer and other diseases to teach laymen to diagnose the early symptoms of these diseases. . . .

And how does the code of ethics cover the question of what to tell the patient with an incurable disease, such as certain forms of cancer? A survey of Philadelphia physicians in 1953 showed that the majority of physicians do not tell a patient that he has cancer, although they always tell some member of his family.[2] They may tell the patient himself under special circumstances—if the lesion is usually curable, as, for example, skin cancer; if the patient needs to make special provision for dependents; or if the patient would otherwise refuse treatment.

The problem of truthfulness in medicine is not new, because the best therapy and absolute honesty do not always go hand in hand. But the present glare of publicity has subjected medical matters to a close scrutiny and has shown very clearly the difficulties of early diagnosis of cancer. The solution for this ethical problem is, of course, a cure for the disease.

The Irreducible Minimum

Human nature being what it is (and it has not improved noticeably . . .), the medical profession will probably always include a certain irreducible minimum of physicians who are more concerned with their own interests than with those of the patient or the profession. For a number of reasons it is getting easier to cover up mediocre medical care or outright racketeering. Improvements in anesthesia and pre- and postoperative care have reduced the risks of operation so much that an unscrupulous surgeon no longer fears to perform unnecessary ones. In large cities a physician may know very few of his patients per-

[2] W. T. Fitts, Jr., and I. S. Ravdin, "What Philadelphia Physicians Tell Patients with Cancer," *J.A.M.A.*, Vol. 153 (November 7, 1953), p. 901.

sonally, and the loss of this relationship removes an important check on professional ethics. Unnecessary operations and illegal abortions are not new problems, but they may become more prevalent if their safety increases and if the personal element in medicine is gradually reduced.

The medical profession has taken steps to safeguard the public against the unscrupulous physician. For example, hospitals throughout the country have set up tissue audit committees to examine carefully all tissue removed at operation. If such tissue is found to be normal, the surgeon is called to account. If he continues to remove more normal tissue than is justified, his operating privileges are suspended.

The American Medical Association has aimed to protect the public against unethical medical practices by instigating the establishment of grievance committees in the constituent and component medical societies. By January 1953 all of the forty-eight state associations, the District of Columbia, and Hawaii had provided committees for hearing and acting on complaints from the public. . . .

A Look to the Future

The medical profession in the United States has always been distinguished by a strong streak of individuality and independence, the counterpart probably of the same pioneer spirit which originally marked the commerce and industry of the New World. Nowhere is this individualism more apparent than in the profession's emphasis on the sanctity of the doctor-patient relationship. Both the constitution and the Principles of Ethics of the AMA reflect the high regard in which that relationship is held and show the determined efforts of the profession to preserve it intact. . . .

The essence of the doctor-patient relationship is the promise of the doctor to take complete responsibility for a patient once he has accepted his care, and the freedom of the patient in the choice of his physician. Once the physician's responsibility is divided between consultants, other specialists, and laboratory physicians, the strength of the doctor-patient relationship is weakened. Multiple practice is effecting a virtual revolution in medicine because of the fragmentation in responsibility that goes with it. . . .

There is another sense in which a patient may "slip between the specialists." When a physician limits his practice to a specialty, he does not normally take emergency calls unrelated to his field, usually because he is incompetent to do so. This means, however, that a patient may be unable to locate the type of doctor he needs or may be refused medical care by several doctors and feel justifiably neglected. The profession has finally recognized its responsibility in this regard by setting up night and emergency services organized by the county medical societies throughout the country. . . .

To replace this loss of an intense individual responsibility, it will probably be necessary to develop a greater sense of the collective responsibility of the profession to society. The absorption of the average physician in his own demanding practice has made him peculiarly blind to the inadvertent gaps in medical care that have arisen through social and economic forces outside his immediate acquaintance. . . .

INSURANCE PLANS

The negative attitude of organized medicine and its failure to experiment with insurance plans and related projects have been most unfortunate. The control of medical care is likely to slip out of the hands of the medical profession—as it nearly did during the thirties and forties in the campaign for socialized medicine—if it fails to keep abreast of the health needs and desires of society.

SOCIAL MEDICINE

The positive philosophy of "social medicine" (not socialized medicine) as developed in England has been slow to penetrate in this country. The importance of social medicine as a separate discipline is still highly debatable, but its emphasis on the preventive aspects of medical care supplies a real need and brings a much larger horizon to medicine. According to social medicine, the duty of the physician is not just to the individual patient but to the community at large—the body social, as it were; and the physician should study not only individual pathology but the social pathology which is recorded in the statistical annals of many disciplines. His scope will then reach out into the fields of statistics, sociology, anthropology, and psychology. This is not a new concept, but the attitude of promoting health as well as curing disease has not been sufficiently emphasized in American medicine, nor the responsibility of the physician for the health of the community as a whole. . . .

We do not share the view that a code of ethics should be inviolate and unchanging. Moral truths may be unchanging but their application varies as social and economic factors change. The relatively new problem of scientific research on humans (the controlled "clinical trial") is an example of a new ethical problem not specifically covered by the older codes.

. . . Only by eliminating unfair competition between members can a profession establish a high standard of ethics. The early history of codes and rules of ethics indicates that they have been primarily a method of asserting internal professional discipline. When the conditions of competition change, the codes necessarily change with them.

The current problems now facing the medical profession would seem to make it imperative that the problems and history of medical ethics be well understood by physicians everywhere. There is at present relatively little information about ethical problems imparted in the medical curriculum. Many ideals and attitudes are passed along unconsciously from teacher to student, but this may not be enough in an era when ethical attitudes are no longer forced upon doctors by close and intimate contact with patients. Possibly the answer lies in a greater stress on moral character in the selection of medical students and in a greater stress on the teaching of ethical principles in medical schools.

๛๛๛๛

Trial by Combat in American Courts*

DAVID DRESSLER

David Dressler (1907-   ) is professor of sociology and social welfare at Long Beach State College in California. He has written many professional articles and books related to the law and the handling of offenders. He has worked with lawyers and judges and was executive director of the New York State Division of Parole.

The average criminal trial, said the late Judge Jerome Frank, is a "sublimated brawl." A decade ago, few of Judge Frank's colleagues bothered to defend their profession when he made the charge in his crusading book, *Courts on Trial;* today many progressive lawyers and judges are battling for the very reforms he championed, and in some Federal and state courts the ancient rituals are changing. But

* From *Harper's Magazine*, 222 (April 1961), pp. 31-36 with omissions. Used by permission of *Harper's Magazine* and the author.

even now in the United States, despite our prevailing respect for the scientific search for truth, trial techniques are as unscientific as an appendectomy performed with a tomahawk. With the sensational Finch murder trial in court for the *third* time in California, the law is still "a ass, a idiot," as Mr. Bumble put it—if not worse.

Unfortunately for advocates of reform, most lawyers are proud of this instance of cultural lag. Our so-called adversary theory against which Judge Frank inveighed sets the rules of trial procedure. It stems from medieval trial by combat and is basic both to English common law and to American legal codes. In the old days accuser and accused met on the field of battle and had at each other with sword or lance. If the accused fell, he was guilty. If the accuser died, that proved he didn't have a just cause to begin with. Thus was "truth" revealed.

Today, instead of fighting with lethal weapons, we use legal arguments. Where combatants formerly met face to face, they now have surrogates—attorneys—who fight for them. The judge acts as referee, theoretically protecting the contenders against foul blows. The jury decides which "side" fought the better fight. But fight it is and the object is to win, not necessarily to reveal the truth.

The heart of the adversary system—and the source of many of the evils which the reforms now in progress aim to eliminate—is "surprise," a technique which some lawyers call "trial from ambush." The intent of surprise is to time a sudden blow so as to throw the opposition off balance and overwhelm it before it can recover.

An example of a successful surprise is the following: A Chicago attorney, Luis Kutner, was in Federal Court defending William Henderson, who had been charged with piracy on the high seas. Henderson had boarded a sight-seeing motor launch operating on Lake Michigan and, when it left its moorings, pulled a pistol and robbed the passengers. At trial, thirty erstwhile passengers positively identified the defendant as their assailant. Kutner cross-examined diffidently, as if his cause were hopeless. He presented no evidence on his own, and listened respectfully as United States Attorney Al Bosworth summed up and rested his case, by which time Henderson's guilt was plain as a wart.

Then Kutner addressed Judge James H. Wilkerson: "Your Honor, the defense moves for a directed verdict of acquittal, on grounds this court lacks competent jurisdiction." Under Federal law, counsel pointed out, the port of registry of a vessel determines jurisdiction. "The boat in question is registered out of Milwaukee. Chicago is therefore not the venue of the crime."

The judge ordered acquittal.

Now, as he told me in an interview, Kutner knew all along that the case belonged in a Milwaukee court. He could have moved for change of venue before the trial opened in Chicago. Instead, he let it run its course. He allowed the prosecution to rest its case, confident it had won. Then he sprang his trap. He knew that once the evidence was in and the directed verdict on record, double-jeopardy laws would prohibit the Government from retrying the case in Milwaukee. In the eyes of the law, Kutner's conduct was entirely ethical. Under the adversary theory he was an advocate, which is to say he was obliged to be strictly partisan. As a partisan, he was entitled to use surprise.

A Jury of Potato Peelers

Tongue in cheek, attorneys insist that the adversary system guarantees revelation of all facts bearing on an issue, and so it furthers the scientific method in trial practice. A lawyer buried beneath a mountain of books in the Los Angeles County Law Library told me, "I am here seeking the matter that will win a certain action. My opponent is here, too, with the same purpose. I search with fervor and frenzy. Nothing favorable to my position will escape me. The same is true of my opponent, dammit! He and I will search and together we will bring in facts so plain that even a jury of potato peelers and peanut vendors will understand them."

Maybe. But when I headed the New York State Division of Parole, I had been in and out of courts for seventeen years and most of the time I felt those potato peelers and peanut vendors were licked. They would not get at the truth because it lay hidden behind a curtain of flimflam and obfuscation. Each attorney was out to help his side and his side only, at almost any cost. Each wanted the jury to believe that he and he alone was the bearer of the Holy Grail, while his opponent was a knave out to suppress the truth. Each witness swore he was telling nothing but the truth, even when his story was directly contrary to what a witness for the other side swore was true. No witness was permitted to tell all he knew, although under oath to tell "the whole truth." No witness could tell what he did tell in his own way. The attorney on his side suggested by his questions what the witness should say. In cross-examination the opposing lawyer tried to trap him into saying something else. Each counselor hoped to cajole the jury into disregarding everything the other lawyer or witnesses said. The net outcome, all too often, probably was that the talesmen agreed with the wag who said that cases are decided only "according to the preponderance of the perjury." They voted for the side that seemed to tell fewer lies.

Juries might get at the truth if counsel researched cases scientifically. When two research men investigate causes of cancer they make a hypothesis and check it with an open mind. They may pursue different courses but they clear their findings with each other.

Not so in criminal trial practice. According to the late eminent attorney, Charles P. Curtis, the counsel who sets out to build evidence "will waste a lot of time if he goes with an open mind." Unlike a scientist, he will not sit down with his opposite number and say, "Here is what I found. What did you find? We are both after the same thing—truth. What can we agree on, in the interest of justice?" Instead, he squirrels away his evidence, citations, and arguments—his putative "facts"—hoping his opponent will be overwhelmed by them in the courtroom.

An attorney told a Bar Association audience: "Of course surprise elements should be hoarded. Your opponent should not be educated as to matters concerning which you believe he is still in the dark. Obviously, the traps should not be uncovered. Indeed, you may cast a few more leaves over them so that your adversary will step more boldly on the low ground believing it is solid."

The leaves over the low ground are yellowed pages of musty law books containing ancient trial decisions, which serve as precedents. Precedents are hallowed. What was good enough for great-great-grandpappy is all the better today because it is aged-in-the-book. The contemporary counselor who has a talent for digging these vintage morsels becomes a scholar in the law, highly respected and extravagantly paid. More important, he gains an advantage. The older a precedent, the less likely it is his adversary will find it, too. In court, before an amused jury, the opposing lawyer is trapped and the victory may go to the legal scholar.

What makes such tactics more deplorable is that the precedents often fail to go to the heart of a matter. They award a decision, not on the essence of a case—that is, whether the defendant is guilty or not—but more frequently on mere technicality. If, as happened in one Florida case, the judge simply has to leave the bench to answer the call of nature while counsel is summing up for the jury, the opposing lawyer will make no demur. He has an early precedent up his sleeve that holds if a judge has to go, the trial should be recessed, even though all the evidence is in and only summation is in progress. Then, if the verdict is against his side, the lawyer will jostle the precedent loose and demand a new trial.

There are literally hundreds of thousands of technicalities that have won cases in the past. Many of them are contradictory. The lawyer who can't find the special one that fits his case had better turn in his diploma. The best known compendium of such judicial precedents is Dean John H. Wigmore's monumental treatise, *Evidence*. First published in 1923, it now runs to five volumes of 5,500 pages listing 42,000 precedents still guiding criminal practice. Some go back more than a hundred years.

In one case, the advocate found just what he needed to defend his client, a North Carolinian who had fired across the state line and killed a man in Tennessee. When North Carolina attempted to charge him, the attorney cried foul. The act, he pointed out, was completed in Tennessee, and the law requires a man be tried where the act was completed. North Carolina had to agree. Tennessee then tried to extradite the killer as a fugitive from justice. Impossible, counsel fumed. Since his client had never been in Tennessee how could he be a fugitive from that state? Tennessee gave up. Thus, remarks Roscoe Pound, dean of legal philosophers, "The state which had him could not try him, while the state which could try him did not have him and could not get him."

Legal Hit-Run

If, by amazing mischance, a counselor finds no precedent, *circa* 1800, to prove his case, he might try another form of surprise, the hit-run tactic. He may fire an improper question at a witness, knowing it must be withdrawn. It will be expunged from the record but not from the recollection of the jurors.

When the Teamsters' president James R. Hoffa was tried for bribery in 1957, his attorney, Edward Bennett Williams, was content to have eight Negroes on the jury. I was an observer in the court and saw John Cye Cheasty, a prosecution witness, come up for cross-examination. Out of a clear sky, Williams asked him if he had not once been engaged by a bus line to investigate the National Association for the Advancement of Colored People during a Florida labor dispute.

The horrified prosecutor jumped to his feet, protesting that the question was altogether immaterial to the matter at issue. The judge sustained the objection and ordered the jury to disregard the question —one of many neat legal fictions is that jurors can forget what they have heard. Actually, the damage was done. It seems reasonable to assume that at least eight veniremen considered Cheasty's testimony as the biased mouthings of an enemy of labor and minorities.

Soon after, another dramatic surprise staggered the prosecution. Ex-champion Joe Louis sauntered into the courtroom, put an arm around Hoffa, and explained to newsmen, "I just came over to say hello to my friend Jimmy." Acquittal for the friend of the oppressed followed.

While in the Hoffa case surprise benefited the defense in court, the prosecution usually has a distinct advantage in preparing certain surprises before trial. For example, the findings of the police laboratory are available to it, rarely to the defense.

In one Los Angeles case, a defendant charged with murder convinced his attorney he was absolutely innocent. Although some attorneys consider it their duty to defend guilty clients, and the canons of the bar hold that this is the one way to assure that mitigating circumstances will be put before a jury, this particular attorney prefers not to handle such cases. He feels he cannot win unless he goes into court convinced in his own mind he is defending an innocent man. At trial, the state produced a police witness who testified he photographed the latent print of the palm of a hand, found on the window sill over which the slayer climbed to gain entrance. The print was the defendant's. Had defense been apprised of this before trial, it might have prepared a better argument in favor even of a guilty client. Taken by surprise, it surrendered the decision to the prosecution. Almost certainly a guilty man was convicted in this instance, but it is our theory that even a guilty man is entitled to the best possible defense.

A case which is still moot as this is written offers another illustration, this time in a situation where we do not know whether the defendant was guilty or innocent. In the first trial early last year of Dr. R. Bernard Finch and Carole Tregoff Pappa for the murder of the physician's wife, the district attorney let Dr. Finch, called by the defense, testify to details of the fatal struggle. He alleged his wife came at him with a gun, he seized it in self-defense and it was accidentally discharged, killing Mrs. Finch. Thereupon the prosecutor on the seventy-first day of the trial brought in tape recordings of an interview between the physician and police shortly after his arrest. On the tape, Dr. Finch gave testimony directly contrary to what he had just given on the stand. Neither the accused nor his counsel knew the interview was recorded. The prosecutor had hoarded the tapes for just such a purpose. It would seem that if a trial is intended to discover truth, both sides should have known of the existence of the tapes. Each side would insist that the truth ought to be brought into court. How could it hurt, then, to reveal it before the trial?

Nevertheless, when I asked a Los Angeles police official whether police findings should not be shared with the defense, he replied, "Do the Dodgers give the Giants their signals?" No, but human beings are not baseballs, trials are not baseball games, and the stakes are not pennants. The liberty and perhaps the life of a defendant is at stake in every criminal trial. Police science should be employed in the interest of truth and justice, not to win a battle for one side.

Peeking at the Claws

Because adversary methods sanction a battle of wits rather than a search for truth, a few leaders in the law have become restive. They know that we have at hand methods of finding evidence scientifically, that trials can be made more truthful and just than they usually are at present. Largely as a result of their efforts, the American Bar Association has at long last instituted reforms in the adversary method, though much more remains to be done. The first attack was on surprise. To minimize the unfairness and inefficiency of this technique, the American Bar Association produced what it calls "discovery."

Judge Frank likened surprise to a cat-and-mouse game. He thought the mouse should at least have "a peek at the cat's claws." That peek is now provided by discovery. This is, in essence, legal machinery by which one side is required to inform the other, in advance of trial or sufficiently in advance during trial, that certain evidence will be introduced. Forewarned, the other side has time to prepare its case. . . .

Most discovery is in the interest of the defense, since it is the prosecution that brings the charge and believes it has evidence to sustain it. But some disclosure favors the prosecution. In several states the defense is required to notify the prosecutor when it plans to plead not guilty by virtue of insanity. Michigan, Arizona, Ohio, Kansas, Wisconsin, require that the prosecution be notified if the defense claims an alibi. . . .

Does discovery make it harder to convict the guilty? Not so, says Maryland's Supreme Court. "We are not impressed by the fear. . . . It apparently has not had that effect."

Professor Abraham S. Goldstein, of Yale Law School, in an article prepared for *The Yale Law Journal* this winter, suggests a safeguard if it be feared that discovery will tip the balance to the side of the defense. In return for discovery the accused could be required to waive immunity from self-incrimination. He could be required to take the stand. That would give the prosecution an opportunity for its own discovery, direct from the man who, by the prosecution's presumption, knows most about the crime. Professor Goldstein holds the law could be so written as not to conflict with the Constitutional guarantee that a defendant may not be forced to testify against himself.

The trend toward discovery is impressive but as yet limited. It continues to meet with resistance by a majority of attorneys. Professor W. T. Morgan, of Harvard Law School, has explained why: "Some of the finest legal minds today are anxious for revolutionary changes in procedure, but they are as voices crying in the wilderness compared to the great unleavened mass of lawyers who are abundantly satisfied with things as they are. With even a slight modification of procedure in civil and criminal cases the United States could dispense with half her lawyers. The average citizen, therefore, need not expect the legal profession to commit hari-kari."

He Defends the Widow and Orphan Unless . . .

It will take an entirely new generation of lawyers, trained in a loftier philosophy, to bring a more effective justice into our courts. Most attorneys today come from law schools that imbue them with the theory of winning decisions at almost any cost. They have been taught to use not only surprise but every other questionable advantage which a complacent judge, himself a product of such schools, will allow.

Logic argues that a witness belongs to neither side. He should mount the stand to tell what he knows, whatever the outcome. But budding lawyers study textbooks that teach them to consider witnesses either "friendly" or "hostile." According to such texts, the hostile witness is an outsider and, as Charles P. Curtis says in *The Ethics of Advocacy*, "A lawyer is required to treat outsiders as if they were barbarians and enemies.". . .

We have barely emerged from the era of the self-made lawyer, who needed only a mail-order law book and a fireplace in front of which to study. That was good enough in Abe Lincoln's day, but we can do better today. This is an age of specialization, but one in which we believe the specifics of professional practice should be superimposed on a foundation of general education. Yet over half of today's attorneys are trained in the law without learning to understand the society for which law is created. They do not have college degrees. The majority attended schools of a type which a Columbia University dean called "vocational bargain basements." An investigator for the American Bar Association reported in 1954 that of nine law schools he inspected, six "showed no impact of the modern world whatsoever."

But a measure of improvement is on the way. The great universities now require a liberal-arts base for the law degree. They teach law as an institution of society, as a philosophy, a science, and a craft. When enough of their students have been graduated, law will be practiced with a sense of responsibility for the ethics of modern life. At any rate, there is a chance that lawyers will accept the obligation to make law serve society.

A Daumier print shows a lawyer arguing in court. Nearby sit a woman and child. The caption reads: "He defends the widow and orphan, unless he is attacking the orphan and the widow." That's trial by combat under adversary rules. We require much better in our time. Chief Justic Arthur T. Vanderbilt, of New Jersey, put it this way:

"Justice in our courts shall be a search for truth, and not a mere battle of wits."

ᘛᘚᘛᘚᘛ

The Colleges, Ethics, and the Public*

RALPH E. HIMSTEAD

Ralph E. Himstead (1893-1955) was an authority on constitutional law, academic freedom, and civil liberties. After teaching at Cornell College and Syracuse University, he became General Secretary of the American Association of University Professors, and editor of the Bulletin of the A.A.U.P., 1936-1955.

In the discussion of any subject, definition of terms is important. In this discussion the terms which need definition are college, ethics, and public.

A college has been defined as "a society of scholars, or friends of

* From *The Annals of the American Academy of Political and Social Science*, 280 (March 1952), pp. 133-141 in part. Used by permission.

learning, incorporated for study or instruction, especially in the higher branches of knowledge." The basic concept is a community of scholars. This, at least, is the basic concept of what a college should be. Later in this article there will be discussed in some detail what a college is and what a college is not, in relation to what its ethical functions may be.

Ethics is concerned with morality, with the ideals of morality, with ideal human character, and with ideal human action. The questions with which ethics deals concern the nature of the *summum bonum* and the validity of the criteria of its achievement. Ethics has been defined as "a system of moral principles." Thus, we have individual ethics, social ethics, professional ethics, and other kinds of ethics, which govern the moral actions of individuals in their personal relationships and in their social and professional relationships. There have been, and are, various theories of ethics—the egoistic, the altruistic, and the perfectionistic; and two conceptions of its nature—absolute and relative. Those who view ethics as absolute affirm an unchanging moral code. Those who view it as relative regard the standards of moral conduct as subject to change with human development. With these theories and views of ethics, this article is not concerned. The term "ethics" as used in this article means those principles the observance of which contribute to the highest good.

The term "public" as used in this article means the whole of the population of a nation, state, or community and not merely those portions of the public directly related to our colleges—students, parents, alumni, benefactors—with which the college has special and direct relationships and which may be regarded as having special claims on the services of colleges.

Relationships Between Colleges and Public

This article is concerned with the relationship of the work of colleges to the public with special reference to the principles conducive to the highest good of the public. That the work of our colleges affects the public cannot be questioned. Through the process of educating successive generations of youth, our colleges have contributed, and are contributing, greatly to the welfare of the public by helping to lift the level of enlightenment of our citizenry. Indeed, it may be said that the state of the public is in large part determined by the state of our colleges.

Is the work of our colleges affected by the public? The answer is clearly in the affirmative. It may, therefore, also be said that the state of our colleges depends on the state of the public. This has always been true, but is more so today than ever before, when we have so many lay spokesmen for education who hold themselves out as specialists in higher education and who speak with certitude concerning what our colleges should teach and how they should teach it. These self-appointed spokesmen are frequently influential in forming public opinion, and our colleges are influenced by public opinion.

Our colleges are also not infrequently influenced by pressures from representatives of special interests, or segments of the public, in reference to what is taught, how it is taught, and by whom it is taught. Those who bring such pressures on colleges either do not understand what a college is or, possessing this understanding, disregard it. What such pressure groups wish of our colleges is not education but indoctrination. They would have our colleges become agencies of propaganda for certain views and beliefs—economic, political, social, or religious. They would subvert our colleges. Because most colleges are in need of money, and the pressures to influence their work are frequently made by prospective donors or by persons thought to be prospective donors, or by influential legislators or by persons influential with legislators, such pressures are frequently successful. To the extent that they are successful, our institutions of higher education are corrupted, and the institution concerned is no longer worthy of the name college or university.

What Is the Ethical Responsibility of Colleges?

Concern about ethics and morals is not new, nor are the conditions which justify such concern new. Both are familiar phenomena. Efforts to lift the level of the standards of ethics and morals have always been regarded as necessary and desirable and should always be so regarded. This does not mean that every individual should become a "reformer," or that all of our institutions—educational, governmental, and commercial—should become ethical societies, seeking reform. It does mean, however, that individuals, as individuals, and those who administer and are a part of our institutions should be aware of the ethical implications of their work, in relation to the general welfare.

As regards our institutions of higher education, it is the thesis of this article that the greatest contribution they can make to the ethics and the morals of the public is to maintain their integrity as institutions of higher education and to adhere faithfully to their purpose, namely, the pursuit of scholarship and the instruction of youth. Those whose profession is the education of youth at the higher levels should also seek at all times to "educate" the public concerning the nature of an institution of higher education and concerning the values to the public of maintaining the integrity of these institutions and of their adhering faithfully to their functions.

While there is general verbal concurrence in the conception of a college defined above, experience has made it clear that in the day-to-day work of our colleges this conception is frequently more honored in the breach than in the observance; that what educators permit to be done to our colleges, without protest, belies what they say they believe a college should be. The reason may be an imperfect understanding of what a college is or the lack of courage to speak and act in accordance with their understanding and convictions.

It is sometimes helpful to an understanding of what something is to note with some particularity what it is not. Experience has shown this to be so in defining institutions of higher education. Organizationally speaking, institutions of higher education have many things in common with other institutions. They are incorporated; they have governing boards; they have administrative officers; they have employees, for, legally speaking, their faculties are employees. Boot and shoe factories and other commercial corporations have similar organization. They are incorporated, have governing boards, administrative officers, and employees. Because our colleges and universities have organizational aspects in common with commercial corporations, they are frequently regarded as analogous in other respects to commercial corporations. This confusion is serious as regards the welfare of higher education and of the public, for attitudes toward, and actions taken in reference to, institutions of higher education resulting from this confusion are of a kind likely to impair the integrity and subvert the purpose of these institutions. It is pertinent, therefore, to note and to emphasize what an institution of higher education is not.

An institution of higher education is not a commercial enterprise. It is not in the business of manufacturing, processing, or selling commodities. It is not a proprietary institution. Its character is eleemosynary, strictly eleemosynary. An institution of higher education, even though state supported, is not an arm or branch of the state government and should not be so regarded or administered. An institution of higher education is not a political party. It is not an ethical society. It is not a church. It is an educational institution, and as such is *sui generis*. Its purpose is scholarship, which means research and reflection, and the education of youth. Its concern is with the life of the mind, with the attainment of intellectual excellence. This fact is basic in the thesis of this article.

Educational Goals Conducive to Morality

Intellectual excellence is not unrelated to ethics and morals. In one of the most familiar passages in John Henry Newman's series of lectures in 1852 on "The Idea of a University," he said,

> Liberal Education . . . makes not the Christian, not the Catholic but the gentleman. It is well to be a gentleman; it is well to have a culti-vated intellect, a delicate taste, a candid, equitable, dispassionate mind, a noble and courteous bearing in the conduct of life;—these are the connatural qualities of a large knowledge; they are the objects of a university.

Concerning the values of liberal education to the student, he said,

> He profits by an intellectual tradition, which is independent of par-ticular teachers, which guides him in his choice of subjects, and duly interprets for him those which he chooses. He apprehends the great outlines of knowledge, the principles on which it rests, the scale of its parts, its lights and its shades, its great points and its little, as he otherwise cannot apprehend them. Hence it is that his education is called "liberal." A habit of mind is formed which lasts through life, of which the attributes are, freedom, equitableness, calmness, moder-ation, and wisdom; or what in a former discourse I have ventured to call a philosophical habit. This then I would assign as the special fruit of the education furnished at a university, as contrasted with other places of teaching or modes of teaching. This is the main purpose of a university in its treatment of its students.

An institution of higher education administered in accordance with Cardinal Newman's conception of a university would be unique in the United States today—unique in many desirable ways. Such an institu-tion would never be imperiled as many of our institutions of higher education are today imperiled by anti-intellectualism, evidenced in part, but only in part, by the overemphasis on intercollegiate athletics and the resultant practice of subsidizing and professionalizing football and basketball in the guise of scholarships. This practice has given many of our students a sense of values which, educationally speaking, are false. These false values explain the susceptibility of some students to the kind of corruption currently revealed at a number of colleges and universities. These students are the victims of an immoral anti-intellectualism, for the development of which educators are in large part responsible.

While the attributes of an educated person—devotion to freedom, equitableness, calmness, moderation, wisdom, cultivated intellect and dispassionate mind—do not guarantee morality, since they are themselves attributes of ideal human character they are conducive to morality. The truly educated person seeks freedom, has a sense of moral and ethical values, and has respect for truth and justice—the greatest of our moral virtues. . . .

Moral Obligation to Public

We of the academic profession have the privilege of helping to educate young men and women for life in a free society. In our special academic disciplines we must, if our colleges are to make the greatest moral contributions to the public, insist upon intellectual integrity, intellectual excellence, and basic knowledge. We must do more. We must also be specialists in freedom and instruct our students in the values of freedom. To do less is to be unworthy of our calling; to do less is to fail to meet a clear moral obligation to the public.

FOR FURTHER STUDY

Medicine

"Crisis in American Medicine," *Harper's Magazine* 221 (October 1960: 124-168. (A Special Supplement edited by Marion K. Sanders.)

Fletcher, Joseph. *Morals and Medicine*. Princeton: Princeton U. Press, 1954. (Beacon paperback, 1960.)

Hawley, Paul R. "Too Much Unnecessary Surgery," *U. S. News and World Report*, 34 (February 20, 1953): 47-55 (Interview with Dr. Paul R. Hawley, Director of American College of Surgeons).

Opinions and Reports of the Judicial Council 1964. Chicago: American Medical Association, 1964.

Sanders, Theodore M., M.D. "What Doctors Can Do To Cut the Cost of Medical Care." *Harper's Magazine*, 228 (May 1964): 16, 22, 24, 26.

Law

East, Sara Toll (ed.). *Law in American Society*. New York: Wilson, 1963. (The Reference Shelf, Vol. 35, No. 2.)

George, B. J., Jr. "A New Approach to Criminal Law," *Harper's Magazine*, 228 (April 1964): 183-188.

Gossett, William T. "Human Rights and the American Bar," *The American Scholar*, 22 (Autumn 1953): 411-422.

Pike, James A. *Beyond the Law: The Religious and Ethical Meaning of the Lawyer's Vocation*. New York: Doubleday, 1963.

Pollitt, Daniel H. "Timid Lawyers and Neglected Clients," *Harper's Magazine*, 229 (August 1964): 81-86.

Education

Bertocci, Peter A. *Education and the Vision of Excellence*. Boston: Boston U. Press, 1960.

National Education Association of the United States. *Opinions of the Committee on Professional Ethics*. Washington, D. C.: The Association, 1964.

Smith, Huston. "Values: Academic and Human," in *The Larger Learning*, ed. Marjorie Carpenter. Dubuque: Wm. C. Brown, 1960.

Ulich, Robert. "Ethics and Education" in *Moral Principles of Action*, ed. Ruth Nanda Anshen. New York: Harper, 1952, Ch. 18.

CHAPTER 18

ETHICS IN
AN INDUSTRIAL SOCIETY

*For a New Code of Business Ethics**

CLARENCE B. RANDALL

Clarence B. Randall (1891-   ), former president
and chairman of the board of Inland Steel Company,
has held many important business and government
posts. He is the author of articles and books including *A Creed for Free Enterprise*, 1952, and *The Folk-
lore of Management*, 1961.

The subject of business ethics, which has been smoldering for some
months, has burst into flame. Sparked originally by such events as the
prosecutions and convictions in the electrical industry and the fall from
grace of a member of the New York Stock Exchange, this fire has fed
rapidly on highly combustible material which it has encountered in the
field of public opinion. Sensing the possibility of a major conflagration,
the Kennedy Administration has sounded an all-out alarm.

Secretary of Commerce Hodges recently made a most courageous
and forthright address on the subject in Miami, and the Pentagon has
announced that it will firmly enforce a new policy directive requiring
the very highest moral standards on the part of all who are engaged in
military development and research activities.

* Clarence B. Randall, *New York Times Magazine*, April 8, 1962, pp. 24, 127-128.
Copyright © 1962 by The New York Times Company. Reprinted by permission.

Above all, President Kennedy himself did exactly the right thing when he placed the responsibility where it belongs: mainly, on industry itself. He appointed a committee of distinguished business men from all sections of the country to serve as his Business Ethics Advisory Council. They have now presented to him a report which poses very searching inquiries, indeed, to the industrial community.

From these and other signs it is clear that industry in this country is facing a moral crisis. The American people are taking a new, hard look at us and are asking themselves whether by any chance the whole lot of us are dishonest.

They demand urgently to know whether we operate behind a pious facade, whether our public posture is a fraud, whether deep down inside we are completely antisocial in our purposes. We are not yet convicted in the public mind, but a heavy cloud of suspicion surrounds us.

We must face this issue squarely, as indeed the electrical industry itself has. In my opinion, we must at once do one of two things. If our ethical practices are in fact shameful, we must change them forthwith, and make it clear that we have done so. If conscience tells us that they are completely above reproach, we must offer a new declaration of faith to the American people, and then by our conduct demonstrate the complete integrity of our purposes.

No man of senior years, like myself, can fail to sense that the moral climate in industry today is greatly improved over what we knew in earlier years, but this is partly because it was so bad in the period when we first went to work. We remember all too vividly practices which prevailed then, and which we would now like to forget.

For example, in the steel industry, I knew a time when it was common for one company to endeavor continuously by subversive means to steal the research secrets of its competitors. This was done in many ways, with all the stealth of a Communist agent. Technicians in other laboratories would be suborned and for a fixed payment per month, delivered in rolls of bills at secret rendezvous, would turn over copies of blueprints or duplicates of new formulae. A second and even more effective way was simply to hire away the chief chemist or other research officer by doubling his pay, on condition that he would bring his secrets with him.

During the Great Depression, these methods were applied to sales. The vice president of a company whose pay had been severely cut was an easy mark for the competitor who offered a big increase. When he changed jobs, he brought his little black book with him, and revealed the secret rebates which he had been giving customers. The trouble was that his aroused former employer often hired him back at the end of the first year, and when he returned he crossed up his new employer and took his new little black book with him.

There was another kind of venality—a betrayal of trust within a company for a cold cash payment. I was once trapped in the midst of one such nasty situation where, for every carload of steel scrap shipped to the steel plant, the inspector was paid handsomely for not looking beneath the top layer. Nor was this enough. A further shocker was in store for me, because I found that the shipper who had bought the inspector had also bought the court.

Bribery of public officials, the crude buying of legislators, was also widely practiced in earlier days. The notorious black bag was not a fiction in my day but reality, and devious indeed were the mental processes by which otherwise high-minded men justified the practice. For example, I knew a company which for years secretly put a particular member of the legislature on its payroll for $400 a month (that was real money then) with the justification that he was making a great personal sacrifice in accepting the office. I do not recall, however, that he ever voted for a measure of which the company disapproved.

And I knew another corporation in which the officer who handled the taxes was directed by the president to get the assessment reduced, and not to report back. He did in fact get the assessment down. He did it by meeting the assessor in a hotel room. And he did not tell the boss what he had done—but he did tell me.

Now most of those crude and crass practices have disappeared from American business practice—most, but not all. For example, the large-scale pirating of trade secrets in big industry is no longer resorted to. In steel, at least, technical information is now openly and freely exchanged. Advances based upon research by one company become available to all. Competitors have learned that they gain more that way than they lose. Nevertheless in new industries which depend heavily on design factors and advanced technology, or in fields where only a few large companies carry on research programs, I suspect that the stealing still goes on.

Graft, unhappily, is still practiced by many at the municipal level, in such cases as buying off an alderman for an alley permit and this is very wrong. Though undoubtedly rare, money may still sometimes actually pass to a member of a state legislature, or of Congress, to influence his attitude.

I regret, too, that in all candor I must record the unsavory fact that there is a related area of business endeavor where the state of morality is very low indeed, and where there is a stain on the conscience of industry which needs to be removed, and removed soon. I mean the bribery of officials in the governments of new countries in the under-developed parts of the world.

In the course of my government service, I visited many of these areas. I know whereof I speak, and I say that there are many otherwise respectable companies which still buy their way in when it comes to securing a mineral concession or establishing an operation in a remote part of the world.

This must stop, and it can only be accomplished by self-discipline. Surprisingly enough, I happen to have grave doubt whether it is a violation of any present Federal law for an American citizen to corrupt an officer of a foreign government, but that fact merely highlights the challenge to our business leadership. I reject the argument that other nations are doing it, and therefore we must if we are to compete. Better to lose the business than to deny our heritage. The entire prestige of our country, and its ability to preserve our way of life in the world, is at stake. Those precious values must not be jeopardized by individual dishonor.

In the host countries, someone always knows the facts. What could be more tragic than for us to lose an air base that is vital to our national security because of moral turpitude on the part of American business? What will be our position when some demagogue from the desert calls his people to arms with the cry, "Drive the filthy Americans into the sea. We have been robbed of our ancient heritage"?

Either we have a code of morals, or we do not. If we do, it is for universal application, and must be adhered to in all circumstances, regardless of the impact on earnings. This is the acid test of our integrity.

That was the moral point at issue in the investigations of the electrical industry—setting artificially high prices to keep profits up. It is perhaps unfair to pass judgment upon those cases without personal knowledge of the facts, but who among us can avoid it, when so much is at stake?

For myself, there is no doubt whatever that serious mistakes were made. Things were done which have prejudiced the continuing development of the private-enterprise system, and this is bad for all of us. How could this have come to pass? How may one explain these incredible circumstances? All that an outsider may do is to speculate.

Conceivably, for example, these were mistakes of the head, and not of the heart, committed by overzealous executives. It might be argued that here were men who in their daily lives were decent, law-abiding citizens, and who responded to the highest loyalty they knew, the desire to advance the interests of their companies. In other words, it is possible that they put corporate welfare above that of their country merely because they knew no better. It is possible that they simply did not understand the vital function of a free market in a democratic society.

If this were the answer, it would still be bad. To hold the confidence of our public, we in industry must not only have the moral courage to do the right, but sufficient insight to know the right. Our minds must be clear, as well as our consciences.

This hypothesis does not ring true, however. These executives were men of long years of service and broad experience, and it is hard to believe that they did not know that they were violating the law. Our moral crisis is there, either way.

But beyond these proved and punished aberrations there are large, new, somewhat peripheral areas of moral problems of such comparatively recent origin that the issues have not yet been sharply defined, nor full corrective measures taken. Here the impeccable conduct of the many is being placed in jeopardy by the rascality of the few.

This is a partial list:

(1) *Lack of truth in advertising.* There is still an occasional business buccaneer who misrepresents the quality of the product, or who understates the price by concealing the fact that there are indispensable accessories which will also be required.

(2) *The credit racket.* There are still unscrupulous vendors who overpersuade the unwary buyer of modest means by the no-payment-down, take-all-the-time-you-need pitch. The true interest charge on the deferred balance is not revealed, and the seller makes his money out of the financing of the debt rather than as legitimate profit on the merchandise.

(3) *The union agent racket.* There are still evil-minded employers who cross the palm of the organizer, and buy exemption from legitimate worker grievances thus cheating the employes and rejecting the responsibilities of orderly collective bargaining.

(4) *Denial of promotion on merit to minority groups.* There are still those who give lip service in public to the doctrine of fair opportunity for all workers, regardless of creed or color, but who deny it in actual practice.

(5) *Expense account cheating.* No well-informed observer can doubt for a moment that the Federal Government is still being deprived of large sums of revenue by the unscrupulous padding of income tax deductions claimed as business expenses. The honest citizen pays more than his share of the tax load when the man who cheats pays less.

In listing this catalogue of corporate sins one must, in fairness, point out that industry is not alone in having its moral lapses. The commercial world has no monopoly on character weakness. There are newspaper reporters who state as fact that for which they have no documentation; there are clergymen whose conduct is such that they have to be unfrocked; there are scholars who must be dismissed from faculties; there are surgeons who split fees, and lawyers who are disbarred.

But the human frailty of others can never justify moral turpitude in business. The American people are entitled to expect the very best from us at all times. We have no present alternative other than to submit forthwith all our practices to the most intensive re-examination, done in an atmosphere of heart-searching humility, and thereafter we must have the fortitude to do the right, wherever that may take us. We can and must set off a moral and spiritual reawakening which will touch every segment of American life.

Here is a unique challenge for our trade associations. Let our two great groups, the National Association of Manufacturers and the United States Chamber of Commerce, seize the initiative in denouncing obvious misconduct and in proclaiming new codes of ethical conduct. Then let the trade groups, industry by industry, promote the doing of the right as zealously as they now promote the sale of the product.

Above all, let each corporate officer determine in his own heart that never again will he put expediency above principle, never again let a chance for a quick profit stifle the dictates of his conscience.

Only thus can the survival of private enterprise in this troubled world be assured.

Forms of Irresponsibility*

W. H. FERRY

W. H. Ferry (1910-   ) is Vice-President of The
Fund for the Republic and Staff Administrator of the
Study of the Economic Order at the Center for the
Study of Democratic Institutions at Santa Barbara.
He has had a varied experience including work as a
newspaper editor and public relations director deal-
ing with a number of large business concerns.

Americans regard freedom and justice as by-products, pleasant acci-
dents of a specially endowed industrial community. Freedom and
justice, in this view, grow in the cracks, in the interstices of society. It
is true that many American values came into existence and flourished in
just this way. But, in the new and complicated conditions of society, so
naive a method scarcely merits confidence. Many have noticed the
cracks are closing up, the interstices becoming fewer. In the view of
some, for example, freedom and justice flourish only where the labor
union is not, as in the opinion of others they flourish where the corporation is not. But both are omnipresent. There is still another view, that
freedom and justice are natural American phenomena, reliable and constant as the dew, not to be affected by courts or cold wars. Though the
citizenry is commanded to transform the country into a garrison and
to fight, if need be, to the end of civilization in the name of freedom
and justice, Americans are enjoined not to plan for their survival and
enhancement in the common life.

This is a wrong-headed way to look at freedom and justice. Addic-
tion to the freedom-by-accident dogma leads to most of the forms of
irresponsibility with which this paper is concerned. Americans have
got things in reverse when they devote close to 100 per cent of their
time and thought to housekeeping problems. Here the corporation is
especially culpable. Keeping a nation of 185 million people adequately

* From *The Annals of the American Academy of Political and Social Science*,
343 (September 1962): 65-74 with omissions. Reprinted by permission of The
Academy and the author.

supplied with goods and services is, of course, a necessary means to the general welfare, as well as one with its incidental fascinations and rewards. But the corporation customarily sees itself as an end, not a means. The trouble occurs when the economic machine, including the corporation, comes to be regarded as the be-all and end-all. From such a conception of the economic order flows much of the confusion about national purpose, much of the bewilderment about Soviet progress, and most of the forms of irresponsibility now depreciating the general welfare.

A few definitions will make the ensuing discussion more intelligible.

By "responsible" is mainly meant the capability to distinguish right from wrong, and also accountability, both legal and moral, for actions taken and actions not taken.

It is to be noted that this definition has two parts. The first is personal and has to do with what managers learned in Sunday school. The second part, accountability, is nonpersonal and has to do with the corporation's duty to the common good, the main elements of which, it may be recalled, are peace, order, freedom, and justice.

By "irresponsible" is mainly meant the antithesis of responsible. Irresponsibility is characterized by unethical and morally distasteful behavior. Irresponsibility is marked by short views, self-righteousness, hypocrisy, and disdain for the common good. . . .

The Common Uncommon Men

In taking up the forms of corporate irresponsibility, such well-publicized conflict of interest situations as those involving the Chrysler Corporation and the Prudential Insurance Company will be passed over. The togetherness that brought so much sadness upon the electrical-supply companies will be alluded to only mildly and delicately. Yet it must be remarked that the crowded dramatis personae of this case tend to bring in question Crawford Greenewalt's statement in *The Uncommon Man*[1] that "A disposition on the part of a single individual within the organization to be a scoundrel would encounter tough going. The number of people he would have to persuade to join him on the primrose path would, I think, dishearten the most determined."

However, what is irresponsible is not necessarily illegal, and these matters are referred to for the light they throw on the common law of the corporation, by which is meant that body of precedent and accepted practice by which the corporation more and more demands that it be

[1] New York: McGraw-Hill, 1959, p. 27.

judged. Some of the most advanced corporate practitioners of social responsibility were, after all, involved in the widespread thimblerigging in the electrical-supply industry. . . .

Advertising is so willing an accomplice of corporate irresponsibility that it must expect to appear often in a catalogue of this kind. Consider advertising's discovery and methodical exploitation of the teen-age market. Here are clearly drawn the lines of battle between those who would sell and those who would train, between the manipulators in one phalanx, and school, church, and mother in the other. Consider, too, advertising's part in the fateful paradox of Mr. Smith as consumer and Mr. Smith as union member. As consumer, he is cajoled, pounded, and motivationally motivated to buy. As union member, Mr. Smith is solemnly warned to beware of union leaders who tell him that he needs wage increases if he is going to buy what he is cajoled, pounded, and motivationally motivated to buy.

Planned obsolescence is one of the more obvious forms of irresponsibility. Waste is inevitable in any form of organization. But it is a triumph of irresponsibility to elevate waste to a principle in a society which, even though affluent, is yet far from providing a minimum decent life for all its citizens.

Critics are sure to remind us that the United States, after all, is the best-off of nations, and measurably better off in all respects in this generation than last. But these comments are not directed at our history or accomplishments. They are aimed at aspects of the economic order that, at a crucial stage, are actively hindering progress toward a society that will be open, free, and just in the best sense of those words and able to play its part in a world order whose new and radically altered dimensions are clear to all who are willing to look.

A cherished corporate legend is that governmental bureaucracy is inefficient, full of featherbedding dullards, and tends toward venality but that the bureaucracy of the large company comprises high-minded and overworked gentlemen whose eyes are on a brighter star. This line is one of the main strands of the political irresponsibility of corporations. Though it might, at first glance, seem merely an engaging self-deception, it, in fact, tears away at respect for law and government, which are the joint creations of people for their own good, and aggrandizes the private company as somehow superior both in aim and practice. Closely related to the managerial theory of dunderhead government is that of corporate perfectionism. This is the insistence that the corporation never makes a mistake, so that, when something goes wrong, the fault may always be found elsewhere—in some government office, in the perfidy of unions, in unfair competition from beyond the seas, or in the fickleness of the public. A quaint consequence of this theory is that those few who make the corporate mistake—for mistakes are made—suffer little, and those many who had nothing to do with the decision suffer much. Thus, a mistaken judgment about a new product does not result in firing the managers who made the judgment but in laying off the employees who were not involved in it. Anyone can count on his thumbs the mistakes that have been acknowledged by corporations; there is no need to enlarge this point. . . .

Technology and Employment

The irresponsibility of political short views is readily illustrated by considering the corporate attitude toward technology and employment. The United States is moving into an epoch in which most of the ancient evils, drudgery, want, war, can be eliminated or minimized. The venerable rule which says "the more machines, the more jobs" is being repealed. The probable effects of automation are a matter of surmise. But what is not a surmise is that there will be a very great deal of automation and that traditional ways of coping with such developments— collective bargaining, for example—are clearly inadequate. What shall we do when we can meet all our needs with half or a quarter of the available supply of labor? This dark issue is lingering just over the horizon, its harbingers already among us in nests of technological unemployment. Americans are beginning, also, to understand that automation means more centralized decision-making, more and more influence in the hands of fewer and fewer people. What has the corporation to say about these momentous problems? Up to this point virtually all that has been heard has been the usual pieties about things working themselves out and not interfering with progress. This is not an easy matter to think about, to be sure, yet it is sad that the great corporations appear not to be willing to make the effort.

A different style of political irresponsibility is harshly illuminated by United States problems in Latin America and in the other less-developed parts of the world. No one acquainted with the behavior of Western corporations on their pilgrimages for profit during the last fifty years can really be surprised to learn that the African explosions now taking place are doing so in an anti-American and anti-capitalist context. For many years, these continents have been happy hunting grounds for corporate adventurers, who have taken out great resources and great profits and left behind great poverty, great expectations, and great resentment. Gunnar Myrdal[2] points out that capitalist intervention in underdeveloped countries thus far has almost uniformly had the result of making the rich richer and the poor poorer—a spectacular record of political irresponsibility on a global scale. These unfriendly raids on the resources of others, of course, have their domestic counterpart in undiminished raids on our own timber, oil, and grazing lands and mineral deposits.

The immediate future should tell whether corporate leaders are repentant and now willing to share in the social and money costs of building up the backward parts of the world. But the corporation is not well equipped to play anything but a secondary role to government and international agencies in the tasks that must be undertaken in these areas. A far from uncharacteristic article, "International Intelligence for the International Enterprise," by J. J. Beauvois, in *The California Management Review*[3] discloses why this is so. In eight pages, Mr. Beauvois, a management consultant, suggests only once that the international company seek to understand the history and aspirations and culture of the people of underdeveloped countries. He advises that the maximum intelligence be garnered about economic and political conditions and the prospects of profit and concludes by saying that the international manager of the 1960's will have two responsibilities—one to stockholders, the other to America's part in the cold war. A new and sensitive nation might be excused for finding a few flaws in this approach.

The Corporation and War

A closely related category of irresponsibility is the posture of the corporation on questions of war and peace. The prospect of the destruction of civilization is looking the country dead in the eye. The contribution of our industrial potentates to the debate on this crucial issue, as far as one is aware, is almost exactly zero. Threadbare rhetoric about the malevolence of the Russians and the unimpeachable rightness of our side does not count. In Russia, one expects submission and silence from Soviet commissars about such matters. But should Americans expect silence and submission from their own industrial leaders? . . . It is difficult to recall a single constructive suggestion from corporate headquarters for hastening disarmament or, indeed, any enthusiasm for the

[2] *Rich Lands and Poor* (New York: Harper, 1958).
[3] Vol. 3, No. 2 (Winter 1961), p. 39.

general idea. The evidence, alas, all seems to be to the contrary, that business has no interest in disarmament.

Nor can any other step toward peace by the corporation be named nor a single criticism of official policy. The businessman's passion for frugality in government which is so aroused when public works or federal aid to education are mentioned is extinct where the arms budget is concerned. . . .

Government of Corporations

Americans rightly believe that the quality of life under their self-governing system is superior to that under a tyranny or under a despot, however well intentioned. This is what we say the cold war is all about. Aside from the deep conviction that constitutional democracy is the only just form of government, Americans point to the particular virtues with which it endows the common life: openness, freedom, opportunity, choice. The benevolent despotism of the corporation can include many advantages like utter security, but all are achieved at the price of some of the virtues just mentioned. Perhaps it is too much to ask of corporate life that it improve those exposed to it, that it make better men of them, so to speak. But it is not too much to ask that it not make worse men of them. In a despotism, the quality of life is inevitably smudged, or changed, or degraded. What the despot can give he can take away. Though his sanctions may never be used, they are always ready at hand.

Now, without fitting the metaphor into contemporary circumstances too tightly, one can still ask about the quality and texture of corporation life in this context. Managers do not like the answers given by social scientists, by novelists and playwrights, and by outsiders generally. Yet few indeed are the answers provided by the hand of corporate experience, and, so, we are pretty much left with the impression passed on by the sociologists and novelists. That they frequently strike a responsive note reflects what we learned in school and in experience about life on well-run baronies. It is not that the inhabitants of such fiefdoms had particularly onerous lives, it is that their condition was decided by someone else. It is one thing to choose an empty and ordinary life and another to have no choice in the matter. It is unacceptable to argue that today's corporate man can always quit, for the simple reason that he can only go to another corporation. It is irresponsible to argue that the quality of life in the corporation has no connection with its neofeudal government. The present mode of corporate government is a potent teacher of political apathy and nonparticipation.

The irresponsibilities here enumerated make up a substantial indictment, but they are intended to show structural defects and not moral turpitude in managers. The principal defect is that of the theory of a mature political economy; no one understands what the corporation is all about, its place in the economic order, and the purpose of the economic order itself in a constitutional democracy. Nietzsche said: "The commonest stupidity is in forgetting what we are trying to do." Today's world is hazardous and radically novel. The continuing irresponsibility of the corporation is its reliance on the belief that what it was trying to do a half-century ago is its manifest duty in Year 17 of the Atom Age.

๛๛๛๛๛

A Statement on Business Ethics
and a Call for Action*

THE BUSINESS ETHICS ADVISORY COUNCIL

> The Business Ethics Advisory Council is a group of outstanding businessmen, educators, clergymen, and journalists whose aim is to help the American business community develop and carry out programs for the improvement of business ethics.

The ethical standards of American businessmen, like those of the American people, are founded upon our religious heritage and our traditions of social, political, and economic freedom . . .

* From *The Annals of the American Academy of Political and Social Science,* 343 (September 1962): 137-140. Reprinted by permission.

As the ethical standards and conduct of American private enterprise have improved, so also has there developed a public demand for proper performance and a keen sensitivity to lapses from those standards. The full realization by the business community of its future opportunities and, indeed, the maintenance of public confidence require a continuing pursuit of the highest standards of ethical conduct.

Attainment of this objective is not without difficulty. Business enterprises, large and small, have relationships in many directions—with stockholders and other owners, employees, customers, suppliers, government, and the public in general. The traditional emphasis on freedom, competition, and progress in our economic system often brings the varying interests of these groups into conflict, so that many difficult and complex ethical problems can arise in any enterprise. While all relationships of an enterprise to these groups are regulated in some degree by law, compliance with law can only provide a minimum standard of conduct. Beyond legal obligations, the policies and actions of businessmen must be based upon a regard for the proper claims of all affected groups.

Moreover, in many business situations, the decision that must be made is not the simple choice between absolute right and absolute wrong. The decisions of business frequently must be made in highly complex and everchanging circumstances, and at times involve either adhering to earlier standards or developing new ones. Such decisions affect profoundly not only the business enterprise, but our society as a whole. Indeed, the responsible position of American business—both large and small—obligates each participant to lead rather than follow.

A weighty responsibility therefore rests upon all those who manage business enterprises, as well as upon all others who influence the environment in which business operates. In the final analysis, however, the primary moral duty to establish high ethical standards and adequate procedures for their enforcement in each enterprise must rest with its policy-making body—its board of directors and its top management.

We, therefore, now propose that current efforts be expanded and intensified and that new efforts now be undertaken by the American business community to hasten its attainment of those high ethical standards that derive from our heritage and traditions. We urge all enterprises, business groups, and associations to accept responsibility—each for itself and in its own most appropriate way—to develop methods and programs for encouraging and sustaining these efforts on a continuous basis. We believe in this goal, we accept it, and we encourage all to pursue its attainment.

Some Questions for Businessmen

The following questions are designed to facilitate the examination by American businessmen of their ethical standards and performance. They are intended to illustrate the kinds of questions that must be identified and considered by each business enterprise if it is to achieve compliance with those high ethical standards that derive from our heritage and traditions. Each reader will think of others. No single list can possibly encompass all of the demands for ethical judgments that must be met by men in business.

1. GENERAL UNDERSTANDING:

Do we have in our organization current, well-considered statements of the ethical principles that should guide our officers and employees in specific situations that arise in our business activities, both domestic and foreign? Do we revise these statements periodically to cover new situations and changing laws and social patterns?

Have those statements been the fruit of discussion in which all members of policy-determining management have had an opportunity to participate?

Have we given to our officers and employees at all levels sufficient motivation to search out ethical factors in business problems and apply high ethical standards in their solution? What have we done to eliminate opposing pressures?

Have we provided officers and employees with an easily accessible means of obtaining counsel on and resolution of ethical problems that may rise in their activities? Do they use it?

Do we know whether our officers and employees apply in their daily activities the ethical standards we have promulgated? Do we reward those who do so and penalize those who do not?

2. COMPLIANCE WITH LAW:

Having in mind the complexities and everchanging patterns of modern law and government regulation:

What are we doing to make sure that our officers and employees are informed about and comply with laws and regulations affecting their activities?

Have we made clear that it is our policy to obey even those laws which we may think unwise and seek to have changed?

Do we have adequate internal checks on our compliance with law?

Have we established a simple and readily available procedure for our officers and employees to seek legal guidance in their activities? Do they use it?

3. CONFLICTS OF INTEREST:

Do we have a current, well-considered statement of policy regarding potential conflict of interest problems of our directors, officers, and employees? If so, does it cover conflicts which may arise in connection with such activities as: transactions with or involving our company; acquiring interests in or performing services for our customers, distributors, suppliers, and competitors; buying and selling our company's securities; or the personal undertaking of what might be called company opportunities?

What mechanism do we have for enabling our directors, officers, and employees to make ethical judgments when conflicts of interest do arise?

Do we require regular reports, or do we leave it to our directors, officers, and employees to disclose such activities voluntarily?

4. ENTERTAINMENT, GIFTS, AND EXPENSES:

Have we defined our company policy on accepting and making expenditures for gifts and entertainment? Are the criteria as to occasion and amount clearly stated or are they left merely to the judgment of the officer or employee?

Do we disseminate information about our company policy to the organizations with which we deal?

Do we require adequate reports of both the giving and receiving of gifts and entertainment; are they supported in sufficient detail; are they subject to review by appropriate authority; and could the payment or receipt be justified to our stockholders, the government, and the public?

5. CUSTOMERS AND SUPPLIERS:

Have we taken appropriate steps to keep our advertising and sales representations truthful and fair? Are these steps effective?

How often do we review our advertising, literature, labels, and packaging? Do they give our customers a fair understanding of the true quality, quantity, price, and function of our products? Does our service as well as our product measure up to our basic obligations and our representations?

Do we fairly make good on flaws and defects? Is this a matter of stated policy? Do we know that our employees, distributors, dealers, and agents follow it?

Do we avoid favoritism and discrimination and otherwise treat our customers and suppliers fairly and equitably in all our dealings with them?

6. SOCIAL RESPONSIBILITIES:

Every business enterprise has manifold responsibilities to the society of which it is a part. The prime legal and social obligation of the managers of a business is to operate it for the long-term profit of its owners. Concurrent social responsibilities pertain to a company's treatment of its past, present, and prospective employees and to its various relationships with customers, suppliers, government, the community, and the public at large. These responsibilities may often be, or appear to be, in conflict, and at times a management's recognition of its broad responsibilities may affect the amount of an enterprise's immediate profits and the means of attaining them.

The problems that businessmen must solve in this area are often exceedingly perplexing. One may begin his reflections on this subject by asking—

Have we reviewed our company policies in the light of our responsibilities to society? Are our employees aware of the interaction between our business policies and our social responsibilities?

Do we have a clearly understood concept of our obligation to assess our responsibilities to stockholders, employees, customers, suppliers, our community, and the public?

Do we recognize and impress upon all our officers and employees the fact that our free-enterprise system and our individual business enterprises can thrive and grow only to the extent that they contribute to the welfare of our country and its people?

FOR FURTHER STUDY

American Academy of Political and Social Science. *The Ethics of Business Enterprise*. Philadelphia: The Academy, 1962, *The Annals*, 343 (September 1962): 1-140.

Bartels, Robert (ed.). *Ethics in Business*. Columbus: Bureau of Business Research Monograph Number 111, The Ohio State University, 1963, 180 pp.

Baumhart, Raymond C. "How Ethical Are Businessmen?" *Harvard Business Review*, 39 (July-August, 1961): 6-19, 156-176.

Hall, Cameron P. *On-the-Job Ethics*. New York: National Council of Churches, 1963. (Report on a Study Project in six major occupations, 148 pp.)

Lerner, Max. *America as a Civilization*. New York: Simon and Schuster, 1957, Vol. I. Ch. V, "Capitalist Economy and Business Civilization," 265-352.

Smith, Richard Austin. "The Incredible Electrical Conspiracy," *Fortune*, 63 Part I (April 1961): 132-180; Part II (May 1961): 161-224.

Spurrier, William A. *Ethics and Business*. New York: Scribner, 1962.

Wirtenberger, Henry J. *Morality and Business*. Chicago: Loyola U. Press, 1962.

CHAPTER 19

ETHICS
AND THE MASS MEDIA

ᘛ᚜ᚘᚘᚘᚘᚘᚘᚘᚘᚘᚘᚘᚘᚘᚘᚘᚘᚘᚘᚘᚘᚘᚘ

What Is Wrong With TV—
*and With Us**

CHARLES A. SIEPMANN

Charles A. Siepmann (1899-   ) is Chairman of the
Department of Communications in Education at
New York University (Washington Square). He
is the author of several books and a consultant to
the Ford Foundation. Some years ago he was Vice
President in charge of programing for the B.B.C.

At a luncheon meeting during the convention of the National Asso-
ciation of Broadcasters in Chicago the other day, a Congressional guest,
Representative Walter E. Rogers of Texas, got a standing ovation.
Why? Because he is the author of a bill designed to prevent the Federal
Communications Commission from regulating the amount of advertis-
ing on the air, and the House had approved the bill, 317 to 43.

But does the public approve? What, in broadcasting, is the "public
interest," and who shall determine it? What, in other words, would
constitute a true national policy for broadcasting and how could it be
implemented?

* From *New York Times Magazine*, April 19, 1964, pp. 13, 112-114. Copyright
© 1964 by The New York Times Company. Reprinted by permission.

A national policy implies a national consensus—something that all of us can agree to. Personal preferences are here beside the point. Such a policy can only be defined by analyzing (1) the distinctive potentialities of the television medium and (2) the compelling needs of our society —meaning needs shared by us all, as individuals and as citizens.

Television is distinctive in its universal reach. No other medium can transport us all simultaneously to the scene of action anywhere on earth. This universal reach creates a corresponding dependence. This is why we all turn to television in times of common need as we did during the four days that shook the world last November. Television is distinctive also as a new language, a new art-in-the-making with extraordinary power to quicken the senses and focus the mind on reality.

Television, then, will be true to itself as it exploits these distinctive properties and reckons with their implicit cultural and moral obligations. Its universal reach gives it its opportunity—to serve the common interest. But this is also its limitation. For, given an audience comprising the whole nation, only shared interests can be served—and not even all of these. Even rough justice is possible only by providing programs that offer *variant exposure to the widest practicable range of commonly shared interests*. Hence the test of true service is not the size of the audience at a given hour, but the overall variety of interests provided for throughout a day or week.

But we are already in trouble as we unconsciously confuse the interests (tastes) of the public with the public interest, which is what broadcasting, under law, is charged to serve. For the public interest has little to do with our appetites and desires, however widely shared. It has everything to do with our needs, as human beings and citizens of this democracy. In both realms our whims and appetites must be subordinate to our needs and duties (to ourselves and others) if we are to survive.

Consideration of our needs, moreover, has this advantage: Tastes differ, and any policy that seeks fairly to reconcile the myriad conflicting tastes and interests of a nation is foredoomed to failure. But our needs can be defined, and in terms that are, surely, acceptable at the bar of reason. What, then, are they, and from what do they stem?

They stem from our common humanity—from the chance that nature offers each of us to become a human being, transcending the beast that lurks in each of us. This, I suggest, involves the endless refinement and exercise of our distinctively human, suprabestial faculties. Broadly defined, these needs would seem to be as follows:

(1) *The need for relaxation.* Laughter, amusement, even idle frivolity are legitimate needs because they are psychological necessities. They have always been so.

(2) *The need for expansion of our horizons of knowledge and awareness*—of people, their condition and their interaction with one another, their arts and their inventions—the all-embracing world of knowledge in a contemporary sense. (As it equips us to vote responsibly, such service meets our civic as well as our individual needs.)

(3) *The need not only for knowledge but for experience in depth,* comprising all that invites our understanding of what lies below the surface of events and of all meaning, including the meaning of life itself. This, pre-eminently, is the realm of the artist, the philosopher, the divine. But it is essentially a dimension of experience common to us all, forced on us inescapably the moment we use our minds and our imaginations. Awe, suffering, love, ecstasy are elements of this experience.

(4) *Practical needs in our day-to-day living.* There exists a storehouse of knowledge and experience here which, if made the property of all, would transform the happiness and health of millions. The extent and variety of such knowledge is vast—the rearing of children, healthy diet, marital relations, mental health and medical services, at one end of the scale; and at the other, such relatively trivial needs as how to cook and fill out income tax forms—the infinities of "how to do it" knowledge.

If we aspire to be human beings and to pay more than lip service to democracy and its claims on us, these are the four necessary components of a humanistic diet. Exclude any one of them, and we risk intellectual and emotional pellagra.

Television, then, serves us well as it meets all of these four needs at various levels of understanding. And with three networks available, we have the physical facilities for *nationwide satisfaction of each of these needs for three-and-three-quarter-hours a night, seven days a week, between the hours of* 6-11 *P.M. alone!* (Actually, more is possible, for more than one need can be met in a single program. "The Merchant of Venice," for example, and "The Defenders" both offer relaxation *and* experience in depth.)

Apply this yardstick, and how does television measure up? People will differ widely as they appraise the worth of any given program.

But if we apply the above criteria, consensus is surely possible on some patent defects of present service.

For a start, the time devoted to light entertainment, especially in evening hours, is wildly disproportionate, amounting to more than provision for all the other needs combined. Much of it is a great deal better than some critics are ready to admit, but the sheer amount of it precludes enjoyment of other interests for which millions are hungry and to which millions are entitled.

A network president has described present practice as cultural democracy. On the same principle we should presumably have economic democracy if department stores cleared their shelves of all but their best-selling lines.

Consider next, not content, but modes of communication. Age-old in its hold on popular imagination is the drama. Television drama is a distinctive art. Its power to portray the human situation, hold up a mirror to reality, communicate experience in depth has been proven again and again. Its quantity and, many claim, its quality have declined, and we are scarcely compensated for this by the spate of dated films now on the air, such enjoyment as they provide being heavily discounted by exasperation at the endless intrusion of crude commercials.

They are cheaper, of course, and in television it is revenue that counts. A distinctive art form of wide popular appeal has been virtually discarded in the interests of the profit ledger.

And what of news? For years it was conspicuous by its absence at convenient hours. The defect has recently been somewhat remedied— in terms of the time devoted to it. But what of its quality? In New York City the newspaper strike of 1962-63 forced readers to rely on broadcast news, and the experience resulted in reassessment of its worth. Before the strike 83 per cent of a sample interviewed thought it excellent. After 100 days without a newspaper people changed their minds. Only 16 per cent now thought it excellent. Sixty-eight per cent spoke of radio and television news as *poor*.

News apart, sustained analysis and comment on national and world events remain conspicuously absent. Many-sided discussion, representing the full spectrum of diverse opinion, is all but nonexistent. Television apparently knows better than Jefferson who claimed that "a nation that expects to be ignorant and free expects what never was and never will be."

Of daytime dramas, with their distorted image of reality, the less said the better. But here again it is less their presence on the air that invites censure than the alternatives of useful service which, by their profusion, they crowd out. It is the unbalanced diet—*absence* of service in our four categories of need—that here again makes a mockery of television as a responsible service to the nation.

Television's performance warrants analysis on another count as well, that of hypocrisy. It has long and insistently claimed that it gives the public what it wants. Whether one thinks this constitutes service in the public interest or not, let us put the industry to its own test. There is known to be widespread dissatisfaction with television on two grounds, of which the first is the excess of murder and mayhem on the air. God knows we have our bellyfull of it, as the reader can verify by sampling any weekday's output of the networks.

Thus in one evening, picked at random, there were two horror shows, two war films, two Westerns, four crook stories and six murders. Yet an exhaustive study of television's audience, sponsored by C.B.S., shows that even the *average* viewer "thinks that programs depict too much imitable violence." Twenty-five per cent of parents think children would be better off without television; 66 per cent cannot think of any example where children have benefited from it; 29 per cent cite examples where it harmed them.

It is the *average* viewer, again, who claims that there are too many commercials. Forty-three per cent would prefer to have none, while 24 per cent so resent them that they would pay for television to be rid of them. Here are matters on which broadcasting has a clear mandate from the people to speed reforms—and has responded with contemptuous disregard.

And as for advertising, we now have the preposterous situation of an industry that has for years claimed freedom from regulatory interference (on the ground that it can regulate itself) protesting violently when the F.C.C. proposes to adopt and to enforce the generous limits of advertising time which the industry itself had formulated but has not bothered to enforce. Such is the cynical hypocrisy of TV.

But not all television is commercial. There is educational television, too, broadcast by stations undistracted and uncontaminated by the lure of money.

The first educational television station went on the air in 1957. Today there are 85. Progress has been slow partly because ETV was assigned a majority of frequencies in the ultrahigh-frequency band to which most receivers cannot be tuned without the added cost of an "adapter." The stations are variously supported and operated by school systems, universities and by the local community. Mostly they perform local services and reflect local life and talent. All are in more or less desperate financial need—at least as they aspire to rounded program service of high quality over extended hours.

But, thanks to the Ford Foundation, local production resources are supplemented by five hours of program material a week supplied by the National Educational Television Center. For the next three years the center is to receive $6 million to produce programs of first-rate professional quality, at least half of which are to cover public and international affairs. Thus the imbalance of commercial television is partly redressed, and continuous exposure to experience in vital areas of need becomes available to an ever larger potential audience.

ETV is only now beginning to hit its stride. Critics continue to speak of it as dull and unimaginative and compare it unfavorably with commercial television in its professional standards of production. It is also criticized as lacking a unified philosophy with program output proportioned to the priorities of need.

But it has many superb programs already to its credit and it is young. In areas where it has become more or less established it has regular viewers ranging from 10 to 25 per cent of the population that its signals reach. Its need is for more money and for what money alone can assure in significant numbers—men of talent and imagination at its controls.

What, in the light of this analysis, are the broad outlines of the picture? On the commercial side (ETV is too young to appraise fairly) it is the picture of an industry rising intermittently to triumphant heights of responsible service but committed in its day-to-day operations to a warped and false philosophy—and a disingenuous philosophy at that— as it belies its own claim that it gives the public what it wants.

Television in the public interest does not mean coralling a peak audience for every hour on the air. Dragging or luring the horse to the water is not its business. Its function is to keep the well full and uncontaminated; let the horse drink as and when it wills. We get entertainment aplenty, though even here the range of interest is artificially confined by adherence to proven stereotypes of lowest-common-denominator tastes. But even if all of it were rich and varied, we get too much of it.

Programs suffer from a fatal disproportion, with the result that vital needs and varied competing interests shared by millions get short shrift.

In all but entertainment we get spotty, intermittent service. Yet it is only by continuous exposure that we acquire new interests, new insights, new awareness. Television takes us as we are (and that in the mass aggregate)and thereby keeps us where we are, denying that which we have it in us to become.

The pride and supposed virtue of private enterprise is that it is enterprising and takes risks. Television plays it safe. Its short-term gains are writ large in its profit-and-loss account. What of the long-term consequences—to television and to our society? "Style is the last morality of mind"? The trouble with television's style is that it is vulgar.

What lies at the root of the trouble? It is in large part the unique role that advertising plays in broadcasting as its major source of revenue. This gives the sponsor a degree of control over programs that is near absolute—in marked contrast to his control over newspaper and magazine content.

Thus a disastrous distortion of our system of broadcasting has taken place. The interests of the public have been subordinated to the interests of the sponsor. Sponsored programs are programs designed to expose commodities to the largest number of potential buyers. The tail of merchandising wags the dog of programing in the public interest.

But this is only part of the truth. For broadcasters are not so much in thrall to sponsors as they claim to be. They are, at least in some measure, masters in their own house—as they plow back into programs of which sponsors fight shy some part of their enormous profits. It is the Midas touch that plagues the broadcaster. Not profits, but profits without limit, determine program policy—and profits derived from a source that makes merchandising, not programing, its primary objective. Admittedly, not all television stations make big money. But enough do to support the contention that men making private profit through privileged access to a public property have obligations to serve the public interest first and foremost.

The profits of the television industry are in fact staggering. Total revenues in 1962 were nearly half a billion dollars—up 12.7 per cent over 1961. In 10 years profits have risen $5\frac{1}{2}$ times. In 1962, 81 per cent of V.H.F. (very high frequency) stations made a profit, and one-fourth of these earned over $1 million. As to networks, C.B.S. has topped all previous profits in each succeeding year but two since 1957. Its profits for the third quarter of 1963 nearly doubled those for the same period in 1962. Not even faintly comparable increase in varied service to our needs has followed.

What can be done about it all? Will the answer come from the broad-casting industry—through self-regulation? If it be true that "by their fruits ye shall know them," the prospect seems bleak.

Promise (as measured by speeches of industry spokesmen and publicity releases) and performance (as measured by the criteria we have applied) are too contradictory to warrant hope or confidence. Supposedly educated men seem, in television, to lose their standards of morality, taste, honor and responsibility somewhere between home and the office. "Am I my brother's keeper?"—the question that has troubled the conscience of mankind for centuries—gets from television the contemptuous answer, "No," as it conflicts with money-making.

Given the crisis of our times, the desperate premium on our society's collective intelligence and moral standards, the men at the controls of television are perilously near to fiddling while Rome burns. Reluctantly one concludes that in television private enterprise and true service in the public interest are incompatible.

Can the industry be controlled? The Communications Act provided that it should be, established the F.C.C. and gave it broad, discretionary powers. But in 30 years, only two chairmen have stood up like David to this Goliath. License renewal—even of stations in flagrant default on the program service they promised as applicants—has been the norm for years. Until appointment to the F.C.C. is removed from the political spoils system and goes to men of high intelligence coupled with proven integrity and devotion to the public interest, it is naive to hope for better things.

And even then we should not hope for too much. Prescription by an agency of government of what should be broadcast (other than in terms as broad and permissive as our four basic needs of men) is undesirable and probably impracticable. At best, the F.C.C. can only protect the public interest by fighting a rear-guard action against flagrant violation of such regulation as it imposes. You cannot, beyond a point, legislate the morality of men whose perspectives blind them to the inescapable association of responsibility with power.

Can Congress act? It can, indeed. Some have proposed a statutory requirement that there be an hour or more, in each of the three major segments of the day, aimed at audiences other than those seeking light entertainment. Others propose a limit on profits—as quid pro quo for privileged use of facilities neither privately owned nor primarily intended as lubricants for the machinery of commerce. Sponsors, again, could be deprived, as in Britain, of any power to dictate program content, and limited to buying time on the air as they buy space in newspapers. These and similar brakes on the wheels of avarice are possible.

But *will* Congress act? Many of its members are parties of interest—as owners or shareholders of radio and television stations. More still are too beholden to the broadcaster (for providing free time to address their constituents) to risk forfeiting such patronage. Their sympathy is indicated by their votes on the Rogers bill on radio-TV advertising.

Is pay TV the answer? Why should it be? The lure of profit is as compelling here as in our present system. And pay TV would be exempt from even the nominal control of programs now vested in the F.C.C. For when viewers pay for what they get it is unthinkable that government should prescribe what they should be allowed to pay for.

What of educational television? Given financial backing, programing wholly devoted to our societal and cultural needs would be feasible and is in fact in the making. Educational television is a potential countervailing force. But the very notion of a palliative is ill-conceived, for only the concerted effort of *all* our mass media, combined with our educational resources, is likely to see us through the troubled years ahead.

Time is no longer with us, but against us. The price of social and cultural immaturity grows more disastrous by the day. And anyhow, is commercial television to be given a free hand, its record of always too little and too late to be rewarded by unconditional surrender of publicly owned frequencies?

What, finally, can be looked for from the public? Television has lulled it into a fatal complacency. Its perspectives reflect the patterns of "service" that it has been offered. Custom as much as conscience "doth make cowards of us all." It is incredible what we get used to. (Little more than 30 years ago the radio sponsor dared not intrude into our homes after shopping hours; at 7 P. M. all advertising on the air ended!) What, moreover, can we expect of a public 65 per cent of which condoned television's foulest hour—the quiz scandals?

Flaccid, indifferent and unaware (because not made aware), it accepts what it is given—what is easy on the eye and ear, what gives no offense. Unchallenged, unstimulated, offered no leadership, it drifts out on television's soporific tide toward the fog banks of the mind that obscure the realities that face us. Television has made non-think popular.

These are lugubrious conclusions. But they perhaps direct us to the heart of the whole matter. For in television's mirror, surely, we see our own faces reflected with only minor distortion. What is wrong with television (though this gives the broadcaster no alibi) is in large part what is wrong with us. The notion that anything goes for a fast buck, tolerance and even enjoyment of brutality gratuitously thrown on the screen, non-think—these and like characteristics are not peculiar to television, for all that it aids and abets them. They are part of the temper of the people.

Television represents no more than the visible outcropping of an ugly seam that runs from coast to coast under the surface of our culture—alienation from our true selves and our tradition through misplaced materialist preoccupations. The times cry out for a regeneration, a new commitment and a new morality in our society. It is to this alone that we can look for redirection of television in the public interest. "The fault, dear Brutus, is not in our stars but in ourselves that we are underlings."

FOR FURTHER STUDY

Arons, Leon and May, Mark A. (eds.). *Television and Human Behavior: Tomorrow's Research in Mass Communication*. New York: Appleton-Century-Crofts, 1963.

Elliott, William Y. (ed.). *Television's Impact on American Culture*. East Lansing: Michigan State U. Press, 1956. (See especially Ch. 6, "Television and the American Character—A Psychiatrist Looks at Television" by Eugene David Glynn, M.D.)

Frank, Josette. *Children and TV*. New York: Public Affairs Committee, 1962. (Pamphlet No. 323.)

Himmelweit, Hilde T., *et al. Television and the Child*. New York: Oxford U. Press, 1958. (A Study sponsored by the Nuffield Foundation. Pamphlet Reprint of Chs. 1-4, 1961.)

Koenigil, Mark. *Movies in Society*. New York: R. Speller, 1962.

Minnow, Newton N. "The Broadcasters Are Public Trustees," in *Vital Speeches*, 27 (June 15, 1961): 533-537.

Schramm, Wilbur (ed.). *The Science of Human Communication*. New York: Basic Books, 1963.

Tyler, Poyntz (ed). *Television and Radio*. New York: Wilson, 1961. (The Reference Shelf, Vol. 33, No. 6.)

CHAPTER 20

MARRIAGE AND SEX

∽∾∽∾∽∾∽∾∽∾∽∾∽∾∽∾∽∾∽∾∽∾∽∾∽

*Sex Fictions and Facts**

SYLVANUS M. DUVALL

Sylvanus M. Duvall (1900-   ) has taught in the
fields of the social sciences and religion at George
Williams College since 1933. His specialty is in family
and marriage relations, and his writings include
Before You Marry; Men, Women, and Morals; and
The Art and Skill of Getting Along With People.

"I don't know what to do about Bill. I'm very fond of him. He's only
20, but he's had a generous share of women. He regards sex as simply
a game, and me as just another female body.

"When I'm with him, I become terrified at my own capabilities.
When he touches me, I feel the most ecstatic joy imaginable, and all
my previous 'proper' feelings are lost in one wish—to make him happy.
Do you see what I am up against? What shall I do?"

Two generations ago, this 16-year-old girl and her boy friend might
have been strongly tempted by their desires. But they would have had
few questions about what they should do. A clear social standard would
have guided their conduct. The code would have supported the girl's
reluctance. It would also have allowed the boy (albeit mistakenly) to
sow his "wild oats" with disreputable women. But it certainly would
not have allowed him to "proposition" a "respectable" girl. And her

* From "Sex Fictions and Facts: A Social Scientist Destroys Some Myths,"
Look Magazine, 24 (April 12, 1960): 47-48, 50, 52. Reprinted by permission.

278

standards would have required her, however great the temptation, to recoil with horror and shock. Today, she has little guidance beyond the vague feeling that, to him, she is only "another female body."

How responsible are the parents, teachers and clergy of these young people? Do we provide adequate help in developing some kind of standards for our youth to live by? The answer is "no," probably because, as adults, we often have been baffled and bewildered ourselves. We have come to feel that young people should know the biological facts about sex, and to regard the subject without shame or embarrassment. But beyond that, we are uncertain and confused.

A few years ago, for example, if a high-school girl became pregnant, there was little uncertainty about what to do. She was dismissed, quietly, but in disgrace. Today, school authorities are unsure. They are concerned about the effects of her impropriety upon the other students. But if they act forcibly, they worry: "What will we be doing to the girl?" Rare indeed is the program of either school or church that comes to grips with the issues of sexual behavior. Education regarding sound sex standards under present conditions has made little progress.

Even our greater knowledge has added to our dilemma. Only those who have strong prejudices feel sure of themselves.

Until our growing scientific knowledge about sex has been evaluated and digested, hesitancy and uncertainty are not only inevitable, but highly desirable. We have, however, reached a point where many of our confusions about sexual conduct can and must be cleared up.

Here are some of the commoner fictions about sex, and the facts concerning them:

FICTION:
Sex is essentially beautiful and good.

FACT:
Sexual experience occurs on different levels.

To say that sex is beautiful and good is as meaningless as to say that liquids are nourishing and delicious. It is a pleasing bit of nonsense that once served a useful purpose—to counteract the opposite fiction that sex is essentially nasty and vulgar. Among human beings, sex can be beautiful and good, or neurotic and vicious; it can be delightful, or unpleasant and boring. It is not *essentially* any of these.

Sex may be compared in some ways to pigments. In the hands of a Leonardo da Vinci, colors become masterpieces of beauty that point to the divine. In other hands, they become ugly and degrading, or a kind of cheap whitewash to be daubed over any back fence. Most people will produce neither masterpiece nor monstrosity. The relationship will be just sex, sometimes a joyous union of two selves, and sometimes an annoying concession. Great artists in any medium are rare.

FICTION:
The success of a marriage depends upon the achievement of satisfactory sexual relationships.

FACT:
In many successful marriages, satisfactory sexual adjustments are achieved late or not at all.

In a study of 792 marriages, Dr. Lewis Terman found that many happy couples had poor sexual adjustments. Professor Judson Landis studied 409 couples who had been married for twenty years or more, and discovered that one out of eight such couples had never worked out a satisfactory sexual adjustment. On the other hand, E. T. Krueger encountered many divorced couples whose sexual relationships had become increasingly satisfactory, right up to the time of their divorces. Undoubtedly, satisfying sex relationships can enrich a marriage and therefore help to hold it together. But basic personality defects cannot be cured, nor can fundamental differences be resolved, through sex, no matter how satisfying. Sexual intercourse is not, and cannot be made, a substitute for maturity, character, mental health or basic agreement on fundamental issues.

FICTION:
A person who is really in love will not be sexually interested in anyone else.

FACT:
Most men and many women are polyerotic.

Often a wife will feel that her husband no longer loves her if he shows a normal interest in other women. But no matter how honest and genuine our love for our mates may be, we will find others of the opposite sex who are physically attractive to us.

If we understand this possibility in advance, we can usually handle such problems without feeling guilty or assuming that it is necessary to yield to temptation. People who find each other attractive can often continue to work happily together without indulging in sex, just as a treasurer can continue to handle honestly large sums of money that he might be tempted to steal. Those who remain faithful to their marriage partners do so, not because attraction to others is absent, but because of their own moral standards.

FICTION:
Sexual intercourse is a need of all people who are physically potent.

FACT:
Sexual outlets are a need of all normally developed males, but these do not have to occur through sexual intercourse. The body itself, through nocturnal emission, provides for all the outlet that is physically necessary.

Sexual intercourse is a normal *desire* of all developed and potent males, and of many females. Sexual intercourse, like a mink coat or a swanky sports car, can become a "need" for those suffering from certain kinds of emotional distortion. This need is emotional, rather than biological. The philanderer is driven, not by the strength of his physical urges, but by some abnormality of personality. His real need may be to overcome feelings of inferiority, to find a "mother image," to express hostility toward women or meet some other neurotic demand.

The same principle holds generally true for sexually lax women. The unwed mother is often someone who is love-hungry and emotionally deprived. Like her male counterpart, she is usually a woman with a personality deficiency, not a normal biological need.

In our culture, sexual laxity is most common among those (1) who are immature and feel inadequate, rejected and unloved, (2) who lack strong ties with family and friends, and (3) who lack the religious and other spiritual roots that give people a sense of personal dignity.

FICTION:
Sexual restrictions impose an unnecessary hardship upon unmarried women.

FACT:
According to the Kinsey studies, only a small proportion of women are so highly sexed that lack of sexual relationships is distressing.

The great majority of women apparently have little desire for sexual relationships, unless and until this desire has been awakened by considerable experience. What they do want is companionship and love. Sexual relationships that cannot provide for the kind of security that women in our culture can usually get only through marriage may arouse more hungers than they satisfy.

FICTION:

Intelligent people can protect themselves against venereal infections and unwanted pregnancies.

FACT:

Venereal infections and unwanted pregnancies are much more common than supposed.

Despite great gains in medical science, venereal infections are the second most widespread class of disease in the United States, and syphilis has been increasing steadily for the past few years.

People who cohabit are safe from venereal infections only if both are free from the disease to begin with and if both remain strictly monogamous. One girl who had sexual relations only with her lover was dismayed to find herself infected. A "venereal tracer" was put on the case, and this is what he found: The boy had consorted with only one other, a girl to whom he had once been engaged. She had consorted with five other men, all of whom she knew well. These five in turn had had contacts with 19 women, some of whom had been promiscuous in their relations. It turned out that the girl who thought her relationship had been limited to one person had had indirect contact through him with at least 92 others.

Few potent couples who consort sexually succeed in protecting themselves from pregnancies. Reported illegitimate births in the United States have increased from 141,600 in 1950 to over 200,000 in 1957, an increase that is more than twice as great as that for legitimate births. Many more such births are not recorded. It has been estimated that up to a million abortions are performed every year on women who were not successful in protecting themselves from unwanted pregnancies. Even among those supposedly best able to protect themselves, married college students, about two thirds of their first pregnancies were unplanned. Studies on this subject indicate that the vast majority of American couples are not able to protect themselves adequately against unwanted pregnancies.

FICTION:

Sex relationships are private affairs.

FACT:

Because of possible infection and pregnancy and of other repercussions, sex relationships outside of marriage rarely can be private affairs.

These supposedly "private" affairs can affect:

1. The various health departments and the taxpayers who support them, since, as we have seen, venereal infections are the second most common class of disease in America.

2. The general public, which bears the costs of illegitimacy. In 1959, the estimated cost of supporting illegitimate children through aid to dependent children was more than $200,000,000, plus many additional millions for other forms of public and private relief.

3. The families of the couple. There is almost no end to the distress of such families: the anxious telephone calls; the painful conferences; the work and effort to find a suitable place for the birth; the dashing of parental hopes for a wedding of which all could be proud; the difficulties of explaining to, or concealing the truth from, friends and neighbors; the financial burden.

4. The marriage. The effects of adultery vary greatly, depending upon economic resources and social position and the extent to which it is either accepted or concealed. Sometimes, families break up, and children are taken from their parents by court order.

5. The child. Those who assert that sexual relationships are private affairs rarely consider the rights of the baby. For the fortunate child who is adopted at birth into a good family, the results of illegitimacy may be negligible. For the child who must grow up in a one-parent home, or who is otherwise neglected, the results can be psychological scars that may ruin his life.

If sex conduct cannot be private, neither is it likely to be secret. In any group, such as a business-office staff, campus or social set, the sex standards and conduct of its members soon become common knowledge. Every person should assume that his or her sexual behavior will sooner or later become known to associates.

FICTION:
It is practically impossible for a young person to avoid sex relationships before marriage.

FACT:
Premarital sex is often the exception rather than the rule.

From 1915 to 1959 inclusive, there have been published 36 studies of premarital sex behavior, in addition to numerous observations and reports, including some intensive interview studies. Premarital virginity among men was found to be as low as 27 per cent and as high as 68 per cent; among women, it was as low as 53 per cent and as high as 93 per cent. The strongly religious among Jews, Catholics and

Protestants were found to observe standards of sexual conduct conspicuously higher than does the general population.

FICTION:

The girl who refuses to give in to her boy friend may lose him.

FACT:

The girl who yields decreases, rather than increases, her chances for a good marriage.

1. Often a boy will talk about or even promise marriage, only as a way of getting what he wants. If a girl yields, he may brag to his friends about his conquest, and thus diminish her chances with someone else who might be really interested in marriage.
2. The boy himself may doubt the suitability for marriage of a girl who would yield: "If she gives in to me, to how many others has she given in also?"
3. The "love" that they feel toward each other may be mainly sexual desire. Since both have what they really want, why marry?
4. The boy may want to marry, but fears the responsibilities of marriage. As long as the wedding date lies in the vague future, he can remain interested. But if there are sex relationships, he faces the real possibility of a pregnancy forcing him into a marriage for which he is not yet ready, and he may break off while he still can.
5. One or both may feel guilty and blame the other; the resulting quarrels may break up the relationship.

These facts help to explain what is so puzzling to many engaged couples—that the establishment of sex relationships has cooled their love, rather than increased it.

FICTION:

Our traditional sex standards are definitely on the way out.

FACT:

Our sex code is being extensively violated, but not more so than our moral standards in other areas of life.

Comparison of the Kinsey findings on laxity in sex conduct with reports of corruption in business, government and labor points to a surprising conclusion: Americans observe their sex standards better than they do the moral standards in any other area that has been carefully studied. If we were to compare violations of the sex standards with traffic violations, for example, the differences in favor of the sex code would be even more striking. Yet no one suggests that our traffic regulations are, or should be, on the way out.

The crucial question about any code of behavior is not the extent to which it is observed, nor even its future outcome, but its desirability: An increase in alcoholism, the use of narcotics or the steady march of totalitarian ideals may indicate a "wave of the future," but this would not make them less evil. Morality demands loyalty, not to a practice or even a trend, but to what is good. The basic issue about sex behavior is: What is desirable?

Sexual enjoyment must be limited by the need for protection against exploitation, venereal infections and irresponsible pregnancies. It must provide for love and sound family life. No code regarding sex or any other area of life can completely avoid injustices, unhappiness and frustrations. A good sex code is the best compromise between divergent and often conflicting values that we can devise.

FICTION:
Young people are well informed about sex.

FACT:
Young people seem no better informed about the matter than they were twenty years ago.

Freedom to discuss the stars without embarrassment does not make one an astronomer. Two studies—one of 13,528 representative young people made in 1937, and a second of 8,500, made twenty years later —reveal a shocking fact. In 1937, 30 per cent got their sex knowledge from their parents, and 8 per cent, from their schools. In 1957, only 24 per cent got their sex knowledge from their parents; only 6 per cent, from the schools. Most of their sex information (and misinformation) came from youthful associates.

Interestingly, this striking loss in the sources of information was not due to lack of desire for knowledge. In the 1957 study, 74 per cent wanted sex education made a regular part of the school curriculum, and this same eagerness for knowledge has been found in study after study, both of young people and their parents. But it has not resulted in any significant improvement in the sex knowledge of our youth.

FICTION:
The solution to our problem is more "sex education" for our youth.

FACT:
We should concentrate on deeper human values.

An adequate biological knowledge of sex is part of the education that every well-informed person should have. But a knowledge of anatomy and physiology will no more solve our problems than a greater understanding of automobile mechanics will markedly improve safety on the highways. Something far deeper than mere textbook information is required. If sex education is to contribute significantly to good living, it must be focused upon relationships and standards of behavior. As a start, maturing young people should learn how sex affects their developing emotional life. They should know the differences between mere sexual urges and an adequate kind of love. Sex education should give them guidance in what to expect of others and how to handle difficult situations.

Young men are often under heavy pressure from their "gang" to have premarital relationships, often regarded as evidence of "manhood." Girls are under far greater pressure from their boy friends than was true two generations ago, and instances of suitors actually forcing sexual attentions on their girls have become startlingly common. Yet girls receive little guidance from their elders on what to do, and little support from them in their efforts to maintain moral standards. But let them "get into trouble," and the sky falls in.

The basic problem of sex today is what it always has been—to integrate it properly into the whole of life. We have erred in the past by imposing undue restrictions. Since we found it hard to accept sex as a real and proper part of life, we made it a kind of disreputable relative who had to be acknowledged, but was admitted through the back door and had to live in the cellar. No wonder that we have had not only revolt, but a constant emphasis, by well-intentioned but mistaken people, that sex is necessarily wholesome and good.

Today, the problems of sex arise mainly not out of undue restrictions, but from the assumption that sex can run "hog-wild" without being significantly related to the rest of our lives. Sex is thereby dissociated from its relationships to, and its effects upon, the values and goals of our society. We fail to understand that sex is part of the total personality structure.

This separation of sex from the totality of life is seen not only in those who wish to relax the sexual code, but in those who seek to defend it. The "case for chastity" is often unconvincing, largely because it is stated in terms of limited personal risks and disadvantages, rather than in terms of the kind of persons we wish to be, the kind of family relations that will most enrich our lives, the kind of society we want to live in, and the permanent values to which we are committed.

Certainly, one of the major reasons for chastity before marriage, and fidelity after, is the preservation of the best kind of family life.

The task of the educator and the religious leader is not to beat the drums on behalf of a misguided liberalism, or to seek a resurrection of the past taboos. It is, instead, to help people, young and old, to fit their sex interests and behavior into a total and constructive concept of self and life, and to develop the moral standards that are required by valid personal, social and lasting goals. We rightly begin by discarding the fictions that still delude us; but before us lies the far greater task of developing those deeper insights that will enable us to make sex a happy and meaningful part of our lives.

FOR FURTHER STUDY

Barron, Jennie Loitman. "Too Much Sex on Campus," *Ladies Home Journal*, 81 (January-February, 1964): 48, 52.

Duvall, Evelyn Millis. *Why Wait Till Marriage?* New York: Association Press, 1965.

Duvall, Evelyn Millis, and Hill, Rueben. *When You Marry*. New York: Association Press, 1962 (with chapters in collaboration with Sylvanus M. Duvall).

Farnsworth, Dana L. "A Reasonable Basis for Sexual Morality in Our Society," in *The Student Seeks an Answer*, ed. John A. Clark. Waterville: Colby College Press, 1960, Ch. XIII.

Fitch, Robert E. "A Common Sense Sex Code," *Christian Century*, 81 (October 7, 1964): 1233-1235.

Fletcher, Joseph. *Morals and Medicine*. Boston: Beacon Paperback, 1960.

Gordon, Albert I. *Intermarriage: Interfaith, Interracial, Interethnic*. Boston: Beacon Press, 1964.

Hechinger, Grace, and Hechinger, Fred M. "College Morals Mirror Our Society," *New York Times Magazine*, April 14, 1963, pp. 22, 120, 122.

Landis, Judson T., and Landis, Mary G. *Building a Successful Marriage*. 4th ed.; Englewood Cliffs: Prentice-Hall, 1963.

Marriage and Family Living, Journal of The National Council on Family Relations, includes many articles written by specialists in the fields of marriage, sex problems, and family relations.

Pike, James A. *If You Marry Outside Your Faith*. New York: Harper, 1962, 159 pp.

CHAPTER 21

MORALITY
AND RACE RELATIONS

Letter from Birmingham City Jail*

MARTIN LUTHER KING, JR.

Martin Luther King, Jr. (1929-   ), minister and
president of the Southern Christian Leadership Conference, won the Nobel Peace Prize in 1964. He is an
outstanding leader in the Negro nonviolent struggle
for equal rights. One of his books is *Stride Toward
Freedom*, 1958.

You deplore the demonstrations that are presently taking place in
Birmingham. But I am sorry that your statement did not express a
similar concern for the conditions that brought the demonstrations into
being. I am sure that each of you would want to go beyond the superficial social analyst who looks merely at effects, and does not grapple
with underlying causes. I would not hesitate to say that it is unfortunate
that so-called demonstrations are taking place in Birmingham at this
time, but I would say in more emphatic terms that it is even more
unfortunate that the white power structure of this city left the Negro
community with no other alternative.

In any nonviolent campaign there are four basic steps: (1) collection

* Excerpts reprinted from pamphlet of the American Friends Service Committee, Philadelphia, Pa., copyright © 1963 by Martin Luther King, Jr. Reprinted by
permission of Joan Daves.

of the facts to determine whether injustices are alive; (2) negotiation; (3) self-purification; and (4) direct action. We have gone through all of these steps in Birmingham. There can be no gainsaying of the fact that racial injustice engulfs this community. Birmingham is probably the most thoroughly segregated city in the United States. Its ugly record of police brutality is known in every section of this country. Its unjust treatment of Negroes in the courts is a notorious reality. There have been more unsolved bombings of Negro homes and churches in Birmingham than any city in this nation. These are the hard, brutal, and unbelievable facts. On the basis of these conditions Negro leaders sought to negotiate with the city fathers. But the political leaders consistently refused to engage in good faith negotiation. . . .

You may well ask, "Why direct action? Why sit-ins, marches, etc.? Isn't negotiation a better path?" You are exactly right in your call for negotiation. Indeed, this is the purpose of direct action. Nonviolent direct action seeks to create such a crisis and establish such creative tension that a community that has constantly refused to negotiate is forced to confront the issue. It seeks so to dramatize the issue that it can no longer be ignored. . . .

We know through painful experience that freedom is never voluntarily given by the oppressor; it must be demanded by the oppressed. Frankly I have never yet engaged in a direct action movement that was "well timed," according to the timetable of those who have not suffered unduly from the disease of segregation. For years now I have heard the word "Wait!" It rings in the ear of every Negro with a piercing familiarity. This "wait" has almost always meant "never." It has been a tranquilizing thalidomide, relieving the emotional stress for a moment, only to give birth to an ill-formed infant of frustration. We must come to see with the distinguished jurist of yesterday that "justice too long delayed is justice denied." We have waited for more than three hundred and forty years for our constitutional and God-given rights. The nations of Asia and Africa are moving with jet-like speed toward the goal of political independence, and we still creep at horse and buggy pace toward the gaining of a cup of coffee at a lunch counter.

I gue it is easy for those who have never felt the stinging darts of segregation to say wait. But when you have seen vicious mobs lynch your mothers and fathers at will and drown your sisters and brothers at whim; when you have seen hate filled policemen curse, kick, brutalize, and even kill your black brothers and sisters with impugnity; when you see the vast majority of your twenty million Negro brothers smothering in an air-tight cage of poverty in the midst of an affluent society; when you suddenly find your tongue twisted and your speech stammering as you seek to explain to your six-year-old daughter why she can't go to the public amusement park that has just been advertised on television, and see tears welling up in her little eyes when she is told that Funtown is closed to colored children, and see the depressing clouds of inferiority begin to form in her little mental sky, and see her begin to distort her little personality by unconsciously developing a bitterness toward white people; when you have to concoct an answer for a five-year-old son asking in agonizing pathos: "Daddy, why do white people treat colored people so mean?"; when you take a cross country drive and find it necessary to sleep night after night in the uncomfortable corners of your automobile because no motel will accept you; when you are humiliated day in and day out by nagging signs reading "white" men and "colored"; when your first name becomes "nigger" and your middle name becomes "boy" (however old you are) and your last name becomes "John," and when your wife and mother are never given the respected title "Mrs."; when you are harried by day and haunted by night by the fact that you are a Negro, living constantly at tip-toe stance never quite knowing what to expect next, and plagued with inner fears and outer resentments; when you are forever fighting a degenerating sense of "nobodiness";—then you will understand why we find it difficult to wait. There comes a time when the cup of endurance runs over, and men are no longer willing to be plunged into an abyss of injustice where they experience the bleakness of corroding despair. I hope, sirs, you can understand our legitimate and unavoidable impatience.

You express a great deal of anxiety over our willingness to break laws. This is certainly a legitimate concern. Since we so diligently urge people to obey the Supreme Court's decision of 1954 outlawing segregation in the public schools, it is rather strange and paradoxical to find us consciously breaking laws. One may well ask, "How can you advocate breaking some laws and obeying others?" The answer is found in the fact that there are two types of laws: There are *just* laws and there are *unjust* laws. I would be the first to advocate obeying just laws. One has not only a legal but moral responsibility to obey just laws. Conversely, one has a moral responsibility to disobey unjust laws. I would agree with Saint Augustine that "An unjust law is no law at all."

Now what is the difference between the two? How does one determine when a law is just or unjust? A just law is a man-made code that squares with the moral law or the law of God. An unjust law is a code that is out of harmony with the moral law. To put it in the terms of

Saint Thomas Aquinas, an unjust law is a human law that is not rooted in eternal and natural law. Any law that uplifts human personality is just. Any law that degrades human personality is unjust. All segregation statutes are unjust because segregation distorts the soul and damages the personality. It gives the segregator a false sense of superiority and the segregated a false sense of inferiority. To use the words of Martin Buber, the great Jewish philosopher, segregation substitutes an "I-it" relationship for the "I-thou" relationship, and ends up relegating persons to the status of things. So segregation is not only politically, economically, and sociologically unsound, but it is morally wrong and sinful. Paul Tillich has said that sin is separation. Isn't segregation an existential expression of man's tragic separation, an expression of his awful estrangement, his terrible sinfulness? So I can urge men to obey the 1954 decision of the Supreme Court because it is morally right, and I can urge them to disobey segregation ordinances because they are morally wrong.

Let us turn to a more concrete example of just and unjust laws. An unjust law is a code that a majority inflicts on a minority that is not binding on itself. This is *difference* made legal. On the other hand a just law is a code that a majority compels a minority to follow that it is willing to follow itself. This is *sameness* made legal.

Let me give another explanation. An unjust law is a code inflicted upon a minority which that minority had no part in enacting or creating because they did not have the unhampered right to vote. Who can say the legislature of Alabama which set up the segregation laws was democratically elected? Throughout the state of Alabama all types of conniving methods are used to prevent Negroes from becoming registered voters and there are some counties without a single Negro registered to vote despite the fact that the Negro constitutes a majority of the population. Can any law set up in such a state be considered democratically structured?

These are just a few examples of unjust and just laws. There are some instances when a law is just on its face but unjust in its application. For instance, I was arrested Friday on a charge of parading without a permit. Now there is nothing wrong with an ordinance which requires a permit for a parade, but when the ordinance is used to preserve segregation and to deny citizens the First Amendment privilege of peaceful assembly and peaceful protest, then it becomes unjust.

I hope you can see the distinction I am trying to point out. In no sense do I advocate evading or defying the law as the rabid segregationist would do. This would lead to anarchy. One who breaks an unjust law must do it *openly*, *lovingly* (not hatefully as the white mothers did in

New Orleans when they were seen on television screaming "nigger, nigger, nigger") and with a willingness to accept the penalty. I submit that an individual who breaks a law that conscience tells him is unjust, and willingly accepts the penalty by staying in jail to arouse the conscience of the community over its injustice, is in reality expressing the very highest respect for law.

Of course there is nothing new about this kind of civil disobedience. It was seen sublimely in the refusal of Shadrach, Meshach, and Abednego to obey the laws of Nebuchadnezzar because a higher moral law was involved. It was practiced superbly by the early Christians who were willing to face hungry lions and the excruciating pain of chopping blocks, before submitting to certain unjust laws of the Roman Empire. To a degree academic freedom is a reality today because Socrates practiced civil disobedience.

We can never forget that everything Hitler did in Germany was "legal" and everything the Hungarian freedom fighters did in Hungary was "illegal." It was "illegal" to aid and comfort a Jew in Hitler's Germany. But I am sure that, if I had lived in Germany during that time, I would have aided and comforted my Jewish brothers even though it was illegal. If I lived in a communist country today where certain principles dear to the Christian faith are suppressed, I believe I would openly advocate disobeying these anti-religious laws.

I must make two honest confessions to you, my Christian and Jewish brothers. First I must confess that over the last few years I have been gravely disappointed with the white moderate. I have almost reached the regrettable conclusion that the Negroes' great stumbling block in the stride toward freedom is not the White Citizens' "Counciler" or the Ku Klux Klanner, but the white moderate who is more devoted to "order" than to justice; who prefers a negative peace which is the absence of tension to a positive peace which is the presence of justice; who constantly says "I agree with you in the goal you seek, but I can't agree with your methods of direct action"; who paternalistically feels that he can set the time-table for another man's freedom; who lives by the myth of time and who constantly advises the Negro to wait until a "more convenient season." Shallow understanding from people of good will is more frustrating than absolute misunderstanding from people of ill will. Lukewarm acceptance is much more bewildering than outright rejection. . . .

You spoke of our activity in Birmingham as extreme. At first I was rather disappointed that fellow clergymen would see my nonviolent efforts as those of the extremist. I started thinking about the fact that

I stand in the middle of two opposing forces in the Negro community. One is a force of complacency made up of Negroes who, as a result of long years of oppression, have been so completely drained of self-respect and a sense of "somebodiness" that they have adjusted to segregation, and of a few Negroes in the middle class who, because of a degree of academic and economic security, and because at points they profit by segregation, have unconsciously become insensitive to the problems of the masses. The other force is one of bitterness and hatred and comes perilously close to advocating violence. It is expressed in the various black nationalist groups that are springing up over the nation, the largest and best known being Elijah Muhammad's Muslim movement. This movement is nourished by the contemporary frustration over the continued existence of racial discrimination. It is made up of people who have lost faith in America, who have absolutely repudiated Christianity, and who have concluded that the white man is an incurable "devil." I have tried to stand between these two forces saying that we need not follow the "do-nothingism" of the complacent or the hatred and despair of the black nationalist. There is the more excellent way of love and nonviolent protest. I'm grateful to God that, through the Negro church, the dimension of nonviolence entered our struggle. If this philosophy had not emerged I am convinced that by now many streets of the South would be flowing with floods of blood. And I am further convinced that if our white brothers dismiss us as "rabble rousers" and "outside agitators"—those of us who are working through the channels of nonviolent direct action—and refuse to support our nonviolent efforts, millions of Negroes, out of frustration and despair, will seek solace and security in black nationalist ideologies, a development that will lead inevitably to a frightening racial nightmare.

Oppressed people cannot remain oppressed forever. The urge for freedom will eventually come. This is what has happened to the American Negro. Something within has reminded him of his birthright of freedom; something without has reminded him that he can gain it. Consciously and unconsciously, he has been swept in by what the Germans call the Zeitgeist, and with his black brothers of Africa, and his brown and yellow brothers of Asia, South America, and the Caribbean, he is moving with a sense of cosmic urgency toward the promised land of racial justice. Recognizing this vital urge that has engulfed the Negro community, one should readily understand public demonstrations. The Negro has many pent-up resentments and latent frustrations. He has to get them out. So let him march sometime; let him have his prayer pilgrimages to the city hall; understand why he must have sit-ins and freedom rides. If his repressed emotions do not come out in these nonviolent ways, they will come out in ominous expressions of violence. This is not a threat; it is a fact of history. So I have not said to my people, "Get rid of your discontent." But I have tried to say that this normal and healthy discontent can be channeled through the creative outlet of nonviolent direct action. Now this approach is being dismissed as extremist. I must admit that I was initially disappointed in being so categorized.

But as I continued to think about the matter I gradually gained a bit of satisfaction from being considered an extremist. Was not Jesus an extremist in love? "Love your enemies, bless them that curse you, pray for them that despitefully use you." Was not Amos an extremist for justice—"Let justice roll down like waters and righteousness like a mighty stream." Was not Paul an extremist for the gospel of Jesus Christ—"I bear in my body the marks of the Lord Jesus." Was not Martin Luther an extremist—"Here I stand; I can do none other so help me God." Was not John Bunyan an extremist—"I will stay in jail to the end of my days before I make a butchery of my conscience." Was not Abraham Lincoln an extremist—"This nation cannot survive half slave and half free." Was not Thomas Jefferson an extremist—"We hold these truths to be self evident that all men are created equal." So the question is not whether we will be extremist but what kind of extremist will we be. Will we be extremists for hate or will we be extremists for love? Will we be extremists for the preservation of injustice—or will we be extremists for the cause of justice? In that dramatic scene on Calvary's hill three men were crucified. We must never forget that all three were crucified for the same crime—the crime of extremism. Two were extremists for immorality, and thus fell below their environment. The other, Jesus Christ, was an extremist for love, truth, and goodness, and thereby rose above His environment. So, after all, maybe the South, the nation, and the world are in dire need of creative extremists. . . .

. . . I must honestly reiterate that I have been disappointed with the Church. I do not say that as one of those negative critics who can always find something wrong with the Church. I say it as a minister of the gospel, who loves the Church; who was nurtured in its bosom; who has been sustained by its spiritual blessings and who will remain true to it as long as the cord of life shall lengthen.

I had the strange feeling when I was suddenly catapulted into the leadership of the bus protest in Montgomery several years ago that we would have the support of the white Church. I felt that the white ministers, priests, and rabbis of the South would be some of our strongest allies. Instead, some have been outright opponents, refusing to understand the freedom movement and misrepresenting its leaders; all too many others have been more cautious than courageous and have remained silent behind the anesthetizing security of stained glass windows.

In spite of my shattered dreams of the past, I came to Birmingham with the hope that the white religious leadership of this community would see the justice of our cause and, with deep moral concern, serve as the channel through which our just grievances could get to the power structure. I had hoped that each of you would understand. But again I have been disappointed.

I have heard numerous religious leaders of the South call upon their worshippers to comply with a desegregation decision because it is the law, but I have longed to hear white ministers say follow this decree because integration is morally right and the Negro is your brother. In the midst of blatant injustices inflicted upon the Negro, I have watched white churches stand on the sideline and merely mouth pious irrelevancies and sanctimonious trivialities. In the midst of a mighty struggle to rid our nation of racial and economic injustice, I have heard so many ministers say, "Those are social issues with which the Gospel has no real concern," and I have watched so many churches commit themselves to a completely other-worldly religion which made a strange distinction between body and soul, the sacred and the secular.

So here we are moving toward the exit of the twentieth century with a religious community largely adjusted to the status quo, standing as a tail light behind other community agencies rather than a headlight leading men to higher levels of justice. . . .

Maybe again I have been too optimistic. Is organized religion too inextricably bound to the status quo to save our nation and the world? Maybe I must turn my faith to the inner spiritual Church, the church within the Church, as the true *ecclesia* and the hope of the world. But again I am thankful to God that some noble souls from the ranks of organized religion have broken loose from the paralyzing chains of conformity and joined us as active partners in the struggle for freedom. They have left their secure congregations and walked the streets of Albany, Georgia, with us. They have gone through the highways of the South on torturous rides for freedom. Yes, they have gone to jail with us. Some have been kicked out of their churches and lost the support of their bishops and fellow ministers. But they have gone with the faith that right defeated is stronger than evil triumphant. These men have been the leaven in the lump of the race. Their witness has been the spiritual salt that has preserved the true meaning of the Gospel in these troubled times. They have carved a tunnel of hope through the dark mountain of disappointment.

I hope the Church as a whole will meet the challenge of this decisive hour. But even if the Church does not come to the aid of justice, I have no despair about the future. I have no fear about the outcome of our struggle in Birmingham, even if our motives are presently misunderstood. We will reach the goal of freedom in Birmingham and all over the nation, because the goal of America is freedom. Abused and scorned though we may be, our destiny is tied up with the destiny of America. Before the pilgrims landed at Plymouth, we were here. Before the pen of Jefferson etched across the pages of history the majestic words of the Declaration of Independence, we were here. For more than two centuries our foreparents labored in this country without wages; they made cotton "king"; and they built the homes of their masters in the midst of brutal injustice and shameful humiliation—and yet out of a bottomless vitality they continued to thrive and develop. If the inexpressible cruelties of slavery could not stop us, the opposition we now face will surely fail. We will win our freedom because the sacred heritage of our nation and the eternal will of God are embodied in our echoing demands. . . .

. . . Over the last few years I have consistently preached that non-violence demands that the means we use must be as pure as the ends we seek. So I have tried to make it clear that it is wrong to use immoral means to attain moral ends. But now I must affirm that it is just as wrong, or even more so, to use moral means to preserve immoral ends. . . .

Education Is the Answer*

JAMES FULBRIGHT

Senator James Fulbright (1905-   ) was a Rhodes
Scholar and served as president of the University of
Arkansas, 1939-1941. He was a member of the
Seventy-Eighth Congress, 1943-1945, and since 1945
has been a United States Senator. He has distin-
guished himself as chairman of the Senate Foreign
Relations Committee.

The following is from a discussion in the Senate on
the report of the Civil Rights Commission that dealt
with voting rights and the need for new legislation.

There will not be a change in mass proportions from that situation
through enactment of more bills of this nature. The change will be by
means of the slow process of education and as a result of people acquiring greater interest in both State and national affairs. . . .

Mr. President, racial relations in the South, at which this proposed
legislation is directed, will be sacrificed again on the altar of political
expediency. Before the Supreme Court desegregation decision of 1954,
we were making real progress in creating better racial relations in the
South. The lines of communication were open between the races, and
real progress was being made in bringing about better economic and
social conditions for the colored people. These accomplishments were
made sometimes at the expense of similar treatment for the white people.
For example, in my State, since 1945, 60 per cent of our school construction money has been devoted to building modern educational facilities for the Negro schoolchildren. I realize that this emphasis was
necessary to live up to the spirit of the "separate but equal" doctrine
laid down in Plessy against Ferguson. The spirit of improvement which
prevailed in the South before the 1954 Supreme Court decision has been
badly trampled and abused by that decision and the subsequent agita-
tion from groups outside the South. The dangerous atmosphere of

* From *Congressional Record*, Vol. 106. Pt. 3, March 1, 1960, pp. 3703-3704.

resentment and distrust between the North and the South and the Negro and the white races cannot be cleared by enactment of additional sectional and class legislation. The split between the races created by the current political approach to racial problems may take generations to heal. It will never heal unless we accept the fact that progress in this area can be achieved only through good will, education, and mutual respect, which cannot be achieved through legislation or judicial orders. The South must be left alone, to handle the problem as any human relationship problem must be resolved; by patience, understanding, and, above all, education. The continued treatment of our section as a conquered territory will create more fear, distrust, and turmoil and set back racial relations even further. Throughout the civil rights controversy over the last few years there has been a tragic misunderstanding of human instincts and impulses. The citizens of the South are prisoners of their environment. When sudden change is attempted to be imposed upon attitudes or principles deeply imbedded within them by inheritance, tradition or environment they, as any other similar group, are likely to react almost as by involuntary reflex, and often violently. This is the basic factor which all proponents of this coercive legislation overlook, or refuse to recognize. It is a basic sociological truism that no law can be effective which does not take into consideration the conditions and attitudes in the community for which it is designed. Certainly the conditions and attitude of the South have not been considered or recognized in the present proposals.

Mr. President, I reiterate that we need national unity and harmony among our people at this time more than any period in our history. The proposals before us would widen the cleavage which now exists between the North and the South and the white and the Negro races. It is indeed a tragic period in our history that when our national responsibilities are so demanding we must be so driven by internal dissension to the point of paralysis. What a dismal commentary upon the democratic way. So it must appear to the observing world.

Mr. President, much has been said here and I think there has been considerable agreement upon the importance of education in this field. I was glad that the Senate a few weeks ago passed a bill to assist the educational system of this country. I call attention of the Senate to an article in this morning's Washington Post which bears upon this whole problem. I would like for those who are so interested in the proposed legislation, to give equal interest to education. . . .

FOR FURTHER STUDY

Ashmore, Harry S. *An Epitaph for Dixie*. New York: Norton, 1958.

Brink, William, and Harris, Louis. *The Negro Revolution in America*. New York: Simon and Schuster, 1964.

Clark, Kenneth Bancroft. *The Negro Protest*. Boston: Beacon Press, 1963, (James Baldwin, Malcolm X, Martin Luther King talk with Kenneth B. Clark).

Gordon, Milton M. *Assimilation in American Life: The Role of Race, Religion, and National Origins*. New York: Oxford U. Press, 1964.

Haselden, Kyle. *Racial Problems in Christian Perspective*. New York: Harper, 1959, Torchbook edition, 1964.

Killian, L. M., and Grigg, C. M. *Racial Crisis in America*. Englewood Cliffs: Prentice-Hall, 1964.

Myrdal, Gunnar. *An American Dilemma: The Negro Problem and American Democracy*. New York: Harper & Row, 1962. (New Preface by Gunnar Myrdal and a review of recent developments by Arnold Rose.)

Tussman, Joseph, ed. *The Supreme Court on Racial Discrimination*. New York: Oxford U. Press, 1963.

CHAPTER 22

MORALITY AND THE STATE

Ethical Standards in
American Legislative Chambers*

HUBERT H. HUMPHREY

Hubert H. Humphrey (1911-   ) taught political
science for a number of years before entering politics. In 1945 he was elected Mayor of Minneapolis,
in 1948 United States Senator from Minnesota, and in
1964 Vice-President of the United States. He was a
member of the Senate Subcommittee on Ethics in
Government.

A medieval English quatrain, brought to the attention of our Subcommittee on Ethics by Senator Douglas, has real meaning for our
times. Commenting on the way in which the common lands were en-
closed and taken over by the nobility of England, the poet wrote:

The law locks up both man and woman
Who steals the goose from off the common
But lets the greater felon loose
Who steals the common from the goose.

Politics is not practiced in a vacuum; and the activities of politicians
reflect, albeit with some distortion, the prevailing standards of American

* From *The Annals of the American Academy of Political and Social Science*,
280 (March 1952): 51-59 with omissions. Reprinted by permission of the Academy
and the author.

society, particularly of American business. Nevertheless, transgressions or practices that might be overlooked in business life assume far greater importance in public life because of the greater magnitude of the consequences. For instance, the businessman who uses pull to "get it wholesale" for a friend is regarded as doing a favor; but a Congressman who uses pull to get a contract for a constituent is often regarded as having committed a crime. If the businessman is rewarded, few eyebrows are raised; the Congressman who accepts gifts is regarded as having compromised himself.

American Attitude Toward Politics

It has become almost a truism today to equate politics with corruption. Nor is this a new phenomenon in our society. A member of the continental Congress joined in an attempt to corner the market on flour, despite the rigors being suffered at Valley Forge. Artemus Ward amused Lincoln by saying: "I am no politician, and my other habits are good." More recently, the National Opinion Research Center discovered that five out of every seven Americans believed it impossible for a professional politician to be honest, and only 18 per cent of America's parents were willing to let their sons enter political careers. This is a revealing if startling commentary on the public attitude toward politics.

American public office has little tradition of honor behind it. In part, this can be traced back to the axiom: "That government is best which governs least." Americans have habitually ignored the government as much as possible and too frequently left office-seeking to those who stood to gain personally from it. Too many people still cherish this early, idyllic concept of the government—or act as if it were still attainable. At bottom, the solution to the problem of corruption in legislative bodies lies in an alert, participating and interested citizenry. Public opinion must not wait for the disclosure of glaring transgressions before rousing itself to action: it must constantly support men of integrity, ability, and candor. Only the active participation of a large proportion of the electorate in political activity—through the medium of political parties—can supplant the power of organized pressure groups on the one hand and backroom politics and personal favoritism on the other. When the people leave politics to be the plaything or special interest of a few, the public can expect that it will be played with and serve the special economic and political interests of the participants. Democratic or representative government is everyone's business if it is to be an honorable pursuit. If the people want clean and honest government, the minimum price is an active and continuing interest in political parties and political processes.

Blaming the public for complacency does not solve our problems. Legislative bodies have all too often tolerated corruption in their midst. Even where flagrant violations of law have been proved and the miscreants jailed, too frequently no disciplinary measures have been taken. In this vein it should be pointed out that men who stoop to smear tactics, demagoguery, and general confusion of the issues in order to gain public office cannot be expected to change suddenly once they are sworn in. They cannot be trusted with the government of this country or any of its states. While most of the responsibility for correcting such abuses is up to the public, legislative bodies themselves should also act. Callous disregard of the intelligence of the public and the integrity of political office should be punished by voters and legislators alike.

With this background in mind, let us turn now to the problems which face the legislator who attempts to abide by a "code of ethics" in his conduct. Unfortunately, there are no clear-cut criteria or solutions in this field. Certain practices are obviously unethical—but the honest legislator is tormented by a twilight zone into which many of his actions unavoidably fall. I shall set forth the problems as I see them, suggest some solutions, but give no final answer.

Financial Problems

One of the major danger zones in legislative ethics is centered on finance. The costs of waging political campaigns have become exorbitant and the salary and allowances of office are usually insufficient to cover the expenditures required.

MOUNTING COSTS OF CAMPAIGNS

Twenty-nine years ago a senator from Michigan was forced to resign because of public pressure after a Congressional investigating committee publicized the fact that he had spent $195,000 on his campaign. In 1950, the national committee of one of the parties is said to have spent $100,-000 for one half hour on television and radio. According to the *Congressional Quarterly*, $10,000,000 was spent to elect the Eighty-second Congress. Even so, loopholes in the law enabled many expenditures to go unreported. Two of the successful candidates are each said to have had spent in their behalf campaign contributions amounting to more than $2,000,000. This is $1,925,000 more than either will be paid during his six-year term.

The chief cause of this tremendous rise in costs is the importance of radio and television time. A good TV personality is a must for successful campaigning in many sections of the country today. For liberal candidates the importance of radio and television is emphasized by the conservatism of the national press. In 1948, for example, thirteen states were without a single daily paper supporting Truman.

The expense of campaign headquarters, posters, advertisements in the press and by special campaign sheets; the cost of staging rallies and public meetings; the innumerable special projects carried out in a state-wide campaign—these total to a staggering figure.

OBLIGATIONS INCURRED

It is obvious from the foregoing figures that conscientious candidates often face the dilemma of either accepting disproportionate contributions from particular groups or persons or of not having enough money to make an effective and successful campaign. Many questions arise. Where can the candidate solicit funds? What is his obligation to special interests or groups which help him? What degree of personal independence can he maintain? Should he limit the amount he will accept from one individual or group? How much of a claim on his time has a firm whose president has contributed heavily to his campaign? Do his supporters believe in his policies or are they expecting something concrete in return?

Thus the matter of campaign funds is central to the whole issue of ethics. Present laws place a $3,000,000 ceiling on the amount any one national committee can spend during a calendar year and a $5,000 limit on individual contributions. These figures are totally unrealistic. There are dozens of devices used to get around the law—in fact, it is almost impossible accurately to estimate the cost of a national campaign. Evasions of the law through the formation of separate committees and by splitting donations among the members of a family are common. Often the statutes are not enforced. In many cases, the bulk of the expenditures is never reported, nor are the sources of much of the money. The result has been a very unwholesome atmosphere.

Totalitarians, both of the left and of the right, attack democracy as a farce and fraud where special interests govern. It is perhaps unrealistic to expect successful candidates not to feel a certain responsibility to their financial angels. But we can at least demand a full disclosure of who—and how angelic—they are. I am therefore unequivocally for requiring publication of all campaign contributions right down to the last dollar. This would include, not only donations to candidates, but also those to all participating committees.

POSSIBLE REMEDIES

To supplement this essential first step, study should be given to other methods of dealing with the problem. Persuasive evidence was received by the Senate Subcommittee on Ethics in favor of direct public support for political campaigns. The difficulties in working out such a policy are not insurmountable. It has been proposed that the government could pay for legitimate campaign expenses. This is not as revolutionary as it may sound. Theodore Roosevelt recommended that the Congress provide "an appropriation for the proper and legitimate expenses of each of the great national parties." In the 1920 campaign William Gibbs McAdoo stated: "If the National Government paid the expenses of the national campaigns and specified the legitimate objects for which expenditures might be made, politics would be purified enormously."

Similar to direct subsidy is the proposal to set up a public corporation—or trust fund—to aid in providing all bona fide candidates with access to the public eye and ear. Safeguards would assure emphasis on rationality and limitation to legitimate expenses. In addition to public funds, the corporation might also receive and administer private contributions. Many persons who do not give directly to parties or candidates might be willing to contribute to such a public corporation. Such a public corporation or trust fund is now being sponsored by a group of interested citizens in Minnesota. It will be interesting to watch the response such a project receives. This is an experiment in American politics—and a worthy one.

In any case, efforts should be made to broaden the base of the campaign structure. Some have suggested that the tax laws should be amended to allow deduction of small contributions, perhaps up to $100, for income-tax purposes. It is argued that government, by not permitting such deductions, is discriminating against its own vital processes and undermining its support. Another step to help candidates which could be undertaken with only minor disruption would be a qualified extension of the franking privilege. A further proposal would make free radio and television time available at stated periods during the campaigns. Since ownership of the airways is vested in the public, such a requirement in the licensing of broadcasting stations would be perfectly valid. Should this prove too great a burden on them, stations might be asked to denote a stated proportion of the total time contracted for. Both Canada and Great Britain provide free radio time to candidates, while in the Netherlands, prior to the Nazi invasion, radio stations were owned by the parties.

All of the above proposals, of course, require elaboration and further study. I mention them, not necessarily as an advocate, but to stimulate thinking and discussions.

EXPENSES OF OFFICE

Unfortunately, financial problems do not end with the election. The Congressman also has abnormal expenses after he takes office. He must maintain a residence in Washington without losing touch with his constituency. This means frequent short visits home. Many members of Congress maintain two residences—one in their state and another in Washington. Travel expenses are high, and the government pays for only one trip per session. As a public figure, a Congressman has pressing social obligations. He is fair game for solicitors for all worthy causes—and even small contributions add up. Office budgets have not kept pace with the ever increasing volume of mail, to say nothing of providing adequate professional assistance. To do a conscientious job, the legislator must dig into his own pocket. The high cost of political campaigns plus the ever increasing cost of living in Washington, along with added office expenses, may well serve to make Congressional service a special prerogative for the rich. Surely a person of moderate means finds it increasingly difficult to make ends meet.

SUPPLEMENTARY INCOME

There is little likelihood of forthright action to meet these problems. The fear of public opinion recently forced repeal of the tax exemption on the $2500 expense allowance Congress voted itself in 1946. Congress is therefore not likely to vote salary increases. Hence, many legislators seek outside means of supplementing their income. Except for the independently wealthy, important ethical problems arise.

Lawyers may resort to fees or legal retainers. This raises the question of influence. Similarly, it comes up when business connections are not severed, since frequently members have access to confidential information from which they can gain financially.

Many Congressmen accept fees for speaking engagements. In a sense, this is in line with their duty to keep the public informed about important issues—but it is also an important drain on their time and energy. I have often been criticized for going out and making talks here and there. Certainly I have no desire to travel around the country on week ends and leave my family and my job. But I am the father of four children, I must maintain property in two places, I must be able to meet hospital bills and similar emergencies, I must make frequent trips back to Minnesota, costing a minimum of $200 each, and I must pay additional expenses of office. This would be impossible if I had no outside income. My choice is either to make the speeches and earn the money or to leave the Senate.

Acceptance of additional income cannot, at present, be outlawed. But one simple step would be a strong deterrent to shady or undercover dealings: full disclosure of all sources of income. I am now co-sponsoring legislation which would require all members of Congress to disclose their incomes, assets, and all dealings in securities and commodities. These reports should be made generally available. Then, I believe, it would become politically unhealthy for legislators to handle matters from which they stood to gain personally.

The Obligations of Office

A Representative or Senator is not merely a legislator. He is, increasingly, an investigator. And he has always been errand boy and helper for his constituents. Let us explore the problems arising from each of these functions in turn.

The major problems connected with legislation deal with determination of values, personal and political obligations, and lobbying. The scope of this article permits only a suggestive listing. To start with, should a legislator vote as he thinks best for the country, even though he knows that it will be contrary to the wishes of the majority of his constituents? Democratic theorists have reached no consensus on this problem of representation. To say that the people know what is best does not provide us with a rule of action.

Even more puzzling, perhaps, is the problem presented by legislation where what is best for the country as a whole affects particular constituencies adversely. Take, for example, the question of reciprocal trade. I have had to face the fur farmers of my state who have stood to lose as a result of my votes in support of the program. I can sympathize with the representatives of some of the states whose industries have suffered from the low tariff rates. They are really in a dilemma.

PARTY LOYALTY

Turning now to political obligation, what loyalty does a Congressman owe his party? Political independence, though long cherished as a virtue, has had disastrous consequences in the past. For instance, our failure to enter the League of Nations, despite clear commitments by both parties, led to twenty years of isolationism and abetted the rise to totalitarianism abroad. The traditional vagueness of party platforms obscures substantial differences, and elections have seldom provided mandates for action. Lack of party discipline often makes even clearly recognized objectives impossible to attain. The need for greater responsibility is manifest in the present refusal of a nominally Democratic Congress to carry out the President's domestic program.

PRESSURE GROUPS

Intimately connected with the issue of party responsibility is the problem of lobbies and organized pressure groups. These have, in part, usurped traditional party functions in the field of policy determination. Yet the present hue and cry about lobbies largely neglects this basic issue. It is focused not on the root but on the results. We are concerned not with increasing party responsibility, but with regulating lobbies. The shortcomings of this approach are obvious, though understandable. . . .

Lobbies, despite their well-known evils, perform useful functions in political life. I like to know how proposed legislation affects the needs of people—the lobbies tell me. I like to hear about conditions which need correcting—the lobbies tell me that too. But I also want to know just whom these lobbies represent: how many people, where they get their funds, how they make their policy decisions, and what their other activities are. Therefore, I should like to see tighter, better-enforced laws, which would trace funds back to their sources. I have introduced a bill which would help tighten one of the loopholes. Then the public, as well as responsible legislators, could make decisions with better understanding of what is involved.

INVESTIGATIVE FUNCTION

The investigative function of Congress, although firmly established for some years, has recently threatened to overshadow the legislative function. Members have taken advantage of Congressional immunity to make spectacular charges on the floor, and probing committees have made sweeping revelations. While much good has been accomplished, the reputations of honest and able men have sometimes been irreparably and irresponsibly damaged and the prestige of the government has been considerably lowered.

Administrative officials attacked on the floor of either house should have protection equal to that afforded congressional members; and agency heads who are subject to personal attack on the floor should be given an opportunity to make an immediate or early reply. Similarly, private citizens should have the right to reply in the *Congressional Record*. Immunity from suit rewards irresponsibility with protection, and prevents recourse for damaged reputations. . . .

ETHICS OF USING INFLUENCE

If a Congressman desires to assist a constituent, he can express personal interest in three ways. The first will merely ask that the constituent be given every consideration and that the matter in which he is interested be expedited. The second kind of pressure is stronger and may say: "I know Mr. X and I can vouch for his integrity. He is honest, able, and fulfills certain requirements. Anything you can do for him will be appreciated." The third, and rarely used, kind of pressure says: "I know everything about this case. If I were in your spot I would grant the request, and I think you ought to do it." It is the last that gives rise to the ethical questions, particularly when it is accompanied by the implicit threat of an appropriation cut or legislative reprisal.

Whenever a legislator uses pressure in a case, he cannot help having some effect upon the responsible officials. The extent of his influence depends upon both the Congressman and the administrator. It is reported that at one time in TVA whenever a job applicant had a letter in his behalf from a Senator or Congressman, that job application was turned down. This may be exaggerated, but it does happen. Other administrators find it difficult to say no. A part of the influence of the legislator will depend on his committee assignment. If he deals with legislation or appropriations touching the department concerned, he has, of course, a power which may be abused.

The responsibility of the legislator is to act as an inspection or screening committee with regard to requests that come into his office. He must make sure in his own heart and conscience that he is seeking to advance cases only on their merits and that he has no personal economic interest. This is more difficult, however, where political considerations are involved. How can he draw the line between proper and improper personal interests when those interests are essentially political in character?

Raising Ethical Standards

The foregoing treatment has been suggestive rather than comprehensive in nature. I have skirted flagrant violations of ethics which have already been brought to public attention in favor of noting some of the causes of legislative corruption and bringing into focus some of the problems which face those legislators who honestly try to serve their country. The usual American remedy is "there ought to be a law." Yet the law cannot deal effectively with every range of human activity. Many of the ethical questions cannot be solved by legislation—remedies must instead be sought in a new consciousness of the dignity of public office and a higher sense of civic duty. All of us, as citizens, can achieve this through awareness of the difficulties and active support of all efforts to raise legislative standards. We can require, as the price of our support, declarations similar to the following code of "Ten Congressional Commandments" which Senator Benton presented in his testimony before the Subcommittee on Ethics, and to which I fully subscribe:

1. In the same sense in which a judge debars himself from decisions in which he has a direct personal financial stake, so I shall debar myself from legislative decisions, or, if I take action or choose to vote I shall fully disclose the nature of my interest.

2. I shall never use my office to exert extra-legal pressure over the decisions of executive or administrative agencies.

3. I shall treat witnesses who testify before committees on which I sit with courtesy and fairness, following self-imposed limitations which for centuries have been the hallmark of the judicial process.

4. I shall not abuse my privilege of Congressional immunity; I shall not say things on the floors of Congress that I am not prepared to say outside, nor shall I betray the official confidence of the Congress, or any committee thereof.

5. I shall not indulge in personal vilification of any kind, but I shall not hesitate to criticize public figures and public policies with determination and courage whenever facts of public nature justify such criticism.

6. I shall not vote on any issue without an attempt to consider the voiceless interest of the unorganized in our society.

7. I shall strive constantly to interpret interests of my constituents in the perspective of the total national interest.

8. I shall try to be loyal to the promises of my political party, and thus to strengthen party teamwork and party responsibility in the Congress.

9. I shall not waste my own or my colleagues' time with irrelevant and inconsequential talk in committee or on the floor.

10. Whether as a member of the majority or minority, I shall attempt in my actions and words to educate and clarify, never to obscure or confuse.

FOR FURTHER STUDY

Brandt, Richard B. (ed.). *Social Justice.* Englewood Cliffs: Prentice-Hall, 1962.

Cahn, Edmond. *The Predicament of Democratic Man.* New York: Macmillan, 1961.

Commager, Henry Steele. "Can Democracy Produce Excellence," in *Challenge of the Sixties, Critical Issues and Decisions, Series 11,* ed. Harold F. Breimyer. Washington, D. C.: U. S. Department of Agriculture, 1963.

Falk, Richard A. "The Relations of Law to Culture, Power, and Justice," *Ethics* 72 (October 1961): 12-27.

Ginsberg, Morris. "The Concept of Justice." *Philosophy* 38 (April 1963): 99-116.

Gordis, Robert. *Politics and Ethics.* Santa Barbara: Center for the Study of Democratic Institutions, 1961.

Hook, Sidney. " 'Welfare State'—A Debate That Isn't," New York: *New York Times Magazine* (November 27, 1960): 27, 118-119.

Rawls, John. "The Sense of Justice." *The Philosophical Review,* 72 (July 1963): 281-305.

CHAPTER 23

THE THERMONUCLEAR AGE
AND THE QUEST FOR PEACE

ຈດ·ຈດ·ຈດ·ຈດ·ຈດ·ຈດ·ຈດ·ຈດ·ຈດ·ຈດ·ຈດ·ຈດ·ຈດ·ຈດ·ຈດ·ຈດ·ຈດ·ຈດ·ຈດ

Introducing a
*Nobel Peace Prize Winner**

GUNNAR JAHN

Gunnar Jahn (1883-   ) is chairman of the Nobel
Committee of the Norwegian Parliament.

Shortly after the atomic bombs had wrought their destruction in
Hiroshima and Nagasaki, Albert Einstein summed up the situation in
the following words:

> The time has come now, when man must give up war. It is no
> longer rational to solve international problems by resorting to war.
> Now that an atomic bomb, such as the bombs exploded at Hiroshima
> and Nagasaki, can destroy a city, kill all the people in a city, a small
> city, the size of Minneapolis, say, we can see that we *must* now make
> use of man's powers of reason, in order to settle disputes between
> nations.
> In accordance with the principles of justice we must develop inter-

* From the address of Introduction delivered at the University of Oslo, Norway,
December 10, 1963, on the occasion of the presentation of the Nobel Prize for
Peace to Linus Pauling. From *Science and Peace* (Center for the Study of Democratic Institutions, Santa Barbara: The Fund for the Republic, 1964), pp. 2-5 with
omissions.

national law, strengthen the United Nations, and have peace in the world from now on. . . .

In 1946, at the request of Albert Einstein, Linus Pauling, together with seven other scientists, formed the Emergency Committee of Atomic Scientists, of which Einstein was chairman. The most important task of the committee was to bring to the notice of people everywhere the tremendous change that had taken place in the world after the splitting of the atom and the production of the atomic bomb had become facts.

"It was a crusade of people who were children in all political questions," in the words of the author Robert Jungk. The hope cherished by mankind that, once World War II was over, an age of peace and disarmament would follow had not been fulfilled. Before long, differences between East and West emerged in all their stark reality, as the cooperation engendered in time of war crumbled away to dust, to be replaced by suspicion and mutual fear of aggression.

The result was the armaments race between the two great powers, to see who could produce the most effective nuclear weapons. Gradually the "balance of terror" became the tacitly accepted safeguard against war and a guarantee of peace. The armaments race created an atmosphere that not only made it difficult to work for the promotion of disarmament and peace but also threatened to muzzle freedom of speech. . . .

The United States tested its first hydrogen bomb in November 1952, and the Soviet Union followed suit in August 1953. The cold war had now entered upon a still more uncompromising phase, but the voice of Linus Pauling was not to be silenced. Tireless and undaunted, and supported in his views by numerous scientists, he continued to draw attention to the fearful destruction and mass annihilation of human life that might result if hydrogen bombs were used. . . .

In 1957 he drew up an appeal which attracted the attention of the public more than anything he had done previously. The appeal was signed immediately by more than 2,000 American scientists. Later it was signed by more than 11,000 scientists in all from forty-nine different countries. And in January 1958 Pauling and his wife, Ava Helen Pauling, submitted the appeal to the then Secretary-General of the United Nations Organization, Dag Hammarskjöld.

In this same year, without entering into any prior agreement, the Soviet Union, followed by the United States and Great Britain, discontinued nuclear tests. Just what effect the warnings of scientists, first and foremost Linus Pauling and Albert Schweitzer, may have had in this connection would be difficult to say with any certainty. But it is undeniable that both of them, together with other scientists, had helped to familiarize people with the dangers that nuclear tests involve. Every government is bound to take public opinion into consideration whether it is openly expressed or not. . . .

In 1963, however, after what had long appeared to be a state of permanent deadlock, discussions on a nuclear test-ban finally made some headway when the United States, the Soviet Union, and Great Britain entered into an agreement. This was signed in Moscow on July 23, 1963, and came into effect on October 10, 1963. Most countries have now joined, the most important exceptions being France and China. The agreement covers all tests with nuclear weapons, apart from underground detonations.

No one would suggest that the nuclear test-ban is the sole work of Linus Pauling. But does anyone believe that the treaty would have been reached if there had been no responsible scientist who, tirelessly, unflinchingly, year in and year out, impressed on the authorities and on the general public the real menace of nuclear tests?

Science and Peace*

LINUS PAULING

Linus Pauling (1901-   ) was a member of the staff of the California Institute of Technology for more than forty years. In 1963 he became a member of the staff of the Center for the Study of Democratic Institutions. He received the Nobel Prize for Chemistry (1954) and the Nobel Prize for Peace (1963). He has published about 100 articles and a book on the subject of world peace.

I believe that there will never again be a great world war—a war in which the terrible weapons involving nuclear fission and nuclear fusion would be used. And I believe that it is the discoveries of scientists upon which the development of these terrible weapons was based that are now forcing us to move into a new period in the history of the world, a period of peace and reason, when world problems are not solved by war or by force, but are solved in accordance with world law, in a way that does justice to all nations and that benefits all people.

I remind you that Alfred Nobel wanted to invent "a substance or a machine with such terrible power of mass destruction that war would thereby be made impossible forever." Two thirds of a century later scientists discovered the explosive substances that Nobel wanted to invent—the fissionable substances uranium and plutonium, with explosive energy ten million times that of Nobel's favorite explosive, nitroglycerine, and the fusionable substance lithium deuteride, with explosive energy fifty million times that of nitroglycerine.

The first of the terrible machines incorporating these substances, the uranium-235 and plutonium-239 fission bombs, were exploded in 1945, at Alamogordo, Hiroshima, and Nagasaki. Then in 1954, nine years later, the first of the fission-fusion-fission superbombs was exploded, the 20-megaton Bikini bomb, with energy of explosion one thousand

---

* From *Science and Peace, The Nobel Peace Prize Lecture* (Santa Barbara: Center for the Study of Democratic Institutions, The Fund for the Republic, 1964), pp. 6-12 with omissions.

times greater than that of a 1945 fission bomb. This one bomb, the 1954 superbomb, contained less than one ton of nuclear explosive. The energy released in its explosion was greater than that of all of the explosives used in all of the wars that have taken place during the entire history of the world, including World War I and World War II.

Thousands of these superbombs have now been fabricated; and today, eighteen years after the construction of the first atomic bomb, the nuclear powers have stockpiles of these weapons so great that if they were to be used in a war hundreds of millions of people would be killed, and civilization itself might not survive the catastrophe.

Thus the machines envisaged by Nobel have come into existence, and war has been made impossible forever.

The world has now begun the metamorphosis from its primitive period of history, when disputes between nations were settled by war, to its period of maturity, in which war will be abolished and world law will take its place. The first great stage of this metamorphosis took place only a few months ago—the formulation by the governments of the United States, Great Britain, and the Soviet Union, after years of discussion and negotiation, of a treaty banning the testing of nuclear weapons on the surface of the earth, in the oceans, and in space, and the ratification and signing of this treaty by nearly all of the nations in the world.

I believe that the historians of the future may well describe the making of this treaty as the most important action ever taken by the governments of nations, in that it is the first of a series of treaties that will lead to the new world, from which war has been abolished forever.

We see that science and peace are related. The world has been greatly changed, especially during the last century, by the discoveries of scientists. Our increased knowledge now provides the possibility of eliminating poverty and starvation, of decreasing significantly the suffering caused by disease, of using the resources of the world effectively for the benefit of humanity. But the greatest of all the changes has been in the nature of war—the several millionfold increase in the power of explosives, and corresponding changes in methods of delivery of bombs.

These changes have resulted from the discoveries of scientists, and during the last two decades scientists have taken a leading part in bringing them to the attention of their fellow human beings and in urging that vigorous action be taken to prevent the use of the new weapons and to abolish war from the world.

The first scientists to take actions of this sort were those involved in the development of the atomic bomb. In March 1945, before the first nuclear explosion had been carried out, Leo Szilard prepared a memorandum to President Franklin Delano Roosevelt in which he pointed out that a system of international control of nuclear weapons might give civilization a chance to survive. A committee of atomic scientists with James Franck as Chairman on June 11, 1945 transmitted to the U.S. Secretary of War a report urging that nuclear bombs not be used in an unannounced attack against Japan, as this action would prejudice the possibility of reaching an international agreement on control of these weapons.

In 1946 Albert Einstein, Harold Urey, and seven other scientists formed an organization to educate the American people about the nature of nuclear weapons and nuclear war. This organization, the Emergency Committee of Atomic Scientists (usually called the Einstein Committee), carried out an effective educational campaign over a five-year period. The nature of the campaign is indicated by the following sentences from the 1946 statement by Einstein:

> Today the atomic bomb has altered profoundly the nature of the world as we know it, and the human race consequently finds itself in a new habitat to which it must adapt its thinking. . . . Never before was it possible for one nation to make war on another without sending armies across borders. Now with rockets and atomic bombs no center of population on the earth's surface is secure from surprise destruction in a single attack. . . . Few men have ever seen the bomb. But all men if told a few facts can understand that this bomb and the danger of war is a very real thing, and not something far away. It directly concerns every person in the civilized world. We cannot leave it to generals, senators, and diplomats to work out a solution over a period of generations. . . . There is no defense in science against the weapon which can destroy civilization. Our defense is not in armaments, nor in science, nor in going underground. Our defense is in law and order. . . . Future thinking *must* prevent wars.

During the same period and later years many other organizations of scientists were active in the work of educating people about nuclear weapons and nuclear war; among them I may mention especially the Federation of American Scientists (in the United States), the Atomic Scientists' Association (Great Britain), and the World Federation of Scientific Workers (with membership covering many countries).

On July 15, 1955 a powerful statement, called the Mainau Declaration, was issued by fifty-two Nobel Laureates. This statement warned that a great war in the nuclear age would imperil the whole world, and ended with the sentences: "All nations must come to the decision to renounce force as a final resort of policy. If they are not prepared to do so they will cease to exist."

A document of great consequence, the Russell-Einstein Appeal, was made public by Bertrand Russell on July 9, 1955. Russell, who for years has remained one of the world's most active and effective workers for peace, had drafted this document some months earlier, and it had been signed by Einstein two days before his death, and also by nine other scientists. The Appeal began with the sentence:

> In the tragic situation which confronts humanity, we feel that scientists should assemble in conference to appraise the perils that have arisen as a result of the development of weapons of mass destruction.

and it ended with the exhortation:

> There lies before us, if we choose, continual progress in happiness, knowledge, and wisdom. Shall we, instead, choose death, because we cannot forget our quarrels? We appeal, as human beings, to human beings: Remember your humanity, and forget the rest. If you can do so, the way lies open to a new Paradise; if you cannot, there lies before you the risk of universal death. . . .

Would a great war, fought with use of the nuclear weapons that now exist, be a catastrophe to all humanity?

Consideration of the nature of nuclear weapons and the magnitude of the nuclear stockpiles gives us the answer: It is Yes.

A single 25-megaton bomb could largely destroy any city on earth and kill most of its inhabitants. Thousands of these great bombs have been fabricated, together with the vehicles to deliver them.

Precise information about the existing stockpiles of nuclear weapons has not been released. The participants in the Sixth Pugwash Conference, in 1960, made use of the estimate of 60,000 megatons. This is 10,000 times the amount of explosive used in the whole of World War II. It indicates that the world's stockpile of military explosives has on the average doubled every year since 1945. My estimate for 1963, which reflects the continued manufacture of nuclear weapons during the past three years, is 320,000 megatons. . . .

No dispute between nations can justify nuclear war. There is no defense against nuclear weapons that could not be overcome by increasing the scale of the attack. It would be contrary to the nature of war for nations to adhere to agreements to fight "limited" wars, using only "small" nuclear weapons—even little wars today are perilous, because of the likelihood that a little war would grow into a world catastrophe.

The only sane policy for the world is that of abolishing war.

This is now the proclaimed goal of the nuclear powers and of all other nations.

We are all indebted to the governments of the United States, the Soviet Union, and Great Britain for formulating a test-ban agreement that has been accepted by most of the nations of the world. As an American, I feel especially thankful to our late President. It is my opinion that this great international agreement could not have been formulated and ratified except for the conviction, determination, and political skill of President Kennedy.

The great importance of the 1963 test-ban treaty lies in its significance as the first step toward disarmament. To indicate what other steps need to be taken I shall quote some of the statements made by President Kennedy in his address to the United Nations General Assembly on September 26, 1961:

> The goal [of disarmament] is no longer a dream. It is a practical matter of life or death. The risks inherent in disarmament pale in comparison to the risks inherent in an unlimited arms race. . . .
>
> Our new disarmament program includes . . . : First, signing the test-ban treaty by all nations . . . ; Second, stopping production of fissionable materials and preventing their transfer to [other] nations . . . ; Third, prohibiting the transfer of control over nuclear weapons to other nations; Fourth, keeping nuclear weapons from outer space; Fifth, gradually destroying existing nuclear weapons; and Sixth, halting . . . the production of strategic nuclear delivery vehicles, and gradually destroying them.

The first of these goals has been approached, through the 1963 treaty, but not yet reached. By a vote of 97 to 1 the Political Committee of the United Nations General Assembly has approved a resolution asking that the eighteen-nation Disarmament Committee take supplementary action to achieve the discontinuance of all test explosions of nuclear weapons for all time. We must strive to achieve this goal.

The fourth action proposed by President Kennedy, that of keeping nuclear weapons from outer space, has been taken in the United Nations, through a pledge of abstention subscribed to by many nations. . . .

Is there no action that we can take immediately to decrease the present great danger of outbreak of nuclear war through some technological or psychological accident or as the result of a series of events such as that even the wisest national leaders could not avert the catastrophe?

I believe that there is such an action, and I hope that it will be given consideration by the national governments. My proposal is that there be instituted with the maximum expedition compatible with caution a system of joint national-international control of the stockpiles of nuclear weapons, such that use could be made of the American nuclear armaments only with the approval both of the American government and of the United Nations, and that use could be made of the Soviet nuclear armament only with the approval both of the Soviet government and of the United Nations. A similar system of dual control would of course be instituted for the smaller nuclear powers, if they did not destroy their weapons.

Even a small step in the direction of this proposal, such as the acceptance of United Nations observers in the control stations of the nuclear powers, might decrease significantly the probability of nuclear war. . . .

To illustrate the threat I may mention the plans to use nerve gases that, when they do not kill, produce temporary or permanent insanity, and the plans to use toxins, such as the botulism toxin, viruses, such as the virus of yellow fever, or bacterial spores, such as of anthrax, to kill tens or hundreds of millions of people.

The hazard is especially great in that, once the knowledge is obtained through a large-scale development program such as is now being carried out, it might well spread over the world, and might permit some small group of evil men, perhaps in one of the smaller countries, to launch a devastating attack.

This terrible prospect could be eliminated now by a general agreement to stop research and development of these weapons, to prohibit their use, and to renounce all official secrecy and security controls over microbiological, toxicological, pharmacological, and chemical-biological research. Hundreds of millions of dollars per year are now being spent in the effort to make these malignant cells of knowledge. Now is the time to stop. When once the cancer has developed, and its metastases have spread over the world, it will be too late.

The replacement of war by law must include not only great wars but also small ones. The abolition of insurrectionary and guerrilla warfare, which often is characterized by extreme savagery and a great amount of human suffering, would be a boon to humanity.

There are, however, countries in which the people are subjected to continuing economic exploitation and to oppression by a dictatorial government, which retains its power through force of arms. The only hope for many of these people has been that of revolution, of overthrowing the dictatorial government and replacing it with a reform government, a democratic government that would work for the welfare of the people.

I believe that the time has come for the world as a whole to abolish this evil, through the formulation and acceptance of some appropriate articles of world law. With only limited knowledge of law, I shall not attempt to formulate a proposal that would achieve this end without permitting the possibility of the domination of the small nations by the large nations. I suggest, however, that the end might be achieved by world legislation under which there would be, perhaps once a decade, a referendum, supervised by the United Nations, on the will of the people with respect to their national government, held, separately from the national elections, in every country in the world.

It may take many years to achieve such an addition to the body of world law. In the meantime, much could be done through a change in the policies of the great nations. During recent years insurrections and civil wars in small countries have been instigated and aggravated by the great powers, which have moreover provided weapons and military advisers, increasing the savagery of the wars and the suffering of the people. In four countries during 1963 and several others during preceding years democratically elected governments with policies in the direction of social and economic reform have been overthrown and replaced by military dictatorships, with the approval, if not at the instigation, of one or more of the great powers. These actions of the great powers are associated with policies of militarism and national economic interest that are now antiquated. I hope that the pressure of world opinion will soon cause them to be abandoned, and to be replaced by policies that are compatible with the principles of morality, justice, and world brotherhood.

In working to abolish war we are working also for human freedom, for the rights of individual human beings. War and nationalism, together with economic exploitation, have been the great enemies of the individual human being. I believe that, with war abolished from the world, there will be improvement in the social, political, and economic systems in all nations, to the benefit of the whole of humanity. . . .

Now we are forced to eliminate from the world forever this vestige of prehistoric barbarism, this curse to the human race. We, you and I, are privileged to be alive during this extraordinary age, this unique epoch in the history of the world, the epoch of demarcation between the past millennia of war and suffering and the future, the great future of peace, justice, morality, and human well-being. We are privileged to have the opportunity of contributing to the achievement of the goal of the abolition of war and its replacement by world law. I am confident that we shall succeed in this great task; that the world community will thereby be freed not only from the suffering caused by war but also from hunger, disease, illiteracy, and fear through the better use of the earth's resources, the discoveries of scientists, and the efforts of mankind; and that we shall in the course of time be enabled to build a world characterized by economic, political, and social justice for all human beings, and a culture worthy of man's intelligence.

FOR FURTHER STUDY

American Friends Service Committee. *Speak Truth to Power*. Philadelphia: American Friends Service Committee, 1955.

Bennett, John C. (ed.). *Nuclear Weapons and the Conflict of Conscience*. New York: Scribner, 1962.

Butterfield, Herbert. *International Conflict in the Twentieth Century*. New York: Harper, 1960.

Cousins, Norman. *In Place of Folly*. New York: Washington Square Press, 1962.

Gross, Ernest A. *The United Nations Structure for Peace*. New York: Harper, 1962.

Hocking, William Ernest. *Strength of Men and Nations*. New York: Harper, 1959.

Lerner, Max. *The Age of Overkill: A Preface to World Politics*. New York: Simon and Schuster, 1962.

Millis, Walter. "A Demilitarized World and How to Get There," *Saturday Review*, 47 (September 12, 1964): 18-23, 30-32.

Thompson, Kenneth W. *Christian Ethics and the Dilemmas of Foreign Policy*. Durham: Duke U. Press, 1959.

PART FOUR

A FRAMEWORK FOR A
MORAL PHILOSOPHY

CHAPTER 24

FREEDOM, DETERMINISM,
AND RESPONSIBILITY

*Of Liberty and Necessity**

DAVID HUME

David Hume (1711-1776), a Scotchman and a leading empiricist, wrote on philosophy, politics, and
history. He is recognized as one of the keenest critical minds of the Enlightenment. His influence is still
strong, especially among logical positivists and philosophical analysts.

We come now to explain the *direct* passions, or the impressions which
arise immediately from good or evil, from pain or pleasure. Of this
kind are, *desire and aversion, grief and joy, hope and fear.*

Of all the immediate effects of pain and pleasure, there is none more
remarkable than the *will;* and though, properly speaking, it be not
comprehended among the passions, yet, as the full understanding of its
nature and properties is necessary to the explanation of them, we shall
here make it the subject of our inquiry. I desire it may be observed,
that, by the *will,* I mean nothing but *the internal impression we feel,
and are conscious of, when we knowingly give rise to any new motion
of our body, or new perception of our mind.* This impression, like the
preceding ones of pride and humility, love and hatred, it is impossible
to define, and needless to describe any further; for which reason we

* From *A Treatise of Human Nature* (1738), Book II, Part III, Sec. 1.

shall cut off all those definitions and distinctions with which philosophers are wont to perplex rather than clear up this question; and entering at first upon the subject, shall examine that long-disputed question concerning *liberty and necessity*, which occurs so naturally in treating of the will.

It is universally acknowledged that the operations of external bodies are necessary; and that, in the communication of their motion, in their attraction, and mutual cohesion, there are not the least traces of indifference or liberty. Every object is determined by an absolute fate to a certain degree and direction of its motion, and can no more depart from that precise line in which it moves, than it can convert itself into an angel, or spirit, or any superior substance. The actions, therefore, of matter, are to be regarded as instances of necessary actions; and whatever is, in this respect, on the same footing with matter, must be acknowledged to be necessary. That we may know whether this be the case with the actions of the mind, we shall begin with examining matter, and considering on what the idea of a necessity in its operations are founded, and why we conclude one body or action to be the infallible cause of another.

It has been observed already, that in no single instance the ultimate connection of any objects is discoverable either by our senses or reason, and that we can never penetrate so far into the essence and construction of bodies, as to perceive the principle on which their mutual influence depends. It is their constant union alone with which we are acquainted; and it is from the constant union the necessity arises. If objects had not an uniform and regular conjunction with each other, we should never arrive at any idea of cause and effect; and even after all, the necessity which enters into that idea, is nothing but a determination of the mind to pass from one object to its usual attendant, and infer the existence of one from that of the other. Here then are two particulars which we are to consider as essential to necessity, viz. the constant *union* and the *inference* of the mind; and wherever we discover these, we must acknowledge a necessity. As the actions of matter have no necessity but what is derived from these circumstances, and it is not by any insight into the essence of bodies we discover their connection, the absence of this insight, while the union and inference remain, will never, in any case, remove the necessity. It is the observation of the union which produces the inference; for which reason it might be thought sufficient, if we prove a constant union in the actions of the mind, in order to establish the inference along with the necessity of these actions. But that I may bestow a greater force on my reasoning, I shall examine these particulars apart, and shall first prove from experience that our actions have a constant union with out motives, tempers, and circumstances, before I consider the inferences we draw from it.

To this end a very slight and general view of the common course of human affairs will be sufficient. There is no light in which we can take them that does not confirm this principle. Whether we consider mankind according to the difference of sexes, ages, governments, conditions, or methods of education; the same uniformity and regular operation of natural principles are discernible. Like causes still produce like effects; in the same manner as in the mutual action of the elements and powers of nature.

There are different trees which regularly produce fruit, whose relish is different from each other; and this regularity will be admitted as an instance of necessity and causes in external bodies. But are the products of Guienne and of Champagne more regularly different than the sentiments, actions, and passions of the two sexes, of which the one are distinguished by their force and maturity, the other by their delicacy and softness?

Are the changes of our body from infancy to old age more regular and certain than those of our mind and conduct? And would a man be more ridiculous, who would expect that an infant of four years old will raise a weight of three hundred pounds, than one who, from a person of the same age, would look for a philosophical reasoning, or a prudent and well concerted action?

We must certainly allow, that the cohesion of the parts of matter arises from natural and necessary principles, whatever difficulty we may find in explaining them: and for a like reason we must allow, that human society is founded on like principles; and our reason in the latter case is better than even that in the former; because we not only observe that men *always* seek society, but can also explain the principles on which this universal propensity is founded. For is it more certain that two flat pieces of marble will unite together, than two young savages of different sexes will copulate? Do the children arise from this copulation more uniformly, than does the parents' care for their safety and preservation? And after they have arrived at years of discretion by the care of their parents, are the inconveniences attending their separation more certain than their foresight of these inconveniences, and their care of avoiding them by a close union and confederacy?

The skin, pores, muscles, and nerves of a day-labourer, are different from those of a man of quality: so are his sentiments, actions, and manners. The different stations of life influence the whole fabric, external and internal; and these different stations arise necessarily, because uniformly, from the necessary and uniform principles of human nature. Men cannot live without society, and cannot be associated without government. Government makes a distinction of property, and establishes the different ranks of men. This produces industry, traffic, manufactures, lawsuits, war, leagues, alliances, voyages, travels, cities, fleets, ports, and all those other actions and objects which cause such a diversity, and at the same time maintain such an uniformity in human life.

Should a traveller, returning from a far country, tell us, that he had seen a climate in the fiftieth degree of northern latitude, where all the fruits ripen and come to perfection in the winter, and decay in the summer, after the same manner as in England they are produced and decay in the contrary seasons, he would find few so credulous as to believe him. I am apt to think a traveller would meet with as little credit, who should inform us of people exactly of the same character with those in Plato's republic on the one hand, or those in Hobbes's *Leviathan* on the other. There is a general course of nature in human actions, as well as in the operations of the sun and the climate. There are also characters peculiar to different nations and particular persons, as well as common to mankind. The knowledge of these characters is founded on the observation of an uniformity in the actions that flow from them; and this uniformity forms the very essence of necessity.

I can imagine only one way of eluding this argument, which is by denying that uniformity of human actions, on which it is founded. As long as actions have a constant union and connection with the situation and temper of the agent, however we may in words refuse to acknowledge the necessity, we really allow the thing. Now, some may perhaps find a pretext to deny this regular union and connection. For what is more capricious than human actions? What more inconstant than the desires of man? And what creature departs more widely, not only from right reason, but from his own character and disposition? An hour, a moment is sufficient to make him change from one extreme to another, and overturn what cost the greatest pain and labour to establish. Necessity is regular and certain. Human conduct is irregular and uncertain. The one therefore proceeds not from the other.

To this I reply, that in judging of the actions of men we must proceed upon the same maxims, as when we reason concerning external objects. When any phenomena are constantly and invariably conjoined together, they acquire such a connection in the imagination, that it passes from one to the other without any doubt or hesitation. But below this there are many inferior degrees of evidence and probability, nor does one single contrariety of experiment entirely destroy all our reasoning. The mind balances the contrary experiments, and, deducting the inferior from the superior, proceeds with that degree of assurance or evidence, which remains. Even when these contrary experiments are entirely equal, we remove not the notion of causes and necessity; but, supposing that the usual contrariety proceeds from the operation of contrary and concealed causes, we conclude, that the chance or indifference lies only in our judgment on account of our imperfect knowledge, not in the things themselves, which are in every case equally necessary, though, to appearance, not equally constant or certain. No union can be more constant and certain than that of some actions with some motives and characters; and if, in other cases, the union is uncertain, it is no more than what happens in the operations of body; nor can we conclude anything from the one irregularity which will not follow equally from the other.

It is commonly allowed that madmen have no liberty. But, were we to judge by their actions, these have less regularity and constancy than the actions of wise men, and consequently are further removed from necessity. Our way of thinking in this particular is, therefore, absolutely inconsistent; but is a natural consequence of these confused ideas and undefined terms, which we so commonly make use of in our reasonings, especially on the present subject.

We must now show, that, as the *union* betwixt motives and actions has the same constancy as that in any natural operations, so its influence on the understanding is also the same in *determining* us to infer the existence of one from that of another. If this shall appear, there is no known circumstance that enters into the connection and production of the actions of matter that is not to be found in all the operations of the mind; and consequently we cannot, without a manifest absurdity, attribute necessity to the one, and refuse it to the other.

There is no philosopher, whose judgment is so riveted to this fantastical system of liberty, as not to acknowledge the force of *moral evidence*, and both in speculation and practice proceed upon it as upon a reasonable foundation. Now, moral evidence is nothing but a conclusion concerning the actions of men, derived from the consideration of their motives, temper, and situation. Thus, when we see certain characters or figures described upon paper, we infer that the person who produced them would affirm such facts, the death of Caesar, the success of Augustus, the cruelty of Nero; and, remembering many other concurrent testimonies, we conclude that those facts were once really existent, and that so many men, without any interest, would never conspire to deceive us; especially since they must, in the attempt, expose themselves to the derision of all their contemporaries, when these facts were asserted to be recently and universally known. The same kind of reasoning runs through politics, war, commerce, economy, and indeed mixes itself so entirely in human life, that it is impossible to act or subsist a moment without having recourse to it. A prince who imposes a tax upon his subjects, expects their compliance. A general who conducts an army, makes account of a certain degree of courage. A merchant looks for fidelity and skill in his factor or supercargo. A man who gives orders for his dinner, doubts not of the obedience of his servants. In short, as nothing more nearly interests us than our own actions and those of others, the greatest part of our reasonings is employed in judgments concerning them. Now I assert, that whoever reasons after this manner, does *ipso facto* believe the actions of the will to arise from necessity, and that he knows not what he means when he denies it.

All those objects, of which we call the one *cause* and the other *effect*, considered in themselves, are as distinct and separate from each other as any two things in nature; nor can we ever, by the most accurate survey of them, infer the existence of the one from that of the other. It is only from experience and the observation of their constant union, that we are able to form this inference; and even after all, the inference is nothing but the effects of custom on the imagination. We must not here be content with saying, that the idea of cause and effect arises from objects constantly united; but must affirm, that it is the very same with the idea of these objects, and that the *necessary connection* is not discovered by a conclusion of the understanding, but is merely a perception of the mind. Wherever, therefore, we observe the same union, and wherever the union operates in the same manner upon the belief and opinion, we have the idea of cause and necessity, though perhaps we may avoid those expressions. Motion in one body, in all past instances that have fallen under our observation, is followed upon impulse by motion in another. It is impossible for the mind to penetrate further. From this constant union it *forms* the idea of cause and effect, and by its influence *feels* the necessity. As there is the same constancy, and the same influence, in what we call moral evidence, I ask no more. What remains can only be a dispute of words.

And indeed, when we consider how aptly *natural* and *moral* evidence cement together, and form only one chain of argument betwixt them, we shall make no scruple to allow, that they are of the same nature, and derived from the same principles. A prisoner, who has neither money nor interest discovers the impossibility of his escape, as well from the obstinacy of the gaoler, as from the walls and bars with which he is surrounded; and in all attempts for his freedom, chooses rather to work upon the stone and iron of the one, than upon the inflexible nature of the other. The same prisoner, when conducted to the scaffold, foresees his death as certainly from the constancy and fidelity of his guards, as from the operation of the axe or wheel. His mind runs along a certain train of ideas: the refusal of the soldiers to consent to his escape; the action of the executioner; the separation of the head and body, bleeding, convulsive motions, and death. Here is a connected chain of natural causes and voluntary actions; but the mind feels no difference betwixt them in passing from one link to another; nor is less certain of the future event than if it were connected with the present impressions of the memory and senses by a train of causes cemented together by what we are pleased to call a *physical necessity*. The same experienced union has the same effect on the mind, whether the united objects be motives, volitions, and actions, or figure and motion. We may change the names of things, but their nature and their operation on the understanding never change.

I dare be positive no one will ever endeavour to refute these reasonings otherwise than by altering my definitions, and assigning a different meaning to the terms of *cause, and effect, and necessity, and liberty, and chance*. According to my definitions, necessity makes an essential part of causation; and consequently liberty, by removing necessity, removes all causes, and is the very same thing with chance. As chance is commonly thought to imply a contradiction, and is at least directly contrary to experience, there are always the same arguments against liberty or free-will. If any one alters the definitions, I cannot pretend to argue with him till I know the meaning he assigns to these terms.

The Dilemma of Determinism*

WILLIAM JAMES

William James (1842-1910) had training in medicine
and taught physiology and psychology at Harvard
before turning to philosophy. He was one of the
founders of the system of philosophy known as
pragmatism. His lectures and books have had widespread influence on twentieth-century thought, especially in the United States.

A common opinion prevails that the juice has ages ago been pressed
out of the free-will controversy, and that no new champion can do
more than warm up stale arguments which every one has heard. This
is a radical mistake. I know of no subject less worn out, or in which
inventive genius has a better chance of breaking open new ground,—
not, perhaps, of forcing a conclusion or of coercing assent, but of deepening our sense of what the issue between the two parties really is, of
what the ideas of fate and of free-will imply. . . . [O]ur first act of
freedom, if we are free, ought in all inward propriety to be to affirm
that we are free. . . .

With this much understood at the outset, we can advance. But not
without one more point understood as well. The arguments I am about
to urge all proceed on two suppositions: first, when we make theories
about the world and discuss them with one another, we do so in order
to attain a conception of things which shall give us subjective satisfaction; and, second, if there be two conceptions, and the one seems to
us, on the whole, more rational than the other, we are entitled to suppose that the more rational one is the truer of the two. . . .

To begin, then, I must suppose you acquainted with all the usual
arguments on the subject. I cannot stop to take up the old proofs from
causation, from statistics, from the certainty with which we can foretell one another's conduct, from the fixity of character, and all the

* William James, *The Will to Believe and Other Essays in Popular Philosophy*
(New York: Longmans, Green, 1897), pp. 145-183 with omissions.

rest. . . . Old-fashioned determinism was what we may call *hard* determinism. It did not shrink from such words as fatality, bondage of the will, necessitation, and the like. Nowadays, we have a *soft* determinism which abhors harsh words, and, repudiating fatality, necessity, and even predetermination, says that its real name is freedom; for freedom is only necessity understood, and bondage to the highest is identical with true freedom. . . .

[Determinism] professes that those parts of the universe already laid down absolutely appoint and decree what the other parts shall be. The future has no ambiguous possibilities hidden in its womb: the part we call the present is compatible with only one totality. Any other future complement than the one fixed from eternity is impossible. The whole is in each and every part, and welds it with the rest into an absolute unity, an iron block, in which there can be no equivocation or shadow of turning.

> With earth's first clay they did the last man knead,
> And there of the last harvest sowed the seed.
> And the first morning of creation wrote
> What the last dawn of reckoning shall read.

Indeterminism, on the contrary, says that the parts have a certain amount of loose play on one another, so that the laying down of one of them does not necessarily determine what the others shall be. It admits that possibilities may be in excess of actualities, and that things not yet revealed to our knowledge may really in themselves be ambiguous. Of two alternative futures which we conceive, both may now be really possible; and the one become impossible only at the very moment when the other excludes it by becoming real itself. Indeterminism thus denies the world to be one unbending unit of fact. It says there is a certain ultimate pluralism in it; and, so saying, it corroborates our ordinary unsophisticated view of things. To that view, actualities seem to float in a wider sea of possibilities from out of which they are chosen; and, *somewhere*, indeterminism says, such possibilities exist, and form a part of truth.

Determinism, on the contrary, says they exist *nowhere*, and that necessity on the one hand and impossibility on the other are the sole categories of the real. Possibilities that fail to get realized are, for determinism, pure illusions: they never were possibilities at all. There is nothing inchoate, it says, about this universe of ours, all that was or is or shall be actual in it having been from eternity virtually there. The cloud of alternatives our minds escort this mass of actuality withal is a cloud of sheer deceptions, to which "impossibilities" is the only name that rightfully belongs.

The issue, it will be seen, is a perfectly sharp one, which no eulogistic terminology can smear over or wipe out. The truth *must* lie with one side or the other, and its lying with one side makes the other false.

The question relates solely to the existence of possibilities, in the strict sense of the term, as things that may, but need not, be. Both sides admit that a volition, for instance, has occurred. The indeterminists say another volition might have occurred in its place: the determinists swear that nothing could possibly have occurred in its place. Now, can science be called in to tell us which of these two point-blank contradicters of each other is right? Science professes to draw no conclusions but such as are based on matters of fact, things that have actually happened; but how can any amount of assurance that something actually happened give us the least grain of information as to whether another thing might or might not have happened in its place? Only facts can be proved by other facts. With things that are possibilities and not facts, facts have no concern. If we have no other evidence than the evidence of existing facts, the possibility-question must remain a mystery never to be cleared up.

And the truth is that facts practically have hardly anything to do with making us either determinists or indeterminists. Sure enough, we make a flourish of quoting facts this way or that; and if we are determinists, we talk about the infallibility with which we can predict one another's conduct; while if we are indeterminists, we lay great stress on the fact that it is just because we cannot foretell one another's conduct, either in war or statecraft or in any of the great and small intrigues and businesses of men, that life is so intensely anxious and hazardous a game. But who does not see the wretched insufficiency of this so-called objective testimony on both sides? What fills up the gaps in our minds is something not objective, not external. What divides us into possibility men and anti-possibility men is different faiths or postulates,—postulates of rationality. To this man the world seems more rational with possibilities in it,—to that man more rational with possibilities excluded; and talk as we will about having to yield to evidence, what makes us monists or pluralists, determinists or indeterminists, is at bottom always some sentiment like this. . . .

Nevertheless, many persons talk as if the minutest dose of disconnectedness of one part with another, the smallest modicum of independence, the faintest tremor of ambiguity about the future, for example, would ruin everything, and turn this goodly universe into a sort of insane sand-heap or nulliverse, no universe at all. Since future human volitions are as a matter of fact the only ambiguous things we are tempted to believe in, let us stop for a moment to make ourselves sure whether their independent and accidental character need be fraught with such direful consequences to the universe as these.

What is meant by saying that my choice of which way to walk home after the lecture is ambiguous and matter of chance as far as the present moment is concerned? It means that both Divinity Avenue and Oxford Street are called; but that only one, and that one *either* one, shall be chosen. Now, I ask you seriously to suppose that this ambiguity of my choice is real; and then to make the impossible hypothesis that the choice is made twice over, and each time falls on a different street. In other words, imagine that I first walk through Divinity Avenue, and then imagine that the powers governing the universe annihilate ten minutes of time with all that it contained, and set me back at the door of this hall just as I was before the choice was made. Imagine then that, everything else being the same, I now make a different choice and traverse Oxford Street. You, as passive spectators, look on and see the two alternative universes,—one of them with me walking through Divinity Avenue in it, the other with the same me walking through Oxford Street. Now, if you are determinists you believe one of these universes to have been from eternity impossible: you believe it to have been impossible because of the intrinsic irrationality or accidentality somewhere involved in it. But looking outwardly at these universes, can you say which is the impossible and accidental one, and which the rational and necessary one? I doubt if the most ironclad determinist among you could have the slightest glimmer of light on this point. In other words, either universe *after the fact* and once there would, to our means of observation and understanding, appear just as rational as the other. There would be absolutely no criterion by which we might judge one necessary and the other matter of chance. Suppose now we relieve the gods of their hypothetical task and assume my choice, once made, to be made forever. I go through Divinity Avenue for good and all. If, as good determinists, you now begin to affirm, what all good determinists punctually do affirm, that in the nature of things I *couldn't* have gone through Oxford Street,—had I done so it would have been chance, irrationality, insanity, a horrid gap in nature,—I simply call your attention to this, that your affirmation is what the Germans call a *Machtspruch*, a mere conception fulminated as a dogma and based on no insight into details. Before my choice, either street seemed as natural to you as to me. Had I happened to take Oxford Street, Divinity

Avenue would have figured in your philosophy as the gap in nature;
and you would have so proclaimed it with the best deterministic conscience in the world. . . .

And this at last brings us within sight of our subject. We have seen
what determinism means: we have seen that indeterminism is rightly
described as meaning chance; and we have seen that chance, the very
name of which we are urged to shrink from as from a metaphysical
pestilence, means only the negative fact that no part of the world,
however big, can claim to control absolutely the destinies of the whole.
But although, in discussing the word "chance," I may at moments have
seemed to be arguing for its real existence, I have not meant to do so
yet. We have not yet ascertained whether this be a world of chance or
no; at most, we have agreed that it seems so. And I now repeat what I
said at the outset, that, from any strict theoretical point of view, the
question is insoluble. To deepen our theoretic sense of the *difference*
between a world with chances in it and a deterministic world is the
most I can hope to do; and this I may now at last begin upon, after all
our tedious clearing of the way.

I wish first of all to show you just what the notion that this is a
deterministic world implies. The implications I call your attention to
are all bound up with the fact that it is a world in which we constantly
have to make what I shall, with your permission, call judgments of
regret. Hardly an hour passes in which we do not wish that something
might be otherwise; and happy indeed are those of us whose hearts
have never echoed the wish of Omar Khayam—

> That we might clasp, ere closed, the book of fate,
>   And make the writer on a fairer leaf
> Inscribe our names, or quite obliterate.
>
> Ah! Love, could you and I with fate conspire
> To mend this sorry scheme of things entire,
>   Would we not shatter it to bits, and then
> Remould it nearer to the heart's desire?

Now, it is undeniable that most of these regrets are foolish, and quite
on a par in point of philosophic value with the criticisms on the universe of that friend of our infancy, the hero of the fable The Atheist
and the Acorn,—

> Fool! had that bough a pumpkin bore,
> Thy whimsies would have worked no more, etc.

Even from the point of view of our own ends, we should probably make a botch of remodelling the universe. How much more then from the point of view of ends we cannot see! Wise men therefore regret as little as they can. But still some regrets are pretty obstinate and hard to stifle,—regrets for acts of wanton cruelty or treachery, for example, whether performed by others or by ourselves. Hardly any one can remain *entirely* optimistic after reading the confession of the murderer at Brockton the other day: how, to get rid of the wife whose continued existence bored him, he inveigled her into a desert spot, shot her four times, and then, as she lay on the ground and said to him, "You didn't do it on purpose, did you, dear?" replied, "No, I didn't do it on purpose," as he raised a rock and smashed her skull. Such an occurrence, with the mild sentence and self-satisfaction of the prisoner, is a field for a crop of regrets, which one need not take up in detail. We feel that, although a perfect mechanical fit to the rest of the universe, it is a bad moral fit, and that something else would really have been better in its place.

But for the deterministic philosophy the murder, the sentence, and the prisoner's optimism were all necessary from eternity; and nothing else for a moment had a ghost of a chance of being put into their place. To admit such a chance, the determinists tell us, would be to make a suicide of reason; so we must steel our hearts against the thought. And here our plot thickens, for we see the first of those difficult implications of determinism and monism which it is my purpose to make you feel. If this Brockton murder was called for by the rest of the universe, if it had to come at its preappointed hour, and if nothing else would have been consistent with the sense of the whole, what are we to think of the universe? Are we stubbornly to stick to our judgment of regret, and say, though it *couldn't* be, yet it *would* have been a better universe with something different from this Brockton murder in it? That, of course, seems the natural and spontaneous thing for us to do; and yet it is nothing short of deliberately espousing a kind of pessimism. The judgment of regret calls the murder bad. Calling a thing bad means, if it mean anything at all, that the thing ought not to be, that something else ought to be in its stead. Determinism, in denying that anything else can be in its stead, virtually defines the universe as a place in which what ought to be is impossible,—in other words, as an organism whose constitution is afflicted with an incurable taint, an irremediable flaw. The pessimism of a Schopenhauer says no more than this,—that the murder is a symptom; and that it is a vicious symptom because it belongs to a vicious whole, which can express its nature no otherwise than by bringing forth just such a symptom as that at this particular spot. Regret for the murder must transform itself, if we are determinists and wise, into a larger regret. It is absurd to regret the murder alone. Other things being what they are, *it* could not be different. What we should regret is that whole frame of things of which the murder is one member. I see no escape whatever from this pessimistic conclusion, if, being determinists, our judgment of regret is to be allowed to stand at all.

The only deterministic escape from pessimism is everywhere to abandon the judgment of regret. That this can be done, history shows to be not impossible. The devil, *quoad existentiam*, may be good. That is, although he be a *principle* of evil, yet the universe, with such a principle in it, may practically be a better universe than it could have been without. On every hand, in a small way, we find that a certain amount of evil is a condition by which a higher form of good is bought. There is nothing to prevent anybody from generalizing this view, and trusting that if we could but see things in the largest of all ways, even such matters as this Brockton murder would appear to be paid for by the uses that follow in their train. An optimism *quand même*, a systematic and infatuated optimism like that ridiculed by Voltaire in his Candide, is one of the possible ideal ways in which a man may train himself to look on life. Bereft of dogmatic hardness and lit up with the expression of a tender and pathetic hope, such an optimism has been the grace of some of the most religious characters that ever lived.

> Throb thine with Nature's throbbing breast,
> And all is clear from east to west.

Even cruelty and treachery may be among the absolutely blessed fruits of time, and to quarrel with any of their details may be blasphemy. The only real blasphemy, in short, may be that pessimistic temper of the soul which lets it give way to such things as regrets, remorse, and grief.

Thus, our deterministic pessimism may become a deterministic optimism at the price of extinguishing our judgments of regret.

But does not this immediately bring us into a curious logical predicament? Our determinism leads us to call our judgments of regret wrong, because they are pessimistic in implying that what is impossible yet ought to be. But how then about the judgments of regret themselves? If they are wrong, other judgments, judgments of approval presumably, ought to be in their place. But as they are necessitated, nothing else *can* be in their place; and the universe is just what it was before,—namely, a place in which what ought to be appears impossible. We have got one foot out of the pessimistic bog, but the other one sinks all the deeper. We have rescued our actions from the bonds of evil, but our judgments are now held fast. When murders and treacheries cease to be sins, regrets are theoretic absurdities and errors. The theoretic and the active life thus play a kind of seesaw with each other on the ground of evil. The rise of either sends the other down. Murder and treachery cannot be good without regret being bad: regret cannot be good without treachery and murder being bad. Both, however, are supposed to have been foredoomed: so something must be fatally unreasonable, absurd, and wrong in the world. It must be a place of which either sin or error forms a necessary part. From this dilemma there seems at first sight no escape. . . .

FOR FURTHER STUDY

Beardsley, Elizabeth L. "Determinism and Moral Perspectives," *Philosophy and Phenomenological Research*, 21 (September 1960): 1-20.

Beloff, John. *The Existence of Mind.* London: MacGibbon & Kee, 1962, Ch. 5.

Compton, Arthur H. "Science and Man's Freedom," *The Atlantic Monthly*, 200 (October 1957): 71-74.

Hook, Sidney (ed.). *Determinism and Freedom.* New York: New York U. Press, 1958, Part I, "Determinism in Philosophy," Part III, "Determinism and Responsibility in Law and Ethics." (Also Collier Book BS37, 1961.)

Kenner, Lionel. "Causality, Determinism and Freedom of the Will," *Philosophy*, 39 (July 1964): 233-248.

Mandelbaum, Maurice. "Determinism and Moral Responsibility," *Ethics*, 70 (April 1960): 204-219.

Morgenbesser, Sidney, and Walsh, James (eds.). *Free Will.* Englewood Cliffs: Prentice-Hall, 1962.

Pears, D. F. (ed.). *Freedom and the Will.* New York: St. Martin's Press, 1963.

Taylor, Richard. "I Can," *The Philosophical Review*, 69 (January 1960): 78-89.

CHAPTER 25

ADVENTURE AND DISCOVERY IN MORALS

∿∿∿∿∿∿∿∿∿∿∿∿∿∿∿∿∿∿∿∿

*Experiments in Living**

A. MACBEATH

A. Macbeath (1888-   ) is the author of a number
of books. He was professor of logic and metaphysics at The Queen's University, Belfast, from
1925 to 1954, and later taught moral philosophy at
Edinburgh University.

I have . . . argued that the good life is not good in spots or patches to
which the rest of it is mere means, but throughout; that the moral
ideal is not a distant end to be reached sometime in the future, but a
way of life which can be progressively realised and may be being
realised here and now; that the duties in connection with what are
called the lower goods are not lower or less urgent duties; that, in
fact, morality is not concerned with a separate sphere of activities;
that moral duties are not a separate class of duties, duties to be morally
good or to improve character as such. Character is improved and
moral goodness realised by doing whatever is right in the circumstances, whether it be the humblest domestic duty or ruling an empire,
whether it be removing the rubbish that disfigures a street or "the
rubbish that lies in the way to knowledge." I have thus tried to break

* From *Experiments in Living*. London: Macmillan & Co. Ltd., 1952, pp. 432-455
with omissions.

down the separation between moral duties, on the one hand, and social, economic, political, religious or legal duties, on the other. In all spheres of life, duties arise and they are moral duties. In all of them the moral judgement is the final judgement. Moral considerations are not restricted to a limited sphere or to the application of a limited set of rules—rules which are usually regarded as mainly negative, kept in a special compartment, and acknowledged in general terms. Morality is not concerned merely with the impartial administration of the law, but also with the justice of the law which is administered; not just with keeping promises or contracts, but also with the kind of promises which should be made and the kind of contracts which should be entered into; not merely with telling the truth, but also with intellectual integrity in weighing evidence and reporting facts; not just with making a return for services rendered, but also with what is a fair return for what services, and so on. It is mainly with regard to the latter of these alternatives that we find differences of opinion between different peoples, whereas most ethical theorists concern themselves mainly with the former which do not normally profoundly stir or deeply perplex the moral agent, and which remain vague and general until they are articulated in a way of life in which they are brought into relation with the latter. It seems to me that the same principle of moral judgement applies to both, and that, in trying to formulate it, we must not neglect the more concrete, complex and controversial issues.

I have also argued that the way in which we get knowledge of the moral characteristics of things, whether of rightness or goodness, resembles the tentative groping, and the growing vision, of the natural or empirical scientist rather than the crystal-clear intuitions and the incorrigible judgements of the mathematician.

Now these general considerations, and the formal structure of the moral life which I have described, apply to all men and all morality, and they are compatible with the enormous diversity which we find in the operative ideals or ways of life, and, therefore, in the particular judgements of rightness and goodness, of different peoples. Is there, then, any test which we can apply to discover whether one way of life is better than another, whether one operative ideal is a more adequate expression of the formal ideal which they are all attempts to embody? In particular, can we discover any evidence of progress in this respect from the more primitive to the more advanced societies? And, if so, along what lines does it proceed and what criterion of progress does it imply?

If my account of the moral life has been in principle sound, moral goodness consists in loyalty to the recognised or operative ideal. This is possible for every man in every society, whatever its stage of development or way of life may be. Accordingly, with one possible exception which I shall mention later, there has been no evolution or development of morality from the most primitive men known to history or anthropology to the most civilised men that we know, in the sense that the meaning of moral goodness has changed or that it is more possible at one stage or in one society than in another. It is difficult to say whether there has been any progress in moral goodness, in the sense that more advanced people are morally better, i.e. live up to their own ideals more consistently, than primitives; but there is no reason to believe that this is so. To discover how far different peoples live up to their own ideals would entail an enquiry which has not yet been conducted; and, no doubt, there are great differences between different primitive and between different civilised peoples in this respect. It is true that the higher the recognised ideal, the greater the demands it makes on those who acknowledge it, the more difficult it is to live up to its requirements, and, therefore, the less likely it is that people as a whole will do so consistently. It is also true that among some peoples there are more stimuli to moral steadfastness, which make it more likely that they will conform to the requirements of their recognised ideal; but mere conformity is no guarantee of moral goodness. It may also be thought that the nature of the operative ideal of a society may be some indication of the moral goodness of its members, because one condition of developing the insight necessary to recognise a higher ideal is that men should conscientiously perform the duties which they already recognise; while persistent failure to live up to an ideal tends to discredit the ideal itself, so that it ceases to be recognised as such; but, as we shall see, other conditions are also necessary for the recognition of higher ideals. Taking everything into consideration, then, there is little evidence to suggest that the more advanced peoples are either morally better or morally worse than the more primitive.

Accordingly, if we are to find development or progress at all, we must look for it in the nature of the ideals entertained rather than in the consistency and conscientiousness with which they are realised, that is, in moral enlightenment rather than in moral goodness. It seems to me essential, for our understanding of both morality and progress, that we should distinguish clearly between moral goodness and moral enlightenment. Moral goodness consists in loyalty to the operative or recognised ideal, whatever the content of this ideal may be; and, therefore, it does not change. But the content of the ideal itself changes. It may be more or less enlightened, richer and more comprehensive or narrower and more circumscribed, its parts more or less consistent, its provision for the needs of human nature more or less adequate. Therefore the acts in which moral goodness manifests itself and the ends which the morally good man pursues change. We have seen that the general form of every operative ideal is a way of life in which different people co-operate to realise the ends which are dictated by their nature as self-conscious persons. I think we may say that the development which has taken place in the conception of the moral ideal consists in an increasingly adequate grasp of what is implied in such co-operation, of what it means to be a person and of what is involved in membership of a co-operative community of persons.

This development has been mainly along two closely interconnected lines. The one has been an extension of the number of those who are included in the community to which the way of life and the rights and duties which it involves apply, an extension which continued till all men are, at least in theory, included in its scope, and, therefore, entitled to be treated as persons. The other has been a changing conception of the nature of personality and of the relations between persons which are necessary to express this nature, and provide scope for its development. Progress in enlightenment has not consisted merely, as is sometimes suggested, in giving a different answer to the question "Who is my neighbour?" but also in a different conception of what is meant by neighbourliness, not merely in an extension of the group who are believed to share in the common humanity, but also in a deepening of the significance of what is involved in the common humanity. Indeed, it may well be that a change in the way of life which is shared by a group is a condition of the extension of the group who share in it, and especially of its extension to include all mankind. There are peoples whose ways of life and scales of value have to be remodelled to make such extension possible.

Consider, e.g., the way of life of the Crow Indians. Their way of life is based on principles of mutual helpfulness and friendly co-operation between the members of the in-group. Quarrelling and fighting between them are strongly disapproved. But the whole structure of the group-life, the relations between individuals within it, the constitution of its societies, its scale of values, and even the content of its religious visions, were dominated by the military spirit and the pre-eminence of the military virtues. This assumed that members of other groups were to be treated as enemies, and the presence of such enemies was a presupposition of the whole structure of the way of life. Extend the principles of friendly co-operation which prevailed between members of the in-group to their relations to their neighbours and the whole pattern and scale of values of their way of life will collapse, as in fact happened when the United States government forbade them to make war on their neighbours.

Here, then, we seem to have one test which can be applied to different ways of life to discover their adequacy. Any way of life whose general structure or scale of value does not admit of being extended to mankind as a whole, without denying the common humanity of some men and their right to be treated as persons, must be regarded as unsatisfactory; and the more remodelling it needs to make this extension possible, the more unsatisfactory it is.

There are other ways also in which development in enlightenment has taken place, and these lines of development condition, and are conditioned by, the extension of the size of the group and the deepening grasp of the nature of personality. For a way of life does not grow up in a vacuum. It is developed in interaction with, and in response to, a natural and supernatural environment, and the form which it takes is partly determined by the beliefs entertained about that environment. It is, therefore, liable to be modified not only by the degree of insight into the nature of personality, but also by the extent and accuracy of the knowledge available about the nature of the environment in which life is lived. Accordingly, the development of the conception of the moral ideal is largely the result of increasingly accurate knowledge of matters of fact about nature and man and supernature. And the development in one of these lines influences, and is influenced by, development in the others. For the way of life which is the embodiment of the ideal is a relatively integrated whole in which the different aspects mutually modify, as well as support, one another. We may also get progress in the degree of integration of the way of life, in the adjustment of the institutions which in their interrelation constitute it. Here the line of advance has been from a way of life whose unity consists merely in the functional interdependence of its parts towards one which is rationally coherent. Without such integration, clashes of interests and conflicts of loyalties are bound to occur and to give rise to frustration, unhappiness, and inefficiency in action. Similar results follow from failure in comprehensiveness, i.e. failure to make provision for some of the major needs of human nature, and, in this respect too, progress is possible. In the main, however, it would seem that the way in which progress in moral enlightenment or the conception of the moral ideal has come about is not so much through the development of new powers of moral insight as through the emergence of conditions in which such powers of moral insight as men have can function effectively.

Bearing in mind these general considerations, and in particular the interaction of the different lines of development, let us look a little more in detail at some of the lines of progress in moral enlightenment, see the conditions under which they take place, the principle or principles, if any, on which they proceed, the direction in which they tend, and their significance for further progress.

The increase in the size of the group to whom moral considerations apply seems to come about in part, at least, through peaceful contacts in intertribal trade and commerce, and, perhaps even more, through the conquest of one group by another. Not that either commerce or conquest produces greater moral insight, but they provide opportunities for contact and co-operation, and, wherever such opportunities exist, there is a tendency for men to come to recognise one another as persons, and to take an interest in one another's welfare. In many forms of contact, especially contact which is brought about forcibly through conquest, there are many forces which militate against such recognition, forces which lead to such institutions as slavery or a caste system, under which some individuals tend to be treated as things rather than persons. But the greatest barrier to the mutual recognition of people as persons is ignorance. This arouses fear and suspicion which lead, at worst, to hostility and, at best, to indifference to one another's interests. When this barrier is removed through contact, especially contact which involves co-operation, even if it is in the first instance forcibly brought about, opportunities are created for man's natural interest in man to assert itself. Co-operation tends to be found good, social sentiments develop, and man's natural interest in the welfare of others finds expression. . . .

The other great barrier to the recognition of other people as persons and to paying regard to their welfare, is lack of imagination, of capacity to put oneself in the other person's place, to realise what he is thinking and feeling. Among all peoples much selfishness is the result of thoughtlessness, of lack of imagination. In breaking down this barrier, the example and the teaching of specially gifted individuals, who are more sensitive and sympathetic to the feelings of others, and have more imaginative appreciation of their position and point of view, play an important part. The great moral teacher is he who opens our eyes so

that we come to recognise what we had hitherto been unable to see
for ourselves, but which we acknowledge when he points it out. He
makes us feel that he knows us better than we know ourselves. But if
the insight of our best moments and the impulses to which it gives rise
are to survive, they must be embodied in customs and institutions, and
become part of our way of life. These act as reminders to us in the
days of gloom of the vision of the hours of insight; and they provide
stimuli to moral steadfastness when the vision is dim and the impulse
to well-doing weak.

Once the moral implications of men's common humanity are recognised and pointed out and acted on by some individuals, others will
come to acknowledge what they might have failed to realise if left to
themselves. Thus a social conscience comes to be developed; and, if it
is embodied in institutions and organisations, even those who have little
inclination to respect the common humanity or the rights of others
cannot help, from time to time, being reminded of them and even being
troubled by their own neglect of them. A social conscience, whether
in relation to the members of one's own or another society, is just the
inability to be content, however adequately one's own needs, material
and spiritual, are provided for, as long as other people are without the
conditions necessary for their welfare or deprived of opportunities to
develop their personalities. And among the conditions which favour
the development of such a conscience, the most important are contact
and a vivid imagination. . . .

Another influence, which has played a considerable part, if not in
bringing about, at least in strengthening, the belief that all men are
persons owing duties to one another, is religion and religious institutions, especially those of the universal and monotheistic religions. Even
within the limited group, religion is, as we have seen, one of the great
cohesive forces which serve to unite men into a common brotherhood;
but it is also one of the chief barriers which divide groups from one
another. When, however, the believer regards his God as the creator
and preserver of all men, this has a profound influence in breaking down
the barriers which prevent him from regarding other men as persons
like himself. It may well be that the recognition of men's common
humanity is as much the cause as the effect of monotheism. But whether
it be the cause or the effect of this recognition, monotheism helps to
conserve and support the belief that all men are persons, and that they
owe duties to one another. For the association of this belief with the
profoundest emotional reactions and the most deeply cherished convic-

tions of believers in a universal God, acts as a reminder to men of their common humanity and their duties to one another.

Thus, through increasing contacts and co-operation between peoples, and a deepening imaginative appreciation of one another's feelings, and with the support and sanction of the monotheistic religions, the group to which moral considerations apply has extended, slowly and intermittently, until, in theory at least, it includes all men.

Consider next the progress which we find in the content of the moral ideal, the changes in the quality, as distinct from the extent, of the common life in which it is embodied, and the ways in which these have altered men's ideas of their duties.

Increasingly accurate knowledge of nature and of the consequences of actions have led to modifications of men's ideas of what they ought to do. For example, once it is recognised that ill-health and death are due to natural causes and not to the malevolence of fellow-men, one barrier to the formation of social sentiments and friendly relations has been removed. Similarly, certain views about the effects of actions, such as that telling the truth to your neighbour will put him in possession of the means to use magic against you, or that the scalps of other people are necessary to make crops grow, make a marked difference to the sort of actions which are considered right; and, so, a more accurate knowledge of the consequences of actions and of their effects on people's welfare plays an important part in the progress of men's conception of the good life.

An even more important effect of growing knowledge is a change in men's ideas as to what is inevitable, part of the human lot, and, therefore, to be tolerated and accepted with resignation. The primitive is apt to regard many of the causes of his frustration and unhappiness as inevitable; and this applies not only to natural conditions, but to many aspects of his social environment. He sees no alternative to them; and he does not think anyone is responsible for them. So the idea that it might be possible to change them does not occur to him. Accordingly, his ideal tends to be to change himself into line with them, an ideal of self-discipline and resignation to the nature of things. And this attitude is strengthened when he regards the nature of things as the expression of a superhuman purpose; and especially when he believes that this purpose is good, though he may be unable to understand how it is so. But, with growing knowledge comes an increasing sense of power over his environment, and his ideal tends to become one of mastering and controlling and changing it so as to bring it into line with his desires.

Thus, there emerges a new and more conscious attitude to change. The idea of progress takes shape, and men try not only to master and control their natural environment, but also to change their social institutions, if not in the light of a consciously held ideal, at least so as to remove some of the major ills of life.

Now this growing dominance of mind over nature and social structures has resulted in very great gains; for many of the ills which men have been accustomed to accept as inevitable are preventable by human wisdom and goodwill. But the change of attitude may be carried too far. There is a danger that men may regard themselves as completely masters of their fate, set up their uncriticised desires as the directors of evolution, and forget that there is a constitution of the universe to which the proper attitude is one of recognition and acceptance, and into conformity to which they ought to discipline themselves. In particular, there is the danger that, either directly or through their mastery of nature, they may try to control their fellowmen, that they may regard people as objects to be understood and mastered and used for their purposes, instead of recognising them as persons, independent centres of purposes, to be accepted and respected. The danger of adopting this attitude is specially great when people are concerned with large masses of men to whom their relations are largely impersonal and mechanical. An attitude of humility and deference, even of reverence, is becoming in our relations with another personality; for it is something which has value in itself and not just in relation to our purposes; and this attitude is inconsistent with that of mastery and control. I believe nothing is more necessary or perhaps more difficult in the modern world than to distinguish clearly between the occasions on which these different attitudes are appropriate; for without a recognition that there are ideals and values which are rooted in the nature of man and the constitution of the universe, and, therefore, to be accepted and appreciated, the reforming spirit is in danger of losing its direction.

There have been two other lines of development which in part preceded, and which provide a supplement and corrective to, the attitude of mastery and control which is embodied in the idea of progress. The first is an increasing emphasis on the inner life, on motives and intentions and the spirit in which actions are performed. This is the one sense, to which I referred above, in which there seems to me that there has been development in the meaning of moral goodness from the more primitive to the more advanced societies. In the main, the primitive tends to think of moral goodness as doing what is believed to be right rather than as doing it from a good motive. It is not so much that he lays all the emphasis on the external action as that he fails to distinguish as clearly as we do between the external action and the spirit in which it is done, just as he often fails to distinguish between accident and design, or between the unforeseen consequences of an action and those which are deliberately willed. It is true that in relatively small communities, in which there is little difference between the ideas as to what is right entertained by different individuals, the performance of the external action may be taken by a man's neighbours as a rough indication of his motives. It is also true that field workers among primitives give us less information than we would wish about the extent to which, in their moral judgements, primitives take account of motives; and that the more thoroughly primitive ways of life are investigated by trained experts, the more account they are found to take of motives, as we have seen, for example, in Malinowski's account of the Trobrianders, Junod's account of the Bantu, and Hogbins' account of the inhabitants of Wogeo. But when due allowance has been made for these considerations, there is little doubt that most primitive peoples pay insufficient attention to the inner aspect of the moral life; and that one of the most important developments from the more primitive to the more advanced peoples has consisted in the discovery of the inner life and the consequent importance attached to conscientiousness and purity of motives.

The other closely connected line of development has been an increasing appreciation of the individuality of the moral agent as a self-governing, responsible personality, with a right of private judgement and entitled to some measure of tolerance and freedom to conduct his life in his own way. . . .

In all matters of fundamental importance freedom of choice and initiative is very strictly limited. For, in the conditions of life of most primitive people, unity is necessary to survival and unity is apt to be interpreted as uniformity; non-conformity is regarded as dangerous and, therefore, the would-be reformer is apt to be classed with the rebel and treated accordingly. No doubt the most difficult problem with which any people is confronted is that of reconciling freedom for initiative and the expression of creative impulses, which justice to the individual demands, with the requirements of social order, which regard for the common good demands. Every way of life, primitive or civilised, is an attempt to solve this problem; but among most primitives the scales tend to be very heavily weighted in favour of social order and the common good rather than justice to the individual and opportunities for initiative and self-expression.

Whether an individual can effect any changes in the way of life of his people, and, if he can, to what extent he can do so, depends not merely on his personal qualities, but also on the position which he occupies in the community. Specially gifted individuals who are in positions of political or religious authority sometimes bring about important changes; but, in the main, such changes as come about in the institutions and ways of life of primitive groups are not the results of conscious planning; the emergence of the idea of progress in social and political conditions, the attitude of the reformer who sets out deliberately to change the beliefs and institutions of his people in the light of a consciously entertained ideal, is, as we have seen, one of the significant changes in the advance from the more primitive to the more advanced peoples. And this development is not unconnected with increasing respect for personality, for the need for tolerance of individual differences and the desirability of opportunities for initiative and the expression of creative impulses. Here, too, the line of progress has been in the direction of a more widespread recognition of individuals as self-governing, responsible persons, to be persuaded rather than coerced, to be provided with opportunities for developing their powers rather than directed.

The last line of progress which I want to mention concerns the development which we find in men's conception of the supernatural. We have seen that even the most primitive men believe themselves to be in contact with something in their environment which they regard as supersensible, superhuman, or supernatural, something which evokes in them a profound emotional reaction, and to which they consider it necessary to adjust themselves. Here the line of progress has not been towards a greater certainty of the reality of the supernatural, but towards a different conception of its character. Just as we find man, as his insight into himself and his fellows grows, drawing a clearer distinction between the inner and the outer aspects of his life, and tending more and more to regard the inner or spiritual self as the real self, and its values as the highest values; so, in his thinking of his cosmic environment, we find him distinguishing more sharply between the natural and the spiritual, and interpreting the supernatural in more personal and spiritual terms, till in the end he comes to conceive it as a personal or supra-personal being who is the embodiment of perfect wisdom and goodness, a being who is regarded not so much as an external judge or law-giver, much less in terms of mere power, operating on men through hope or fear, but rather as a being whose very existence is a condemnation of moral imperfection and weakness, and arouses in man a desire for moral purity and perfection, a being whose character evokes rev-

erence and loyalty and provides a standing challenge and encouragement
to man to try to realise the highest ideals which he finds in his moral
consciousness, and to transform himself and his world so as to approximate more closely to their requirements. At-one-ment with the supernatural then becomes his highest ideal, that which calls forth his supreme
loyalty.

In this way, religion, as it renews its vitality in the insight of its great
teachers, has shown a wonderful capacity for absorbing into itself and
putting in a cosmic setting the values and ideals which the developing
moral consciousness reveals. The cosmological and metaphysical
framework into which the values are fitted may change from age to
age, but the reality of the values and the need for loyalty to them remain; and the added significance which religion confers on them provides a support of the moral will and an incentive to right-doing the importance of which cannot be over-estimated. Nevertheless, as Bowman
has pointed out, the lesson of history seems to be that "when morality
and religion fail to synthesise, morality may hold its own against religion, but religion will have the utmost difficulty in maintaining itself
against morality." Certainly not the least significant of the triumphs of
the moral spirit has been the gradual moralisation of the concept of
the supernatural, and the line of progress has been towards conceiving
the relation of man to the supernatural as a relation between persons, a
relation in which the value and dignity of personality is respected and
enhanced.

What we seem to find, then, is this. From whatever point of view we
consider the progress in enlightenment or in the conception of the
moral ideal from the more primitive to the more advanced peoples, it
seems to take the form of an increasing recognition of the fundamental
importance of personality and of the distinction between persons and
things. Increasingly accurate knowledge of matters of fact, and increasing communications and contacts and co-operation between
individuals and peoples, provide conditions in which moral insight can
function more effectively; and, as it does so, we find men slowly, intermittently and haltingly, but none the less surely, coming to recognise
other men as persons, independent, responsible, self-governing individuals. Things we try to master and control and use. Their value consists
in ministering to our purposes. Persons are subjects of purposes, not
just objects of the purposes of other people. They are separate centres
of spiritual life, independent expressions of the moral consciousness.
This characteristic of men as persons is what Temple has in mind when

he writes of the moral equality of men, and what the advanced religions refer to when they say that all men are equal in the sight of God.

This moral equality of men is, of course, compatible with many differences between them in other respects. Men differ in physical and mental capacity, in knowledge and experience, in wisdom and moral goodness, and so on; but they are equal in a sense which is deeper than all their differences. They are all subjects not objects, persons not things, ends not means. They are self-conscious moral beings, having in themselves a principle of self-government which gives them a worth and dignity which entitle them to our consideration and respect. Only as we recognise this do we understand them as they really are. It is this fundamental moral equality of men as persons which is the justification of their equality before the law, equality of civil and political rights, equality of educational opportunity, and so on. The ideal to which the growing recognition of it points is that of a community of persons co-operating as persons. In this ideal we find the criterion of progress in moral enlightenment, the criterion by which we can test the adequacy of different ways of life. This ideal seems to be operative in the minds of all men so far as they are rational moral beings, however dim and obscure their grasp of it and however imperfect their understanding of its requirements may often be. Its operation is the mainspring of progress, and of dissatisfaction with things as they are. We find it adumbrated in the constitution of the simplest primitive institutions and in the moral symmetry of the principle of reciprocity which underlies all primitive ways of life. At the other end of the scale, it forms the basis of Kant's conception of a Kingdom of Ends and of Christ's idea of the Kingdom of God. The difference which we find between these extremes is twofold, consisting partly in the extension of the group who are recognised as persons, and partly in a deepening of the meaning of what it is to be a person, a deepening which has come about through a clearer grasp of the inner life and of the distinction between persons and things.

The principle of which this ideal is the expression I have called the principle of justice or equity. It seems to me an objective or rational principle. The moral equality of men as persons is not something which depends on us, not something which we want or create. It is something which we discover or recognise and have to accept. Our recognition of it may be within narrow limits and confined to moments of insight when our vision is unclouded by passion and prejudice. In such moments we find we have no option but to recognise others as self-governing moral beings like ourselves, with independent lives and purposes of their own, and our natural interest in them and their welfare takes the form of a desire not to direct and control them and impose our will upon them, but to co-operate with them, to provide opportunities for them to realise their purpose and develop their personalities. But if the spark which flickers in such moments of insight is not to die, but to develop into a steady flame, it must be caught and embodied in patterns of behaviour and institutions and a way of life, which will act as constant reminders of it, till it becomes part and parcel of our habits of thinking and feeling and acting, not so much something which is at the focus of consciousness as what forms the background in the light of which we see everything else. Even then, there will be many forces in us and around us which militate against its continued recognition and its realisation, and the effort to be true to it requires a constant warfare from which there is no discharge. There is, however, another side to this picture which is no less important. The real test of the genuineness of our vision in what we take to be our moments of insight is whether the values and principles and ideals which it reveals can be embodied in a way of life in which they can be reconciled with others which we also recognise. The attempt to effect such a reconciliation may mean a more or less radical reconstruction of our accepted way of life and it may also involve a modification of the new values and ideals themselves; but, until we see how it can be done, we have not really grasped the meaning of these values and ideals themselves, and, unless it can be done, they cannot be accepted as they stand as genuine and worthy of our loyalty. The real difference between the genuine vision of the moral pioneer and the wishful thinking of the utopian dreamer is that the former can, and the latter cannot, be translated into an operative ideal; and the reason why it cannot is not that it is too ideal, but that it is not ideal enough, because it has not grasped the inner nature and possibilities of the actual, what human nature has in it to be and is striving to become.

No doubt the individual who believes he sees values hitherto either wholly or partially unrecognised, rightly considers it his duty to work for their recognition and realisation, even if he cannot see in detail how the way of life of his people has to be reconstructed to give expression to them; and he may be performing a very useful function in his one-sided emphasis on them. But the final test of their validity is their capacity to be incorporated in an operative ideal. And the moral pioneer himself may be unsure of the genuineness of his vision till he has succeeded in persuading at least some others of the worth of the values which he is seeking to realise. He is often acutely conscious that, in pursuing them, he is taking a risk, and that the risk is a moral risk. It is not only a venture of faith, but a venture which may not succeed and may not deserve to succeed, because the insight on which it is based is partial and imperfect. There is such an element of faith in all moral living, but it is specially prominent in the lives of moral and social reformers.

I have already referred to the distinction which is sometimes drawn between two kinds of duty—one concerned with the conscientious discharge of the requirements of existing institutions and ways of life, and the other concerned with the remoulding of the operative ideal so as to bring it nearer to the formal ideal—and I pointed out that both rest ultimately on the same principle and tend to merge into one another. In a relatively stable society, most of the duties of most people belong to the former class, and the moral goodness of most individuals consists in the conscientious discharge of such duties; but the best men in every society feel it their duty to do more than the accepted pattern of the way of life of their people requires, or than others have a right to expect of them. Thus such people are already on the way to raising the requirements of the accepted pattern. The reformer who tries consciously to alter the operative ideal so as to make it more consistent, or to embody new values in it, is only carrying the process a stage further. While there is a difference of emphasis between the two attitudes, they may both be found alternating in the life of the same person; and when duties of the former kind are performed in a spirit of loyalty to the former ideal, which the accepted way of life is an attempt to express, they tend to pass into the latter class.

In a period of transition such as we are living in today, when traditional values are questioned and established institutions are crumbling, and people are trying consciously to reconstruct many of their institutions and, therefore, the way of life which in their interrelation they constitute, duties of the second kind tend to be much in evidence, and their determination is apt to be a cause of moral perplexity to many individuals. In such circumstances, it is essential that men should examine the foundations of the moral and social order and bring to light the fundamental principle which justifies traditional values and institutions, so far as they are justifiable; and which points the direction in which they should be modified, so far as they require modification. The principle which our analysis has revealed as the basis of moral and social obligations may be stated, "Be a person and recognise and treat others as persons." That, however, is only a formal principle and, before we can understand its nature and requirements fully, we must, as

I have already said, try to embody it in a detailed way of life more completely than has yet been done; but many of its conditions are already clear, and what is necessary is to grasp it more clearly, apply it more consistently, and extend it to the whole range of human relationships.

FOR FURTHER STUDY

Blanshard, Brand. *Reason and Goodness*. New York: Macmillan, 1961, Ch. 15 "The Rational Temper."

Bryson, Lyman. "Rational Ethics" in *Patterns of Ethics in America Today*, ed. F. Ernest Johnson. New York: Collier Books, 1962, Ch. 5.

Frankel, Charles, "Is It Ever Right to Break the Law?" *New York Times Magazine*, January 12, 1964, pp. 17, 36, 39, 41.

Rice, Philip Blair. *On the Knowledge of Good and Evil*. New York: Random House, 1955, Ch. 1, "The Method of Experience."

Sockman, Ralph W. *The Morals of Tomorrow*. New York: Harper, 1931, Ch. 11, "Moral Authority for Free Minds," Ch. 12, "The Margins of Moral Experiment."

Toulmin, Stephen Edelston. *An Examination of the Place of Reason in Ethics*. Cambridge, England: U. Press, 1950. Ch. 11, "The Logic of Moral Reasoning."

Wilson, John. *Reason and Morals*. Cambridge, England: U. Press, 1961 Part III, "A Method for Morals."

CHAPTER 26

BRINGING OUR
MORALS UP-TO-DATE

‹ᴓᴕᴓᴕᴓᴕᴓᴕᴓᴕᴓᴕᴓᴕᴓᴕᴓᴕᴓᴕᴓᴕᴓᴕᴓᴕᴓᴕᴓᴕᴓᴕᴓᴕᴓᴕᴓᴕ›

*New Values for Old**

EUGENE RABINOWITCH

Eugene Rabinowitch (1901-   ), a prominent bio-physicist, is editor of the *Bulletin of the Atomic Scientists*. Since 1947 he has been research professor at the University of Illinois. He is the author of various monographs and articles.

That the scientific revolution of our time has shrunk the world to the dimensions of a single country is a commonplace. Passengers travel across oceans in four or five hours. Spending a weekend in Bali or the Congo is a matter of expense, not of time.

The bringing together of all men by science means, however, much more than merely shrinking the physical distances which separate them. Science brings closer together their ways of living and makes their problems increasingly interrelated.

Science itself knows no nation or class. It poses the same problems to scientists whatever their national allegiance and gives answers independent of their ideologies. As national and individual lives are shaped increasingly, all over the world, by science and technology, the differences imposed on human existence by ideological or economic com-

* From *Journal of the American Association of University Women*, 57 (May 1964), pp. 171-173. Reprinted by permission.

mitments recede in significance. Many problems now call for common international effort. Some of them cannot be solved on any narrower scale; such are the problems of the world population pressure, of hunger and disease; such is the paramount problem of our time, that of preventing the catastrophe of nuclear war; such are the problems posed by worldwide economic interdependence, or by unequal distribution of raw materials.

The effective integration of mankind by the scientific revolution is superimposed on the traditional crazy quilt map of separate sovereign states. The gulf between the planned and regulated communist society and the societies based on political and economic freedom divides this map into areas, separated by moats as deep and unbridgeable as have ever been those separating true believers from infidels!

Mankind thus lives, in our times, on two different levels. One is the traditional level of separate self-centered units, which pursue their ideological or power interests (or, more often, a combination of both) as if they were the summum bonum: What is good for one automatically becomes bad for the other. The other level is that of "one world," welded together by common interests, created and continuously expanded by science.

Murder Became a Virtue

The ethical values by which mankind lives have developed in response to the needs of circumscribed, self-sufficient communities. These communities have cultivated by education and imposed by compulsion restraints on individual behavior appropriate to national survival and growth. They have fostered the ideals of conformity and obedience needed to maintain discipline within a society, of readiness to sacrifice everything, including one's life, in the service of this society.

Inhibitions imposed on man's behavior within his own community disappear in conflict with other groups. In war, murder ceases to be a crime and becomes a virtue. We still have among us a national hero whose claim to this title is from having killed, singlehandedly, almost a hundred enemies in World War I! Our press made national heroes out of the crew of the *Enola Gay*, who killed, with a single atom bomb, almost a hundred thousand Japanese in Hiroshima. We see potential heroes in SAC bombardiers or Polaris missile crews, standing by to kill tens of millions of Russians or Chinese at a moment's notice.

In the past, a certain moral justification could be derived from the acceptance by a soldier in war of the risk of being killed himself by the enemy; but in a future atomic war, the millionfold murderers hidden in atomic submarines or hardened missile silos will be the best-protected and least exposed members of their nations.

All semblance of a moral code valid for an individual in war has been destroyed by the inexorable development of military science. Now the concept of "good" and "evil" must be applied not to individuals, but to the organisms which dominate them: Societies and states. Yet we are not out of the age when the behavior of states is supposed to be free from moral compunction. The proposition is still generally accepted that the proper motivation of national behavior is national interest. "Good" is what serves the interest of the state and enhances its power; "bad" is what weakens it.

In several recent crises, we have heard representatives of the American, British, or French Government telling their anxious citizens that *"Whatever we have decided to do was dictated, above all, by the interest of our nation"* and this was supposed to be reassuring! Any suspicion that a national government may be motivated by other than selfish national considerations is to be avoided. Otherwise large groups in the nation will look at their rulers as weaklings or traitors!

Attempts to "Civilize" War

Of course, this scale of values has not remained unchallenged. We have seen attempts to "civilize" wars by imposing certain *don'ts* on warring nations, but we have also seen all these *don'ts* violated by civilized states, from the sinking of passenger ships by German submarines in World War I to the killing of thousands of civilians by American, British, and German bombers in World War II.

We have seen attempts to establish supranational authorities, the League of Nations, the World Court, the United Nations, but we have also witnessed nations refusing to submit themselves to these authorities —Portugal in Angola, France in Algeria, the Soviet Union in Hungary, India in Kashmir. Who can doubt that the United States, if confronted, say, with a UN majority decision that the Panama Canal must be turned over to Panama (or internationalized) would refuse to submit? Every nation wants every other nation to abide by the UN Covenant, but makes exception for itself! As long as this attitude persists, international relations continue on the traditional level: Everyone for himself and the devil take the hindmost.

We have seen "foreign assistance" programs develop in America, in Europe, in the Soviet Union. They reflect a growing sense of responsibility of prosperous (or at least technically advanced) countries for the fate of the less advanced ones. But we have also seen that in order to make this help palatable to public opinion, it has had to be represented as the cheapest way to forward the economic and military interests of the assisting nation, and we now witness strong popular pressure for the emasculation of American foreign aid programs.

The United Nations, the World Court, and the foreign aid program belong to the "other level" of international relations, the level on which nations are bound together by common interests, more important than their divisive national aims. They are early signs of life of an international community that is aborning, but is not yet born.

New Loyalty Before New Law

It is easily said that what is needed now is strengthening of the UN Charter, widening of the jurisdiction of the World Court, or a comprehensive disarmament treaty. All these are formal, legal requirements, and we have been recently reminded, in the controversy about Civil Rights, that no law is better than the will of the people to obey it. The UN Charter is far stronger than the attitudes of nations permit it to be in practice. Its strengthening will be either impossible or illusory as long as slogans such as "my country, right or wrong" have not lost their power over men's minds and emotions.

We do need laws and treaties binding nations to the community of mankind, but to make these bonds strong we need, first of all, a massive re-education, a worldwide revision of values and loyalties, making the "one world" concept a reality in the minds of men, before it can become a reality in law. The power of a legal "superstructure" depends on the strength of its ethical basis in the people's minds.

No nation will be safe in the future unless all nations accept a new set of ethical values adequate to survival in the scientific age. This can be, at best, a slow process, but until it is far advanced, we, our children, and our children's children will live in the shadow of a nuclear catastrophe. All that it is in our power to do is to start moving in the right direction.

In family, in school, in college, in church, and in the lecture hall, we must fight for this new scale of values to be laid down in the minds of the coming generations. We do not need to destroy their patriotism, their love and loyalty to their country, but we must build up a higher devotion, a greater love, and an overriding loyalty to mankind. One does not need to be a bad Virginian to be a good American, so one does not need to be a bad American to be a good member of the world community. The national interests of the United States must be recognized as bound up with the material and spiritual advancement of mankind as a whole, as the interest of an Iowan or a New Yorker lies, first of all, in the well-being of the United States as a whole.

A New Strength

It will be argued that if we embark on such a revision of our values, we will weaken the position of the United States in the present fiercely competitive world, that as long as Europeans, Russians, or Chinese fill their textbooks with glorification of their own deeds and instill exclusive loyalty to their own state, religion, or ideology, we cannot but do the same. But this is not true. When changed conditions call for new attitudes, the groups which first understand the new situation and sail, as it were, before the winds of change are apt to assert and not to lose their leadership. We do not need to undertake unilateral disarmament, or yield in all international or ideological conflicts. Without giving up our present strength, we must build beside it a new strength, on a higher level.

Here is one example. We have hundreds of thousands of men in uniform protecting American interests all over the world. We also have a few thousand Peace Corps Volunteers helping new nations to become viable. On the traditional scale of values, the Peace Corps is a small frill, which can be viewed with benevolence, but is of little importance and could be easily dispensed with, while our armed forces provide a vital guarantee of our survival as a free people. And yet our hope for future leadership lies more heavily on the few thousand Peace Corps Volunteers than on hosts of soldiers, sailors, and airmen.

The latter can only maintain an uneasy truce, a worldwide paralysis of the power struggle, but the Peace Corps is a nucleus from which a stable future world can grow. The scale of ethical values which makes some young Americans devote their best years to serving the interests of mankind is closer to that on which a stable, viable world can be ultimately established than the traditional scale, with its emphasis on service to one's own nation, religion, or political system.

The Peace Corps is only a small example. But it shows the direction in which we must go if we decide to make the common welfare of mankind our paramount national aim, in realization that there is no security for our own country except in a permanently peaceful world, that there is no lasting prosperity for our nation except in the framework of an advancing, hopeful, viable humanity.

᠉᠊᠊᠊᠊᠉

Ethical Frontiers*

WALTER G. MUELDER

Walter G. Muelder (1907-   ) is dean and professor of social ethics at Boston University School of Theology. His writings include *Foundations of a Responsible Society*.

In the revolutionary world situation the ethical frontiers run the whole extent of the cultural spectrum from the family to the international political community. I shall refer briefly to four clusters of new issues which challenge traditional patterns of social ethics. All of these have implications for and are involved in the unity of mankind. These four are: (1) the frontier of productive abundance; (2) the frontier of family life; (3) the frontier of mass communications; and (4) the frontier in nuclear warfare.

A. *The Frontier of Productive Abundance*

This frontier is the product of technology and social organization. The possibility of a worldwide abundance has aroused all nations to pursue the new technology and to explore various new types of social organization. Each nation seeks to raise its standard of living through

* From *Patterns of Ethics in America Today*, F. Ernest Johnson (ed.) (New York: Harper, 1960), pp. 167-177. Copyright © 1960 by The Institute for Religious and Social Studies.

industrialization and agricultural transformation. This means that the ethical ideas of freedom and justice, for example, are being filled with assignments in productivity looking toward abundance. It means that in the United States some are perplexed by the problem of how "to survive sanely and morally in the midst of the orgy of goods."

The new situation challenges, in either case, the older ideas of distributive justice which emphasized equity in the distribution of scarce goods by emphasizing a responsible development of an adequate production of goods. Thus far the world religions have had greater effect on the ethics of distribution than on production. Many unforeseen problems arise when one seeks not only a just division of an existing pie which is too small but even more the baking of an adequate pie. Where abundance is a possibility, poverty is an especially mortal sin. Since the rate of creating abundance is so uneven in the world we have the particularly perplexing dilemma of learning how to live with it at home and learning how to help achieve it soundly abroad.

There is no doubt that the concentration on abundance at home— even in minimal welfare terms—challenges the old religiously rooted values of renunciation, self-denial, and poverty. High consumption affects the morality of thrift and saving and the attitude toward the passing day. If sensuality is the inordinate love of transient good, then, sensuality has become a major vice of American consumers. This type of sin challenges the nation to an effective education in values suitable to a responsible democracy. Indulgence in a high rate of vulgar consumption has the additional effect of creating widespread complacency toward all burning issues, including a sense of irresponsibility toward those parts of the world that are hopelessly frustrated by unspeakable scarcity.

It is not too early to be concerned about the gospel of higher and higher levels of consumption at earlier and earlier stages of family life. It is not too early to consider the national profile of longer vacations, longer weekends, more holidays and the attendant transformation of the gospel and discipline of work into a vulgar hedonism of comfort, security, and bodily excitement. But an even more urgent problem is the question of who or what will guarantee the rate of income needed to sustain personal and family spending at the high rate now becoming habitual. This issue has important bearings on the economics of longevity, retirement, and welfare for older persons. Who is responsible, the family or the community? If both, in what proportions? Shall the responsibility for abundant production be left to private enterprise primarily while the responsibility for equitable distribution, security, and welfare are assigned primarily to government? What is a sound pattern of responsibility?

While we are wrestling with the social ethics of abundance at home, we are challenged to even more radical thoughts on the international economic and political aspects of abundance. Giveaway schemes have limited usefulness. Sharing is a virtue, but it does not automatically illuminate the questions of how much, to whom, when, what kind, and for what ends? In a world where technical change so profoundly affects cultural patterns, responsible giving and responsible receiving must be integrally conceived. In such a world bilateral arrangements may upset the balances of sound multilateral agreements. There is probably no area of life which is more crucial for the stability and development of human welfare than that of the right motivation and the intelligent management of international trade. Here is perhaps the major challenge to the re-education of the peoples of the world.

B. *The Frontier of Family Life*

Technical advances, high levels of employment, education, and woman's freedom to express herself in every phase of culture have developed a profound crisis in family life. The family has become vulnerable to an unprecedent degree.

When cries of family crisis are raised, some defenders point to the improvement of family living as indicated by the rapid development of the suburbs, the one-family houses, the earlier marriages, the larger number of children, the family television set, the revived interest in church activities, and the like. These are important data. There is, despite these developments, an ethical frontier in family life. It means that basic decisions are required which bear on the quality of the family bond, relations of the marriage partners to each other, and the role of the family in the nurture of children in responsible economic and political life.

The economic freedom of women, the labor-saving devices in housekeeping and cooking, and the family security provided by the community have removed many of the older family bonds and have, therefore, placed the greatest stress on the individual adjustment of the marriage partners to each other. For these reasons the psychological and spiritual bonds—the qualitative ones of personal respect, compatibility, and motivation for marriage—have to bear the strains of modern life. Individualistic or egocentric goals on the part of either partner make the marriage relationship highly vulnerable.

This vulnerability of the psychological bond is accentuated by the new tensions that develop on a massive scale because of the large number of working wives and mothers. There are many issues here, but I should like to select one for special emphasis. It is the relationship between the functional status system of the work-a-day world and the mutuality-status system of the family order. Men and women have always played complementary roles. Increasingly they are playing competing roles. These roles affect status in the world of work outside the home and increasingly affect status in the family itself. Since the roles we play influence the profiles of our characters, a study of these has a bearing on the ethics of family life.

Formerly, in the one-income family, the husband confronted two orders of status in which he alternated, one from 7 a.m. to 5 p.m. and the other from 5 p.m. to 7 a.m. On his job his status was measured by his efficiency. He was constantly confronted by the challenge to measure up to objective performance expectations or lose whatever standing he had with his associates who were also his competitors. At 5 p.m. he went home to his family, to relaxation, renewal, and rest. He left the order of competition to enter the order of mutuality. In the family he *had* his status born not of efficiency but of love. Here was emotional security, the wife knowing her role in a complementary society of primary acceptance, and accepting this role in maintaining the traditional values of home life. The family was thus a solidarity group within which status, rights, and obligations were defined in terms of membership as such, and by differences in age, sex, and biological relatedness. As Talcott Parsons and others have so clearly shown, this basis of relationship and status in the family precludes any major emphasis on standards of functional performance such as are typical in work situations away from home.

When both husband and wife work outside the home they tend to bring to the most intimate relationships of family life the ethos of the occupational world. In so doing they put the psychological bonds of the marital ties to the greatest test, apart from sheer disloyalty. As we have said, status and function are closely correlated in the occupational world. This relationship stresses competition in performance and achievement. Within the family the solidarity of life must be protected against the kinds of tensions that accompany severe competition for status between the members. This protection was provided when occupational role and family role were clearly separate from each other. However, when the marriage partners are proving themselves from evening to morning in relation to each other and the children, after having competed with others all day in the occupational world, they are caught in a never ending round of insecurity and anxiety.

In the love of true marriage and family life the aggressive tendencies of each partner are reversed and the "thou" of the other overshadows the "ego" of the self. Consequently, when both marriage partners work outside the home, there is a danger that occupational patterns of function and status will undermine the basis of family solidarity. This threat may be all the more acute in those homes where the woman's achievement in the occupational world is conspicuously more successful than the man's. She may injure both his self-respect and his formal status with the further result of diminishing the emotional support she offers to her husband. The tensions of conflicting roles, even when the working wife is not competitive or aggressive within the home, create difficulties for her. The two roles—and there may be several—create a dilemma. On the one hand, she is supposed to be full of drive, self-assertion, competitiveness, and aggression—an achiever; on the other hand, her role calls for a relaxation of these assertive requirements, and more stress on efforts to please, on protecting or nurturing, on passivity and receptivity.

When conflict between these two sets of values is not resolved by right motivation, understanding, acceptance, education, and love the family is endangered. For both men and women in our culture at the present time this aspect of family life constitutes a major frontier. What is at stake is not the right of women to work outside the home. What is at stake is the meaning of family life itself.

C. The Mass Communications Frontier

A third ethical frontier of contemporary culture is in mass communications. Like the economy of abundance and the dilemmas of family roles, it has been created by basic achievements in technology and social organization. How important are mass communication media? It is easy both to overestimate and to underrate them. The means of communication, in any case, deeply influence the spiritual life of man, the quality of his choices and appreciations, the going standards of valuation, and the character of democratic action in politics. Mass communications, over a long period of time, may prove to have more influence on the spirit of man than the improvement of social and economic standards of production and consumption. This power is due to its all-pervasive character, bathing the mind and emotions in a continuous sea of images, sounds, signs, and meanings, but its methods are controlled increasingly by bigness and centralization which characterize so much of our practical and economic existence.

Recent studies lift up two kinds of basic moral questions with respect to the above situation. First, how can the freedom of the person and the vitality of culture be conserved and yet the whole community be served with information and entertainment? Secondly, how can personal responsibility in decision-making be enhanced in the use and organization of mass media of communication? These questions are too large to be disposed of adequately here, but certain facets of their challenges can be underscored.

The development of television has intensified the aggressiveness of advertising and has invaded the privacy of the home and the viewer as newspapers never could. What are the respective rights of the listener and viewer and of the advertiser, and what are the ethical limitations upon the broadcaster? When television and the movie producers combine to play directly before livingroom audiences—taking much of the time formerly devoted to movie-going in addition to the hours already devoted to TV—the personality and character-shaping power of this medium of communication will be even greater. Naturally this developing situation raises the question how the quality of personal integrity is to be conserved. There is the closely related problem of balancing the claims of personal privacy and the right of the public to know. When the press, radio, and television attend a legislative hearing or investigation there are the conflicting claims of the public and the rights of accused persons to a fair trial since details shared with the public may tend to prejudice the verdict. In other situations there are the competing values of a completely libertarian policy in radio and television over against some degree of control by government.

These moral problems are especially complex because they are lock-stitched into the whole fabric of the social order. A man once asked, "Why do so many newspapers take the viewpoint of big business?" The reply was, "Because newspapers *are* big business." The same response belongs to all the major institutions which are developing the mass media of communication. What rights do stations and advertisers have in slanting the news to favor their interests? How can we be protected from both manipulation and conformism? Who have responsibilities in these matters?

A recent study by Wilbur Schramm shows that there are essentially two basic philosophies of mass communication, the libertarian and the authoritarian. The older authoritarian pattern has a special subtype, the Soviet control system. The older libertarian philosophy has as a modern subtype what may be called the concept of social responsibility. If the classical libertarian view had as its backdrop the authoritarian patterns of state and church, the newer social responsibility philosophy of freedom has as its backdrop the Soviet pattern of authority.

It is difficult to formulate a satisfactory and workable policy, but certain goals may set the sights for ethical deliberation: (a) keeping alive in persons and the public a critical and creative response to what is seen and heard; (b) providing means for the expression of free and independent response; (c) providing access to relevant facts and conflicting opinions and interpretations; (d) raising social conflict from the plane of violence to the plane of discussion; (e) insuring the rights of minorities to be heard; (f) clarifying the distinction between reasonable governmental intervention and a governmental monopoly that uses the media as an instrument of social policy; (g) clarifying the distinction between a negative kind of freedom based on liberty from external control and one that is positively devoted to the enhancement of personality. Cutting across a number of these goals is the difficulty of gratifying the desire of many to broadcast or print their opinions in view of the scarcity of channels and the expensiveness of setting up a newspaper office, or a radio, or television station and providing programs. These are a few of the issues on the frontier of social responsibility as it affects the opportunities for men and women to communicate with each other.

D. *The Frontier of Nuclear Weapons*

The final frontier which must be taken account of is in the development of sound national and international policies for the use and control of nuclear energy. Testing nuclear weapons may be used as a specific instance.

Man's immemorial dilemmas regarding militarism and military defense are intensified by the vast destructiveness of nuclear weapons, by the involvement of civilians on a gigantic scale, by the threats of increasing and cumulative radiation and their effects on generations yet unborn, and by the lethal effect of tests on innocent persons and unborn children in places far removed from the test sites. In addition to these problems are the mounting evidences of an arms race which steps up the conflicts among nations to unprecedented proportions.

In the arms race national pride and hysterical fear combine to threaten the balances in all levels of education. Natural science and technology may undermine curriculum developments in the humanities and social science. These are the disciplines whose weakness has exacerbated the international conflict. The dysfunctions incident to an imbalance of natural science and technology increases the influence of the military sectors of society to the detriment of democracy.

Our initial response must be that just as the civilian side of government must maintain its clear dominance over military power and organization, so in the total educational effort spiritual, social, and moral disciplines must be dominant over natural science and technology. If the battle against poverty and disease is to be won the sciences must be encouraged, but if the battle against tyranny and exploitation is to be won, the moral and behavioral sciences must be given a leading position in higher education.

If there is to be any worthy future for mankind that future must be spiritually and morally grounded. There is a moral difference between the Communist organization of society and its procedures and those of the "free world." This moral difference resides not only in the diverse ends which are pursued, but even more basically in the relating of means to ends; for the ends are predetermined in the means. Methods determine outcomes. Is it not one of the greatest condemnations of the Soviet system that it holds to an ethic which says that for an alleged good end "anything" is allowed? This resort to "anything" necessary may mean repudiation of the pledged word, slave labor camps, liquidation of farmers, violent purges of political opponents, and many other forms of ruthless expediency. The goal allegedly is the classless society; the means are dictatorship by the party and ruthless suppression of opposition.

Having said this of the Soviet Union must we not also say that it would be immoral for *any* nation to adopt the maxim: for an alleged good end "anything" is allowed? Furthermore, must we not say that in nuclear weapons of the kind now being tested and envisaged we have a means which makes possible the ultimate in human destruction? If this be the case are we not in the moral dilemma of embracing the ethics of current Communism: for an alleged good end (the defense of the nation or the Western world) anything is allowed?

If, then, it is wrong to engage in nuclear warfare, it follows that we are not justified in making nuclear weapons tests. To us belongs the moral challenge—moral, not expedient—of finding other ways to communicate a fundamental sense of responsibility for peace, freedom, and justice among nations. This is our moral frontier—with no guarantees of what lies beyond—except the universality of human nature, its needs and aspirations, and our capacity to help satisfy them in terms that respect the dignity of underdeveloped nations.

The moral challenge to the churches, temples, and synagogues is of unprecedented seriousness. Are they willing to risk what is necessary to make the judgment on nuclear weapons which is required if the nation is to make the judgment which the world is clearly yearning for? Our religious bodies can make their major impact on social change and process when they assert their spiritual and moral (and when necessary their material) autonomy in society. In making strategic decisions religious bodies must be fully aware of the social dilemmas in their accommodation to state and community; they must rediscover their prophetic leadership in thousands of churches—not only at national headquarters; and they must be prepared to sacrifice heavily in order to assert their freedom from secular institutions of power.

FOR FURTHER STUDY

Agar, Herbert. *A Time for Greatness*. Boston: Little, Brown, 1943, Part Two, "What Must We Discard, What Conserve?"

Fromm, Erich. *The Sane Society*. New York: Rinehart, 1955.

Hocking, William Ernest. *Strength of Men and Nations*. New York: Harper, 1959, Preamble and Ch. 5, "Our Double Morality."

Huxley, Julian. *The Human Crisis*. Seattle: U. of Washington Press, 1963, Essay 1.

Johnson, F. Ernest (ed.) *Patterns of Ethics in America Today*. New York: Collier Books, 1962.

Rader, Melvin. *Ethics and the Human Community*. New York: Holt, Rinehart and Winston, 1964, Ch. XIV, "Crisis," Ch. XV, "The Basis of Renewal."

Warburg, James P. *The West in Crisis*. New York: Doubleday, 1959, Ch. 11, "The Foundation for Success."

CHAPTER 27

HINDUISM, BUDDHISM, CONFUCIANISM, AND ISLAM

*Selections from Hindu Writings**

THE RULE OF ACTION

Arjuna said: "With these perplexing words thou only confusest my understanding; therefore tell me with certainty the one way by which I may reach bliss."

The Blessed Lord said: "In this world there is a twofold path, as I before said, O sinless one: that of yoga by knowledge, of the Sankhyas; and that of yoga by action, of the Yogis.

"Man winneth not freedom from action by abstaining from activity, nor by mere renunciation doth he rise to perfection. Nor can any one, even for an instant, remain really actionless; for helplessly is every one driven to action by the qualities born of nature. Who sitteth, controlling the organs of action, but dwelling in his mind on the objects of the senses, that bewildered man is called a hypocrite. But who, controlling the senses by the mind, O Arjuna, with the organs of action without attachment, performeth yoga by action, he is worthy. Perform

---

* "The Rule of Action," "The Rule of Devotion," "The Good Man and the Evil," are from *The Bhagavad Gita*, trans. Annie Besant (Wheaton, Illinois: The Theosophical Press, 1929); "The General Duties of Man" is from *The Vishnu Purana*, trans. H. H. Wilson (Calcutta: H. C. Dass, 1894); "Karma" is from *The Garuda Purana*, Manmatha Nath Dutt, ed. (Calcutta: Society for the Resuscitation of Indian Literature, 1908; "Many Paths to the One God" is from *The Sayings of Sri Ramakrishna*, compiled by Swami Abhedananda (New York: The Vedanta Society, 1903). The above selections are also found in *The Portable World Bible* (New York: Viking, 1944).

thou right action, for action is superior to inaction, and, inactive, even the maintenance of thy body would not be possible.

"The world is bound by action, unless performed for the sake of sacrifice; for that sake, free from attachment, O son of Kunti, perform thou action. Having in ancient times emanated mankind together with sacrifice, the lord of emanation said: 'By this shall ye propagate; be this to you the giver of desires; with this nourish ye the shining ones, and may the shining ones nourish you; thus nourishing one another, ye shall reap the supremest good. For nourished by sacrifice, the shining ones shall bestow on you the enjoyments you desire.'

"He who on earth doth not follow the wheel thus revolving, sinful of life and rejoicing in the senses, he liveth in vain. But the man who rejoiceth in the Self with the Self is satisfied, and is content in the Self, for him verily there is nothing to do; for him there is no interest in things done in this world, nor any in things not done, nor doth any object of his depend on any being. Therefore, without attachment, constantly perform action which is duty, for, by performing action without attachment, man verily reacheth the Supreme.

"Whatsoever a great man doeth, that other men also do; the standard he setteth up, by that the people go. Let no wise man unsettle the mind of ignorant people attached to action; but acting in harmony with me let him render all action attractive.

"All actions are wrought by the qualities of nature only. Even the man of knowledge behaves in conformity with his own nature; beings follow nature; what shall restraint avail? Affection and aversion for the objects of sense abide in the senses; let none come under the dominion of these two; they are obstructors of the path. Better one's own duty though destitute of merit, than the duty of another, well-discharged. Better death in the discharge of one's own duty; the duty of another is full of danger."

THE RULE OF DEVOTION

The Blessed Lord said: "Those verily who, renouncing all actions in me and intent on me, worship meditating on me, with wholehearted yoga, these I speedily lift up from the ocean of death and existence, O Partha, their minds being fixed on me.

"If also thou art not equal to constant practice, be intent on my service; performing actions for my sake, thou shalt attain perfection. If even to do this thou hast not strength, then, taking refuge in union with me, renounce all fruit of action with the self controlled.

"Better indeed is wisdom than constant practice; than wisdom, meditation is better; than meditation, renunciation of the fruit of action; on renunciation follows peace.

"He who beareth no ill-will to any being, friendly and compassionate, without attachment and egoism, balanced in pleasure and pain, and forgiving, ever content, harmonious with the self controlled, resolute, with mind and reason dedicated to me, he, my devotee, is dear to me.

"He from whom the world doth not shrink away, who doth not shrink away from the world, freed from the anxieties of joy, anger, and fear, he is dear to me.

"He who wants nothing, is pure, expert, passionless, untroubled, renouncing every undertaking, he, my devotee, is dear to me. He who neither loveth nor hateth, nor grieveth, nor desireth, renouncing good and evil, full of devotion, he is dear to me.

"Alike to foe and friend, and also in fame and ignominy, alike in cold and heat, pleasures and pain, destitute of attachment, taking equally praise and reproach, silent, wholly content with what cometh, homeless, firm in mind, full of devotion, that man is dear to me.

"They verily who partake of this life-giving wisdom as taught herein, endued with faith, I their supreme object, devotees, they are surpassingly dear to me."

THE GOOD MAN AND THE EVIL

"Fearlessness, cleanness of life, steadfastness in the Yoga of wisdom, alms-giving, self-restraint and sacrifice and study of the scriptures, austerity and straightforwardness, harmlessness, truth, absence of wrath, renunciation, peacefulness, absence of crookedness, compassion to living beings, uncovetousness, mildness, modesty, absence of fickleness, vigour, forgiveness, fortitude, purity, absence of envy and pride —these are his who is born with the divine properties.

"Hypocrisy, arrogance and conceit, wrath and also harshness and unwisdom are his who is born with demoniacal properties.

"Holding this view, these ruined selves of small understanding, of fierce deeds, come forth as enemies for the destruction of the world. Surrendering themselves to insatiable desires, possessed with vanity, conceit and arrogance, holding evil ideas through delusion, they engage in action with impure resolves. Giving themselves over to unmeasured thought whose end is death, regarding the gratification of desires as the highest, feeling sure that this is all, held in bondage by a hundred ties of expectation, given over to lust and anger, they strive to obtain by unlawful means hoards of wealth for sensual enjoyments.

"Self-glorifying, stubborn, filled with the pride and intoxication of wealth, they perform lip-sacrifices for ostentation, contrary to scriptural ordinance. Given over to egoism, power, insolence, lust and wrath, these malicious ones hate me in the bodies of others and in their own.

"Therefore let the scriptures be thy authority, in determining what ought to be done, or what ought not to be done. Knowing what hath been declared by the ordinances of the scriptures, thou oughtest to work in this world."

THE GENERAL DUTIES OF MAN

Vishnu being worshipped, a man obtains the consummation of all earthly desires and attains to the regions of the celestials and of Brahma and even final liberation. He is the true worshipper of Vishnu who observes duly the duties of the four castes and rules of four Asramas. There is no other means of satisfying Vishnu. He who offers sacrifices, sacrifices to him; he who recites prayers, prays to him; he who injures living beings, injures him; for Hari is identical with all living beings. Therefore, he who observes duly the duties of his caste is said to worship the glorious Janardana. O lord of earth, the Brahmana, the Kshatriya, the Vaisya, the Sudra, by attending to the duties prescribed by his caste, best worships Vishnu. He who does not vilify another either in his presence, or in his absence, who does not speak untruth, does not injure others, pleases Kesava the best. Kesava is best pleased with him, O king, who does not covet another's wife, wealth, and who does not bear ill feeling towards any. O lord of men, Kesava is pleased with him who neither beats nor slays any animate thing. O lord of men, Govinda is pleased with that man who is ever intent upon serving the gods, the Brahmanas and his spiritual preceptor. Hari is always satisfied with him who is ever anxious for the welfare of all creatures, his children and his own soul. Vishnu is always pleased with that pure-minded man whose mind is not sullied with anger and other passions. He best worships Vishnu, O king, who observes the duties laid down by scripture for every caste and condition of life; there is no other mode.

KARMA

A man is the creator of his own fate, and even in his foetal life he is affected by the dynamics of the works of his prior existence. Whether confined in a mountain fastness or lulling on the bosom of a sea, whether secure in his mother's lap or held high above her head, a man cannot fly from the effects of his own prior deeds.

This human body entombs a self which is nothing if not emphatically a worker. It is the works of this self in a prior existence which determine the nature of its organism in the next, as well as the character of the diseases, whether physical or mental, which it is to fall a prey to.

A man reaps that at that age, whether infancy, youth or old age, at which he had sowed it in his previous birth. The Karma of a man draws him away from a foreign country and makes him feel its consequence even in spite of his will. A man gets in life what he is fated to get, and even a god cannot make it otherwise.

MANY PATHS TO THE ONE GOD

You see many stars at night in the sky but find them not when the sun rises; can you say that there are no stars in the heaven of day? So, O man! because you behold not God in the days of your ignorance, say not that there is no god.

As one and the same material, water, is called by different names by different peoples, one calling it water, another eau, a third aqua, and another pani, so the one Sat-chit-ananda, the everlasting-intelligent-bliss, is invoked by some as God, by some as Allah, by some as Jehovah, by some as Hari, and by others as Brahman.

As one can ascend to the top of a house by means of a ladder or a bamboo or a staircase or a rope, so diverse are the ways and means to approach God, and every religion in the world shows one of these ways.

Different creeds are but different paths to reach the Almighty. Various and different are the ways that lead to the temple of Mother Kali at Kalighat (Calcutta). Similarly, various are the ways that lead to the house of the Lord. Every religion is nothing but one of such paths that lead to God.

As the young wife in a family shows her love and respect to her father-in-law, mother-in-law, and every other member of the family, and at the same time loves her husband more than these; similarly, being firm in thy devotion to the deity of thy own choice (Ishta-Devata), do not despise other deities, but honour them all.

Bow down and worship where others kneel, for where so many have been paying the tribute of adoration the kind Lord must manifest himself, for he is all mercy.

The Sat-chit-ananda has many forms. The devotee who has seen God in one aspect only, knows him in that aspect alone. But he who has seen him in manifold aspects is alone in a position to say, "All these forms are of one god and God is multiform." He is formless and with form, and many are his forms which no one knows.

The Vedas, Tantras, and the Puranas and all the sacred scriptures of the world have become as if defiled (as food thrown out of the mouth becomes polluted), because they have been constantly repeated by and have come out of human mouths. But the Brahman or the Absolute has never been defiled, for no one as yet has been able to express it by human speech.

The magnetic needle always points towards the north, and hence it is that the sailing vessel does not lose her course. So long as the heart of man is directed towards God, he cannot be lost in the ocean of wordliness.

Verily, verily, I say unto thee, he who longs for him, finds him. Go and verify this in thine own life; try for three consecutive days with genuine earnestness and thou are sure to succeed.

God cannot be seen so long as there is the slightest taint of desire; therefore have thy small desires satisfied, and renounce the big desires by right reasoning and discrimination.

Knowledge and love of God are ultimately one and the same. There is no difference between pure knowledge and pure love.

The master said, "Everything that exists is God." The pupil understood it literally, but not in the right spirit.

Selections from Buddhist Writings*

THE FOUNDATION OF THE KINGDOM OF RIGHTEOUSNESS
(The First Sermon Ascribed to Gautama Buddha)

And the Blessed One thus addressed the five monks: "There are two extremes, monks, which he who has given up the world ought to avoid.

"What are these two extremes? A life given to pleasures, devoted to pleasures and lusts; this is degrading, sensual, vulgar, ignoble, and profitless.

"And a life given to mortifications; this is painful, ignoble, and profitless.

"By avoiding these two extremes, monks, the Tathagata has gained the knowledge of the middle path which leads to insight, which leads to wisdom, which conduces to calm, to knowledge, to Sambodhi (supreme enlightenment), to Nirvana.

"Which, monks, is this middle path the knowledge of which the Tathagata has gained, which leads to insight, which leads to wisdom, which conduces to calm, to knowledge, to Sambodhi, to Nirvana?

"It is the noble eightfold path, namely: right views, right intent, right speech, right conduct, right means of livelihood, right endeavour, right mindfulness, right meditation.

"This, monks, is the middle path the knowledge of which the Tathagata has gained, which leads to insight, which leads to wisdom, which conduces to calm, to knowledge, to perfect enlightenment, to Nirvana.

"This, monks, is the noble truth of suffering: birth is suffering; decay is suffering; death is suffering; presence of objects we hate is suffering; separation from objects we love is suffering; not to obtain what we desire is suffering.

"In brief, the five aggregates which spring from grasping, they are painful.

* "The Foundation of the Kingdom of Righteousness" (from the *Mahavagga*) is from *The Life of Gotama the Buddha*, E. H. Brewster (London: Kegan Paul, Trench Trubner, 1926—New York: E. P. Dutton, 1926); "The Nine Incapabilities," (from *The Pasadika*), and "The Aryan Eightfold Path (from the Maha Satipatthana Suttanta) are from *Dialogues of the Buddha*, trans. T. W. and C. A. F. Rhys-Davids (London: Henry Frowde, Oxford University Press, 1938). Copyright vested in Pali Text Society. The above selections are also found in *The Portable World Bible* (New York: Viking, 1944).

"This, monks, is the noble truth concerning the origin of suffering: verily it originates in that craving which causes the renewal of becomings, is accompanied by sensual delight, and seeks satisfaction now here, now there; that is to say, craving for pleasures, craving for becoming, craving for not becoming.

"This, monks, is the noble truth concerning the cessation of suffering. Verily, it is passionlessness, cessation without remainder of this very craving; the laying aside of, the giving up, the being free from, the harbouring no longer of, this craving.

"This, monks, is the noble truth concerning the path which leads to the cessation of suffering. Verily, it is this noble eightfold path, that is to say, right views, right intent, right speech, right conduct, right means of livelihood, right endeavour, right mindfulness and right meditation."

THE NINE INCAPABILITIES
(Words Ascribed to Gautama Buddha)

The brother who is arahant, in whom the intoxicants are destroyed, who has lived the life, who has done his task, who has laid low his burden, who has attained salvation, who has utterly destroyed the fetter of rebirth, who is emancipated by the true gnosis, he is incapable of perpetrating nine things:

1. He is incapable of deliberately depriving a living creature of life.
2. He is incapable of taking what is not given so that it constitutes theft.
3. He is incapable of sexual impurity.
4. He is incapable of deliberately telling lies.
5. He is incapable of laying up treasure for indulgence in worldly pleasure as he used to do in the life of the house.
6. He is incapable of taking a wrong course through partiality.
7. He is incapable of taking a wrong course through hate.
8. He is incapable of taking a wrong course through stupidity.
9. He is incapable of taking a wrong course through fear.

These nine things the arahant in whom the mental intoxicants are destroyed, who has lived the life, whose task is done, whose burden is laid low, who has attained salvation, who has utterly destroyed the fetter of becoming, who is emancipated by the true gnosis, is incapable of perpetrating.

THE ARYAN EIGHTFOLD PATH

The Exalted One said:

"And what, bhikkhus, is the Aryan truth concerning the way that leads to the cessation of ill?

"This is that Aryan eightfold path, to wit, right view, right aspiration, right speech, right doing, right livelihood, right effort, right mindfulness, right rapture.

"And what, bhikkhus, is right view?

"Knowledge, bhikkhus, about ill, knowledge about the coming to be of ill, knowledge about the cessation of ill, knowledge about the way that leads to the cessation of ill. This is what is called right view.

"And what, bhikkhus, is right aspiration?

"The aspiration towards renunciation, the aspiration towards benevolence, the aspiration towards kindness. This is what is called right aspiration.

"And what, bhikkhus, is right speech?

"Abstaining from lying, slander, abuse and idle talk. This is what is called right speech.

"And what, bhikkhus, is right doing?

"Abstaining from taking life, from taking what is not given, from carnal indulgence. This is what is called right doing.

"And what, bhikkhus, is right livelihood?

"Herein, O bhikkhus, the Aryan disciple, having put away wrong livelihood, supports himself by right livelihood.

"And what, bhikkhus, is right effort?

"Herein, O bhikkhus, a brother makes effort in bringing forth will that evil and bad states that have not arisen within him may not arise; to that end he stirs up energy, he grips and forces his mind. That he may put away evil and bad states that have arisen within him he puts forth will, he makes effort, he stirs up energy, he grips and forces his mind. That good states which have not arisen may arise he puts forth will, he makes effort, he stirs up energy, he grips and forces his mind. That good states which have arisen may persist, may not grow blurred, may multiply, grow abundant, develop and come to perfection, he puts forth will, he makes effort, he stirs up energy, he grips and forces his mind. This is what is called right effort.

"And what, bhikkhus, is right mindfulness?

"Herein, O bhikkhus, a brother, as to the body, continues so to look upon the body, that he remains ardent, self-possessed and mindful, having overcome both the hankering and the dejection common in the world. And in the same way as to feelings, thoughts and ideas, he so looks upon each, that he remains ardent, self-possessed and mindful, having overcome the hankering and the dejection that is common in the world. This is what is called right mindfulness.

"And what, bhikkhus, is right rapture?

"Herein, O bhikkhus, a brother, aloof from sensuous appetites, aloof from evil ideas, enters into and abides in the first Jhana, wherein there is cogitation and deliberation, which is born of solitude and is full of joy and ease. Suppressing cogitation and deliberation, he enters into and abides in the second Jhana, which is self-evoked, born of concentration, full of joy and ease, in that, set free from cogitation and deliberation, the mind grows calm and sure, dwelling on high. And further, disenchanted with joy, he abides calmly contemplative while, mindful and self-possessed, he feels in his body that ease whereof Aryans declare: 'He that is calmly contemplative and aware, he dwelleth at ease.' So does he enter into and abide in the third Jhana. And further, by putting aside ease and by putting aside malaise, by the passing away of the happiness and of the melancholy he used to feel, he enters into and abides in the fourth Jhana, rapture of utter purity of mindfulness and equanimity, wherein neither ease is felt nor any ill. This is what is called right rapture.

"This, bhikkhus, is the Aryan truth concerning the way leading to the cessation of ill."

Selections from the Islam Scriptures*

THE MOST HIGH

Praise the name of thy Lord The Most High,
Who hath created and balanced all things,
And who hath fixed their destinies and guided them;
Who bringeth forth the pastures,

* From *The Koran*, trans. J. M. Rodwell (London: Bernard Quaritch, 1876).

Then reduceth them to dusky stubble.
We will teach thee to recite the Koran, nor aught shalt thou forget,
Save what God pleaseth; he verily knoweth alike the manifest and what
    is hidden;
And we will make easy for thee the easiest way.

Warn therefore; verily the warning is profitable:
He that feareth God will receive the warning,—
And the greatest wretch only will turn aside from it,
Who shall be burned at the terrible fire;
Then shall he not die therein, and shall not live.
Happy he who is purified by Islam,
And remembereth the name of his Lord and prayeth.
But ye prefer this present life,
Though the life to come is better and more enduring.
This truly is in the books of old,
The books of Abraham and Moses.

THOSE WHO STINT

Woe to those who stint the measure:
Who when they take by measure from others, exact the full;
But when they mete to them or weigh to them, minish—
Have they no thought that they shall be raised again
For a great day,
A day when mankind shall stand before the Lord of the worlds?

MORAL AND RITUAL PRESCRIPTIONS

There is no piety in turning your faces towards the east or the west,
    but he is pious who believeth in God and the last day and the angels
    and the scriptures and the prophets; who for the love of God dis-
    burseth his wealth to his kindred, and to the orphans, and the needy,
    and the wayfarer, and those who ask, and for ransoming; who
    observeth prayer, and payeth the legal alms, and who is one of
    those who are faithful to their engagements when they have en-
    gaged in them, and patient under ills and hardships and in time of
    trouble: these are they who are just, and these are they who fear
    God.
O believers! retaliation for bloodshedding is prescribed to you: the free
    man for the free, and the slave for the slave, and the woman for

the woman: but he to whom his brother shall make any remission is to be dealt with equitably; and a payment should be made to him with liberality.

This is a relaxation from your Lord and a mercy. For him therefore who after this shall transgress, a sore punishment!

But in this law of retaliation is your security for life, O men of understanding! Haply ye will fear God.

It is prescribed to you when any one of you is at the point of death, that if he leave goods, he bequeath equitably to his parents and kindred; this is binding on those who fear God:—

Whoso then after he hath heard what a bequest is shall change it, the guilt of this shall be on those only who alter it; verily, God heareth, knoweth:

But he who feareth from the testator any mistake or wrong, and shall make a settlement between the parties—that then shall be no guilt in him; verily, God is forgiving, merciful.

O believers! a fast is prescribed to you, as it was prescribed to those before you, that ye may fear God,

For certain days. But he among you who shall be sick, or on a journey, shall fast that same number of other days: and for those who are able to keep it and yet break it, there shall be as an expiation the maintenance of a poor man. And he who of his own accord performeth a good work, shall derive good from it: and that ye fast is good for you—if ye but knew it.

As to the month Ramadan in which the Koran was sent down to be man's guidance, and an explanation of that guidance, and an illumination, as soon as any one of you observeth the moon, let him set about the fast; but he who is sick, or upon a journey, shall fast a like number of other days. God wisheth you ease and wisheth not your discomfort, and that you fulfil the number of days, and that you glorify God for his guidance: and haply you will be thankful.

And when my servants ask thee concerning me, then verily will I be nigh unto them—will answer the cry of him that crieth, when he crieth unto me: but let them hearken unto me, and believe in me. Haply they will proceed aright.

You are allowed on the night of the fast to approach your wives: they are your garment and ye are their garment. God knoweth that ye have mutually defrauded yourselves therein; so he turneth unto you and remitteth unto you. Now, therefore, go in unto them with full desire for that which God hath ordained for you; and eat and drink until ye can discern a white thread from a black thread by the daybreak: afterwards fast strictly till night, and go not in unto them, but pass the time in the Mosques. These are the bounds set up by God: therefore come not near to transgress them. Thus God maketh his signs clear to men: haply they will fear him.

Consume not your wealth among yourselves in vain things; nor offer it to judges as a bribe that ye may consume a part of men's wealth unjustly, while ye know the sin which ye commit.

They will ask thee of the new moons. Say: They are periods fixed for man's service and for the pilgrimage. But there is no piety in entering your houses at the back, but piety consists in the fear of God. Enter your houses then by their doors; and fear God: haply ye shall be prosperous.

ᵔᵔᵔᵔᵔ

Selections from Confucianist Writings*

THE ANALECTS OF CONFUCIUS

The philosopher Tsang said, "I daily examine myself on three points: whether, in transacting business for others, I may have been not faithful; whether, in intercourse with friends, I may have been not sincere; whether I may have not mastered and practiced the instructions of my teacher."

The Master said, "A youth, when at home, should be filial, and, abroad, respectful to his elders. He should be earnest and truthful. He

* From *The Four Books: Confucian Analects, The Great Learning, The Doctrine of the Steadfast Mean, and the Works of Mencius*, trans. James Legge (China: The Commercial Press, n.d.).

should overflow in love to all, and cultivate the friendship of the good. When he has time and opportunity, after the performance of these things, he should employ them in polite studies."

The Master said, "It is virtuous manners which constitute the excellence of a neighborhood. If a man in selecting a residence, do not fix on one where such prevail, how can he be wise?"

The Master said, "The superior man thinks of virtue; the small man thinks of comfort. . . . The mind of the superior man is conversant with righteousness; the mind of the mean man is conversant with gain."

The Master said of Tsze-ch'an that he had four of the characteristics of a superior man—"in his conduct of himself, he was humble; in serving his superior, he was respectful; in nourishing the people, he was kind; in ordering the people, he was just."

The philosopher Tsang said, "There are three principles of conduct which the man of high rank should consider especially important: that in his deportment and manner he keep from violence and heedlessness; that in regulating his countenance he keep near to sincerity; and that in his words and tones he keep from lowness and impropriety. . . ."

Confucius said, "There are three things which the superior man guards against. In youth, when the physical powers are not yet settled, he guards against lust. When he is strong and the physical powers are in full vigor, he guards against quarrelsomeness. When he is old, and the animal powers are decayed, he guards against covetousness."

Confucius said, "There are three things of which the superior man stands in awe. He stands in awe of the ordinances of Heaven. He stands in awe of great men. He stands in awe of the words of sages."

Tsze-chang asked Confucius about perfect virtue. Confucius said, "To be able to practice five things everywhere under heaven constitutes perfect virtue." He begged to ask what they were, and was told, "Gravity, generosity of *soul*, sincerity, earnestness, and kindness. If you are grave, you will not be treated with disrespect. If you are generous, you will win all. If you are earnest, you will accomplish much. If you are kind, this will enable you to employ the services of others." . . .

Someone said, "What do you say concerning the principle that injury should be recompensed with kindness?" The Master said, "With what then will you recompense kindness? Recompense injury with justice and recompense kindness with kindness."

The Master said, "Alas! there is no one that knows me." Tsze-kung said, "What do you mean by thus saying—that no one knows you?" The Master replied, "I do not murmur against heaven. I do not grumble against men. My studies lie low, and my penetration rises high. But there is heaven;—that knows me!" . . .

From the Son of Heaven down to the mass of the people, all must consider the cultivation of the person the root of everything besides.

THE MIDDLE WAY

My master, the philosopher Ch'ang says: "Being without inclination to either side is called *Chung*; admitting of no change, is called *Yung*. By *Chung* is denoted the correct course to be pursued by all under heaven; by *Yung* is denoted the fixed principle regulating all under heaven. This work contains the law of the mind, which was handed down from one to another in the Confucian school till Tsze-sze committed it to writing and delivered it to Mencius."

What heaven has conferred is called the nature; and accordance with this nature is called the Path of Duty; the regulation of this path is called instruction. The path may not be left for an instant. If it could be left it would not be the path.

There is nothing more visible than what is secret, and nothing more manifest than what is minute. Therefore the superior man is watchful over himself, when he is alone.

While there are no stirrings of pleasure, anger, sorrow, or joy, the mind may be said to be in the state of equilibrium. When those feelings have been stirred, and they act in their due degree, there ensues what may be called the state of harmony. This equilibrium is the great root from which grow all the human actings in the world, and this harmony is the universal path which they all should pursue. Let the states of equilibrium and harmony exist in perfection, and a happy order will prevail throughout heaven and earth, and all things will be nourished and flourish.

The Master said, "Perfect is the virtue which is according to the Mean! Rare have they long been among the people, who could practise it!

"I know how it is that the path of the Mean is not walked in:—The knowing go beyond it, and the stupid do not come up to it. I know how it is that the path of the Mean is not understood:—The men of talents and virtue go beyond it, and the worthless do not come up to it.

"The superior man cultivates a friendly harmony, without being weak. How firm is he in his energy! He stands erect in the middle, without inclining to either side. How firm is he in his energy! When good principles prevail in the government of his country, he does not change from what he was in retirement.—How firm is he in his energy! When bad principles prevail in the country, he maintains his course to death without changing.—How firm is he in his energy!"

The Master said, "The path is not far from man. When men try to pursue a course which is far from the common indications of consciousness, this course cannot be considered the path. When one cultivates to the utmost the principles of his nature, and exercises them on the principle of reciprocity, he is not far from the path. What you do not like when done to yourself, do not do to others.

"In the way of the superior man there are four things, to not one of which have I as yet attained.—To serve my father, as I would require my son to serve me: to this I have not attained; to serve my prince, as I would require my minister to serve me: to this I have not attained; to serve my elder brother, as I would require my younger brother to serve me: to this I have not attained; to set the example in behaving to a friend, as I would require him to behave ᵗo me: to this I have not attained."

The superior man does what is proper to the station in which he is; he does not desire to go beyond this.

In a position of wealth and honour, he does what is proper to a position of wealth and honour. In a poor and low position, he does what is proper to a poor and low position. Situated among barbarous tribes, he does what is proper to a situation among barbarous tribes. In a position of sorrow and difficulty, he does what is proper to a position of sorrow and difficulty. The superior man can find himself in no situation in which he is not himself.

In a high situation, he does not treat with contempt his inferiors. In a low situation, he does not court the favour of his superiors. He rectifies himself, and seeks for nothing from others, so that he has no dissatisfactions. He does not murmur against heaven, nor grumble against men.

Thus it is that the superior man is quiet and calm, waiting for the appointments of heaven, while the inferior man walks in dangerous paths, looking for lucky occurrences.

The duke Ai asked about government.

The Master said, "Let there be the men and the government will flourish; but without the men, their government decays and ceases. With the right men the growth of government is rapid, just as vegetation is rapid in the earth; and moreover their government might be called an easily-growing rush. Therefore the administration of government lies in getting proper men. Such men are to be got by means of the ruler's own character. That character is to be cultivated by his treading in the ways of duty. And the treading those ways of duty is to be cultivated by the cherishing of benevolence.

"Benevolence is the characteristic element of humanity, and the great exercise of it is in loving relatives. Righteousness is the accordance of actions with what is right, and the great exercise of it is in honouring the worthy. The decreasing measures of the love due to relatives, and the steps in the honour due to the worthy, are produced by the principle of propriety. . . ."

What Can We Say About the Orient?*

CHARLES A. MOORE

Charles A. Moore (1901-   ) is a professor of philosophy at the University of Hawaii, chairman of the East-West Philosophers' Conferences, and editor of *East-West Philosophy*. He is author or editor of various articles and books written to help create world understanding.

What can we say . . . about the Orient in general or as a whole? I am convinced that we can say nothing. There is no single Oriental philosophy, no one philosophy of the East. The customary practice of thinking of the East as a unit philosophically is unrealistic, unfair, and certainly untrue to the facts. There is not one concept, method, or type of philosophy that pervades the Orient (or even any single major

* From "East-West Philosophy and World Understanding," in *Asia and the Humanities*, Horst Frenz (ed.) (Bloomington: Comparative Literature Committee, Indiana University, 1959), pp. 83-84, 91-94. Used by permission of the publisher and the author.

country in Asia). Nevertheless, if generalities are demanded, let me mention four or five tendencies that are significantly prominent. There is, first, the general attitude of spirituality or idealism, but even this takes many and seriously varied forms—even within each area. Second, there is the seriousness with which practically all Asians take philosophy, seeing in it the only road to a solution of the practical problems of life, be they the problem of suffering and evil, spiritual unrest, social disorder, or personal maladjustment to life. This is the practical motivation in and of philosophy. Third, there is a deep concern about the inner spirit or state of mind of man, variously expressed as the attitude of non-attachment, the demand for inner serenity, the practice of self-control, the search for peace of mind, the goal of contentment—in a word, the general attitude of inwardness, sometimes extreme, sometimes only as a check on man's tendency toward outwardness and worldly attachment. Fourth, there is the attitude of open-minded acceptance of differing and even seemingly incompatible concepts, methods, ways of life, and ideals, the universal spirit of tolerance. Fifth, there is the ideal of universal love and the Golden Rule—even if Confucius did happen to state it negatively.

. . . [T]here is very little that is inscrutable about the basic general principles of the philosophies of the Asian peoples. Perhaps we in the West—and we in America—cannot see eye-to-eye with some of the extremes of Indian thought: its sense for the infinite, its mysticism, its Yoga, but we can remember that these are the extremes of the relative few, that even they are not irrational, unintelligible, or inscrutable. We will probably have difficulty with the lesser degree of individualism and democracy, as we understand it, throughout Asia. And, with our logical background and our "either-or" mentality, we will undoubtedly have difficulty with the more tolerant synthetic perspective of the Asian mind, with the subtle, technical, and very difficult logical and metaphysical terms and methods resulting from this point of view, and perhaps also with Asia's apparent rejection of the disinterested pursuit of truth as the motivation of philosophy. Also, it is hard for us to think in terms of peace of mind, contentment, inner serenity as the goal we seek in life. As has been said, we in the West have deified discontent. We learned well—possibly too well—the Greek demand for perfection.

On the other hand, the overwhelming philosophical kinship of the West, perhaps chiefly the United States, with the over-all idealism of Indian, Chinese, and Japanese philosophies, should dictate understanding and even friendship—certainly mutual respect. All this is said without attempting to delineate the basic features of our own philosophical tradition. I assume a knowledge of the basic principles of our own philosophy on the part of all of us, although we have seldom attempted—at least in America—to become conscious of the fundamentals of our philosophy or to make a concerted effort to explain it to others. (Herein, by the way, lies much of our difficulty and misunderstanding with the Asian peoples in today's and yesterday's confused and troubled world.)

It may be pertinent to remind ourselves that, for all our science, our interest in Nature, our material values, our elements of naturalism, our concern with life and the worldly welfare of ourselves and our fellow men, there is no denying the great tradition of our underlying idealism, the influence of Christianity and Judaism upon our thought, our culture, and our life, our concern for spiritual values, our devotion to truth, freedom, and moral integrity, our sense of personal idealism. We, too, have a significant synthetic over-all point of view, merging our traditional idealism with the realism of worldly life, our science with our idealism or religion. But, as expressed in the "Great Tradition" of Western philosophy, and as expressed in the great documents of our country, there is no denying the underlying idealism of our mind and our life. In practice we often seem to give the lie to these basic convictions, but, in our deepest mind, we know better than this, and, if I may use the expression, when the chips are down, there is no doubt where we stand.

The realistic fact of some significant differences of perspective and of specific beliefs or emphases between East and West is inescapable, but, once we realize, first, that we have much, very much, in common, in terms of basic attitudes toward reality and life; second, that many seemingly conflicting attitudes and practices are not really so antagonistic or unintelligible as we thought; that in some cases it is merely a matter of emphasis, in some others, a matter of our not understanding the concepts, or methods, or attitudes of the East; and, third, that differences are inevitable—then we can hope for a world in which, with all our differences, we can live together and cooperate as human beings in a spirit of understanding and respect, no matter what our racial extraction, our national loyalties, or the details of our philosophies and religions. This is the practical ideal which we must achieve.

No one would want or expect uniformity of belief and practice the world over—that would deprive mankind of the healthy variety of thought and culture that makes for rich human living—but, without demanding or even seeking uniformity, we can understand and respect differences and thereby live with others in peace and harmony, and mutual respect.

Perhaps a concluding contrast will reinforce my major point. The basic philosophical attitudes of India, China, and Japan—and those of Islam, too—appear to be essentially in harmony with those of the West, and therefore they seem to suggest understanding and friendship. The contrasting conflict of these basic principles with the basic principles of Communism from Marx to Khrushchev—materialism, the economic determination of history, the economic determination of philosophy, of ideas, of truth, of the mind, the supremacy of economic values, dependence upon fear and force, internally and in international relations, dictatorship, the insignificance of the human person, the ethics of expediency and of the end justifies the means, the avowed rejection of ethics as known in all the rest of Asia and in the West, and a complete rejection of God, religion, and the truly spiritual—this conflict of basic ideas and ideals reinforces our friendship with Asia, establishes the basis for Asian friendship with America and the West, the basis for Asian fear and opposition to Communism, and the optimistic hope that, if fundamental philosophical beliefs are to be taken seriously as the foundation of life, then Communism cannot win out in Asia, and, to be specific, India cannot turn to Communism without denying its entire deep-seated idealistic philosophical and spiritual tradition, China cannot remain Communist except under the artificial and seldom enduring, but possibly effective, dictate of force, and the idealism for which we all—we and the people of Asia—stand must eventually re-establish itself as the basis of life in China and remain so throughout Asia—including Japan and the Islamic world—and become the essential link between Asia and the West. This interpretation may well be too optimistic, in view of realistic facts, but it is clearly indicated by a philosophical analysis of the situation.

FOR FURTHER STUDY

Burtt, Edwin A. *Man Seeks the Divine.* New York: Harper, 1957.

Gard, Richard A. *Great Religions of Modern Man.* New York: Braziller, 1961. (Buddhism, ed. Richard A. Gard; Hinduism, ed. Louis Renon; Islam, ed. John Alden Williams.)

Jackson, Barbara Ward. *The Interplay of East and West.* London: Allen & Unwin, 1957, Lecture 3.

Keeton, Morris. *Values Men Live By.* New York: Abingdon, 1960.

Moore, Charles A. "Comparative Philosophies of Life," in *Philosophy and Culture—East and West,* ed. Charles A. Moore. Honolulu: U. of Hawaii Press, 1962, Ch. 10.

Nikhilananda, Swami. *Hinduism: Its Meaning for the Liberation of the Spirit*. New York: Harper, 1958, Ch. 4.

Radhakrishnan, S. *East and West*. New York: Harper, 1956, Lecture 3.

Suzuki, D. T. *Zen Buddhism*. ed. William Barrett. Garden City: Doubleday, 1956, Chs. 1, 4. (Anchor Book.)

Wei, Francis C. M. *The Spirit of Chinese Culture*. New York: Scribner's, 1947.

CHAPTER 28

JUDAEO-CHRISTIAN
ETHICAL IDEALS

Selections from the Old Testament
and the New Testament*

THE TEN COMMANDMENTS: Exodus 20: 1-17

And God spoke all these words, saying,

"I am the LORD your God, who brought you out of the land of Egypt, out of the house of bondage.

"You shall have no other gods before me.

"You shall not make yourself a graven image, or any likeness of anything that is in heaven above, or that is in the earth beneath, or that is in the water under the earth; you shall not bow down to them or serve them; for I the LORD your God am a jealous God, visiting the iniquity of the fathers upon the children to the third and the fourth generation of those who hate me, but showing steadfast love to thousands of those who love me and keep my commandments.

"You shall not take the name of the LORD your God in vain; for the LORD will not hold him guiltless who takes his name in vain.

"Remember the sabbath day, to keep it holy. Six days you shall labor, and do all your work; but the seventh day is a sabbath to the LORD your God; in it you shall not do any work, you, or your son, or your daughter, your manservant, or your maidservant, or your cattle, or the sojourner who is within your gates; for in six days the LORD made heaven and earth, the sea, and all that is in them, and rested the seventh day; therefore the LORD blessed the sabbath day and hallowed it.

"Honor your father and your mother, that your days may be long in the land which the LORD your God gives you.

"You shall not kill.

"You shall not commit adultery.

"You shall not steal.

"You shall not bear false witness against your neighbor.

"You shall not covet your neighbor's house; you shall not covet your neighbor's wife, or his manservant, or his maidservant, or his ox, or his ass, or anything that is your neighbor's."

THE MAN WHO WALKS UPRIGHTLY: Psalm 15

A Psalm of David

O LORD, who shall sojourn in thy tent?
Who shall dwell on thy holy hill?

He who walks blamelessly, and does what is right,
    and speaks truth from his heart;
who does not slander with his tongue,
    and does no evil to his friend,
    nor takes up a reproach against his neighbor;
in whose eyes a reprobate is despised,
    but who honors those who fear the LORD;
who swears to his own hurt and does not change;

who does not put out his money at interest,
    and does not take a bribe against the innocent.

He who does these things shall never be moved.

PROPHETS OF RIGHTEOUSNESS AND JUSTICE

He who walks righteously and speaks uprightly;
he who despises the gain of oppressions,
who shakes his hands, lest they hold a bribe,
who stops his ears from hearing of bloodshed,
and shuts his eyes from looking upon evil.

He will dwell on the heights; his place of defense
  will be the fortresses of rocks; his bread will be
  given him, his water will be sure.

Isaiah 33: 15-16

Thus says the Lord:
  Keep justice, and do righteousness, for soon my
  salvation will come, and my deliverance be revealed.

Isaiah 56:1

For thus says the LORD to the house of Israel:
"Seek me and live; . . .

Amos 5:4

"I hate, I despise your feasts,
  and I take no delight in your solemn assemblies.
Even though you offer me your burnt offerings and
    cereal offerings,
  I will not accept them,
and the peace offerings of your fatted beasts
  I will not look upon.
Take away from me the noise of your songs;
  to the melody of your harps I will not listen.
But let justice roll down like waters,
  and righteousness like an everflowing stream.

Amos 5: 21-24

Woe to those who lie upon beds of ivory,
  and stretch themselves upon their couches,
and eat lambs from the flock,
  and calves from the midst of the stall;
who sing idle songs to the sound of the harp,
  and like David invent for themselves instruments
    of music;
who drink wine in bowls,
  and anoint themselves with the finest oils,
  but are not grieved over the ruin of Joseph!
Therefore they shall now be the first of those to go into exile,
  and the revelry of those who stretch themselves shall
    pass away."

Amos 6: 4-7

He has showed you, O man, what is good; and what does
the Lord require of you but to do justice, and to
love kindness, and to walk humbly with your God.

Micah 6: 8

THE SERMON ON THE MOUNT: Matthew 5

Seeing the crowds, he went up on the mountain, and when he sat
down his disciples came to him.

And he opened his mouth and taught them, saying:

"Blessed are the poor in spirit, for theirs is the kingdom of heaven.

"Blessed are those who mourn, for they shall be comforted.

"Blessed are the meek, for they shall inherit the earth.

"Blessed are those who hunger and thirst for righteousness, for they
shall be satisfied.

"Blessed are the merciful, for they shall obtain mercy.

"Blessed are the pure in heart, for they shall see God.

"Blessed are the peacemakers, for they shall be called sons of God.

"Blessed are those who are persecuted for righteousness' sake, for
theirs is the kingdom of heaven.

"Blessed are you when men revile you and persecute you and utter
all kinds of evil against you falsely on my account. Rejoice and be
glad, for your reward is great in heaven, for so men persecuted the
prophets who were before you.

"You are the salt of the earth; but if salt has lost its taste, how shall
its saltness be restored? It is no longer good for anything except to be
thrown out and trodden under foot by men.

"You are the light of the world. A city set on a hill cannot be hid.
Nor do men light a lamp and put it under a bushel, but on a stand, and
it gives light to all in the house. Let your light so shine before men, that
they may see your good works and give glory to your Father who is in
heaven.

"Think not that I have come to abolish the law and the prophets;
I have come not to abolish them but to fulfil them. For truly, I say to
you, till heaven and earth pass away, not an iota, not a dot, will pass
from the law until all is accomplished. Whoever then relaxes one of the
least of these commandments and teaches men so, shall be called least in
the kingdom of heaven; but he who does them and teaches them shall be
called great in the kingdom of heaven. For I tell you, unless your right-

eousness exceeds that of the scribes and Pharisees, you will never enter the kingdom of heaven.

"You have heard that it was said to the men of old, 'You shall not kill; and whoever kills shall be liable to judgment.' But I say to you that every one who is angry with his brother shall be liable to judgment; whoever insults his brother shall be liable to the council, and whoever says, 'You fool!' shall be liable to the hell of fire. So if you are offering your gift at the altar, and there remember that your brother has something against you, leave your gift there before the altar and go; first be reconciled to your brother, and then come and offer your gift. Make friends quickly with your accuser, while you are going with him to court, lest your accuser hand you over to the judge, and the judge to the guard, and you be put in prison; truly, I say to you, you will never get out till you have paid the last penny.

"You have heard that it was said, 'You shall not commit adultery.' But I say to you that every one who looks at a woman lustfully has already committed adultery with her in his heart. If your right eye causes you to sin, pluck it out and throw it away; it is better that you lose one of your members than that your whole body be thrown into hell. And if your right hand causes you to sin, cut it off and throw it away; it is better that you lose one of your members than that your whole body go into hell.

"It was also said, 'Whoever divorces his wife, let him give her a certificate of divorce.' But I say to you that every one who divorces his wife, except on the ground of unchastity, makes her an adulteress; and whoever marries a divorced woman commits adultery.

"Again you have heard that it was said to the men of old, 'You shall not swear falsely, but shall perform to the Lord what you have sworn.' But I say to you, Do not swear at all, either by heaven, for it is the throne of God, or by the earth, for it is his footstool, or by Jerusalem, for it is the city of the great King. And do not swear by your head, for you cannot make one hair white or black. Let what you say be simply 'Yes' or 'No'; anything more than this comes from evil.

"You have heard that it was said, 'An eye for an eye and a tooth for a tooth.' But I say to you, Do not resist one who is evil. But if any one strikes you on the right cheek, turn to him the other also; and if any one would sue you and take your coat, let him have your cloak as well; and if any one forces you to go one mile, go with him two miles. Give to him who begs from you, and do not refuse him who would borrow from you.

"You have heard that it was said, 'You shall love your neighbor and hate your enemy.' But I say to you, Love your enemies and pray for those who persecute you, so that you may be sons of your Father who is in heaven; for he makes his sun rise on the evil and on the good, and sends rain on the just and on the unjust. For if you love those who love you, what reward have you? Do not even the tax collectors do the same? And if you salute only your brethren, what more are you doing than others? Do not even the Gentiles do the same? You, therefore, must be perfect, as your heavenly Father is perfect."

THE GREAT COMMANDMENTS: Matthew 22: 34-40

But when the Pharisees heard that he had silenced the Sadducees, they came together. And one of them, a lawyer, asked him a question, to test him. "Teacher, which is the great commandment in the law?" And he said to him, "You shall love the Lord your God with all your heart, and with all your soul, and with all your mind. This is the great and first commandment. And a second is like it, You shall love your neighbor as yourself. On these two commandments depend all the law and the prophets."

THE PARABLE OF THE LAST JUDGMENT: Matthew 25: 31-46

When the Son of man comes in his glory, and all the angels with him, then he will sit on his glorious throne. Before him will be gathered all the nations, and he will separate them one from another as a shepherd separates the sheep from the goats, and he will place the sheep at his right hand, but the goats at the left. Then the King will say to those at his right hand, "Come, O blessed of my Father, inherit the kingdom prepared for you from the foundation of the world; for I was hungry and you gave me food, I was thirsty and you gave me drink, I was a stranger and you welcomed me, I was naked and you clothed me, I was sick and you visited me, I was in prison and you came to me." Then the righteous will answer him, "Lord, when did we see thee hungry and feed thee, or thirsty and give thee drink? And when did we see thee a stranger and welcome thee, or naked and clothe thee? And when did we see thee sick or in prison and visit thee?" And the King will answer them, "Truly, I say to you, as you did it to one of the least of these my brethren, you did it to me." Then he will say to those at his left hand, "Depart from me, you cursed, into the eternal fire prepared for the devil and his angels; for I was hungry and you gave me no food, I was thirsty and you gave me no drink, I was a stranger and you did not welcome me, naked and you did not clothe me, sick and in prison and you did not visit me."

Then they also will answer, "Lord, when did we see thee hungry or thirsty or a stranger or naked or sick or in prison, and did not minister to thee?" Then he will answer them, "Truly, I say to you, as you did it not to one of the least of these, you did it not to me." And they will go away into eternal punishment, but the righteous into eternal life.

FROM THE EPISTLES OF PAUL

If I speak in the tongues of men and of angels, but have not love, I am a noisy gong or a clanging cymbal. And if I have prophetic powers, and understand all mysteries and all knowledge, and if I have all faith, so as to remove mountains, but have not love, I am nothing. If I give away all I have, and if I deliver my body to be burned, but have not love, I gain nothing.

Love is patient and kind; love is not jealous or boastful; it is not arrogant or rude. Love does not insist on its own way; it is not irritable or resentful; it does not rejoice at wrong, but rejoices in the right. Love bears all things, believes all things, hopes all things, endures all things.

Love never ends; as for prophecy, it will pass away; as for tongues, they will cease; as for knowledge, it will pass away. For our knowledge is imperfect and our prophecy is imperfect; but when the perfect comes, the imperfect will pass away.

When I was a child, I spoke like a child, I thought like a child, I reasoned like a child; when I became a man, I gave up childish ways. For now we see in a mirror dimly, but then face to face. Now I know in part; then I shall understand fully, even as I have been fully understood. So faith, hope, love abide, these three; but the greatest of these is love.

I Corinthians 13

Let love be genuine; hate what is evil, hold fast to what is good; love one another with brotherly affection; outdo one another in showing honor. Never flag in zeal, be aglow with the Spirit, serve the Lord. Rejoice in your hope, be patient in tribulation, be constant in prayer. Contribute to the needs of the saints, practice hospitality.

Bless those who persecute you; bless and do not curse them. Rejoice with those who rejoice, weep with those who weep. Live in harmony with one another; do not be haughty, but associate with the lowly;

never be conceited. Repay no one evil for evil, but take thought for what is noble in the sight of all. Beloved, never avenge yourselves, but leave it to the wrath of God; for it is written, "Vengeance is mine, I will repay, says the Lord." No, "if your enemy is hungry, feed him; if he is thirsty, give him drink; for by so doing you will heap burning coals upon his head." Do not be overcome by evil, but overcome evil with good.

Romans 12: 9-21

Brethren, if a man is overtaken in any trespass, you who are spiritual should restore him in a spirit of gentleness. Look to yourself, lest you too be tempted. Bear one another's burdens, and so fulfil the law of Christ. For if any one thinks he is something, when he is nothing, he deceives himself. But let each one test his own work, and then his reason to boast will be in himself alone and not in his neighbor. For each man will have to bear his own load. . . .

And let us not grow weary in well-doing, for in due season we shall reap, if we do not lose heart. So then, as we have opportunity, let us do good to all men, and especially to those who are of the household of faith. . . .

Galatians 6: 1-5; 9-10

But be doers of the word, and not hearers only, deceiving yourselves. For if any one is a hearer of the word and not a doer, he is like a man who observes his natural face in a mirror; for he observes himself and goes away and at once forgets what he was like. But he who looks into the perfect law, the law of liberty, and perseveres, being no hearer that forgets but a doer that acts, he shall be blessed in his doing.

If any one thinks he is religious, and does not bridle his tongue but deceives his heart, this man's religion is vain. Religion that is pure and undefiled before God and the Father is this: to visit orphans and widows in their affliction, and to keep oneself unstained from the world.

James 1: 22-27

Do Churches Exert Significant Influence on Public Morality?*

F. ERNEST JOHNSON

F. Ernest Johnson (1884-   ), a professor of education at Teachers College, Columbia University, for
many years, is now editor of the Information Service and executive secretary of the Bureau of Research and Survey of the National Council of
Churches. His books include *The Church and Society* and *The Social Gospel Re-examined*.

Let it be granted at once that the question propounded in my title
admits of no categorical answer. The causes of human conduct and of
social phenomena are multiple, and an appraisal of any one factor must
be based on broad inference, not on conclusive proof. My interest in
the topic is not forensic, but exploratory. I should like to indicate some
of the areas in which the churches may be assumed to be influential in
developing sanctions for public conduct and to make some appraisal
of the quality of such influence as they exert. To this end it is important to consider from a sociological viewpoint the nature and the
limits of the influence of organized religion on social standards. Although the generalizations offered will have primary reference to Protestant Christianity, I believe they are susceptible of wider application.

Scope of Public Morality

I am assuming that the term "public morality" is to be taken as meaning more than *the morality of the public*. It is, to be sure, related to the
sum of the personal morals of the citizenry of the nation. But public
morality denotes the quality of all conduct that is public in character,
conduct in which the community has a recognized stake. Indeed, it is

* From *The Annals of the American Academy of Political and Social Science*,
280 (March 1952), pp. 125-127. Reprinted by permission of the Academy and
the author.

basic to this discussion that public morality is much more than a projection of the standards of private conduct. Those who see in the contemporary "wave of corruption" merely the reflection of a degradation of personal standards are, it seems to me, missing the central fact, namely, that a cultural crisis is upon us in which no clear picture of what public responsibility means can be discerned. I doubt that there is any such phenomenon as a *general* moral disintegration. What confronts all our institutions, especially those of education and religion, is the necessity of making our heritage of beliefs and loyalties relevant to a rapidly changing social structure.

The temptation to explain our present situation in terms of a character debacle is a natural one, but the explanation is too facile. It is a melancholy fact that standards of personal morals do not always reflect comparable standards of public behavior. Men who keep their pledged word and pay their debts may participate without compunction in oppressive political practices. Generous persons who readily give to charity are sometimes insensitive to the antisocial consequences of business policies that are maintained by their own proxies in stockholders' meetings. Rackets are carried on by men who seem to be exemplary in their private lives. All this means that it is not enough to teach conventional morals if we are seeking to raise the level of community life. To the extent, therefore, that the churches and synagogues fail in their educational programs to direct their attention to public morality as such, they may be assumed to have little influence on its standards.

It follows that, reluctant as we of the churches may be to acknowledge it, the churches have not been conspicuously successful in raising the standards of public morality; for the prevailing preoccupation of the churches has been with individual behavior patterns rather than with group behavior. This has been notably the case where politics is concerned. The churches have no doubt been an important factor in maintaining the respectability of public office, particularly in local communities, where "clean government" is often the aim of "Christian citizenship" campaigns. But it is probably safe to say that beyond enforcing standards of common decency, the churches have on the whole played relatively little direct part in the continual building of social-moral standards. That process is the result of stresses and conflicts from which the churches tend to remain aloof. In other words, the ethical significance of the churches' ministry has been socially conservative rather than regenerative. The churches have effected the regeneration of individuals and have given them new resources for living in accord with common sanctions, but they have not, it seems to me, conspicuously influenced those sanctions themselves.

Church and Community Identified

There is a fundamental reason why religion is in general a conservative force. Profoundly social in cultus and ritual, institutional religion has sanctified the universal values of human experience. Viewed in the perspective of history, it has therefore been a steadying rather than a reconstructive force. In primitive society, and indeed until modern times, religious organization and expression tended to be coextensive with the community. Even today in many countries religion goes with nationality and the church is the "community on its knees." The church furnishes a powerful support for a common ethos, but it cannot be expected to be socially regenerative in any profound sense.

This is why, when attention is focused on spiritual and moral faults that have deep cultural roots, such as racial and other group antagonisms, the churches often take such a severe beating. They follow the patterns of social stratification and practice race segregation to such an extent that secular societies and agencies often put them to shame. Thus a strange paradox emerges: the very fact of the church's authentic identification with the "community" it represents tends to fasten upon it the limitations and the faults of that community.

I am speaking here, of course, of the typical church, which includes in its membership the people who come in contact with each other in secular life. It has within its fellowship "some of everybody." It is not a group observing a special moral discipline. Unlike the small "sect," which in addition to a common body of religious beliefs has a way of life all its own, the "church" is held together chiefly by an impulse to worship—supplemented, of course, by certain social and cultural attractions. The church teaches an ethic, but its organizing principle is religious rather than ethical. Its moral standards are shared with the community in which it lives.

It is in the relatively small sects—groups characterized by a discipline that is in contrast to common practice—that the prophetic, reconstructive genius of religion most vigorously expresses itself. Thus we have "peace" churches which defy the community at the point of its greatest sensitiveness—patriotism and self-defense. We have sects whose austere way of life sets at naught the prevailing cultural standards in the interest of what they believe to be "a more excellent way." But the minuteness of the small sects renders their impact on the total social conscience inconsiderable. What the large, representative church body lacks the disposition to do in the way of social regeneration, the small religious group lacks the capacity to do.

This is the great dilemma of religion as a social-moral force in the community. An appreciation of it will prevent us from expecting too much of the church in the way of a direct impact on public morality. After all, the frequent impatient query why the church does not do this or that is really a complaint about the majority of the people, who are responsible for the church's policy.

FOR FURTHER STUDY

Brown, Robert McAfee, and Weigel, Gustave, S. J. *An American Dialogue.* Garden City: Doubleday, 1960.

De Vries, Egbert. *Man in Rapid Social Change,* London: SCM Press, 1961 (Published for the World Council of Churches).

Gardner, E. Clinton. *Biblical Faith and Social Ethics.* New York: Harper, 1960, Ch. 1, "The Field of Ethics."

Gordis, Robert. *A Faith for Moderns.* New York: Block, 1960. Ch. 11, "What Is Man?", Ch. 13, "Morality and Its Foundations."

Johnson, F. Ernest, (ed.). *Patterns of Ethics in America Today.* New York: Collier Books, 1962. Ch. 1, "Ethics of Judaism," Ch. 2, "Ethics of Roman Catholicism," Ch. 3, "Ethics of Protestantism."

Lehmann, Paul L. *Ethics in a Christian Context.* New York: Harper and Row, 1963.

Smith, John E. "Religion and Morality," *Journal of Religion* 29 (April 1949): 85-94.

Tillich, Paul. *Morality and Beyond.* New York: Harper, 1963. (Religious Perspectives, Vol. 9, ed. Ruth Nanda Anshen.)

Wieman, Henry Nelson. *Man's Ultimate Commitment.* Carbondale: Southern Illinois U. Press, 1964.

CHAPTER 29

SOME PRINCIPLES
FOR LIVING

~ひ⁊ぴひひひひひひひひひひひひひひひひひひひひひひひひひひ⁊

Values: The Polestar of Education[*]

BRAND BLANSHARD

> Brand Blanshard (1892-   ) has taught philosophy
> at a number of schools and was professor of philoso-
> phy at Yale University for nearly two decades. He
> has written many articles and books, including *The
> Nature of Thought* (2 vols.), *Reason and Goodness*,
> and *Reason and Analysis*.

In the midst of the universal clamor for more and better technology,
too little is heard about the place of values in higher education. . . .
What do we mean by a value? To define the term is surprisingly
hard; many thinkers have thought it impossible. But it is easy enough
to give examples. As examples of minor values, we could cite such
experiences as toasting one's toes before a pleasant fire, having tea in
the midst of a seminar, watching a world series game on television, and
taking a cool plunge on a hot day. As examples of major values, we
could cite the love of Damon for Pythias or of Darby for Joan, the
hearing with full understanding of Beethoven's Fifth Symphony, the

---

[*] Reprinted by permission of the publishers from Willis Weatherford, editor,
The Goals of Higher Education, pp. 76-96 with omissions, Cambridge, Mass.,
Harvard U. Press, Copyright, 1960, by the President and Fellows of Harvard
College.

experience of Keats on first looking into Chapman's Homer, the experience of Schweitzer in ministering to his African Negroes. Is there anything that all these values have in common? Yes, three things, I think.

In the first place they are all experiences. You may say that there are many things that are valuable besides experiences, and it is true that we commonly talk that way. For economists anything has value that can be exchanged for something else one wants—for example, money or a diamond ring or a grandfather clock. But why should anyone else want these things, and why should you want things they will exchange for? The answer in both cases is the same. It is because these things are means to experiences that are wanted for their own sakes. If somebody wants your grandfather clock, it is because he can set it in his front hall and look at it and gloat over it. Things are always wanted for the sake of experiences, never experiences for the sake of things. . . .

Secondly, these values are not only experiences; they are pleasant experiences. I am inclined to think that every experience valued for its own sake is suffused with a flush of agreeable feeling. This does not mean, of course, that hard work, mental and physical, or even the acute suffering of a bad illness or a bad conscience is not good in a sense; only it is good in a different sense. If we call these things good, it is not because we seek them out for their own sakes, but because they are the means to later states of mind that *are* thus sought; in short, they are instrumental, not intrinsic goods. We admire people who can face suffering with Spartan firmness in the interests of a cause. But if we found a man who cultivated illness or pain for its own sweet sake, we should choose our gambit warily in approaching him; we should assume that he was a crank, and not improbably a psychopath. Indeed, I doubt whether even psychopaths attain this pitch of oddity. . . .

Our conclusion so far is that all goods involve pleasant experiences. Is there anything more that is essential to them? I think there is. And perhaps the best way to see it is to take an example which perplexed John Stuart Mill, one familiar to all students of ethics. He began by saying that pleasure, and pleasure alone, was what made anything good. But he was brought up short by reflecting on the comparative value that this doctrine would assign to the lives of Socrates and a pig. Take first a month in the life of a pig, and make it no ordinary pig but a porcine gourmet whose every gustatory whim is satisfied with the most exquisite dainties of the trough. Then take a month in the life of Socrates, and make it a month in which the good man is tormented by doubt, taxes, and Xanthippe. Which life would Mill rather live? Being a singularly honest man, he voted for Socrates, thereby making untold trouble for himself. For he was by no means certain that Socrates' life was a pleasanter life, while he had no doubt at all that it was more worth living. There must, then, be something other than pleasure that makes it more worth living. What was this? I will not remind you of Mill's answer because, by pretty general agreement, it was wrong. The right answer, I suggest is this: Socrates' life was better because, whether more pleasant or not, it involved a completer fulfillment of powers. Grant the pig as generous a gastronomic capacity as one wishes, still one must admit that its intellectual, moral, and aesthetic horizons are limited, while those of Socrates are all but unlimited. What gave Socrates' life its value was the free play of a magnificent mind, the fulfillment in thought, feeling, and practice of a great intellect and a great heart.

This gives us the clue, I think, to the third component of all values. Besides experience, and pleasant experience, there must be fulfillment of natural faculties or powers. . . . Values are not adventitious to human nature. A value is a value because it speaks to our condition, answers our need, meets and completes some demand of our nature. And the more central and fundamental the demand, the greater is the value attaching to its fulfillment.

In the light of all this, we may describe a value as an experience that is at once pleasant and fulfilling. And our question now is, What is the place of values, so conceived, in education?

The answer is that they should form the polestar of education. For the aim of education is to secure a more worth-while life, in the first instance for those who receive it, in the second for others affected by these; and a more worth-while life is one that is richer in values. But while education should aim at the production of values, it has two branches that serve this purpose in very different ways. The aim of *liberal* education is to qualify us directly to realize such values; the aim of *technological* education is to qualify us for them indirectly. . . .

Now there is a difference between a technologist and a scientist. What is this difference? Presumably, that the technologist studies nature for the sake of controlling it, while the scientist studies it for the sake of understanding it. Thus the horizon of the scientist is wider than that of the technologist; for if a certain kind of knowledge gives no promise of application, the technologist's interest fades while that of the scientist may remain as lively as ever. . . .

This brings us to the second of the two values to be found in the

liberal pursuit of science, taken in the broad sense. The first was illumi
nation. The second is discipline. Our education ought to supply us
with a habit and a method of attacking problems, a habit of orderliness,
clearness, persistence, and precision. How often we must endure per-
formances by persons, too often with degrees after their names, which
require an agonizing re-appraisal of their being educated at all: political speeches without form and void, radio sermons full of sound and
fury, signifying nothing; after-dinner oratory in which the point, if
there is one, is fathoms deep in half-relevant anecdotage! And what
a satisfaction it is, when we are hunting for light on some complicated
issue, to find an article that puts the issue simply, offers its evidence
economically, faces difficulties fairly, and draws a firm conclusion!
The ability to do that is one of the most infallible marks of the educated mind. . . .

We have been considering the disciplines that aim at knowledge.
But what about the study of literature, music, and art? These are now
a recognized part of a liberal education, and their primary aim is plainly
not knowledge. Their aim is to satisfy and educate feeling. We sometimes forget that feeling is as educable as intelligence and that, so far
as happiness is concerned, its cultivation is even more important. What
does the education of feeling mean? Someone has given the answer in
the remark that culture is the adjustment of feeling to its objects and
that education is learning to like and dislike the right things. Such
education is one of our most conspicuous needs. Americans are a
people of strong feelings, freely expressed; they have been called the
Latin branch of the Anglo-Saxon family. Many of us seem to like excitement for its own sake, and if there is insufficient outward occasion for it,
we are adroit at generating it *ad hoc*. When Shriners or Legionnaires
get together, or a birthday or the New Year is to be celebrated, Americans have an inexhaustible repertory of first aids to excitement: brass
bands, paper hats, ticker tape, horns and whistles, snake dances, fancy
costumes, and drum majorettes; and at big games there are trained
cheerleaders to work up our emotions and give them organized vent.
Of course exuberance and high spirits are excellent things. But this
hardly implies that the value of an experience depends on how exciting
it is. May I quote two or three wise sentences from the philosopher A.
E. Taylor? "The mere identification of *any* fundamental activity of
the human spirit with emotion, cut loose from a *specific* object, is the
degradation and, in the end, the paralysis of the emotion itself. Emotions of all kinds so manifestly derive their value for human life from

the character of the object on which they are directed. Emotion in-appropriate or disproportionate to the objective situation by which it is evoked is the bane of life.". . .

We have considered values of the intellect and values of appre-ciation, but have said nothing about the values of conduct or practice. Is not life largely action, and should not college prepare us to act as well as to think and feel? Now if action means mere behavior, the play of arm and leg, there are no values of action, for values are in the mind. Still, we all know that the man of action—the Napoleon of the army or industry or public life—is a distinct type from the thinker or the artist, and a vastly important type who is often lost in the shuffle when education is under review. Can a college turn out such men, or even do much to help them? This is my last question.

Of course there are schools of business administration and welfare work and diplomacy, but no college can reproduce the conditions in which the man of affairs is going to work. So when liberal arts col-leges are criticized because their graduates on entering business have to learn it from the ground up, the charge is both true and negligible. No curriculum ever devised will guarantee a Churchill or a Henry Ford. But that a college can do something even here is suggested by the fact that little Merton College, Oxford, with less than a hundred and fifty students, produced, if I remember rightly, seven archbishops of Canterbury in one century, and that Balliol under Jowett poured out administrators to every part of the empire.

The chief points about the office of the college in training men of action seem to me to be these. First, a training of intelligence *is* a train-ing of will. As William James pointed out, a firm will is largely a matter of controlled attention, of fixing our thought firmly on what must be done, and hence a discipline of thought is itself a preparation for action. Secondly, college life on the practical side is not wholly divorced from the rest of life. It exacts hard tasks, it sets deadlines, it requires the ordering of one's time and the budgeting of one's energies. Teachers are sometimes slack and indulgent about these things, as dot-ing parents are, but the student ought not to be so toward himself. He is enjoying a great privilege which he ought to take most seriously, and if he keeps himself to the mark, that alone will equip him to meet the deadlines of the world. Thirdly, American colleges, rightly I think, value athletics; and the participation in competitive games, if wisely conducted, gives an admirable discipline in taking success modestly, in taking defeat and hard knocks uncomplainingly, and in developing respect for justice, since sportsmanship is justice in play. If Yorktown was lost, as has been alleged, on the playing fields of Eton, at least Waterloo was something. Fourthly, as in the realms of intelligence and appreciation, so too in the realm of action college can marshal models across the stage for whom we feel a self-revealing repulsion or affinity. Here history is the chief resource, not so much social or constitutional history as the old-fashioned kind that makes it largely the biography of great men. We all find it intelligible that General Eisenhower, traversing Napoleon's field of action, should have remarked, "I should have liked to tangle with that fellow," or that he and Montgomery should have gone over Gettysburg together and come up with a reappraisal of Lee. What is more significant is that such people as Goethe, Hegel, and Emerson should also be fascinated by Napoleon; that Mommsen, Froude, and Thornton Wilder should have been fascinated by Caesar; and that Carlyle should have worshiped at the shrines of Cromwell and Frederick. These men of action had deep moral flaws, but they were, after all, among the "quarto and folio editions of mankind," and to read in them is to expand one's ideas of what a mere human being can do. Finally, education not only can inspire action, it can give it perspective and goals. How different the world would be if Napoleon and Hitler had been cultivated minds instead of being the one an outsized Corsican brigand and the other a guttersnipe of genius!

We have reached the end of our argument, and it proves to be as simple as it has been long. Values, we have argued, are experiences that are at once satisfying and fulfilling. The purpose of education is to make us creators and centers of value. Technological education does that indirectly by supplying us tools for the exploiting of nature. Liberal education on its intellectual side provides the values of understanding, which makes us at home in our world. Liberal education on its appreciative side makes us responsive to the best that has been said and painted and built and sung. Liberal education on its practical side puts the wind of emulation in our sails and gives direction to our voyage. Values are the stars by which education may and should steer its course.

The Good Life*

D. W. GOTSHALK

D. W. Gotshalk (1901-   ) has taught philosophy
at the University of Illinois since 1927. His books
include *Metaphysics in Modern Times* and *The
Promise of Modern Life*.

Individuals

Like a domain, the human individual as we have interpreted him has
a distinctive *telos*. His multitude of impulses, desires, and drives are
differentiated into an individual system by his physical structure, his
training, his temperament, and similar factors. This differentiated *telos*,
at each of its diverse stages of growth, determines by its range the
possibilities of value compatible with the individual's being. Ideally,
the good life for the individual would seem to be to realize as he goes
along these value possibilities.

Fundamentally, this really means two things. First and obviously,
it means a life congenial to the individual's nature. The demands of
work and play, education and friends, and of whatever other objects
or pursuits give substance to human life, would come within the individual's physical and psychical capabilities, giving them opportunity
for full but agreeable exertion. These demands would exist in amount
and intensity sufficient to challenge all his powers, but not in a strength
that would overwhelm them. There would be a kind of live wholeness
or integrity to the individual's existence, in contrast to the existence of
the unchallenged or overchallenged, the complacent or the broken
individual, which would lack liveness or wholeness of being.

But the good life as above described has a second meaning. It means
realization of capacities as well as congeniality in the realization. This
brings in the domains, for the capabilities of individuals are not merely
subjective possessions. They are capacities for work, for friendship,
for social undertakings, and usually function within domains with their

---

* From *Patterns of Good and Evil* (Urbana: University of Illinois Press, 1963),
pp. 121-135 with omissions. Used by permission of the publisher.

telic structures and principles of measurement. On this side, the good life or the life really valuable would involve meeting the requirements of the relevant domains. It would be not only doing something you wanted to do, but doing well something that is good to do. It would mean effectiveness as well as gratification. Indeed, only in this way would the individual genuinely realize innumerable possibilities of his being, which are domain possibilities, and bring into his life a certain depth or richness of value to go with the integrity and wholeness that congeniality would give.

I have said that this concept of the good life is an ideal. It is likely to be realized only in a degree. Some there are who doing what they can do and truly want to do are also doing the world's work in superlative fashion. Owing to an almost amazing constellation of factors, good disposition and good luck not least of them, their activities are both personally congenial and socially effective. But how many people are among these? It is important to note in considering such a question that the above concept of the good life does not limit it to a stereotype: a scholar, a banker, a philosopher, an ascetic. The variety that might have a good life in the above sense is very large, as is the variety that might not. An active temperament leading the sedentary life of a scholar might be very miserable, as well as very obnoxious, while a sedentary person forced by family demands to be a salesman or politician might be distraught and incompetent. No doubt, a good life would involve being active and effective in a number of domains. Also, such lives often would involve many of the same domains, since many interests of many human beings coincide. But the possibility of various kinds would remain: farmer, poet, philosopher, king. In any instance, there would be the same two principles, effectiveness and congeniality, but this would be all of the sameness really needed.

"Happiness" is the term customarily employed to describe the substance of the good life for individuals. It is a pleasing term, tempting to use, but unfortunately it has many meanings. There is the happiness of the healthy bullfrog with his lifelong gestalt of immediate satisfactions, and the happiness of the willfully superstitious. Lately many have known the happiness induced by intellectual tranquillizers who supply sedatives to troubled nerves by artificial cheeriness.[1] People

[1] Cf. Norman Vincent Peale, *Stay Alive All Your Life* (Englewood Cliffs, N. J.: Prentice-Hall, Inc., 1957), and also *The Power of Positive Thinking* and *A Guide to Confident Living*; Smiley Blanton, *Love or Perish* (New York: Simon and Schuster Co., 1957); Claude Bristol and Harold Sherman, *TNT, the Power Within You* (Englewood Cliffs, N. J.: Prentice-Hall, Inc., 1957); John A. Schindler, *How to Live 365 Days a Year* (Englewood Cliffs, N. J.: Prentice-Hall, Inc., 1954);

today may be in great trouble, and the medications of the happiness boys may be far better for their troubled souls than other drugs on the market. But to be becalmed on a sea of trouble by such artificial stimulants is not exactly the equivalent of the substance of the good life as we are describing it.

However, "happiness" connotes the sweetness and joy of life, a multitude of agreeable states, small fugitive and very private pleasures as when a very pretty and pleasing young lady friend does one an unexpected favor, as well as the more sustained joys of full-tide private and public accomplishment. All this, as the natural accompaniment of congenial and effective activity, would find place in the good life as here conceived. And as we have just noted, this life would also have the character of being potentially open to individuals of many kinds, as happiness is commonly supposed to be. It would require the realization not necessarily of only grand and "heroic" possibilities, but of such capacities as the individual had in those domains suited to his capacities. Further than this, one might describe the good life . . . after the analogy of fine art. As in fine art, it would be the use of skill and personal resources to create an object (here, a life) radiant with immanent values. Very likely, the steady stream of concentrated intrinsic realizations exhibited in works of art at their best is impossible for any long stretch in the life on an ordinary mortal. But something of the spirit of this realization, and approaches to it, seems possible where congeniality and effectiveness are combined in high degree in a value effort.

Choices

Perhaps some may think that the above is really a concept of the mediocre life, not of the truly valuable life, since it does not necessarily require "heroic" attainment. The answer is that where the capacity range of the individual includes the "truly heroic," then, on the above principles, his life if good would require such attainment. The comparative stature of a life is doubtless a function of the comparative stature of the capacities exercised, but its positive goodness or badness has to do with the realization or nonrealization of the capacities actually possessed by the individual.

It may be objected, however, that our concept does ignore many real difficulties in life. One of these is self-knowledge, or, knowing one's capacities. Individuals are frequently uncertain and often mis-

Hornell Hart, *Autoconditioning* (Englewood Cliffs, N. J.: Prentice-Hall, Inc., 1956).

taken here, and when they come to know their capacities in a rational way, if they ever do, they have usually made so many mistakes or wrong commitments that the jig is up, or nearly so. Nothing remains except to live out one's errors. In general, congeniality—the deeply congenial—often takes a lifetime to discover. And who knows its limits? May not something that seemed at one time against the grain turn out to be surprisingly congenial? What fits one's needs and powers? This is an endlessly recurring question. And what is effectiveness? What is effectiveness in business, in art, in education, in politics, in family life and neighborly associations? And what is an effective proportion between all of these and similar activities? And how are all of these possible in present circumstances?

Perhaps these objections can be best stated in terms of the kind of choices now open to people. Were the individual born an adult, were everything in his life or at least his domain possibilities and personal potentialities spread clearly before him like patterns of good and evil laid on a table, did the individual know how actual circumstances would develop, had he unlimited time to survey all of these things, and had he "real" choice, the good life as we have described it might be relatively easy to achieve, and a common occurrence. But this is not the way things are. We live in a very imperfect world including among its imperfections the limitations of our stages of growth and of our knowledge of ourselves and our circumstances. At the same time, we often *must* make choices. The urgency of need and action will not permit delay. We may not like our work and may not do it very effectively. But we may have to work to "live," and may know of no better work available. We may not think our friends very perfect, nor our physical surroundings including the weather and architecture of our town or country what we would want ideally. But in our situation we may be "stuck" with them. We may not think totalitarianism nor democracy is a very satisfactory form of government, and we may think that nationalism of any type is an abomination of the first order. But we may have been born and reared under a regime with one or more of these political commitments, and have or know nothing better to which to escape. Such imperfections, such occasions for discontent, are genuine and interminable. Does not our description of the good life ignore them? How is such a good life possible when individuals are faced with choices between these real alternatives?

Such questions raise important problems, but I do not think they raise important objections to our concept (or any concept) of the good life. This concept is an attempt to describe what the life of an individual would be *if* it were good, and, while such a life may be difficult to realize or even impossible fully to realize under present circumstances, this does not prove that, if it were realized, it would not be good. Only if some evidence is brought against this, for example, if the things alleged to be ignored in our concept of the good life were claimed to be good (such as man's limited knowledge and circumscribed choices), as they are not, could reference to them be a refutation of our concept of what is good. In general, a value ideal is a description not of what people do or can now do, but of what the good requires. And while this may not describe the actualities of the situation people are in, that was never its intention, nor its proper purpose.

The above questions, however, do raise important problems about historical conditions and the choices people face. Today, in our stalemated world so full of potential terror, the blackness and blankness of life sometimes take on sizable dimensions. The "sick individual in a sick society" is the cliché frequently applied to the typically sensitive person, and through a type of deranged surrealist mind, articulate people often interpret the aberrations of our society, its strong turn to pleasure, excitement, sports, gambling, busy work, and crime, its overorganized sectors of faceless togetherness, its fragmentation into artistic and intellectual and other cults, its myopic overspecialization. The technological utopian and soul-shocked existentialists, so far as they serve as contemporary spiritual guides, illustrate similarly an inward imbalance at the root of a discordant civilization.

Obviously, so far as all of this is true, it indicates a lack of rational command over the conduct of life, and less obviously, but equally, it indicates a kind of widely diffused value undereducation. A people rationally trained in the value areas would not create such an awry world. However, the existence of such a world, if it does exist, should occasion no great surprise when we realize that, while our "scientific" resources for social mischief are being expanded geometrically, a scientific level in the value of education is almost totally lacking in our culture. That scientifically grounded value education, even in saturated form, would eliminate all of the evils of human existence is not being suggested. Imperfections in nearly all of the best value realizations are probably ineradicable this side of Utopia. But that a powerful and effective, scientifically grounded value education could eliminate the wayward, self-centered, and provincial orientations disturbing the more dangerous areas of public life today, and that it could give clear principles also for solving the less explosive issues in the other areas, should be evident from the type of "objective," universal, and overarching patterns that we have seen properly govern the domains of human activity. . . .

Society

To have a good life, to live effectively in a deeply congenial manner, usually requires exertion, good judgment, sustained purpose, considerateness, good temper, and similar traits. But it also requires opportunity. A small prison cell may be a suitable setting for some activities. But it is hardly suitable for the great variety of human activity. Subjective potentialities require objective instrumentalities. A potentiality for statesmanship, commerce, education obviously can become actualized only if certain outer means are available. And while these means often are physical, they are usually controlled by human beings, and are open to individuals only under certain social conditions.

Every human being is born into a social order. This order begins with the family, or at least with the parent-child relation, but it is actually as extensive as the human race. This complex order with its many interior orders provides the setting and chief condition of the individual's existence. Physical circumstances may seem independent of it. Air, sunshine, soil, landscape, storms, the seasons: these may appear to be pure products of nonhuman nature. But the more deeply they affect human life, the more strenuous is the effort to bring them under human dominion. Thus, more and more our physical circumstances are socially modified, and society increasingly supplies the all-encompassing conditions of individual existence. Romantics have dreamed of escaping it. But in a total sense there is no escaping it. Not only is there no place one can go, on earth or elsewhere, independent of society, but for a good segment of the individual's life, such as most of his growing years, he is incompetent to go. For various people at various times a change of local setting may be highly desirable. But this is quite different from a total escape, which would require not only an isolated terrain, but the discarding of all habits and training, including language and learning, since these have been acquired from instruction in a society.

Yet society, besides an inescapable and all-encompassing circumstance, is something itself, a complex of domains with its own form and character. What aim should govern such a complex as the context of the good life of the individual?

Perhaps we can state our answer to this question, most easily in terms of one analysis of human nature our argument has prepared us to accept. According to this analysis, the human being has a twofold nature.

He is a purposive creature with great inner resources capable of development in many directions, as the great variety of his domains attest. He is also a causal creature with limited causal powers living in a vast physical universe. Employing his causal powers and the tools he has invented, and trying where he can to bend physical nature to his uses, he still suffers innumerable reverses, hunger, illness, death, many more. Almost completely confined to a small minor planet at the mercy of the cosmic weather, he has yet to establish an assuredly commanding place for his ends in this world. In sum, the human being is a complex purposive being still immensely insecure in a vast causal universe. Clearly, to be successful, to reach his best on all fronts, his causal position must be greatly strengthened as his telic diversity must be developed in accordance with its principles to full eminence.

So far as the good life of its members is concerned, a good society, I believe, would be specifically devoted to these two tasks. It would be a society whose aim was an inwardly well-developed people in a mechanically secure world. What would this mean? At a minimum, two things.

First, it would mean that as a matter of social habit or general institutional practice each individual would be treated equally and impartially, on his own merits, as an intrinsically purposive creature, or as an originative center of purposive striving. Only under this condition could his capacities develop the inherent range in whose proper exercise the good life consists. But, second, physical potentials progressively unlocked by the natural sciences would be treated as *humane* resources to aid or assist individuals, not, as they frequently are now, to threaten, delude, harm, and even destroy individuals. Only under this condition would technology and the causal sciences genuinely strengthen the human being's mechanical position, and starting at home, here on earth, begin to wipe out the insecurities of this position that still everywhere beset him. Should a society achieve or try to achieve these two conditions it would be doing at least the minimum of what it could do to have an inwardly well-developed people in mechanically secure circumstances.

Two deviations from such a society are obviously possible. In the first, the individual, being treated as a means, would be expected to fit into some *a priori* social pattern. A harmony of activities might result from a conformity induced by force or habit or persuasion. But exploitation for an end extrinsic to the individual would be the rule, and the telic potential of the individual would be leveled to fit this goal. Unity of purpose might be achieved in the society but at the expense of diversity and richness. In the second type, physical resources might be developed extensively but as instruments of partisan competition. The aim would be the triumph of some individual or group at the expense of other individuals or groups, and the causal power of individuals would be thinned or destroyed as necessary for strengthening the power position of a small segment. Richness on a small or provincial scale might be achieved, but at the risk, and even at the expense, of rending or destroying the larger social fabric. Under either society, it seems plain, the good life as a general phenomenon would be simply impossible. A few might seem to have it, for example those whose goals fell easily and effectively within the loops of subservience or exploitation. Yet even such people might be troubled if they should try to look upon their world as a setting in which a human being could act freely or securely, without compromising his possibilities.

The good society, we say, is one whose aim is an inwardly well-developed people in a world as mechanically secure as possible. Morality in it, indeed the good life itself, would be rooted in material being and culminate in inner excellence. Thus, the good life, the congenial and effective life, and the good society as here conceived, sharing an equal concern for inner individual strength and outer public mastery, would be two halves of the same whole. . . .

Finally, it may not be amiss to indicate the conception of religion that fits into our views. Superstition, fear, loneliness, moral failure, self-seeking, are a few of the numerous motives that lead people to join in organized worship. But religion is not necessarily connected with any of these, nor with the regional mythologies that usually adorn it. In essentials its chief feature is veneration of perfection or of the pattern of the good embodied in the supreme form of Being. Such veneration inevitably leads to corroboration of the good life in its other parts. But it would be a mistake, I believe, to think of religion as chiefly concerned with this afterglow. Its primary concern, I think, is with the higher life, the awareness of the form of the good life as enshrined in completeness of being. It is a life that in its fullness the ordinary man usually knows only dimly, in the farthest reaches of consciousness. But a segment of being is given to him at every moment of his existence, and by the power of his brain and the telic impulses of his soul he can foreshadow the whole. Religion springs from this transforming outlook, and transcends ordinary time, change, and circumstance. Its vision is to see the form of the good at a glance in its final embodied perfection from one's tiny window on eternity.

FOR FURTHER STUDY

Gardner, John William. *Excellence*. New York: Harper, 1961.

Gotshalk, D. W. *Patterns of Good and Evil*. Urbana: U. of Illinois Press, 1963.

Krutch, Joseph Wood. "Life, Liberty and the Pursuit of Welfare," *Saturday Evening Post*, 234 (July 15, 1961): 18-19, 56-58.

Lowry, Howard. "The Human Privilege," *The American Scholar*, 28 (Spring 1959): 151-163.

Smith, Huston. "Values: Academic and Human" in *The Larger Learning*, ed. Marjorie Carpenter. Dubuque: Wm. C. Brown, 1960.

Tillich, Paul. *Love, Power, and Justice*. New York: Oxford U. Press, 1954.

Weatherford, Willis D., Jr. (ed.). *The Goals of Higher Education*, Cambridge: Harvard U. Press, 1960.

INDEX

Titles in brackets are supplied by the editors.

4¹7